EMILY POST'S
ETIQUETTE

THE CENTENNIAL
EDITION

EMILY POST'S
ETIQUETTE

THE CENTENNIAL EDITION

LIZZIE POST AND DANIEL POST SENNING

ILLUSTRATIONS BY EIGHT HOUR DAY

TEN SPEED PRESS
California | New York

TO EMILY POST AND ALL THOSE
WHO TAKE CARE WITH EACH
OTHER AND IN DOING SO MAKE
THE WORLD A KINDER PLACE.

CONTENTS

AUTHORS' NOTE

Dear Reader,

Etiquette lives, and we are thrilled to be talking about it with you. This twentieth edition of *Emily Post's Etiquette* is a special one. Its publication marks the 100-year anniversary of Emily's famous book (originally titled *Etiquette in Society, in Business, in Politics, and at Home*), which was first released in 1922. Upon its debut, *Etiquette* was an instant hit. For many, it gave a window into the way America's high society lived and at the same time offered a perspective on practical standards for living well with others, both at home and out in the world. Accessible and aspirational, *Etiquette* was updated and reprinted often in its early years, and has been revised by generations of the Post family since Emily's death in 1960. Whether Emily Post is a famed (or perhaps feared) name from your childhood, or her book a cherished keepsake passed down from a loved one, or new to you, it is an honor and a privilege to present this latest edition to you.

While Emily's status in society was that of an older, wealthy white woman, her advice was anchored in principles that were effective and accessible for all, creating a long-lasting and adaptable foundation for her work. The consistent thread throughout is the idea that etiquette is about taking care of people and helping them feel at ease. What matters is the manner of a person—their kindness, thoughtfulness, and awareness of others—not the particular manners they have learned. As Emily explained, "etiquette is not some rigid code of manners; it's simply how persons' lives touch one another."

The editions of Emily's *Etiquette* were famous for their perspective, humor, and detailed depictions of daily life with all its successes and mishaps. With tales like "How a Dinner Can Be Bungled" and characters such as Mrs. Worldly, Constance Style, Mrs. Kindhart, and the Onceweres, she painted relatable pictures of what to do—or not do. One of her most memorable characters was Mrs. Three-in-One, who was added to the book in 1927 to represent those playing the roles of host, cook, and maid all at once, which was most of Emily's audience. Today, nearly every adult is a Mrs. Three-in-One, and the Post family has added, subtracted, and made many revisions and updates to this book over the past 100 years to respond to changes in American culture. Emily certainly never saw a smartphone, and could not have anticipated the role social media plays in our lives. But even with all the changes and adjustments that our culture has seen in the past century, *Emily Post's Etiquette* still aims to equip you, our dear reader, with a sense of confidence and preparedness for some of the situations you'll encounter at home, at work, in your social life, and when you're out and about.

Every few years, a headline declares that "Etiquette Is Dead," but through our work at the Emily Post Institute, we know that this isn't true. Our weekly podcast, *Awesome Etiquette,* has received thousands of etiquette questions from all kinds of people living all kinds of lives: multiple generations navigating living in the same home, students with group work dilemmas, folks who wish they'd received thank-you notes, people grieving losses or celebrating unions, and everyone and their uncle wanting gift-giving advice for various occasions. From table-setting technicalities to the many ways to use titles and names today to how to appropriately discuss relationship problems, we *all* do care about the interactions we have with others, and the fact that we care is what keeps etiquette alive. As long as we keep asking, "What *is* the right thing to do?" etiquette lives. While tradition has, and always will, play a part in how we behave, good etiquette in any situation will always seek to create a positive and respectful experience for all parties involved.

Many people associate the terms *etiquette* and *manners* with grand houses, elaborately set tables, and tidy, calm, pleasant people—an anachronistic picture that we at the Emily Post Institute aim to shatter, or at least expand dramatically. When etiquette is viewed through a lens of wealth and arcane coded behavior, it is elusive and exclusive. When seen through a lens of consideration, respect, and honesty, it is inclusive and accessible. At times, Emily Post's etiquette advice has been viewed as a mandate—with no room for error or exception—or as a saccharine-sweet dream too idealistic for the world we live in today. But we see it as a barometer of North American social and business behavior—a *response* to what is happening, not a dictator of it or an impossibly perfect ideal. To think of etiquette as elitist or unattainable does a disservice to the universality at its heart. Etiquette is for everyone. We hope to inspire not just fancy dinner parties and handwritten thank-you notes, but also acts of kindness, patience, compassion, awareness, and thoughtful behavior. These are things we all crave and that can spring naturally from sharing food, good company, and thoughtful conversation. Our goal is to provide a sense and understanding of what good etiquette looks, sounds, and feels like in our world today.

There is often more than one "right thing" to do. The reality of our ever-changing circumstances requires us to think about and adjust our courses of action, often in a split second. Etiquette asks us not to rely on strict rules, but to *think,* to consider every aspect of a situation. It encourages us to look for a solution that benefits most, if not all, of the people involved. For all the distinct manners around utensils, handshakes, invitation wording, and knowing who introduces whom, being thoughtful is almost all it takes to show that you care and that you are trying (and hopefully succeeding) to be aware of and respectful toward those around you.

This book celebrates 100 years of *Emily Post's Etiquette.* We hope it will feel like a conversation about etiquette and not like an encyclopedia. We hope that you feel included in these pages, and that you find ways to use the advice to fit your life, your style, and your voice. We hope to entertain you as Emily did, with humor and optimism. We offer suggestions for how to interact with others in ways that are both traditional and contemporary, and to encourage you to engage confidently with the world around you. Rather than continue the tradition of adding many new topics to this book, we have pared down the advice to focus on everyday etiquette and entertaining etiquette. Our guidance on weddings and business can be found in our other books on those topics, and advice on many other specialized topics such as hiking, flag, and pet etiquette can be found online at emilypost.com.

We thank you for the opportunity to carry on the Emily Post tradition of changing with the times, both honing and developing our advice to be more inclusive of the many individuals trying to live well with one another in our collective society. We hope you find these pages useful, encouraging, and fun, and that this new edition will be one you'll be proud to use and maybe someday pass down to a loved one.

Always sincerely yours,
Lizzie Post
Daniel Post Senning

BEST SOCIETY

In 1922, the first chapter of *Etiquette* was about what was then called "Best Society." Emily argued that this group's members were not necessarily those born to high society or to great wealth (even though many assumed this to be true), but was instead made up of "gentlefolk" who took care with each other:

> "Best Society is not at all like a court with an especial queen or king, nor is it confined to any one place or group, but might be better described as an unlimited brotherhood which spreads over the entire surface of the globe, the members of which are invariably people of cultivation and worldly knowledge, who have not only perfect manners, but a perfect manner. Manners are made up of trivialities of deportment which can be easily learned if one does not happen to know them; manner is personality—the outward manifestation of one's innate character and attitude toward life."

Emily continued:

> "Thus Best Society is not a fellowship of the wealthy, nor does it seek to exclude those who are not of exalted birth; but it *is* an association of gentle-folk, of which good form in speech, charm of manner, knowledge of the social amenities, and instinctive consideration for the feelings of others, are the credentials by which society the world over recognizes its chosen members."

As Emily explained, while Best Society's manners could be learned, a perfect manner was something that went deeper, having to do with a person's particular character and how they present themself. She suggested that no amount of money could buy grace or make you a charming person. Instead, taking care with your words, having an interest in how the world operates, and focusing on the people around you (and your impact on them) are what make you a member of Best Society.

Best Society members can be found in any home, on any bus or country road, in any store or park—not just in North America, but around the world. There is no financial threshold, no good-deed checklist to meet, and certainly no secret rules to follow. We might call them emotionally intelligent, or maybe we'd say someone is "good people." No matter the label, Best Society includes people who care, who pay attention, who want to contribute to and feel the goodness of the world around them. Altogether, members of today's Best Society give our collective community a chance not just to survive, but to live well with one another—to take care with one another and feel confident in doing so.

Today we recognize Best Society as being made up of people who are kind, compassionate, and aware. These people speak and act in ways that are inclusive—recognizing that many different lives are lived within each community—and create safe spaces for everyone to be heard and to be themselves. People of Best Society are tenderhearted and fearless all at once. They are aware of their impact beyond the present moment, knowing that the actions they take and the words they say can ripple outward. They see the value and necessity of follow-up action, whether that means self-reflection or outreach. They are equipped with smiles and laughter, bringing a hopeful and positive attitude (when appropriate) wherever they go. And they know how to deliver a good apology—one that is sincere, reflective, and focused, while still exhibiting self-respect. In our fast-paced world, members of Best Society recognize the virtue of patience and that slowing down to think first about a problem can be just as useful as solving it quickly.

In many ways Best Society is the same as it was in Emily's day: an association of gentlefolk who have an instinctual consideration for the feelings of others. All it takes to join is to open your mind and heart to the idea that you can and will choose to be someone who cares about those around you; who tries to participate pleasantly and thoughtfully in your interactions with others as best you can. It's up to each of us to continually work on ourselves and ensure that Best Society remains about substance and character.

CHAPTER 1

What Is Etiquette?

"Whenever two people come together and their behavior affects one another, you have etiquette . . . it is not some rigid code of manners; it's simply how persons' lives touch one another."

Emily Post

Etiquette is for everyone. We experience it whenever people interact. It is the social expectation that we have of ourselves and others. Contrary to the clichéd images of staffed homes, Stepford wives, and silver dining sets, etiquette can be seen in the most humble and simple of interactions and spaces, and even between perfect strangers. While it can be fun to daydream about throwing elaborate parties, good etiquette is, at its core, about treating everyone we encounter well. You don't need money, power, a "higher" education, or deportment classes to demonstrate it. There is no particular time in history or place in the world that defines "real" etiquette. Good etiquette isn't formed in a particular type of household or with one version of parenting. Having good etiquette skills isn't a product of any particular background, class, identity, or religion. No. Etiquette can be learned and employed by anyone, at any stage in life, and is a choice that is available to all of us.

CONSIDERATION, RESPECT, AND HONESTY

Good etiquette rests on a foundation of consideration, respect, and honesty. We might think we know what these words mean—we certainly hear them enough—but viewing them through the lens of etiquette allows us to see that, together, they guide us toward good behavior (or, at least, give us a shot at it).

CONSIDERATION

With regard to etiquette, consideration is thinking about others, as well as yourself, before acting. It's about cultivating an awareness of the people, places, and things around us and our impact on them. Through consideration we show our sympathy and/or empathy for others by exploring how a particular action might affect them. We aren't necessarily making a judgment about a situation, just recognizing the people involved and the impact it may create.

RESPECT

As human beings we deserve regard for our feelings, rights, abilities, perspectives, and traditions. By recognizing this, we can see when our actions or words impact someone positively (upholding respect for them) or negatively (disrespecting them). By following the principle of respect, we honor others, not necessarily because of any special talents, qualities, or ideas they may have, or because we like or understand them, but simply because they exist. Respect builds on consideration by encouraging us to understand how the actions we are weighing impact others. By choosing to show respect for others, ourselves, and the world we live in, we make choices based on our potential impact, and when we choose actions that positively impact others, we build relationships—whether with a stranger as we hold a door, in a boardroom with colleagues, or at the dinner table.

HONESTY

The principle of honesty and how it is applied can make or break our polite path forward. In honesty we find both truth and the ability to build trust by being sincere. As we look at who is involved in a given situation, how they are affected, and how possible actions might positively or negatively impact them, honesty can guide us to make the best choice for that moment. With honesty present in our actions and words, we are believable and genuine. By being honest we can facilitate and maintain trust.

CHARM

There is a certain quality you might say wraps all the above together—charm. Any action can be strong when it is founded upon consideration, respect, and honesty, but when our expression of the action is also wrapped in charm—not a false charm used to trick an audience, but a sincere charm of warmth, wit, humor, tact, kindness, and patience—it will likely result in a smooth and comfortable interaction.

MANNERS AND PRINCIPLES

While many people consider manners and etiquette to be one and the same, we teach that they are more like parts of an equation, with etiquette being the sum of manners and principles. Manners are the behaviors that when executed well can demonstrate the principles in action. Employing one without the other may serve you, but only together can they really result in good etiquette.

ETIQUETTE = MANNERS + PRINCIPLES

The principles of consideration, respect, and honesty can help guide us toward good interactions when the specific manners to follow aren't clear or known. For example, it will always be "polite" or "good etiquette" to greet someone with a genuine feeling of welcome and respect. The gestures and words we use may change over time (and will certainly vary among cultures), but the *sentiment* we wish to convey (respect and welcome) is universal regardless of the particular manners we use to express it.

Manners are specific behaviors. They help us know what is expected of us, and what to expect of others. They change over time and differ by country, culture, and even social group or family. As a culture evolves, new manners emerge, and others become traditions that we either uphold or let become obsolete. Emily's 1922 edition of *Etiquette,* for example, discusses chaperones and "at home" invitations, neither of which are in this edition, as they are not current customs. Think of the traditional global greetings of the kiss on the cheek, the bow, and the handshake. Each is preferred in different parts of the world. All three are meant to indicate welcome, respect, and a sense of trust. While these manners vary across the globe, the principle behind them is the same: a respectful and considerate greeting.

The three principles of consideration, respect, and honesty can be applied to any situation you find yourself in where you don't know the proper manners. Of course, people will have slightly different interpretations of these principles, but when we base our actions on them, even when things go badly, others are likely to understand our good intent. If you think about the people involved in the situation and how they might be affected (consideration), acknowledge the worth and value of those involved by recognizing the effects of possible actions (respect), and choose to move forward in a way you feel authentically good about and that genuinely benefits the most people in the situation (honesty), you're likely to respond appropriately and also to honor and improve your relationship with those involved. In our Emily Post business etiquette programs, we use three goals to easily translate the above principles into action: think before you act, make choices that build relationships, and be sincere in your actions.

THE IMPORTANCE
OF TRADITION

Traditions are an important part of being human. We are hardwired to create rituals around meaningful experiences. Some traditions, such as breaking bread together, getting married, and gift giving on holidays, have been followed for thousands of years. Other traditions are only a few generations old, such as sending holiday cards, which started in the late 1800s. And of course, there are brand-new variations on lots of old traditions, like digital invitations and online guest books. When we take care to uphold traditions, we participate in a shared practice and in so doing we bond with others.

Traditions need to be treated with respect. Honoring a tradition may feel like stepping back in time, but through traditions we can find a sense of history in ourselves—a connection to the past. Lighting a menorah, jumping a broom, saying grace at the table, giving up a seat on the bus, or holding a door can hold deep meaning for us beyond the important human connection it reinforces in the moment. That is, if it does. If a tradition doesn't resonate with you, you don't have to keep it, though you might want to think it through before you abandon a tradition (and when it comes to annual holidays, you'll certainly want to consult family and others who typically join in before pulling the plug on it completely). One of the wonderful things about etiquette today is that it almost never limits us to only one way of doing things.

Etiquette is often discussed in connection with traditions, and it is important and worthwhile to understand why a tradition matters to people (or doesn't). Showing respect for someone's traditions is part of showing respect for them. This is why it's important when adopting or blending a tradition to consider whether you are appropriating (using an aspect of a culture or tradition outside its traditional or respected original use) or honoring it.

The reasons behind a tradition will often provide clues to how to behave in new situations. Consider letter writing and its traditional structure, for example. Today we rely on a similar format for emails and can look to letters for options when composing emails. Looking at the reasons behind our traditions is also often the first step toward finding understanding and compromise when we choose to change or adapt them. Tradition gives us something to guide us as well as something to hold on to as we navigate a changing world.

Elizabeth Post, Emily's granddaughter-in-law, who carried the "etiquette expert" mantle after Emily, from 1960 to 1995, wrote in her preface to the 1969 replica edition of the original 1922 *Etiquette*: "How many of us have ever seen a footman? Or been presented with a PPC card? Or been taught to use a finger bowl? For most of us those are things which are purely out of fiction; to read about them is similar to seeing a rerun of a silent film. It fills us with nostalgia for the golden days gone by—allowing us to forget the discomforts, the prejudices, and the inequalities that were also a part of that life."

It's important to make sure our traditions don't harm anyone. As Elizabeth notes, being filled with nostalgia for certain traditions can lead us to overlook their nastier aspects, which are important to understand so we can move forward and avoid repeating them. A glorious dinner party today can allow us to enjoy gathering and celebrating with one another—however formally—while no longer requiring us to alternate seating or divide activities by binary gender standards of old. It's fine to have an uneven balance between women, men, and nonbinary guests, and anyone who'd like to may head to the study for an after-dinner cigar.

COMBATING RUDENESS
WITH AGENCY AND GRATITUDE

It can be hard to channel your most gracious self when you don't feel like you have much agency or you aren't feeling particularly grateful. Friends, family, coworkers, and even strangers can—intentionally and unintentionally—slight you, behave thoughtlessly or carelessly, or be so flat-out rude that it can deflate your better self. If you want to both stand strong and appreciate, embrace, and contribute to civility in the world around you, listen to and amplify that voice inside that says, *I can and will choose to act with consideration, respect, and honesty toward others. And I'm grateful for the opportunity to do so.* This thought can help you find politeness and the good will to use it when rudeness feels like your only option.

By looking at the world as a series of opportunities to do right by yourself and others, you can flip the narrative in your head from *Ugh, I don't want to make this effort—what's the point?* or even *Do I have to?* to *I'm glad to have this chance to do something positive and effective.* It might be holding a door, taking the time to learn and say a name correctly, or confidently engage in a difficult conversation. Whatever the situation, coming from a place of *I can, I will, and I'm grateful* can put you in a great mindset to solve problems and interact with others in ways that build relationships.

When used for self-assessment, etiquette can be a powerful tool to combat the impact of rudeness. When used to judge or critique others, etiquette ceases to function as a useful guide and manners become effectively useless. If the vast majority of rude behavior is unintentional, then the best way to fight it isn't to judge, but to cultivate awareness of our actions and their impact and choose to act in ways that improve our relationships with others. This is where we can effect the most change. Is it possible to turn a slight into motivation to avoid inadvertently treating someone else the same way? While that may sound a bit Pollyanna, rest assured, it's not. To consistently hold yourself accountable to the standards you wish to see in the world is incredibly hard to do. When we are met with rude behavior, etiquette helps us to step up and respond well, instead of casting judgment or responding offensively.

THE PRACTICE OF GOOD ETIQUETTE

Good etiquette always begins with awareness: awareness of your impact on the world around you. Awareness of all the contributing factors in a situation—the people and things involved that could be affected, the traditions and cultures present, and how to take care with it all. With all the focus on others in etiquette, it's important to note that *you* matter too. You are an important part of the equation. While there may be many times when we will choose to do something that's best for others, even if it's not ideal for us, that doesn't mean we should disrespect ourselves. What may be reasonable and doable for one person may not be for another. When this happens, we must find an alternative solution that works best for everyone, including ourselves. When good etiquette is working well among a group of people, everyone will care both about others and themselves (something that can sometimes—it's true—require the sacrifice of certain impulses and desires).

There will be times when we don't have the bandwidth or capacity to be our best selves. There will be other times when we will be amazed that we do. As we grow and mature (and yes, we can continue to grow and mature long after adolescence), we expand our ability to deal with problems, big and small, as they arise. Ideally, our capacity to be our best selves grows with experience.

Etiquette isn't simply something you learn; it's a practice that you continually do. Simply knowing particular manners and principles doesn't make you a polite person; it's only by consistently using the manners and principles together that you become gracious and are recognized as such. Ultimately, it is in our explicit behavior with others, often through our manners, that people recognize the values and principles that motivate us. Our manners function like a shorthand expression of our values. When you are on time, for example, you demonstrate that you value respect and consideration and keeping your word, as well as other people's time.

Learning and practicing these skills takes time. It is said that there are three steps to mastering a new skill: The first step is to learn what to do. The second step is to practice doing it until you get it right. And the third step is to repeat the action as often as needed until it becomes an ingrained habit. The more you do it, the easier it becomes. Repeating good behavior will help make it second nature to you, and help you avoid making unintended or inconsiderate offenses, often the most common kind. So, take heart and flex your good etiquette muscles. Practice, practice, practice on everyone you encounter, and you'll help make the world a kinder place.

CHAPTER 2

Greetings & Introductions

"A handshake often creates a feeling of liking or of irritation between two strangers. Who does not dislike a 'boneless' hand extended as though it were a spray of sea-weed, or a miniature boiled pudding? It is equally annoying to have one's hand clutched aloft in grotesque affectation and shaken violently sideways, as though it were being used to clean a spot out of the atmosphere."

Emily Post

Let's start at the beginning: our everyday interactions begin with greetings. Whether it's the people we see first thing in the morning, our colleagues at work, or friends we're visiting, we always start an interaction with a friendly and welcoming greeting. Greetings can be the start of a longer interaction, or they can be brief and serve the purpose of acknowledging the people we cross paths with throughout the day. Greetings can kick off introductions, and introductions are one of the etiquette classics that never grow old. In Emily's day, there was much focus on who was being introduced to whom, in what order, when they should be introduced, how to properly say their name and title, and which gesture was appropriate. Today we focus more on encouraging people to actually *make* introductions, and to communicate clearly and respectfully while doing so.

GREETINGS

Hello. Acknowledging those around us with even the slightest greeting is a small but very important part of etiquette. At the least, it's a tiny thing (a nod) and at the most it's a full-on production (shrieks, hugs, and kisses) that helps to unite and bond us. A simple greeting is polite and expected. Without greetings, we're just individuals moving around one another in close proximity. A greeting is a beginning, an entrance into a shared space and conversation—or at least the potential for one.

We show respect when we acknowledge one another's existence. With a greeting, we can make someone's day brighter. A greeting costs us nothing and is easy to deliver. In days of old, greetings were used to indicate that we meant no harm. In today's world, where we can often feel divided from and attacked by those around us, the power of a smile and eye contact can be transformative. It's a simple point of etiquette, but an essential one: greet the people you come into contact with throughout your day. No one is above giving a greeting, and no one is below receiving one.

Throughout the day, we must use our judgment, based on the circumstances, to issue appropriate greetings. When we are greeted well, we feel a sense of acknowledgment. When a greeting is lackluster or absent, we feel the lack of recognition. Choosing which gestures and words to use, and when, will depend on how well you know the other person (if at all) and the formality of the occasion. Enter the kitchen on a lazy Saturday morning and you might get a simple, "Mornin'" or "Hey" as your roommate looks up from their cereal bowl. Enter cousin Babs's house, on the other hand, and you'll be greeted with a chorus of welcome as family members flock to the door, arms extended wide for hugs and kisses galore. And there are times when a good greeting is reserved and soft in its delivery, such as when you're meeting a friend who has received bad news or lost a loved one. (See Chapter 8: Hard Times.)

EXPRESSIONS OF GREETING

Good greetings are often simple. Eye contact and one word or phrase are all you need. For a casual greeting, you might even just use the person's name: "Eddyyyyy!" Your facial expression matters too; you don't always have to smile, but you do want your expression to convey joy, welcome, or respect.

CASUAL	INFORMAL	FORMAL
Hi, Hey, Yo, 'Sup, What's up?, Hey girl hey, Hiya, Howdy, Hey y'all, How's it going?, Mornin', Afternoon, Evenin'	Hello, Hi, Morning, Good morning, Afternoon, Good afternoon, Evening, Good evening	How do you do?; greeting plus name or title, such as: Hello, Mrs. Smith; Good morning, Mr. Shelley; Good afternoon, Madam Secretary; Good evening, sir/ma'am/mx/miss

If you are able to look up, make eye contact (and if you cannot, direct your attention at the other person's face as best you can) with a friendly expression, and say "Hi," "Hey," "Hello," or even just offer a friendly or respectful nod, you've covered the basics for a good greeting. Well done, you! Beyond the basics, you can step it up a notch by adding the person's name: "Hey, Puja." And if you really want to be jolly and vibrant, throw in a buoyant "Hey, Puja! So good to see you! How are you?" Asking about a person's well-being, commenting on how happy you are to "see them" or "be here" all enhance a greeting.

Stepping up the pep is all very "yay," but it's also important to remember that not every greeting needs to be sunshine and sparkles. In fact, not every greeting should be. A good greeting at work might be respectful because of its simplicity. Consider the time, place, occasion, and other people present to deliver a greeting that fits the scene. "Morning, Puj! What's shakin?" said cheerfully with a note of excitement is not how to greet Puja when you're visiting her under difficult circumstances. Nor would it be proper when she's clearly working. But when passing her in the office kitchen or a school hallway, or greeting her in the morning while staying at her house? Yes, absolutely!

One thing we tend to do here in the United States that people from other countries have labeled "strange" is to say, "Hi, how are you?" or "Hey, how's it going?" in passing, not expecting the other person to slow down or respond beyond tossing out a "Good, 'n' you?" as they pass, with them also not expecting you to stop or even respond. Many of us will reply "Good" right back at them as they stroll away. In this context there's nothing rude about this type of casual, in-passing exchange.

Preparing yourself with a greeting that doesn't invite further conversation is smart. It isn't to be standoffish, but so you can greet people well when you don't have time to talk. "Franklin! Good to see you!" is brief, friendly, likely true, short, and is polite when coupled with a friendly wave or nod as you pass him outside the grocery store. He may respond in kind, but he won't likely assume you want to stop to actually chat. On the flip side, when you are the one who cannot stop to chat, it's okay to say so: "Hey, Franklin, good to see you, I'm in a hurry or I'd stop to chat." It's a wonderful way to use politeness as a tool even when you're short on time or busy.

SIR, MA'AM, MISS, AND MX

American etiquette has a long tradition of using the terms *sir, ma'am,* and *miss* to show respect when addressing someone, whether you know them or not. "Good morning, sir," or "Yes ma'am." For many these terms create a sense of respect that is comforting, useful, and full of honor. Forty-four percent of Americans say that they appreciate their use.

For others, these terms don't create a respectful sense of formality but an artificial distance or authority that is unwelcome in casual relationships or everyday encounters where you often hear them. In fact, thirteen percent of Americans say that they do not appreciate these terms being used—that's more than one in ten. Another forty-two percent of the population says the use of these forms of address does not matter to them.

This creates a slight conundrum. What's a person who's trying to be respectful and considerate to their fellow people to do when a "Good evening, miss" or a "Yes, sir" could be either appreciated or offensive. You do your best with what you know. Are you in a region where these forms of address are used frequently? Lean toward using them in your everyday interactions. Do you know your dad, who was in the military, really appreciates it, whereas your sister, who is also in the military, prefers you leave it out of your greetings to her? Respect their preferences. If you aren't in a position to know, and you guess wrong (you say "sir" to someone who cannot stand being called sir or leave out a "ma'am" when answering someone who sees it as a sign of respect) and you see they are upset, or they say so, apologize and do your best not to repeat the error. "I'm sorry, yes, *ma'am.*" It's the best you can do in the moment.

There is another reason that our current use of *sir, ma'am,* or *miss* doesn't fit our entire society well. There isn't an option to use for those who are nonbinary and gender-nonconforming. We wonder if looking to the nonbinary title of *mx* has the potential to provide a solution. Using *mx*—pronounced "mix"—could become a welcome option. "Good morning, mx." "Yes, mx."

If someone makes a mistake, be patient and forgiving. Of course, you can issue a gentle correction if the situation warrants: "Craig, do you have a second? I know 'sir' is often said as a sign of respect, but it makes me feel old. Feel free to just call me Darren." "Severin, we say, 'Yes, ma'am' when responding to Grandma." And accept an apology if it comes your way.

ADDRESSING A GROUP OR CROWD

Traditionally, it was commonplace to address a crowd or group as "ladies and gentlemen," "boys and girls," or "guys and gals." Today, unless you know the gender identities of those in the crowd, you should always address a crowd using more general terms like "My dear friends (or colleagues)," "Good people of _____," "Hello, class," "Patrons," "Attention, everyone," or "Dear guests," and simply leave gender out of it. It should also be noted that even though the term *guys* is considered to be gender neutral, some don't identify with it and may be offended by it, as it traditionally referred to males (the same goes for *dude*).

GESTURES OF GREETING

Our greeting gestures are a critically important part of how we communicate and are sometimes the entirety of our greeting. These important signals can be basic, such as eye contact, a nod, a slight wave, or prayer hands (alternatively placing your hand over your heart). Or they can be delivered with the formal flourish and technical precision of curtsies and bows. Most of us fall in the middle ground, which is where we find fist bumps, handshakes, high fives, and the much-debated hug. Let's break these down and consider how we execute gestures of greeting.

GESTURE	FROM A DISTANCE OR TO STRANGERS	IN CASUAL SETTINGS WITH FRIENDS OR ACQUAINTANCES	WITH FAMILY AND CLOSE FRIENDS	IN BUSINESS OR FORMAL SITUATIONS	GOOD WHEN SOCIAL DISTANCING
Eye contact and smile	X	X	X	X	X
Nod	X	X	X	X	X
Hat tip	X	X	X	X	X
Wave	X	X	X		X
High five		X	X		
Fist bump		X	X		
Handshake		X	X	X	
Hug		X	X		
Cheek kiss		X	X		

THE NOD AND THE HAT TIP

A nod of the head is one of the most common gestures of acknowledgment. The nod shows deference and respect. It's a gesture that demonstrates that we are letting our guard down. It is the opposite of the aggressive jutting out of the chin in a fight posture. A simple tilt of the head downward, with or without eye contact, is a respectful nod.

An upward nod is more of a casual "Hey." It's also used when communicating to someone from a distance. It can occasionally come across as cocky or inviting, so be careful how you use it. The downward nod is more respectful in tone.

The hat tip is a simple version of what used to be the grand gesture of removing one's hat in greeting. We still do remove our hats when greeting someone, but not always (see Removing Hats, page 134). Grab the brim of your hat and lift it slightly off your head, an inch or so at most. This is often accompanied by a downward nod. It's a sign of respect, and a nod to traditions of old. If the interaction is likely to continue and you want to remove your hat completely as a sign of respect, after completing the "hat tip," instead of replacing the hat on your head, just hold it in your hand at your side or with both hands in front of you.

THE WAVE

You know how to wave; it's a baby's first gesture. In a business situation, if handshakes aren't being used, a simple wave—no back and forth, just one motion of the hand—is seen as more respectful than anything with more movement. In very formal situations, you wouldn't wave, but instead give a respectful nod. If you want to prevent the wave from leading to a hug or handshake, don't move forward toward the person as you do it. Instead, keep a respectful distance so as not to encourage a more tactile response.

THE HIGH FIVE AND THE FIST BUMP

Definitely a casual greeting gesture, the high five keeps making a comeback. The only real etiquette with the high five (other than when to use it, even casually) is to make sure you don't (a) leave the other person hanging, (b) hurt the other person with the strength and power of your slap, or (c) miss (so embarrassing!). Also, a weak high five usually deserves a redo for everyone to feel satisfied. ("*Doh!* Let's try that again.") But don't insist or try to make it a thing. ("Oh, that was pathetic. Redo?" "Nah." "Okay.")

The fist bump is the high five of the Gen X, Millennial, and Gen Z generations, completely proper and acceptable in a multitude of situations. Cool, casual, and sometimes with an "explosion" afterward. Make a fist. Bump it. Blow it up.

THE HANDSHAKE

The handshake is the American standard for a respectful gesture of greeting. It is a gesture with deep symbolic roots, and says "I come in friendship, I mean you well, I have no weapon, please take my hand, you can trust me." It is an offer to touch, something that is a rare occurrence among strangers, acquaintances, and colleagues. It is kept brief and contained within a simple gesture, and even so, the act of human contact means so much. When the social distancing measures of the COVID-19 pandemic pulled us apart, one of the biggest questions people asked about etiquette was whether the handshake would come back. Let us assure you, it is as important now as ever. It is a classic that is automatic to a great many. When someone reaches out a hand, it's very difficult to refuse it.

There are five elements to a good handshake: eye contact, a smile or friendly expression, a good grip, the right amount of energy, and letting go at the right time.

1. **EYE CONTACT.** If you are able to stand and make eye contact, do so. If you cannot stand, make solid eye contact. If you cannot make eye contact, direct your attention to the other person's face as best you can. (Sometimes focusing on the mouth or the bridge of the nose can help.)

2. **SMILE.** Have a friendly, relaxed, or respectful expression on your face.

3. **GRIP.** Extend your right arm toward the other person, keeping your fingers together and your wrist turned so your palm is facing to the left. Clasp the other person's hand, crook of your thumb to the crook of their thumb. Clasp your hand around theirs, and they'll close their hand around yours. You're aiming for firm but not too tight—no limp fish or bone-crushing grips. Use the same degree of pressure you would apply to turn a doorknob. And definitely do not place your left hand over your clasped hands, or on the other person's upper arm, shoulder, or hip. Leave your other hand at your side, out of the equation entirely.

4. **SHAKE.** Move your hand up and down, one to three times. It's not a big or vigorous movement, but active enough to feel a connection with the other person.

5. **LET GO.** While letting go too quickly can seem abrupt and unfriendly, holding on too long is awkward and leaves the other person wondering if they will ever get their hand back. They'll be focused on how awkwardly long this handshake is and not on anything that you say during the greeting or introduction.

If someone does not shake hands, for whatever reason—health, culture, ability—they will likely say so, or they will smile kindly and focus on using their words to greet you instead of outright declining your handshake. Roll with it. It's perfectly acceptable for people to choose not to engage in physical contact. If you don't ever or are currently choosing not to shake hands, it's best to clarify for others: "Please excuse me, I don't/can't shake hands, but I'm so happy to meet you."

For those who do shake hands, seize every opportunity for a handshake, no matter the hand offered or the grasp needed to shake it. If you are able, always shake any outstretched hand; it's a sign of respect and helps us to connect. Likewise, if you are comfortable, reach out for a handshake. If someone cannot shake your hand, they'll let you know. Then proceed with using your words and expression along with a wave or respectful nod to create a good and pleasant greeting. When greeting someone who clearly cannot use their arms, a respectful wave is appropriate.

THE HUG

Hugs can be amazing, whether it's the embrace of family members or the warmth and closeness of a friend. In the right time and place, a hug can nourish the soul. Pressing one's body against and wrapping one's arms around another human is intimate. When welcomed, it's wonderful! ("I'm a hugger!" "Me, too!" *BIG HUG*) But for a first meeting? No, probably not. It should only be used between those who are familiar with each other and willing. It's important to note that many people are not huggers. For this group, hugs may be completely uncomfortable or comfortable only with certain people. A person who says, "I'm a hugger" as they go in for a hug—bulldozing over a non-hugger's offer of a handshake—is being rude. This kind of hug is aggressive and inconsiderate. It conveys a lack of consideration or, worse, a dominance that is selfishly unaware at best.

Say a family member expects a hug but you don't want to give one, greeting them from a short distance away (three feet or more) may be enough to stave it off. When someone requests one ("Cleo, my dear. Come over here and give me a hug!"), be more direct ("I'm not feeling huggy today, but I am happy to see you, Uncle"). It's good to get used to dialing it back to another gesture of greeting if needed. If someone doesn't want a hug, don't take it personally.

The hug is such an intimate gesture that, for some, an unwanted one can feel like a violation. When someone doesn't ask, pushes for one, or even forces it, they're communicating that because they think it's okay, they get to press their body against someone else's. Depending on how it's done, it can cross over into sexual harassment or assault. Sound serious? That's because it feels that way to those who are uncomfortable with hugs. For this reason, hugs are better avoided in business situations.

So how can you handle hugs well from the start? Always ask if a hug is welcome: "Hug?" If the other person says, "Yes, of course!" then hug away, you huggy people! But if they say, "No," "High five instead?" "A handshake will work," or "Not feeling a hug today," you must absolutely respect their response. And then deliver the alternate gesture with warmth and friendliness.

THE CHEEK KISS

A kiss on the cheek is more common in Europe and South America than in the United States. There are certain cultures that embrace the kiss on the cheek as a hello, and it's understood and welcomed. Some kisses are done in the air at the side of the cheek (air kisses), especially to avoid lipstick stains or gooey gloss, and are often accompanied by an onomatopoetic smack (mwah!). Some kisses are cheek to cheek, and some are lip to cheek. The number of kisses, the degree or emphasis of the kiss, and which side you start on vary greatly between relatives, friends, generations, and geographic regions. Pay attention and follow suit if you're going in for the cheek kiss.

Never move to the mouth on any of these kisses. If you have established a lip-to-lip kiss with someone, you'll know! You won't have to question it. If you make the mistake of leaning the wrong way and happen to kiss someone on the lips, apologize and move on. (Obviously, no one of good character uses this misstep as a way to actually land a kiss.)

In the United States, we often reserve kisses for romantic partners, close family, and dear friends. Those who kiss everyone they meet should consider the position they put others in when they lean in for kisses with complete strangers or in business scenarios. Remember, it's not only about the person initiating it being okay with it. Remember too that to throw kisses and *mwah mwah*'s out with every greeting can be seen as affectatious and send the opposite signal from the one of closeness that was intended.

WHO GREETS WHOM?

Who greets whom? We frequently hear different versions of this question. For example, what is the obligation of coworkers and roommates (or family) to greet each other upon first seeing one another? Does the person in the room greet the person coming into the room, or does the person entering the space greet the person already in it? What if you don't intend to interact and are just passing through? Do you have to greet people every time you cross paths with them? The things we fret over!

The person entering the room generally has the advantage of knowing that there will be a change in the room once they enter, and is often thought to be responsible for announcing their arrival. "Good morning!" you might say breezily to your coworkers as you walk into the office kitchen for a cup of coffee. That said, many feel that the person in the room is in some ways considered the host of the space, having been there first. And that upon seeing the person who is entering, they should acknowledge this person's entrance and welcome them to the space. "Morning!" they say as their roommate enters the living room.

Then there is the reality: sometimes, the person in the room is busy and doesn't notice the person entering. Other times, the person coming in may not be alone and not stop to greet the person already in the room or, worse yet, not even notice that someone else is present. Both cases could leave someone feeling ignored. Rather than spend too much time worrying about who should do what first, the good thing to do, no matter who you are in the situation, is to take action and greet someone when you notice them.

CROSSING PATHS WITH FRIENDS OR COLLEAGUES

It can be easy to get excited when we see friends, family, or colleagues out and about. While we have all probably done it, you really should avoid shouting at someone from afar to get their attention for a quick hello. It could be startling to the person, and it can also be surprising and disruptive to others around you. If you're really excited and truly want to catch someone, go to them rather than shouting across a crowd or a large area. But sometimes we aren't sure if we should call out to get their attention or not. The distance you are from the person can help you decide how to engage. If you are more than ten or so feet away from someone, use a wave or a nod, if you're closer than that, a verbal greeting might be appropriate—but consider the atmosphere first before shouting out to someone. It is a reality of today that with headphones in or on our ears, smartphones in our hands, and the ability to take a call anywhere, we can miss someone greeting us. We also can't always blame technology. Sometimes we can be like dear Ms. Inher Heade, so consumed in thought that she misses the "hellos" she receives in passing from friends, colleagues, or extended family (or even people she'd like to date!). While any of us can be lost in thought, we want to be sure to apologize if someone tells us we have missed a kind greeting that came our way. "Inher, I saw you at the hardware store yesterday and tried to say 'Hi,' but you didn't see me." "Oh my goodness, Kavia, I'm so sorry. I didn't mean to be so oblivious; I would have loved to have stopped for a chat!" It's a good idea to look up and be aware of our surroundings when we are around others.

FOR FORMAL VISITS AND MEETINGS

While we want our greetings to be warm and welcoming, there are times when we need or want respect to be the main focus rather than delight. If it's a formal social situation, say "How do you do?" and add a handshake if appropriate. In some cases, there is no handshake at all—just the greeting. This would be unusual for a business meeting, but it does sometimes happen socially. If we cannot use a handshake for any reason, a respectful nod of the head while making eye contact will absolutely do. "How do you do?" "Good morning," "Good afternoon," and "Good evening" are the best greetings for formal situations, and are appropriate even without a gesture of greeting accompanying them.

It's also not just about what you say. Our demeanor changes when we enter a formal setting. We stand or sit up straight. We give our full attention to those we are present with, facing them, making eye contact, and using our best listening skills. We wait to speak until we are certain someone is finished, or perhaps in some cases only when we are addressed or invited to speak. This is different from our everyday interactions, and the additional investment of attention and care both recognizes and at the same time helps to create the formality.

THE RUDEST THING

The rudest thing you can do is intentionally ignore someone's greeting. In Emily's day, this was called the *cut direct:* "Hi, Molly," met with no words or eye contact, a completely intentional snub, is totally gasp-worthy and meant to send a message. It's a horrible way to let someone know they don't exist to you (right now, at least). Even if you're crossing paths with someone you dislike, take the "etiquette high road" and never ignore a greeting. "Hi, Kat" is all that's needed in reply. This is a base-level social expectation.

YOUR SMILE

For every *hello, hi,* and *how are you,* the nods, handshakes, and hugs, a smile is probably the best greeting of all. No matter what your teeth look like, or the shape of your lips, when a natural smile—even the tiniest one—spreads across someone's face, there is no mistaking the genuine warmth and pleasure that is expressed. A smile may be the simplest and most universal greeting to use. As Emily wrote in 1922, "a ready smile is more valuable in life than a ready wit; the latter may sometimes bring enemies, but the former always brings friends."

INTRODUCTIONS

The most important thing about introductions is to make them. Never hesitate. Even if you've just reintroduced yourself to someone you've already met, it's still better to make an introduction than not. Introductions are considerate and welcoming. They help to make us feel included and provide us with basic information about a person. Historically, they served as a way to vouch for someone socially or professionally, and worked to establish social networks in all areas of life. Great care was taken with the form of the introduction: who approached whom, what words were chosen, what titles and names were used and in what order, even when the introduction would or could take place. All of these choices communicated a connection worth making if done right, and awkwardness if done wrong.

Today we live in a simpler world. Most introductions are intended to make people feel comfortable and give all involved enough information to interact well with each other. We make all kinds of introductions: self-introductions, group introductions, casual introductions, and formal introductions—verbally, in writing, and via different platforms. And there are formalities to consider when introducing or meeting certain people such as government leaders or military or religious figures. (See Government Titles and Religious Titles, pages 49–52) With all the variations that can be found in introductions, the key is not to worry about making a mistake and instead simply make an introduction, whenever and wherever possible. It's the polite thing to do.

WHEN TO MAKE INTRODUCTIONS

You absolutely must make introductions in these situations:

- When you stop to say hello to someone and you are with a person they haven't met.

- When you are bringing someone to a gathering, group, or someone's home and they don't know the others there. (If it's a long weekend or trip, you must do this throughout the trip whenever you encounter people your guest has yet to meet.) The same goes if you've brought a guest to an event and someone your guest doesn't know arrives later.

- When you have a guest at your club, you want to introduce them to anyone you encounter and interact with—staff included. Not everyone you pass, but certainly the people you speak with, such as the bartender. ("Doug, this is my buddy Frank. We'll take two bourbons, please—on me because of my terrible putting.")

- When you're out with friends and cross paths with another friend or group and decide to join up, all parties should exchange names if they don't already know each other.

- When you are on a date and you run into people you know. (You don't have to announce, "This is my date," but you should say, "This is Julie.")

- When you're hosting a meeting and the people present don't already know each other.

When in doubt, introduce. Introductions are rarely (if ever) *not* appreciated, and always help put people at ease.

INTRODUCTION BASICS

A good introduction acknowledges all the people who are meeting for the first time—typically giving equal attention to each person—and makes known the names, titles, pronouns, and relationships of the parties involved. There is, of course, one overarching rule when it comes to introductions and getting everything right: if you aren't sure, ask. Sometimes the best solution is the simplest one. "How do you like to be introduced?" should remove all doubt. Or you might be more specific: "Kai, may I ask what pronouns you use before I introduce you?" "Do you prefer Kate or Catherine when you are introduced?" "Mary, pardon me for forgetting, but do you use Mrs. or Ms.?" Often, you'll have made someone's day by checking first, and it will always be polite to do so.

In formal and business situations or when addressing your elders, you'll want to pay closer attention to who is introduced to whom. (See Formality in Introductions, opposite page.) For casual and everyday introductions, what matters most is that all parties feel welcome, recognized, and have an understanding of whom they have just been introduced to. A good introduction makes way for easy conversation or the commencement of whatever is to follow on the agenda, whether it's a meeting, party, meal, tour, or date.

If appropriate and known to you, share the names, pronouns, and titles of the people you are introducing. Traditionally you would start formally, then allow others to offer more familiar options: "Mrs. Brown, may I introduce Mr. Sal Ugolini? Mr. Ugolini, this is Mrs. Catherine Brown." "How do you do? Please call me Catherine." Or more casually, "Catherine, this is Sal Ugolini; he was my neighbor when I was growing up. Sal, this is Catherine Brown, my mother-in-law; she is visiting from London." Rather than state, "This is Catherine Brown; she uses 'she/her' pronouns," you would intentionally share a tidbit about the person that allows you to identify their pronouns. You might think it's rude to refer to someone who is present in the third person, and it generally is; but during an introduction it's a natural construction to use.

Today, first names can be enough in many situations, but full names, relationship information, and titles can be helpful. Leaving these out isn't rude, but it can feel abrupt and quickly lead to more questions. For casual introductions, this is normal: "Tim, Chelsea. Chelsea, Tim." But for anyone who's not a pal or casual acquaintance in your life, stepping it up a notch is good.

If you don't know someone's name, pronouns, or title and don't have time to ask for them privately before the introduction, you can say something like, "Dietz, I apologize—I realize I don't know your [pronouns, last name, title] to properly introduce you." Dietz will likely now politely reply with whatever information was missing. "Ah—Dietz Warren. I use *they;* thank you for double-checking." You can then carry on with the introduction: "Dietz and I recently met at . . ."

While interrupting is generally rude, there are times when an interruption is required to make an introduction, such as when you and your mother-in-law run into a friend you grew up with. It is far better to interrupt when your friend starts chatting away than to leave your mother-in-law standing there awkwardly. Seconds can feel like ages when you are silenced by your anonymity, almost like having been transformed into a very large fly on the wall. Best not to put others in this position. Instead, make a quick introduction "Excuse me, Sal; please let me interrupt to introduce my mother-in-law, Catherine Brown . . . ".

FORMALITY IN INTRODUCTIONS

The more formal the circumstances (or people), the more structured and specific the introduction wording should be. It's good to know the formal standards for when you may need to apply them.

WHOM TO INTRODUCE TO WHOM

Many people get tripped up on whom to introduce to whom in a formal introduction. The main thing to remember is to always speak to the "more important" person first (the one you want to honor) and offer to *present* or *introduce* the other person to them. This is often self-evident: socially, it would be the elder of the two parties. In business, the client or guest or the more senior-ranking person is spoken to first. If there is no apparent difference in age or rank between the two, you may start with either.

FORMAL INTRODUCTIONS

Instead of "Let me introduce ____," ask, "May I present ____?" (pronounced "pre-*zent*," not "*prez*-ent" like the gift). This introduction is phrased as a question. In the most formal situations, the introduction typically will be made in one direction with the idea that you are presenting one person to another and not back the other way. In formal introductions, people might shake hands, or they may smile, make eye contact, and give a friendly but respectful nod.

> "Mr. Longnow Distinguished, may I present Mr. Fresh Andnew?"

> "How do you do, Mr. Andnew. Are you enjoying the event?"

> "I am, thank you. I am so grateful Ms. Abouttown invited me this evening."

"How do you do?" is the most formal and traditional response to an introduction. It is more like saying "pleased to meet you" than asking about one's well-being. Emily's Mrs. Oldworld would have never responded to an introduction with, "Pleased to meet you, Mr. Andnew." Even though this is commonly heard in many introductions in formal settings today, it is "incorrect" by old-school standards. Instead, after saying "How do you do?" and the person you've just met's name, you would then ask a more specific question, like in the example above. And that is what the person being presented responds to.

WHAT TO AVOID

In formal introductions, avoid saying "I'd like you to meet ____" (the added "you" makes it quite bossy) or "This is ____" (too informal), or "Can I introduce ____?" (is anyone reminded of their mother saying, "I don't know, *can* you?"). And per Emily herself, definitely never say, "I'd like to make you acquainted with ____." That's just wrong.

CASUAL INTRODUCTIONS

Most of us will rarely, if ever, say, "May I present ____?" and "How do you do?" in our lifetimes, at least not in a serious way. Instead, we're likely to be in a social situation where we might choose from a range of semiformal and casual introductions. For example, a semiformal introduction might sound like, "Jim, may I introduce Ms. Delightful, my partner? Bree, this is Mr. Jim Ratte, my friend from Workout World." Or a little more casually: "Jim, this is Ms. Delightful, my partner. Bree, this is Mr. Jim Ratte, my friend." And even more casually: "Jim, this is Bree, my partner. Bree, this is Jim, my friend from Workout World." And the super casual: "Do you two know each other? Jim, Bree, Bree, Jim."

Should someone mispronounce your name when they have just been given it in an introduction, kindly correct it right away. This is true of a misspoken name, pronoun, or title. "Oh, it's Andnew, not Anjou" or "I should probably tell you it's Andnew instead of Anjou."

ONE PERSON TO A GROUP

A casual introduction of one person to a group can be organic or quite the awkward moment. When walking in to join a pick-up game or interest group alongside a regular member or group leader, you'll likely get introduced, "Hey, team, this is Malcolm. Malcolm, this is Trevor, Kyle, Rhys, Ellen, Tobin, Josh, Carlo, Kelsie, Rodney, Katie, and Ahmed."

But for a casual introduction to a group at a small party, when you walk in the door and ten people shout your name ("ANITA!!!"), and you need to introduce the person you're with, that whole name list can be overwhelming and a real time killer. The person being introduced can feel like they are being put on a social pedestal for all to see, while simultaneously trying to look interested in the ten people whose names are being thrown at them. Frankly, it gets old after four to six names, and the likelihood of remembering everyone is slim.

As an alternative, if there are more than five or six people in a group, as you and your guest walk in the door and everyone shouts "ANITA!!!" respond with, "Hey! Everybody, this is Annie. Annie, this is Tobin, our host, and I'll introduce everyone else as we go around." This gives Annie a chance to say hello to her host—an important move for any guest, especially an unknown but welcomed one—as well as for the host to greet you and Annie. It quickly announces the arrival of a new face to the group and gives Annie a moment to get settled before meeting everyone else.

When meeting a big group, expect a lot of *Heys* and upward nods coming back at you. And don't be afraid to ask for someone's name again if you didn't hear it clearly over the din. You are unlikely to shake everyone's hand, and that's okay.

THE SELF-INTRODUCTION

There are plenty of times when you'll need or want to make a self-introduction, such as at a party where you don't know anyone, at conferences, while dining at a counter or on a long flight, or when joining a new group. We learn how to do this as tots, but as we grow up many people get nervous about introducing themselves. A good, confident self-introduction will go a long way toward starting off on the right foot. From being impressive in the business world to making it easy to approach someone who catches your eye, this can be a great tool in your social skill set.

When the time comes, present yourself well for a self-introduction: stand up straight, lift your head, make eye contact if you can, smile, and give a nod or wave or offer a handshake. Accompanied by a clear and friendly "Hi, I'm Roz," that's all you need—technically. When making self-introductions casually, you can offer your last name, pronouns, where you're from, etc. if you wish. You will also adjust your language to fit the situation. For example, at a bar: "Hi, I'm Roz." On a solo work or vacation trip: "I'm Roz, here on vacation from Tuscaloosa. How about you?" At an event like a wedding where you know few people: "Hi, I'm Roz. I'm the groom's friend from work." While some have been doing it for years, many people are new to the practice of making a self-introduction that includes their personal pronouns. When making self-introductions with your pronouns, it might sound like this: "Hi, I'm Pete. I use he/him." (See Pronouns, page 35, for more on pronouns and introductions.)

SOCIAL TITLES OR HONORIFICS IN INTRODUCTIONS

Social titles, or honorifics, have long been used to help communicate age and relationships. *Ms.*, *Mr.*, *Mrs.*, *Mx.*, *Miss*, and *Master* are the ones most commonly used today. The current system has had two additions over the last century to better reflect our population—*Ms.*, which made its debut in the early twentieth century but then fell out of fashion until the 1970s when it became widely used, and *Mx.*, which first appeared in print in 1977 and has seen greater usage since the 2010s. These additions prove to us that this area of culture *can* and *should* continue to change to reflect American society. Details about each title currently in use follow.

MS. (pronounced "miz"; the plural is *Mss.* or *Mses.* pronounced "mizzes") is used by any adult woman roughly 18 years of age and older. When you are unaware of a woman's title, *Ms.* is the default. The acceptance of *Ms.* meant that adult women had a proper title on par with the male counterpart *Mr.*, a huge win for women's equality. No longer was marital status the defining element of female honorifics. It may be used by married women who choose to keep their last name, or who choose to hyphenate their name with their partner's, or who use their spouse's last name but do not wish to use the title of *Mrs.* The plural may be used to indicate multiple women, or multiple women who share a last name. *The Mss. Bridgers, Haim, and Swift* or *the Mss. Haim.*

MR. (pronounced "mister"; the plural is *Messrs.* derived from the French *Monsieurs*) is used by men and young men (15 years of age and older.) The plural may be used to indicate multiple men, or multiple men who share a last name. *The Messrs. Cobb, Lightfoot, and Rawlings* or *the Messrs. Cobb.* There is also a tradition of *Mr.* being used with a man's first name to indicate both respect and familiarity. A child might say, "Mr. Jeff, I painted a picture for you!" (Also see *Master* below as a title for boys.)

MRS. (pronounced "misiz"; the plural is *Mmes.* derived from the French *Mesdames*) is the traditional title option for married women (but not the only one; see *Ms.* on page 29 for another option). A woman historically took her husband's surname and was then referred to formally by his full name (first and last): Mrs. Richard Malsby. While many women still use this construction, today there are multiple options. While some traditionalists might balk at the thought, the title *Mrs.* can be used by a woman to indicate she is married regardless of the name she uses, or the gender of her spouse. If Estelle Mariano has married Brendan Turner, Mrs. Estelle Mariano is as appropriate today as Mrs. Brendan Turner or Mrs. Estelle Turner. To be polite, if you know someone is married, be sure to ask if they use the title *Mrs.* before assigning it in an introduction. "What title do you use?"

MX. (pronounced "mix"; the plural is *Mxes.* pronounced "mixes") is most commonly used by those who identify as nonbinary and gender-nonconforming people, and by people who identify with it as their title, or who prefer it as their title (there is a difference; see Pronouns, page 35). The plural may be used to indicate multiple people who use the title, or multiple people who use the title and who share a last name. *The Mxes. Goldsmith, Norville, and Russel* or *the Mxes. Norville.* The tradition of using an honorific with a first name to show respect and familiarity applies to *Mx.* as well: "Mx. Brady, Mommy says I get to sit next to you at dinner!"

MISS (pronounced "miss"; the plural is *Misses* pronounced as written) is used for girls up to 18 years old. From Emily's day well into the 1960s, it was used for unmarried women of any age. Today, it is reserved primarily for young girls. The exception to this rule is when *Miss* is paired with a first name to indicate both respect and familiarity. A young child might call his friend's mother "Miss Janie" if he has been invited by Janie to do so. Many female teachers are also called *Miss,* followed by their first name, but it shouldn't be assumed they do so or prefer this.

MASTER (pronounced "master"; the plural is *Masters* pronounced as written) is used for young boys up until about 10 years old. Given that boys are not historically called *Mr.* until age 15, there is a title gap for boys ages 10 to 15. Typically, you would not use a title for boys in that age range, which creates inconsistencies in titles when listing family members (and is especially frustrating when addressing envelopes). Many people are uncomfortable with or don't identify with the term *Master* yet still want to use a title for boys and young men. In an effort to offer an alternative and one that could close the age gap issue, we propose using the term *Young Mr.* for boys up to age 15, the plural of which is *Young Messrs.*

ADDRESSING MARRIED AND LONG-ESTABLISHED COUPLES Many people are used to the construction "Mr. and Mrs. Surname" or "Mr. and Mrs. Husband's First and Surname" to indicate a married couple, yet it doesn't work for everyone and there are other options. For those who share a last name you could also use: *Ms./Mrs. Renee DeBell and Mr. Joe DeBell*, or *Ms./Mrs. Renee and Mr. Joe DeBell*. For those who share a title and last name you might choose: *The Messers. Bennington, the Messers. John and Terrance Bennington, Mr. and Mr. Bennington*, or *Mr. John Bennington and Mr. Terrance Bennington*. When individuals in a couple have different surnames the use of *and* between the names is what indicates they are a married or long-established couple: *Mrs. Gilda Rhein and Mr. Willis Fletcher, Mx. Kowalski and Ms. Towne, the Mses. Frey and Landon* on an invitation would all indicate a married couple. The *and* construction is really very useful, as it allows us to accommodate many preferences around the use of names and titles. (See Postcards, Notes, and Letters, page 94, for more on addressing couples in writing.)

MS. OR MRS. AFTER A DIVORCE? When a woman divorces, she can either go back to her maiden or given name or she may continue to use her married name. Say Cynthia Glass went by Mrs. Albert Rockwell when she was married. If she gets a divorce, she may be Mrs. Cynthia Rockwell or Ms. Cynthia Rockwell or Ms. Cynthia Glass. Nowadays, she would not continue to be Mrs. Albert Rockwell.

MS. OR MRS. ONCE WIDOWED? A widow may choose what to call herself after her spouse has passed. Let's use Cynthia Glass Rockwell as an example again. She may retain her husband's name, Mrs. Albert Rockwell, until she remarries. She could also go by either Mrs. or Ms. Cynthia Rockwell, or Ms. Cynthia Glass.

Take note: Currently *Mrs.* is the only adult title that would identify the person who uses it as both an adult and married. In written and spoken form, the term makes it clear that this person is a married woman. No other titles in our system identify marital status. Men, nonbinary, and gender-nonconforming people have no title options to distinguish themselves as married individuals.

SUFFIXES Suffixes are used to distinguish individuals who have exactly the same name but are of different generations in a family. William Goadby Post senior and William Goadby Post junior would appear as William Goadby Post, Sr and William Goadby Post Jr. (either use a comma or the period for abbreviation, but not both). When indicating a roman numeral (the third, the fourth etc.) use no comma—William Goadby Post III. Once a senior dies, a junior is no longer a junior.

PROFESSIONAL TITLES

Within a professional field or when someone is acting in a professional capacity, professional titles are to be observed, used, and treated with the utmost respect. Some professions carry a tradition of their titles also being used in social situations, such as medical doctors, while other professions use their titles only within their field. The holder of the title will decide when it is used, and their choice should be respected. Dr. Lucinda Lindley, a professor of English, could be "Dr. Lucinda Lindley" both professionally and socially. Either is perfectly correct, and a person will often base their decision on the occasion.

Having a title doesn't entitle you to be rude about enforcing its use, however. "It's *Dr.* English to you" is not pleasant, while "I prefer to use my professional title. Please call me Dr. English" feels more like a gentle correction and an invitation.

Professions for which titles are used in both professional and social situations include physician, judge, elected official or diplomat, professor or person with a doctorate (depending on personal preference), and military officers. (See Professional Titles, Religious Titles, Government Titles, and Military Officers, pages 48–52.)

MILITARY, POLICE, AND FIREFIGHTER TITLES

Introductions for all uniformed personnel should include rank and last name. For a first introduction, the full title is used: "Lieutenant Colonel Yahzee" or "Rear Admiral Schuurman."

In conversation, colonels, admirals, and generals are referred to as "Colonel," "Admiral," or "General," sometimes with a surname. The same is true for noncommissioned officers. For example, all grades of sergeant are addressed as "Sergeant." Warrant officers go by their social titles in social situations ("Mx. Cortez") and their military titles when performing military duties ("Chief Warrant Officer Three Cortez").

MILITARY CHAPLAINS AND DOCTORS. While performing their military duties, chaplains and doctors are called by their rank ("Captain Benjamin Pierce"). In social situations, junior officers who are doctors may continue to use *Dr.*, and military chaplains use *Father, Minister, Pastor, Rabbi, Imam,* or whatever their religious honorific may be.

RETIRED SERVICE MEMBERS. Regular and reserve service members who attain retirement status may continue to use their titles after retirement as directed by their individual service regulations. When introducing retired service members, use the term *retired* the way you would use *former* for a civilian profession: "Retired Air Force Colonel Max Abraham" or "Retired Army Sergeant Major First Name Surname." Service members who do not attain retirement status should not continue to use their titles after being discharged from their service.

POLICE OFFICERS AND FIREFIGHTERS. When a military-style title is used before the name of a police officer or firefighter, add *police* or *fire* before the title if needed for clarity ("Police Sgt. Tricia Lamborn" or "Fire Capt. Peter Lindley"). Otherwise, spell out nonmilitary titles, such as *Detective* or *Chief.* When addressing an on-duty police officer in person, use their rank (if known) and last name: "Officer Sibony," "Sargent Lamborn." If you don't know their last name and can't see it on their uniform, use "Officer." When addressing a firefighter in person, use their rank and last name: "Chief Reynolds," "Lieutenant Doyle." Ranks are often displayed on helmets, coats, sweatshirts, or uniforms. Many firefighters are volunteers and appreciate being recognized for the very serious work they do; calling them by their rank honors their work. Often firefighters and officers will call other members of their departments and teams by their rank outside of work. There is no expectation that these titles be used socially.

NAMES

Names are important, and important to get right. Doing so shows respect and consideration, and allows you to present someone to others as they wish to be known. Who hasn't experienced the frustrating embarrassment of forgetting or getting wrong a name they should know? But even when faced with these very common setbacks, we must still do our best to use people's correct names and make a point of doing so when making introductions. Take care to know which name(s) to use—or avoid, in the case of full names or nicknames—and how to pronounce them. If you know that your sister enjoys her new married name, jump on board and start using it when you introduce her.

In Emily's day, last names were regularly used along with a person's social or professional title in introductions; first names were used only for those you were familiar with. Today, people have a mix of names, nicknames, and titles, and it's not always easy to figure out which to use. Unfortunately, there's no correct answer. Some people go by only their social title and last name to those outside their immediate family and social circle, while others will say things like, "Mrs. Wellborne was my mother. Call me Sheila," indicating that you will cause offense by using "Mrs. Wellborne" when addressing Sheila. If you're unsure, ask discreetly before you have to introduce the person: "How do you prefer to be introduced?"

In very formal situations, you might not use someone's first name, only their professional or social title along with their last name. The person being introduced could then invite you to use their first name ("Please call me Werner.") However today, it's not uncommon to use a first name with a title and surname in more formal introductions, as people find it very useful to know a full name, and it's more common today to be addressed by your first name without having been invited to do so.

Commenting on someone's name when you meet them isn't the most polite thing to do. Names can be unique, interesting, or beautiful to us for many reasons. However, if you have a name that gets noticed, and commented on, it can feel like every interaction starts by highlighting this. For some, this might be welcome; hearing "cool name!" might be fine. But when the comment effectively "others" the person receiving it ("Wow, your name is so *unusual*," or "Wow, where does that name come from? It's beautiful"), even when meant as a compliment, it can come across as exoticizing the person, effectively communicating *You are different, let me comment on it* (see Othering, page 70). It might seem innocent or like enthusiastic curiosity, but receiving this sort of comment frequently can be wearing and make someone feel less a part of the community. Find other things to connect with them about. Remember too, that it's never appropriate to question or negatively comment on someone's choice or potential choice for a baby name, either before or after the baby is born.

It is very common to make mistakes with names. Maybe you don't hear it clearly when a name is said, or you forget, moments into meeting someone, what their name was. It happens. But recovering well is important and can help to avoid causing offense. ("I'm sorry; would you repeat your name, please? I didn't catch it.") Keep the tone upbeat and the fault on you, not the other person. Acting confused or frustrated will not create a friendly introduction. If you mispronounce a name, upon receiving a correction, say the name correctly and thank the person for the correction.

If someone incorrectly says your name during an introduction, you may choose whether to make the correction in the moment ("It's Deborah," or "It's pronounced Deb-OHR-ah") or correct them later on ("I didn't mention it during the introduction, but I should let you know that my name is Deborah, not Debra"). Forgetting a name is also common. You should speak up, but with an apology to recognize your mistake. "I'm so sorry, I have blanked on your name. Do you mind telling me again?" Then say thank you when they do.

Having trouble hearing or pronouncing names? You're not alone. It's not always easy, particularly when a name comes from a language you aren't familiar with. If you have a name that is often difficult for people to hear or pronounce, it's helpful to have a "sounds like" example to help people you meet. If you have a friend, colleague, neighbor, or acquaintance whose name you repeatedly get wrong, it's time to set aside the excuses and get serious about learning how to say it right. Find examples of the correct pronunciation with a quick online search, write the name down phonetically, use something it rhymes with to help remind you, and above all practice until it feels comfortable and sounds right. It is seriously polite and well worth the effort.

Nicknames can be a treasure or torture. They are great when they encourage a bond or remind people of good or funny times, but they can also be careless, unnecessary, even cruel and deeply damaging. Giving someone a nickname works only if they appreciate it and agree to it. A nickname or other name should *never*, under any circumstances, be given to a person because you cannot pronounce their name properly. It's one thing if they offer you an easier alternative, but you should never ask, "Can I just call you DB instead?"

RELATIONSHIPS

Emily's idea of what passed for an appropriate relationship description in 1922 now seems downright comical, in our opinion: ". . . do not, in introducing one person to another, call one of them 'my friend.' You can say 'my aunt,' or 'my sister,' or 'my cousin'—but to pick out a particular person as 'my friend' is not only bad style but, unless you have only one friend, bad manners—as it implies Mrs. Smith is 'my friend' and you are a stranger."

Today, stating your relationship to someone when making an introduction is a helpful reference point, and can sometimes even provide a conversation starter for the people being introduced. "Wyatt, this is Kelson. They are my coworker. Kelson, this is Wyatt, he's my brother-in-law." It's easier in business introductions and family introductions because the relationships are clearly defined: "This is our head of engineering, Simone Callan," or "This is my cousin, Maureen from Oregon."

Today, we are not as sensitive as Emily when introducing someone as a friend, but the principle behind Emily's point is kind. There's no need to rank or differentiate between friends—for example, it would be awkward to say, "This is my friend Toni, and this is my *best* friend, Gonzalo." It's perfectly fine to say, "This is my friend, Toni," to indicate that it's a social relationship, not a familial, romantic, or professional one. You aren't obligated to state how you know someone, but if you don't, be prepared for folks to ask about it as a quick and easy conversational follow-up: "And how do you two know each other?" There are times when confidentiality might be an issue, such as when running into your therapist, an ex, or someone you know from a recovery program. In such a case, it's appropriate to defer with a general comment like "Oh, we know each other from around town." If you find yourself on the other side of such an equation and get the sense that someone does not want to say how they know someone else, don't press further.

PRONOUNS

The pronouns we use are an important part of our identity and as such it's polite to get them right when we are speaking about each other and when making introductions. You might think someone's pronouns are easy enough to tell just by looking at them, but the reality is this isn't always the case. *She/her, he/him*, and *they/them* are the three most commonly used pronouns, and neo-pronouns, (like *zi, zim, hir*, and others) are also circulating. While typically used as a plural pronoun, *they/them* is now used as a singular pronoun as well. For many, these options are a welcome relief, and for others this can be confusing. Emerging and traditional courtesies around introductions can afford us clarity.

There is no one right way or time to present your pronouns. In a self-introduction you could state them clearly, "Hi, I'm Daniel, I use he/him pronouns." In many communities, this is already standard practice, while for others, this is totally new. When making introductions, pronouns can be stated in a follow-up piece of information. "Mom, I'd like to introduce Sam Farmington. They are my teacher." From this, you can gather that Sam's pronouns are *they/them*; now you know to use those pronouns when talking about Sam or introducing them.

If you don't know someone's pronouns, and you need to know them in order to make an introduction, asking is the polite thing to do: "Joan, what pronouns do you use?" Note that you don't ask what pronouns Joan "prefers"—an unfortunately common construction for this question. The idea that certain pronouns are "preferred" is offensive to many people. While preference can play a part for people who use multiple pronouns (like someone who uses or is comfortable with *she/her* and *they/them*, for example), that shouldn't be how you frame your question when first asking.

THEY/THEM	HE/HIS	SHE/HER
Can be used by anyone, but are often used by those who identify as nonbinary.	Used by those who identify with male/masculine-gendered pronouns.	Used by those who identify with female/feminine-gendered pronouns.
("This is Ryan. They are my sibling and I love them to the moon and back!")	("This is Ryan. He is my brother and I love him to the moon and back!")	("This is Ryan. She is my sister and I love her to the moon and back!")

RESPECTING TRANSGENDER AND NONBINARY PEOPLE

For the transgender and nonbinary communities, the topic of pronouns and names in introductions can elicit awkwardness and frustration, or conversely, relief and a sense of belonging. Name and pronoun changes are often part of a person's transition or nonbinary identity, and recognizing any such changes and using a person's correct names and pronouns is key to showing them support, respect, and basic courtesy. The friends, family, and community members of a transgender or nonbinary person may have to make an adjustment from using the pronouns (and perhaps name[s]) the person used in the past to those they have transitioned to using. When relearning someone's pronouns and/or name(s), mistakes can happen, and when they do, an apology and follow-up with the correct name or pronoun is always important. When it comes to referring to people before they transitioned, some people are okay with having their past names and pronouns used, while others are not—it depends on the person as well as the nature of your relationship with them. Listen and, if needed, respectfully ask. "Francis, how would you like me to refer to you when we talk about the time before your transition?" or "Francis, what name would you like me to use when referring to you in stories from our childhood?" The goal of your tone and words should be to honor and respect the person, not to dig up information about their past.

ENHANCING INTRODUCTIONS

Adding small details or points of interest about the people you're introducing is a great way to help start a conversation between them, especially if you can't stay to chat. This is perfect for when you're hosting a party of mixed friends or company who don't already know one another, or when introducing team members to one another. For example: "Jenny, this is Chris. He has been traveling to Japan over the past few years. Chris, this is Jenny. She's gearing up for a monthlong trip to Tokyo and Sapporo this winter." Once the introduction is made, you can stay and participate, or step away with a casual "Excuse me," or "I'll leave you two to talk."

While you can drop just about any fact or point about a person into an introduction, make sure it's something the person would want to be shared. "Lika, this is Julian. He's a commitment-phobe who doesn't want kids. Julian, this is Lika. She's about to freeze her eggs," is not the way to go. Avoid intimate or personal details or anything negative or distressing. It's best to stick with hobbies and interests; jobs and talents are usually safe as well.

ENTHUSIASM IN INTRODUCTIONS

Meeting people can be exciting and often we are trying to put our best foot forward. Today it is quite common to hear an overwhelmingly excited response to an introduction: "OMG! I AM JUST BEYOND THRILLED TO MEET YOU!" It's enough to startle a person. For everyday quick or in-passing introductions, pushing enthusiasm beyond a friendly tone and expression is unneces-sary. You do not have to be *thrilled!!!* to have met Colleen in passing while out to lunch with your friend, especially if it is unlikely that you'll cross paths with Colleen again. In fact, you might make Colleen feel overwhelmed. Take it down a notch, and you can still come across as friendly and welcoming. And while it is often meant to be very, very kind and friendly, if the other person doesn't level up to the enthusiasm thrust upon them, it could throw off the vibe of the introduc-tion. "OMG! I AM JUST BEYOND THRILLED TO MEET YOU!" followed by a classic yet neutral, "Hi. Nice to meet you," would feel off or disjointed.

In 1922, Emily warned of overdoing enthusiasm in greetings and introductions: "And you must not say you are delighted unless you have reason to be sure that she is also delighted to meet you." The idea being that if you were overly enthusiastic, you'd put pressure on the other person to match your enthusiasm, even if they didn't feel it. Saying, "I'm delighted to meet you" after learning little more than their name can seem forced. On the other hand, finally meeting your son's boyfriend, whom he has spoken of proudly for so long, would indeed be a delight, and saying so would be appropriate: "Dean, I'm delighted to meet you at last!"

Our advice is to do your best to (a) not overwhelm those you are meeting for the first time; and (b) not leave someone's reaction to an introduction out on a limb. Meet their enthusiasm partway if you can: "It's really nice to meet you, too!"

KIDS ADDRESSING ADULTS

Traditionally in America, we defer to the formal until we are invited to use the casual, a standard many parents still wish to impart to their children. Teaching children to start with a title and last name (Ms. Neff) and then be invited by an adult to use their first name (Loretta), or a title and first name (Miss Loretta), is still appropriate. It sets kids up well for adult life, as especially in the business world, titles and last names are often used for those in supervisory positions.

BUSINESS INTRODUCTIONS

Business introductions are often more serious and formal than social introductions. In business, it's almost always the relationship (client, vendor, supplier, prospect) or rank that determines who is introduced to whom and how. Introduce honored guests and visitors first, then respect organizational hierarchy. All of the following would be correct:

FORMAL: "Mr. Big Wigg, may I introduce Mr. Junior Weenie to you? He started with us this year on the Helping Hands farm project we are sponsoring. Mr. Weenie, I'd like to introduce you to our CEO, Mr. Big Wigg."

FORMAL WITH GUEST: "Ms. Client, may I present Mr. Big Wigg, our CEO, and Mr. Junior Weenie, the head of Helping Hands?"

CASUAL: "Big Wigg, let me introduce Junior Weenie, our new hire on the Helping Hands project. Junior, this is Big Wigg, our CEO."

There is another element to the business introduction that, while once common in social introductions, is unique to the professional world today: the exchange of cards. Business card exchanges are often part of business introductions and are making a comeback even in our digital world. "May I offer you my card?" might follow an introduction or be part of a parting. To up the formality, you might invoke some international manners by presenting your card, held with both hands face up (the side with your name), with the writing readable to the person receiving it. When receiving cards presented this way, accept the card with two hands. And most importantly: read it in front of the person who handed it to you, and handle it with care. The card should not be immediately placed in a pocket or wallet. After taking a moment to appreciate a card given to you, it is wise to offer a card in return and advisable to keep them handy. For occasions where you expect to exchange a number of cards, consider using a card holder or having a designated place to put them.

WRITTEN INTRODUCTIONS

With so much of our communication taking place via the written word, it's important to feel confident making introductions via email, text, group messages, or team platforms. A letter of introduction used to be of critical importance; today we are more likely to be introduced via email or text.

VIA EMAIL. Depending on the circumstances, you might direct the email to one particular person and introduce the other person to them, or you might address both (or all) of the people needing introductions. Be sure to include full names and, when applicable, job titles, as well as how or why the introduction is being made.

> *Dear Felicia,*
>
> *I'm looking forward to working together. I'd like to introduce Alexander Post (cc'd). He is our head of marketing and will be working with you on next year's roll-out.*

Or:

> *Hi Felicia and Alexander,*
>
> *I wanted to take a moment to connect the two of you. Felicia, this is Alexander Post, our head of marketing. He will be facilitating next year's roll-out. Alexander, this is Felicia Roland of Acme Napkins.*

VIA TEXT MESSAGE. It is now common for business and social introductions to happen via text message. However, unlike with email, especially work email, for which contact information is expected to be shared, a personal cell phone number is not something people are as willing to share. Before you introduce someone via text, make sure sharing numbers is okay with both (or all) parties. For business introductions, you'll be slightly more formal, but for social ones it's okay to be casual. Just have it make sense for the introduction.

Cameron

Hi Ilana and Andria—As promised, connecting the two of you so you can coordinate about the bridal shower. Thank you both so much for offering to throw it for me—I can't wait!

Ilana

Thanks so much for connecting us, Cameron! Andria, so nice to meet you via text! I'll text you in a new thread and we can start making plans.

Andria

Thanks Cameron and hi Ilana, so nice to meet you too! Looking forward to this! Talk soon.

TEAM OR GROUP THREAD. You might also find yourself introducing a new colleague or team member to a work app, like Slack or Teams. The etiquette here is the same as when connecting people via email.

Boss

Good morning, everyone. I'd like to introduce Claudette Jones. She's going to be joining us through the launch of the site to keep an eye on . . .

Claudette

Hi, happy to be here and excited to help with the launch!

WHAT TO AVOID

When it comes to introductions, the biggest mistake most people make is not making the introduction. Yes, anyone can have a moment in which they lapse and leave two completely capable individuals to make self-introductions. And yes, many, many people do this intentionally when they have forgotten someone's name, or they use the one-way introduction, saying only the name they know and leaving the other to self-introduce: "Oh, so great to see you—this is my friend Sarah." "Hi Sarah, I'm Paul." Some couples, business partners, or friends even have silent signals to let one another know who needs to pick up an introduction because the other has forgotten a name. This is helpful in a pinch, but it's not best practice and, in many cases, you'd be fine just admitting you've forgotten a name. "Sarah, this is my friend from cross-fit . . . oh my gosh, I can't believe I'm blanking on your name right now . . ." "Totally understand, it's Paul, nice to meet you Sarah." Here are some other things to avoid during an introduction:

- Remaining seated when you are easily capable of standing

- Not making eye contact, when you can

- Shouting the introduction (unless you're in a loud location that requires it)

- Dropping an introduction on someone and then walking away, which will come across as having dumped the person being introduced off like a problem to be dealt with by someone else

- Saying things like, "You two simply had to meet. You will get along so well!" Well-intentioned though it may be, this leaves little room for you to be wrong and places pressure on the two being introduced. You don't want people to feel forced into being friends. Set them up for a good introduction and then let commonalities emerge on their own.

- Making mistakes with peoples' names, titles, or pronouns. If you're having a moment of forgetfulness, say, "Please forgive me—I shouldn't be, but I'm drawing a blank on your name." If you get a pronoun or name wrong and someone corrects you, make your apology, thank them for the correction, and then move on. Don't keep going on about your mistake; it puts more focus on it and makes you look like you care only about the impression you're making. These are important corrections. Be confident receiving them. Say, "Thank you, I'm so sorry I blanked," or "Thank you, I'm sorry I misspoke." Then be sure to use the correct name, title, or pronoun as the conversation continues.

WHAT COMES AFTER THE INTRODUCTION?

The conversation, of course! Once an introduction has been made, it's up to the two people who have been introduced to strike up a conversation or get a meeting going. You might also, after a brief exchange, end up excusing yourself to go meet or mingle with others. If you haven't been given much to go on to initiate conversation, your best follow-up is a benign but not boring question and a willingness to listen. How their day has been, how they know the host, favorite local spots, a question about your shared experience. Offer a little something yourself, to set up the question. "By day two of this conference, I'm knowing my way around a bit better, how about you?" Like a fisherman with a line, try a few times to see if you can catch a conversation and if not, politely excuse yourself. (See The Three Tiers of Conversation, page 61.)

If an exit is going to follow quickly after an introduction, it can be tempting to "find an excuse" to take your leave. But it's not necessary to do so. "It's been nice meeting you. I'm going to mingle," or "It's been nice meeting you" with a polite nod as you step away is perfectly fine.

REFERENCE GUIDES

GREETINGS

SITUATION	BARE MINIMUM	APPROPRIATE	A BIT MUCH
Walking into a room/ office space and encountering others for the first time that day/ shift	Nod with a slight smile or bright eyes Optional: "Hey" or "Hi"	Nod, smile, and say "Good morning" "Hi," "Hello," or even a passing "How's it going today?"	Loudly calling to someone more than five feet away. Waving your arms exaggeratedly or skipping octaves in your voice
Crossing paths with a friend or acquaintance	Make a walking acknowledgment: nod to those you know with a friendly expression If you choose to speak, a friendly or neutral "Hey" or "Hi" and sometimes the person's name	A greeting and the person's name will do If you're actually stopping, do so out of the flow of pedestrian traffic. If you're taking this much time, it's okay to catch up a bit and ask if the other person is doing well	Grabbing the person's arm as you pass by and forcefully hugging them while exclaiming, "It's been so long!" Peppering them with questions before even knowing if it's an okay time for them to stop and chat
Being introduced to someone in passing	A friendly nod with a smile	A handshake or friendly nod, followed by "Pleased to meet you, Dwayne" A super casual but still polite "Hi," "Hello," "Hey," or "Nice to meet you" could also work You could say, "How's it going?" though in this case you aren't really expecting much of an answer	A far-too-long handshake or hug. Asking in-depth questions of the person you've just met, or inviting yourself to join those you ran into
With store staff when you're out shopping	Eye contact and a smile or nod	A friendly hello	Calling out loudly or aiming for an in-depth conversation about how they are
With staff or service workers in your building	Eye contact and a smile or nod	A friendly "Hello" or "Hey, how's it going?"	Attempts at longer conversations. These are usually passing moments and in the case of staff or service workers, they have a job to do. While polite conversation might be welcome, don't assume it will be or that the person has the time

GOODBYES

With so much focus on good beginnings and how to make a good impression, it's important not to forget that parting well is also good etiquette. If you cut a conversation short or immediately depart after an introduction, you can come across as curt or even rude. If you draw out a good-bye, you will feel the patience of those you are with waning. Pay attention to your timing and be gracious in your tone and your parting will likely be sweet sorrow.

FORMAL	CASUAL
When parting in a formal setting, you can add to or expand the goodbye to dress it up a bit: "Goodbye and take good care," "Good day to you, sir," "It's been such a pleasure, good night," "It's time for me to depart, good evening to you."	"Bye," "See ya," "Later," "I'm out," "Take care," "So long," "See you later," "See you soon," "In a while crocodile!"

MAKING INTRODUCTIONS

1. Identify the necessary formality and which person is "more important" (often the older or more senior-ranking person); speak to them first.

2. Use full names and titles to start, then allow each party to invite others to address them more familiarly.

3. If you're unsure of how someone likes to be identified, ask. "How do you like to be introduced?"

4. Include relationship or interesting information to offer reference points for further conversation or context.

In the following examples, which run from extremely formal (calling your grandmother Mrs. Stately Elder) to very casual (addressing her as Granny), you are introducing your friend to your grandmother.

MOST FORMAL (BY THE STANDARDS OF EMILY'S DAY)

You: "Mrs. Stately Elder, may I present Ms. Diedre Youngblood?"

Mrs. Elder: "How do you do, Ms. Youngblood. Are you in town visiting my granddaughter?"

Ms. Youngblood: "Yes, and I'm ever so grateful to be here. I have always dreamed of visiting New York."

You: "Mrs. Elder, may I introduce Ms. Diedre Youngblood? Ms. Youngblood, Mrs. Stately Elder."

Mrs. Elder: "It's a pleasure to meet you, Ms. Youngblood, and please call me Stately. Are you enjoying your visit to New York?"

Ms. Youngblood: "It's a pleasure to meet you as well, Stately. I am indeed enjoying my time here; your granddaughter knows all the most wonderful places to visit."

MORE CASUAL

You: "Grandmother, this is Diedre Youngblood, my friend. Diedre, this is my grandmother, Stately Elder."

Mrs. Elder: "So nice to meet you, Diedre. Are you enjoying your stay in New York?"

Ms. Youngblood: "Lovely to meet you too, Mrs. Elder. Yes, I am very much enjoying my stay, thank you."

CASUAL

You: "Granny, this is Diedre Youngblood. She's a fantastic writer and a wiz with crossword puzzles. Diedre, this is my grandmother, Stately Elder. She covered the rise of rock 'n' roll in the '60s as a journalist here in New York

Mrs. Elder: "Well, I love meeting another crossword fanatic. Please call me Granny; everyone does."

Ms. Youngblood: "Thank you. Granny, it is lovely to meet you as well. Louisa was telling me all about your writing career, and it sounds so cool!"

SOCIAL TITLES

Please see Social Titles, page 29, for more details on the use of social titles. As a general note, if you do not know someone's social title, ask them before you need to make an introduction or use their name in writing.

TITLE	PLURAL	WHO USES IT	IN WRITING	IN CONVERSATION	NOTES
Mx.	Mxes. Pronounced "mixes"	Nonbinary, intersex, and gender-nonconforming people	*Mx. Riley Smith* *Mx. Smith* *The Mxes. Smith* (relatives, or a married couple) *The Mxes. Smith, Laughlin, and Freedman* (relatives or a group of individuals) *Mx. Riley Smith and Mx. Kai Laughlin (individuals or a couple)*	"This is Mx. Riley Smith, they handle our design work." "The Mxes. Smith and Jones from the architecture firm Redefine Design are attending the wedding."	*Mx.* can also be used when you don't want your gender known.
Ms.	Mss. or Mses. Pronounced "mizzes." Or list each Ms. separately.	Adult women, both married and unmarried	*Ms. Lori Flynn* *Ms. Flynn* *The Mses./Mss. Flynn* (relatives, or married couple) *The Mses./Mss. Flynn and Stone* (relatives, married couple, or individuals) *Ms. Flynn and Ms. Stone* (two individuals or two married women)	"Ms. Lori Flynn has an appointment at one." "The Mss. Flynn and their mother . . ." "The Mses. Flynn and Stone bought the building."	*Mss.* and *Mses.* may be used interchangeably. *Ma'am* is preferable to *Lady* when addressing a woman whose name you don't know, but whose gender identity you do.

TITLE	PLURAL	WHO USES IT	IN WRITING	IN CONVERSATION	NOTES
Mrs.	Mmes. pronounced "mesdames"	Adult married women. Some women use their first name with a partner's last name; others use their partner's first and last name. Some keep their full name but use *Mrs.* to indicate they are married.	*Mrs. Erin Sain* (using given name) *Mrs. Jason Carmichael* (using spouse's full name) *Mrs. Erin Carmichael* (her first name with spouse's surname) *The Mmes. Sain* (relatives, or a married couple) *The Mmes. Sain and Yee* (two separately married women, or a couple) *Mrs. Erin Sain and Mrs. Denisa Yee* (two separately married women, or a married couple who doesn't share a last name but uses the Mrs. title.)	"Mrs. Erin Carmichael is speaking at the event." "The Mmes. Sain will be at the meeting."	A woman chooses to use this title. However it should never be assumed. Default to *Ms.* until you know for certain. You may always ask.
Mr.	Messrs. Pronounced "messers"	Men, young and adult, married and not married. Sometimes used with just a first name to indicate a friendly but respectful relationship	*Mr. Jon Zhou* *Mr. Zhou* *Messrs. Zhou* (relatives, or a married couple) *Messrs. Zhou, Gold, and Raitt* (a group of individual men) *Mr. Jon* (familiar but respectful, used upon invitation) *Mr. Jon Zhou and Mr. Rolph Fipps* (two individual men, or a married couple)	"Mr. Zhou is coming to visit." "The Messrs. Zhou will be on the call." "Messrs. Zhou and Finley, 222 Fountaine Street . . ." "Hi, Mr. Jon!"	*Messrs.* could indicate relatives, spouses who share a last name (or not), or business partners. There is no married honorific for men. *Sir* is preferable to *Mister* when addressing a man whose name you don't know, but whose gender identity you do.

TITLE	PLURAL	WHO USES IT	IN WRITING	IN CONVERSATION	NOTES
Miss	Misses pronounced as spelled	Young women from birth to about 18 years old. Sometimes used with just a first name to indicate a friendly but respectful relationship.	*Miss Linda Ortiz* *Miss Ortiz* *The Misses Ortiz* (young relatives) *Miss Linda* (familiar but respectful, often used in the South upon invitation to do so)	"Miss Ortiz is present." "The Misses Ortiz will visit their father." "The Misses Ortiz, Buckley, and Johnson will attend . . ." (a group of young women) "Hi, Miss Linda!"	Wait to be invited before calling an adult *Miss* and their first name. Miss is used to address a young woman or girl either as a sign of respect or because you do not know her name. "Excuse me, miss?"
Master	Masters pronounced as spelled	Originally unmarried men of any age, now young boys usually 10 years old and younger. Or use the term *Young Mr.* instead	*Master William Blake* *The Masters Blake* (relatives) *The Masters Blake, Gould, and Thompson* (a group of young boys) *Young Mr. William Blake* *The Young Messrs. Blake and Thompson*	"Master William Blake is invited to . . ." "The Masters Blake are attending." "Masters Blake, Gould, and Thompson . . ." "May I introduce Young Mister Blake" "The Young Messrs. Blake and Thompson"	*Master* usually comes up only for formal wedding invitations. For those looking for an alternative option to the term *Master*, replace it with *Young Mr.* for boys up to age 15. *Young man* is used when addressing a boy whose name you do not know but whose gender is known. It is preferable to *boy*.

PROFESSIONAL TITLES

PROFESSION	LETTER ADDRESS	SALUTATION	SPOKEN GREETING	FORMAL INTRODUCTION
Doctor of medicine	Gurinder Singh Wadhwa, M.D. Dr. Gurinder Singh Wadhwa Dr. G. S. Wadhwa	Dear Dr. Wadhwa:	"Dr. Wadhwa"	Dr. Gurinder Singh Wadhwa
Attorney	Susan Baker, Esq. (or J.D., if held) Mr./Mx./Mrs./Ms. Susan Baker	Dear Mr./Mx./Mrs./ Ms. Baker:	"Mr./Mx./Mrs./Ms. Baker"	Mr./Mx./Mrs./Ms. Susan Baker
University professor	Professor Drew Altman Mr./Mx./Mrs./Ms. Drew Altman (or Dr., if held)	Dear Professor Altman: Dear Mr./Mx./Mrs./ Ms. Altman (or Dr., if held):	"Professor Altman" "Dr. Altman" (if held)	Professor Drew Altman (or Dr., if held)

RELIGIOUS TITLES

POSITION	ADDRESSING AN ENVELOPE	SALUTATION	SPOKEN GREETING	FORMAL INTRODUCTION
Pope	His Holiness Pope John Paul the III (contemporary version)	Most Holy Father, *or* Your Holiness,	When speaking with him: "Your Holiness"	Should you ever have to introduce the pope: "His Holiness, Pope John Paul the III"
Catholic Clergy	The Reverend James Morency, initials of order if used	Dear Father Morency:	"Father Morency" "Father"	The Reverend James Morency Father Morency
Imam	The Imam Sharif	Dear Imam Sharif:	"Imam Sharif" "Imam"	The Imam Sharif of the Islamic Center of Tuscon
Rabbi	Rabbi Molly Ritvo (insert academic degrees if held)	Dear Rabbi Ritvo:	"Rabbi Ritvo" "Rabbi"	Rabbi Molly Ritvo, of Ohavi Zedek Synagogue
Protestant Minister/Pastor	The Reverend Peter Plaggie United Church of Christ	Dear Reverend Plaggie: Dear Pastor Plaggie:	"Reverend Plaggie" "Pastor Plaggie"	The Reverend Peter Plaggie Pastor Peter Plaggie
Bishop, The Church of Jesus Christ of Latter-Day Saints	The Bishop Mark McClintock	Dear Bishop McClintock	"Bishop McClintock"	The Bishop Mark McClintock

GOVERNMENT TITLES

POSITION	ADDRESSING AN ENVELOPE	SALUTATION	SPOKEN GREETING	FORMAL INTRODUCTION
President of the United States	The President	Dear Mr./Mx./ Madam President:	First greeting: "Mr./Mx./Madam President"	The President of the United States (of America, when abroad) The President
Vice President	The Vice President	Dear Mr./Mx./ Madam Vice President: The Vice President Sir/Mix/Ma'am	First greeting: "Mr./Mx./Madam Vice President"	The Vice President of the United States The Vice President
American Ambassador	The Honorable Daniel Rooney Ambassador of the United States of America	Dear Mr./ Mx./ Madam Ambassador: Dear Ambassador:	"Mr./Mx./Madam Ambassador"	In the Western Hemisphere: The Honorable Daniel Rooney, Ambassador of the United States of America to Ireland (when away from post) The Honorable Daniel Rooney, Ambassador of the United States of America (when at post)
Foreign Ambassador	His/Her/Their Excellency Allen Post The Ambassador of [Country] Or His/Her/Their Excellency Dr./ Professor/Lord/ etc. . . . Allen Post	Your Excellency: Dear Ambassador: Dear Ambassador Post:	"Your Excellency" "Ambassador" "Ambassador Post"	His/Her/Their Excellency, the Honorable Allen Post, can also add: Ambassador Extraordinary and Plenipotentiary of [Country] Or The Ambassador of [Country]
U.S. Senator	The Honorable Bernard Sanders United States Senate Washington, DC (or district office address)	Dear Senator Sanders:	First greeting: "Senator Sanders" Subsequent greetings: "Senator" "Sir/Mx./Ma'am"	The Honorable Bernard Sanders, Senator from Vermont Personal introduction: "Senator Sanders"

POSITION	ADDRESSING AN ENVELOPE	SALUTATION	SPOKEN GREETING	FORMAL INTRODUCTION
U.S. Representative	The Honorable Peter Welch United States House of Representatives Washington, DC (or district office address)	Dear Mr./Mx./Mrs./Ms. Welch: Dear Congressman/ Congresswoman/ Representative Welch:	"Mr./Mx./Mrs. "Ms. Welch" Technically appropriate and traditionally a higher honor than "Congressman/ Congresswoman/ Representative" however many in this position prefer the latter. Subsequent greetings: "Representative/ Congresswoman/ Congressman" "Sir/Mx./Ma'am"	The Honorable Peter Welch, Representative from Vermont Congressman/ Congresswoman/ Representative Welch Personal introduction: "Representative Welch"
Governor	The Honorable William Senning Governor of Vermont	Dear Governor Senning:	First greeting: "Governor Senning" "Governor"	The Honorable William Senning, Governor of the state of Vermont More casually: Governor Senning
Federal Judge	The Honorable Katherine Wilson U.S. Court of San Diego with spouse: The Honorable Katherine Wilson and Mr. Daniel Wilson	Dear Judge Wilson:	"Your Honor" (in court) "Judge Wilson" (in conversation)	The Honorable Katherine Wilson Judge Wilson

THE USE OF *FORMER:* A commonly asked etiquette question is "How do I address a former president?" The official answer is that for any elected office held by only one person at a time (President/Vice President/Speaker of the House/Governor/Mayor), the individual does not retain the title of that office when they leave it. When speaking *about* this person, you use the term *former* to indicate they no longer hold the position. This is out of respect for the current office holder. For example, "Former President Barak Obama is an excellent writer." When speaking *to* this person, you use their social title, "Mr. George W. Bush, may I present my cousin Ms. Amelia Shaw." If the former office holder still uses a professional title they held prior to taking office, such as Doctor, then it should be used. Other elected positions held by more than one person—where the is no risk of confusion—retain their titles. For the past 30 years it's become common for people (especially the press) to address former presidents as President (Full/Surname) even though this is technically incorrect and can cause confusion. In private—where there is no risk of confusion—many people use these terms to honor the position once held.

THE USE OF *HONORABLE*: Once you are an honorable, you are always an honorable. Any position that affords you this title during your term affords it for life. Senators, representatives, governors, and judges are the most classic examples.

MILITARY OFFICERS

COMMISSIONED OFFICERS IN THE ARMY, AIR FORCE, AND MARINES

LETTER ADDRESS	SALUTATION	SPOKEN GREETING	INTRODUCTION
(Full rank) (Full name) Social Correspondence: Major General Nathan Longford (for official correspondence, include post-nominal branch of service i.e. USAF)	(Basic Rank) (Surname) Dear General Longford:	(Basic Rank) (Surname) "General Longford"	(Full Rank) (Full Name) (Branch of Service) "Major General Nathan Longford, United States Air Force"

The following positions follow this same format:

Lieutenant General (Lt. Gen.), Major General (Maj. Gen.), Brigadier General (Brig. Gen.), Colonel (Col.), Lieutenant Colonel (Lt. Col.), Major (Maj.), Captain (Capt.), First Lieutenant (1st Lt.), Second Lieutenant (2nd Lt.).

COMMISSIONED OFFICERS IN THE NAVY AND COAST GUARD

LETTER ADDRESS	SALUTATION	SPOKEN GREETING	INTRODUCTION
(Full Rank) (Full Name), (Branch of Service) Vice Admiral Kelly Buska, USCG	(Basic Rank) (Surname) Dear Admiral Buska	(Basic Rank) (Last Name) "Admiral Buska"	(Full Rank) (Full Name) (Branch of Service) "Vice Admiral Kelly Buska, United States Coast Guard"

The following positions follow this same format:

Vice Admiral (Vice Adm.), Rear Admiral Upper Half (Rear Adm.), Rear Admiral Lower Half (Rear Adm.), Captain (Capt.), Commander (Cmdr.)

For plurals, add "s" to the main element in the title (Adms. Buska and Jones).

The sections on the opposite page all follow the formats above.

WARRANT OFFICERS

Chief Warrant Officer (Chief Warrant Officer), Warrant Officer (Warrant Officer). There are five grades of warrant officer: Warrant Officer 1 (Warrant Officer), Chief Warrant Officer 2–5 (Chief Warrant Officer Two, Three, Four, or Five)

ENLISTED PERSONNEL IN THE ARMY
(Civilian-Styled Abbreviations)

Sergeant Major of the Army (Sgt. Maj. of the Army), Command Sergeant Major (Command Sgt. Maj.), Sergeant Major (Sgt. Maj.), First Sergeant (1st Sgt.), Master Sergeant (Master Sgt.), Sergeant First Class (Sgt. 1st Class), Staff Sergeant (Staff Sgt.), Sergeant (Sgt.), Corporal (Cpl.), Specialist (Spc.), Private first class (Pfc), Private (Pvt.)

ENLISTED PERSONNEL IN THE AIR FORCE
(Civilian-Styled Abbreviations)

Chief Master Sergeant of the Air Force (Chief Master Sgt. of the Air Force), Chief Master Sergeant (Chief Master Sgt.), Senior Master Sergeant (Senior Master Sgt.), Master Sergeant (Master Sgt.), Technical Sergeant (Tech Sgt.), Staff Sergeant (Staff Sgt.), Senior Airman (Senior Airman), Airman first class (Airman 1st Class), Airman (Airman), Airman basic (Airman)

ENLISTED PERSONNEL IN THE MARINES
(Civilian-Styled Abbreviations)

Sergeant Major of the Marine Corps (Sgt. Maj. of the Marine Corps), Sergeant Major (Sgt. Maj.), Master Gunnery Sergeant (Master Gunnery Sgt.), First sergeant (1st Sgt.), Master Sergeant (Master Sgt.), Gunnery Sergeant (Gunnery Sgt.), Staff Sergeant (Staff Sgt.), Sergeant (Sgt.), Corporal (Cpl.) Lance Corporal (Lance Cpl.), Private first class (Pfc.), Private (Pvt)

ENLISTED PERSONNEL IN THE NAVY
(Civilian-Styled Abbreviations)

Master Chief Petty Officer of the Navy (Master Chief Petty Officer of the Navy), Master Chief Petty Officer (Master Chief Petty Officer), Senior Chief Petty Officer (Senior Chief Petty Officer), Chief Petty Officer (Chief Petty Officer), Petty Officer First Class (Petty Officer 1st Class), Petty Officer Second Class (Petty Officer 2nd Class), Petty Officer Third Class (Petty Officer 3rd Class), Seaman (Seaman), Seaman Apprentice (Seaman Apprentice), Seaman Recruit (Seaman Recruit)

CHAPTER 3

Conversation & Correspondence

"Above all, stop and *think* what you are saying! This is really
the first and last and only rule. If you 'stop' you can't chatter or
expound or flounder ceaselessly, and if you *think*, you will find a
topic and manner of presenting your topic so that your neighbor
will be interested rather than long–suffering."

Emily Post

While Emily's 1922 advice on communications was limited to in-person and telephone conversations, as well as notes and letters, today we communicate in so many different ways: in person; via video; by phone; via text message; by email; with handwritten notes, postcards, and letters; and of course, both publicly and privately online.

We have common practices that can be applied to all forms of communication and all manner of conversations to help make them more pleasant for everyone. However, each medium has its own set of standards, advantages, and drawbacks. With the added fact that each person has their own perspective, style, and preferences, one can see that communication can be ripe for confusion, frustration (sometimes hilarity), and a whole lot of *mis*communication. You might say that in today's world full of miraculous communication options, achieving good communication is nothing short of a miracle!

THE BASICS OF CONVERSATION

While there are many considerations for each method of communication, for the most part they boil down to one main point: *how* you choose to communicate matters. It's easy to think of polite conversation as only talking about the weather, or "nice" and "pleasant" topics. This serves us very well in simple moments, such as a passing greeting to a store clerk, or chatting with a friend after a service or softball game. But our communications, even everyday ones, can be more complicated, important, emotional, and even intense than these simple, quick social moments. These harder conversations can also serve us well and offer the chance to build and strengthen our relationships, when we can be respectful with them. In such situations, we can use politeness as a tool to help us dig into those uncomfortable or difficult moments and work our way through them with consideration, respect, and honesty.

As a society, we have given ourselves more room to discuss, share, and express our thoughts than ever before. We are encouraged to experience our emotions, and not hide our worries behind polite, plastered-on smiles. Yes, sometimes the truth can be brutal and hard, but we have the option to offer truth with benevolent honesty rather than brutal candor. Without denying ourselves, we can balance our impact on others by how we choose to share. In Emily's day, you would hardly be considered smart to share what you're going through with a stranger, and yet who among us hasn't had a perfectly enlightening, maybe even life-changing, conversation on a bus ride, in a waiting room, or on a plane with someone we never saw again? (And yes, the other side of that can be the worst ride or wait as someone blathers on, not noticing that you have no desire whatsoever to talk to them. See Casual Conversations, page 74, for how to decline a conversation with strangers.) By applying the following basics, you can help improve your everyday conversations.

PERSPECTIVE MATTERS

Conversations are built around both speaking and listening, offering and receiving. While it may seem that as long as you speak the same language you should each be understood, it's important to recognize that when talking with others, perspective matters because it can differ and impact how we understand each other. People are varied, to say the least! We have different experiences, ideas, and emotions. Life is ripe for miscommunication, frustration, and hurt—even when you might think, *How could that possibly be confusing or offensive?* For example, asking "What do you do?" is for some the *worst* thing you could have asked to strike up a conversation, while for others it's a chance to discuss their passion.

One thing that can help us in conversation to better understand those we are speaking with, and to be better understood, is to adopt a curious, candid, and optimistic tone when speaking with others. We must take care with our conversations and communications with each other, and recognize the wholeness of the other person or people we are talking to. Reminding yourself that you don't know the entirety of someone's story or perspective leaves room to hear them and not just your version of them. When we treat others this way, we have a greater chance of being heard in return. We have to accept that other people's perspectives *do* matter, and if we encounter differences, we can use etiquette as a tool for bridging the gap. Ultimately no matter where we come from or what our experiences have been, good conversation skills will better our interactions with those around us.

THE MAGIC WORDS

We consider the magic words—*please, thank you, you're welcome, excuse me,* and *I'm sorry*—to be some of the most effective politeness tools at our disposal. Emily described them as being part of "Kindergarten Manners," the behavior lessons we learn in our early childhood years and for good reason. They will work their magic no matter the method of conversation, but what truly makes them magic is how you use and deliver them.

It is the effect these words can have on people and relationships that is indeed magic. They can express intent, show respect, and help to soften an exchange. They should be used everywhere, and will always be considered appropriate when used well. It's equally important whether we are in a restaurant speaking to a server or at home with family and friends. There's always room to improve. When used regularly, and with a sincere and friendly delivery—not with attitude or through gritted teeth or said so sweetly that they are intentionally insincere—these words show respect and consideration for those around you. As we say in our Emily Post children's etiquette programs, "The words themselves aren't magic; the magic is in you."

PLEASE

Please changes a command or demand into a polite request. "Pass the peas" versus "Please pass the peas": the two have different tones and expectations. The former is direct and expectant, the latter a respectful request. You can form a full sentence around *please* ("Jeremiah, would you please pass me the peas?") or use it as a welcoming gesture instead of a command ("Please, come in!"). Like children looking for cookies, adults would be well advised to consider the likelihood of getting what they desire based on the effective use of this simple word.

"Please" can be said in the worst ways and with such attitude that it's obviously insincere. "Puuuh–leeeezzz" with an eye roll means *Give me a break.* When said sternly through gritted teeth, it means, *I'm using the word, but I'm not happy about it.* And it can be said with such a mockingly sweet tone that it's transformed into an insult. Protect your "please." None of these is considered polite. Should you find yourself feeling the negative emotions behind these "faux pleases," consider instead saying what you feel in a different way, if you can.

THANK YOU

Expressing gratitude can have a profound impact on the relationships and everyday exchanges in your life. *Thank you* is the most commonly used expression of gratitude in English, and we should continue to use it frequently. Saying "thank you" acknowledges the other person involved in an exchange and indicates how their actions or the interaction between you has positively impacted you. Both issuing and receiving a thank-you can feel like magic. Thanking someone feels so good, and we are often in a position where both parties wish to express their gratitude. While no one loves going back and forth like a ping-pong ball in a game of gratitude ("Thank you for the flowers," "Thank *you* for hosting," "Thank *you* for coming," "Thank *you* for inviting me"), you can never go wrong with getting your thanks in. And remember, a snarky or sullen "Thanks" is no kind of thank-you in our book. (For thank-you notes, see page 96.)

YOU'RE WELCOME

We use *You're welcome* to recognize gratitude. When you receive gratitude well by issuing a "you're welcome" or other similar phrase, you participate respectfully in one of the most fundamentally important aspects of human behavior: the act of gratitude. While we can be grateful on our own, when we express gratitude toward others, it must be recognized and recognized well. Sadly, many people seem to think there is an arrogance in replying "You're welcome" to someone who has thanked you. As if somehow not issuing a thank-you in return or not showing some kind of modesty in a reply means the gratitude was expected. "You're welcome" is fine to issue on its own. "Thanks for bringing those hoses over." "You're welcome." This is perfectly polite. If you want some other options to acknowledge gratitude, you can try "You are most welcome," or "My pleasure," or "Happy to."

"No problem," "Oh, it was nothing," and "No worries," other replies we hear, are very common. Many languages have a version of "It was nothing" as a standard reply. However, it's worth noting that some people hear these phrases and wonder if perhaps it *would* have been a problem. We often issue these phrases to let the thanker know that the act they are thanking you for was easy for you to do. These phrases are not impolite, though it's worth noting that they don't resonate with everyone, and in the wrong circumstances they could minimize a thank-you. So you don't want to use them every time. By saying "you're welcome," "my pleasure," or "happy to," you can eliminate the chance of minimizing the exchange.

Whatever phrase you choose, accepting someone's gratitude is part of a polite exchange and should not be lost. Following a "Thank you" with "Thank *you!*" may feel right in the moment for something quick, and truly reciprocal, but that second "thank you" has the effect of one-upping the first. For something quick, try following "Thank you" with "You're welcome. *And* thank you."

EXCUSE ME

Excuse me is magic because it acknowledges your impact on others and helps smooth over rough spots. We say "Excuse me, do you mind if I sneak by you?" to pass by someone in a tight space. We say "Excuse me, Pascal" to interrupt or get someone's attention. We say "Please excuse me," sincerely, to excuse behavior such as an inadvertent burp. We say "Excuse me for a moment," to depart a conversation. "Pardon me" is another version that can be equally useful. "Excuse me" is simple and works, but your attitude makes a difference. A snarky, "Ex-cuuuuuse me!" sucks the magic right out of this great phrase.

I'M SORRY

I'm sorry (or *I apologize*) can do both light and heavy lifting when it comes to solving problems and mending relationships. It, too, can be said well and have incredible impact: "Kaitlin, I apologize for missing the deadline. It won't happen again, and if there is anything I can do to compensate for my error, I'd be happy to hear it." "I'm sorry" can be said as a casual but sincere apology ("I'm sorry about that, Camilla") or as a casual but more apologetic version of "excuse me," as in, "Sorry, didn't mean to," as you bump someone in a crowd at a concert. On the other hand, saying "I'm sorry" for everything can also become a habit you don't want to develop. The "sorry" can lose some of its meaning and convey an overactive sense of responsibility; think about what you're really saying and why to keep your apologies impactful.

Saying "I'm sorry" can indicate you are taking responsibility for having wronged someone or done something you didn't mean to: "I'm sorry I hurt you." Or it can be used to sympathize with someone: "I'm so sorry to hear this," or "I'm sorry you're going through this."

A "sorry" that is callously tossed out with little sincerity communicates a lack of consideration and respect. If you're going to deliver what is clearly *not* an apology, it's basically the same as saying, "Sorry, not sorry." Why not take the high road and explain why you aren't able to apologize to this person right now? It is, after all, another option in communication.

How you issue your apology will play a big part in how it is received. Protect your apology. Give it the meaning you intend by keeping it clear. (For more on apologies, see The Good Apology, page 66.)

BODY LANGUAGE AND PERSONAL SPACE

How we hold our bodies, and the gestures we use, and the tone and volume of our voice are all part of how we communicate with and are received by others. Crossed arms, a furrowed brow, a clenched jaw, and pursed lips are not welcoming. It is important to turn toward the people we speak with. You are much more approachable if your eyes are engaged, your face lifted, back upright, and arms relaxed. When we are going about our day, exchanging pleasantries, a relaxed and friendly posture and body language will help to match our desire to be polite and put others at ease around us—even if it's just a brief elevator ride together.

How close or far do you stand when speaking with others? To be polite in our everyday conversations, we want to present ourselves as approachable, or at least at ease, and we want to observe and respect the personal space of others—as well as our own. For most people in the United States, this means keeping about a foot and a half (half a meter) between you and the other person. (That is, of course, unless social distancing is necessary or you're in a very crowded space.) Avoid leaning in too far or being soooo enthralled that you're practically dripping off the other person. Keeping too far away can also be awkward, as it might send the signal that you are unwilling to enter the classic three-foot comfort zone and the other person might wonder if you think they are contagious, foul smelling, or unpleasant in some way. A comedic scene in any movie, but not fun to experience in real life. Remember, that you should never touch someone who is pregnant without asking first--even if you're going for a belly touch, definitely stop and ask first. And respect whatever answer comes your way.

VOCAL TONE AND VOLUME

While our tone can be quite hard to convey via words on a page or screen, we can certainly express it clearly in our spoken conversations. Most of us have a wide range of vocal tones, so which "voice" is the real you? The "sweet" one you use when you answer a call with a smile on your face? The "lazy" one chilling on the couch in your sweats and calling out for the queso dip? The "whiny" one you employ when you just wish other people would fix things for you? Or the "confident" one you wield when you know just how to deliver a pitch, share bad news, flirt, or be fun? Serious, silly, kind, harsh, dismissive, arrogant, defiant, loving, patient, reassuring—there are many different tones we can strike, but when it comes to good etiquette, it's all about getting good at using the tone you want to when it's needed, the one that matches and respects the moment.

One of our biggest pieces of advice when it comes to handling awkward or unfamiliar situations is to rehearse what you want to say so you can hear your tone. Don't know how it's going to sound when you ask your sister not to bring her kids with her to dinner at your place Friday night? Practice out loud. If you are nervous or tense about making this request, your nerves may overshadow your intent. If you are worried or tense about it, and your tone comes across as strict or defensive, your request will have lost its good intention, which was to welcome your sister for a fun, kids-free evening. An unintentionally tense or negative tone can result from working up a conversation in your head. Snapping "I really *need* Friday to be adults only. Will that be a problem for you?" is hardly welcoming and definitely doesn't put the emphasis on having a good time. A relaxed and friendly "Hey, sis, I was hoping to do an adults' evening for Friday. Let me know if you can come and if you need any help finding a sitter" is clear and inviting. It states what you're hoping to achieve as the host for the evening and leaves options open if the plan doesn't work for the guest you're inviting. Tone matters.

We live in a time when we have never had more opportunities to see pictures of ourselves (thank you, selfies). However, unless we are regularly making recordings and videos of ourselves, we don't really have a sense of how we *sound* to others. For example, it can be tough to assess our volume, even if as children we were constantly told to use our "indoor voices." What is an indoor voice? One good way to gauge it is to try to speak loud enough for someone two to three feet away to hear you, and quiet enough so that someone six to eight feet away would not.

It can be quite difficult when someone soft-spoken is trying to chat with someone who has trouble hearing. In these situations, we might find ourselves leaning in or speaking more loudly. Do the best you can to assess what you and the person you are speaking to need. If you have a hard time hearing others, or if certain noises are tough for you to recover from quickly, let the person you're speaking with know. "I have tinnitus—I'm just going to step outside for a moment to let my ears adjust."

Avoid shouting indoors or from room to room. Screaming "MA!" from the kitchen when she's in the living room may be classic in many homes, but it's not exactly the most considerate use of volume.

Whispering should be used only when you need to speak quietly so that you don't disturb others. It should rarely (if ever) be used to keep others from hearing what you're saying. If you can't say something in front of everyone, wait to say it when you have a private moment.

THE THREE TIERS OF CONVERSATION

Polite conversation, good company, table conversation, small talk—whichever phrase you use to describe it, what matters is that we recognize that some topics of conversation are low stakes and easy for virtually any situation (Tier I topics), while others take us into dicier, potentially controversial territory (Tier II topics). And some topics fall into the category of being generally private and therefore brought up with only our nearest and dearest or with trusted professionals (Tier III topics). These tiers are not set in stone, but they do hold up in most situations and help us to appropriately moderate our participation in conversations.

A work colleague may not receive your full thoughts on opposing presidential candidates, but maybe you'll share your belief that voting is essential to being a good citizen. However, at home, among your closest family or friends, you might voice your political thoughts with all the candor and enthusiasm you have for the topic. Being familiar with which topics fall under which tiers and paying attention to your surroundings will aid you well in being a good conversationalist.

TIER I

Tier I topics are low stakes, easy to participate in, and safe for testing conversational waters when on the train or bus, standing in a long line, in some waiting rooms, on a first date, at a charity event, at a work mix 'n' mingle event, with your new mother-in-law, or during your Thanksgiving Zoom call. Tier I topics are the standard small-talk topics and include the weather (a classic), entertainment (music, books, podcasts, plays, performances, TV, movies), sports, hobbies, and shared experiences (such as the food, the event, the atmosphere, or the traffic that morning).

TIER II

Tier II topics are subjects that people can have very different and strong feelings about. These topics include religion, money, sex and romantic relationships, and politics. Conversations about these things aren't forbidden by any means, but have the potential to get personal or even offensive. When broaching Tier II topics, test the waters before getting in too deep. Try introducing a topic before taking a strong stance. Be prepared for your audience to possibly decline the conversation and redirect the topic, or even to be offended by the topic or your opinion on it. There is also the chance, of course, that broaching these subjects could result in a rousing conversation with enthralling ideas. These Tier II topics are important to us, and important to talk about. Asking if it's all right to broach the subject will give your audience an out if they wish, which is thoughtful and polite, and shows your care in approaching something others may feel differently about. ("I know it's not the easiest subject at a dinner table, but I would love to hear your thoughts on last week's debate if you'd be willing to share." "Oh, Mr. Daring, I would indeed, but let's leave our conversation about it until after dinner? I want to savor every bite before I distract my brain with politics.")

TIER III

Tier III topics are really only broached privately with close company: family or friends, or folks who know us well enough and whom we can trust with the shared information. Tier III topics include family, health, personal finances, and anything shared in confidence. Even when we are comfortable talking about these things, it is important to remember that not everyone (including our nearest and dearest) will be interested in hearing about them. Some people might judge (or at least note) your discretion and sense of personal privacy based on how you treat these topics.

When it comes to your family or chosen family, it is important to respect their privacy. We often choose to be our most vulnerable and open selves among these individuals, and trust that our thoughts and actions will be taken with a view and understanding of us as whole people. Though we may be privileged to know what goes on in the lives of those we hold most dear, we must try to understand and respect their personal privacy too by not sharing the intimate details of their personal or family life in public. The same is true for health-related information. People choose what to share for a combination of reasons; sometimes it's about what they are comfortable sharing and other times it's about what someone else is comfortable hearing; not everyone wants to hear about your colonoscopy. Discussions of family matters or personal issues are usually reserved for folks we are very close to.

Notice that the subjects of money and finances fall into both the Tier II and Tier III categories. When money is declared to be strictly a private topic, it limits the sharing of information that can help people increase their financial understanding and personal wealth. By not discussing money, equality and empowerment can suffer. Thinking of money as a Tier II category topic will hopefully encourage more conversation around it. This idea would constitute a change in our culture, however, it will take time for people to find ways in which they are comfortable discussing it. When approaching the subject of money, try to raise it tactfully. "I'm looking to get a better sense of what salaries for my job look like in this market, would you be willing to discuss it?" is more polite than, "What do you make? It's no big deal to share."

Finances are also placed in Tier III because they can be very personal, and there could be confidential reasons to decline talking about them. It's worth asking yourself why you want to discuss them with a particular person now. There could be lots of good reasons to engage with this topic, but it's wise to consider them first. Those who choose to talk about their finances might try to answer tactfully, being open in areas where they feel comfortable and vague where they do not. Abruptly asking, "What's in your portfolio?" will likely always be considered rude, but asking to have a candid conversation about money should not be taboo. ("Would you be comfortable talking about finances? I'm curious about retirement planning.")

TIME, PLACE, AND MODE

Receiving attention from others is a gift, and we should treat it as such. Asking for someone's time or attention is a small ask, but an ask nonetheless. Before you begin, start by asking yourself: *Do I need to discuss this here and now?* We have so many ways to communicate and to schedule a time to talk. Respecting the setting of your conversation is an etiquette point that can get you into trouble if you don't consider it. Think of the tense, whispered conversation at a religious service that gets loud at just the wrong time, the coworker who discusses their sex life in detail at the lunch table, the complaint you vent about someone who ends up being right nearby . . . the list goes on.

Choosing the appropriate time and place applies to written, phone, and video conversations, too. Consider sending a heavy text to someone after their workday ends—seeing a message about something tough but not time-sensitive will add unnecessary anxiety to their day. Rather than answering a video call from someone when you can't really chat well on camera, decline or text them asking for a phone call instead. Consider the nature of the call. If you know a friend isn't doing well, is calling her while you try to prepare dinner and herd the kids around the kitchen respectful of where she's at or your intent to really be there for her?

Make sure the mode of communication you choose is the optimum one for the conversation you're trying to have. Typically, if you're going to be discussing opinions or the why of something, pick up the phone, initiate a video chat, or meet in person. If you're going to communicate the facts and details of a situation (the *who, what, where,* or *when*), use a written medium so you can keep track of the information and details. You might call your friend to discuss her upcoming visit to you, and then text her your address so it's both easy to locate and use directly from her phone. Run a quick check first of the time, place, and mode, and your communication is more likely to be well received.

Many people today would rather text someone than talk to them over the phone or face to face. It's worth noting that we still think of in-person conversations as the richest, most empathetic, and most direct means of communication, and consider less direct means of communication as being less personal. A more personal way of communicating, although tough, can give you more tools to communicate fully and less chance of being misunderstood. It is often the most respectful way of handling a situation.

THE GOOD LISTENER

Sure, you can talk, but can you listen? When you listen, do you hear? Good listening skills are paramount to good manners. Listening (and/or paying close attention to nonverbal communication) allows us to truly participate. If we are simply planning out exactly what brilliant, cutting, or hilarious thing we are going to say next, we aren't really part of a conversation; we are simply waiting to speak. Getting comfortable with the idea that your brilliant remark could go unsaid is a wonderful skill to develop. It takes patience and a little humility to be a good listener, but it's the dream of every friend, partner, coworker, and family member to interact with someone who is. Here are some traits of a good listener:

- Make eye contact when possible. Focusing on someone's mouth or the bridge of their nose are alternatives for those who cannot sustain or make eye contact easily.

- Nod and/or say "mmhmm," "yes," "uh-huh," "aha," "okay" and other short phrases and expressions to show that you are following along.

- Respond with questions or comments: "You know, that reminds me of a time you . . ." "Wait, were you already out of the house at that point, or had you not left yet?" "Wow, how did that make you feel?" Note that you don't want to always be responding with stories or thoughts about your own life. A good listener—and a good conversationalist—will balance this, keeping most of the conversation focused on or relevant to the person speaking.

- Weigh what is important to respond to and what can be left unsaid, rather than responding with every thought you might have.

THE SKILLED TALKER

It can be difficult to pay attention to someone else when your brain is focused on what you're trying to say, but someone who is a "skilled talker" (as Emily liked to call them) will notice the moment they start to lose their audience. Their radar will go off at the slightest stifled yawn, the glazed or drifting eye, or the merely polite response. *High alert—this person is losing interest in the conversation!* Cultivate and listen to that radar so you can stop yourself, "I'm so sorry. I'm going on and on about my toddler. How was your trip to Ohio?" or, "Forgive me, I could go on, but I'd love to hear your perspective." At this point you switch to your good listening skills. This might also be when a skilled talker realizes the conversation is over. While you might try to move on to another subject, ending a conversation is always an option as well: "Eva, I've talked your ear off. Let's go get out on the dance floor!"

A skilled talker also notices when a group conversation needs some expansion. If the conversation seems to be turning into a singles' tennis match, the skilled talker will quickly recognize when only one or two voices are dominating and will encourage others to engage by finding a time to interrupt and ask a question of someone else. "Jill, you've worked in Washington. What do you think?"

One of the things a skilled talker is best at is knowing what they don't know, and being comfortable stating it. "I'll be honest, Courtney, I'm not familiar enough with particle physics to venture a guess, but I'd love to hear more about what you know on the subject."

A skilled talker does not speak of people familiarly to those who don't know them. You'll never catch them saying, "Bob absolutely loved it" when no one present knows Bob. Instead they would say: "My father-in-law, Bob, absolutely loved it." Similarly, a skilled conversationalist is never *surprised* by anyone, because that would mean they'd made assumptions about the person. Instead, they are *interested* or *glad* to find something out. "Oh, I'm so glad to know you love fishing" is much more polite than "I'm surprised *you* love fishing." In every conversation, tact is as essential as honesty.

A considerate conversationalist is also adept at speaking *to* an individual rather than *about* them when they are right there. As a general rule, avoid referring to someone in the third person when they are present. Rather than assume a child with Down syndrome (or any child) can't speak for themselves or shouldn't be spoken to directly, they would ask the child, "And Sophie, how old are you?" rather than asking the parent, "How old is she?" If someone is unable to respond or feeling shy, a parent or friend or their assistant can respond on their behalf. It is imperative to pay the person you are speaking to respect through your direct attention. Same goes if you or the person you are speaking with is using an interpreter. Your eye contact and body language should be addressing the person you are having the conversation with, not the interpreter. (But it's kind to thank the interpreter for their help after the conversation has concluded.)

PROFANITY AND VULGARITY

Swearing, cursing, cussing, colorful language—no matter what you call it, profanity is part of our culture. We may not choose to use so-called curse words personally, or we may pepper them liberally throughout our conversations. The issue isn't so much whether these words are right or wrong to use, but when you choose to use them and around whom. Typically, in public spaces we try to avoid swearing, and definitely try to avoid swearing loudly. At our own restaurant table, at a volume that doesn't go beyond our group space, it is probably not so offensive. Loudly and frequently when small children—little ears!—are nearby: not appropriate. When we really have to watch ourselves is while we are talking in a public space on our phones. If you are lost in conversation, it's easy to forget your whereabouts and speak as though you and the other person are talking in private. We suggest you be more careful.

Because curse words can so easily take the place of other words, you don't want to lean on them to the point of becoming lazy with the rest of your vocabulary. Swear words do have their place, though; studies have shown they can actually reduce pain and relieve stress when said in exclamation. However, lean on them too much and you lose the habit of choosing other effective ways of making your point or expressing yourself. If they become too much a part of our everyday speech, we may have a harder time reining them in when we want or need to. Practice using a range of words to express yourself, and you'll easily be able to switch when needed.

"Vulgar" language covers a lot, but to be polite we typically would keep detailed descriptions of the body and its functions (even if healthy and fun), or describing times of illness, out of our general conversation. Bathroom humor, locker-room talk—save those comments and conversations for friends or family members you can "go there" with.

Respectful, considerate, and kind language never refers to a specific condition in a disparaging way—to do so is horribly disrespectful to those with that diagnosis. "I swear, she is totally bipolar today, so watch out," or "OMG, I have like PTSD from how bad that restaurant was," or "That is so lame," are all inappropriate. Consider whether a colloquial phrase might be offensive before you say it, and never use a real diagnosis or words that have historically been connected with a disability as hyperbole.

Language that is mean or cruel might feel powerful or help you vent in the moment, but the hurt it can cause makes it truly profane and beyond the bounds of decent behavior.

THE GOOD APOLOGY

Accidents will happen and mistakes will be made. How you handle them says a great deal about you, maybe even more than how you handle your successes. Delivering a good apology will help you succeed in your relationships, both in social settings and at work. When you feel confident making an apology and know why you're making it, you can take responsibility and begin the first steps toward repairing the damage. "I'm sorry that I was late and held everyone up," "I'm sorry I was gross, please pardon me," and "I'm sorry that I hurt you" are good places to start.

Avoid the word *if* in an apology. It invalidates the offense or the other party's feelings, and suggests that whatever you did or said might not have actually had the impact it did. It's a form of gaslighting (see page 70) inside an apology. If you're apologizing, there's a reason why, and you should take responsibility for that. Even if it's something small, allow the person impacted to dismiss the offense ("I'm sorry I was a bit quiet tonight." "I didn't notice a thing—it was delightful having you!") rather than suggesting they might dismiss it for you ("I'm sure it wasn't an issue, but I'm sorry I was quiet tonight at dinner").

A good apology also avoids continuing with a *but* to explain your side. You can still add your perspective, but don't use it as a contrast. Rather than saying, "I'm sorry, but I've heard you tell that story to others before, so I thought it would be okay," try "I'm sorry, it was wrong of me to assume. I thought because I've heard you tell that story that it would be okay to tell it tonight. I'm glad you let me know it was a mistake; I won't do it again."

GOOD APOLOGIES	LACKLUSTER APOLOGIES
"I'm sorry my words were offensive and hurt you."	"I'm sorry *if* my words were offensive and hurt you."
"I'm sorry I hurt you."	"I'm sorry I *might have* hurt you."
"I'm sorry I missed the deadline."	"I'm sorry I *may have* missed the deadline."
"I'm sorry for the delay on my end."	"I'm sorry for *any* delay on my end."
"I'm sorry I created stress [worry, frustration] for you."	"I'm sorry *if* I created stress [worry, frustration] for you."
"I'm sorry for my part in this. I should not have done that."	"I'm sorry for my part in this, *but you . . .*"

TO CORRECT OR NOT TO CORRECT?

One of the least impressive things you can do in conversation is correct someone you aren't responsible for: "Actually, it's *hone,* not *home.* A pigeon *homes* in on a location, while a skill or knife is *honed,* as in sharpened." It's certainly helpful to have common misconceptions corrected, but it comes across as pretentious if it isn't coming from someone who is supposed to be teaching you, such as a parent, manager, or teacher. It makes it seem like the corrector is somehow the editor of the conversation, a role they weren't asked to play. There are times and places for pointing out an error, but it's rarely in the moment in front of others unless necessary to correct something about you, such as your name, job title, pronoun, relationship status, or other personal fact.

While there are rules for our grammar and pronunciation, we have many different ways of speaking English here in North America. No one version is perfectly correct, and few people use formal language regularly. Today, we switch from casual to formal speech to manage the different environments and relationships in our lives. To think that every interaction needs perfect grammar or the most formal versions of American English is unrealistic and can come across as out of touch. Unless you have been asked for your input or you are a teacher or are responsible for helping someone with their speech, don't correct others, especially not in front of anyone.

CULTIVATING KINDNESS IN LANGUAGE

Taking the time to cultivate kindness in your language not only means you're being considerate, respectful, and honest in your communications, but it can also help you strengthen your listening skills, patience, and awareness of others. Paying attention to a few language tweaks, and finding ways to implement them, can make a big difference in how others receive and respond to you.

TRADE *YOU* FOR *I.* Taking responsibility for your own behavior, perspective, or experience rather than putting the focus on others is a great way to cultivate kind language. Whenever possible, switch from *you* statements that highlight other people's negative behavior to *I* statements about how you are feeling or have been impacted ("You don't listen" becomes "I don't feel heard"). You can also claim a personal perspective rather than declaring something as an absolute: "Please excuse me, I'm sensitive to cigar smoke. I'm going to move away" versus "Your cigar smoke really smells horrible."

TONE DOWN THE LANGUAGE. De-escalate difficult or angry conversations by saying, "I strongly dislike" instead of "I hate," or "I'm so mad at him" instead of "I'm gonna tear him limb from limb." Language that is based on violence, particularly physical violence, even if it is not meant to target anyone, can significantly impact people. Every time you remove it from the conversation, you help to de-escalate things.

SPEAK IN ACTUALITIES. Is it really *every* time? Does someone *never* do XYZ? When we exaggerate, we leave ourselves less room to reconcile an issue. Painting a fair, realistic picture of what you're experiencing is not only respectful to others involved, but also helps to de-escalate tense conversations. "It's not every time, but it has been too many times recently, and that's why I'm upset." This is an important form of honesty. We have lots of words to minimize the idea of lying (white lies, fibs, harmless lies, prosocial lies) but rather than try to excuse this, why not go for honesty? It's easier to keep track of and builds trust. It may sound hard, but in truth (haha) it's easy to do.

CAREFULLY COMMUNICATE CRITICISM. When you take care with how you deliver negative feedback to someone, it really helps them receive the feedback well. One time-tested strategy is the "compliment sandwich": deliver praise, then the constructive criticism, followed by another positive comment. "Jade, the eye you're bringing to the launch this month is spot-on. I'd like you to bring that much attention to filling out your time slips on the project from here on out. I think the client is going to be really thrilled." Another technique is the "praise, concern, suggest" framework: start with a specific positive, bring up any issues or concerns, and then offer some solutions. "Jade, the press release and social campaign you set up for the launch are fantastic. I have been concerned about getting your time slips for the project in. Would setting a reminder in your calendar to fill it out each day before you head out be helpful?" Critical feedback alone can shut down someone's ability to hear it. Science suggests you can try a three-to-one ratio of positive to negative feedback, being sure to mention at least three positive things for every concern or negative issue you raise as a way to give successful criticism. This ratio helps to keep someone emotionally available to receive the criticism, which is ultimately your goal.

FLIP YOUR LANGUAGE. Rather than saying, "Here's what you're doing wrong," try "This is where you could improve," or "There's room for improvement here." Rather than highlighting a fault, flipping a *don't* to a *do* can inspire growth and act as a healthy challenge. It's certainly a kinder approach.

LEAVE ROOM TO BE WRONG. Shocking as the revelation may be, we are all capable of getting things wrong. Embracing this reality can make it easier to accept and move on when we do.

Some mistakes require reparative action, and knowing everyone makes mistakes can make that easier to do.

BE CLEAR WHEN INVITING SOMEONE TO DO SOMETHING. When making an invitation to a friend or a date, rather than asking if the person would like to "do something sometime" (vague), try asking them with more specificity. Instead of "Want to go for a hike sometime?" try "Want to go for a hike this weekend?" The latter gives the other person something clear to respond to. If the answer is no, you can always suggest another time. A kind ask makes it easy for the person you're asking to respond, whether they are declining or accepting.

DECLINE AND ACCEPT REGRETS GRACIOUSLY. Many of us feel bad when we have to decline a kind offer, whether it's a job, date, event, trip, or even just an invitation to hang out. It can feel awkward to turn down an offer. We know we feel bad when people can't say yes, and we don't love having to put others in this position. However, when we graciously decline ("I won't make it this time, but thanks so much for inviting me. I appreciate it") we take the sting out of someone hearing our "no" and we gain the benefit of giving the person who asked a clear reply. In turn, when the person we're giving our regrets to is kind about receiving them, it makes for a polite moment. "I'm sorry, I can't say yes to a date," can be responded to politely with "Glad I tried anyway," or "No worries. Have a good night," or "Glad to have met you, and have a good rest of your day." These are all far preferable to "What do you mean, no?" or "Oh really, come on—just a coffee?" It's okay to be disappointed that someone turned you down, but that disappointment is for you to manage, not them.

IT'S OKAY TO SAY "I DON'T KNOW." One of the classiest—and most honest—things you can do in a conversation is admit when you don't know something. It's okay not to get a joke, or not to know everything about a subject (or even that a subject existed). Admitting that you don't know something is far better than wading into a conversation when you're already lost. Most people will be more than willing to fill you in or get you acquainted with a topic. "I'm not familiar with that. Can you give me the basics?"

The more you practice cultivating kindness in your language, the more it will become second nature.

GASLIGHTING, "OTHERING," AND PRIVILEGE IN CONVERSATION

The following behaviors can unfortunately show up in conversation and are considered rude even if they're unintentional. Like all rude behaviors, they have negative effects. Even mild versions of these infractions are examples of incivility that are worth eliminating.

GASLIGHTING is when someone disputes the perceived experience of someone else. It happens frequently in conversation, "Oh, you shouldn't worry about that" or "No, that's not what was going on" or "Don't take it so personally," and should be corrected, if not avoided. If someone you are speaking with tells you they are offended by something or experienced a situation in a particular way, it's not your job to revise their experience ("No way—he wasn't hitting on you. That's not his style"). Instead, listen to them ("I didn't notice, but I'm sorry that's how he was with you."). If applicable, ask if there's something you can do to help. That is polite. Trying to erase or change what happened by sharing your perspective isn't. While there are certainly times when we perceive others incorrectly, in gaslighting, the person who was offended says, "This happened," and the other person says, "No, it didn't." This is different from the offended person seeking your input by asking, "Did this just happen? Am I reading it wrong?"

OTHERING happens when you make assumptions that the person you are engaging with isn't part of the same social group, community, or organization as you, or isn't from the same place. Saying to someone who looks or sounds different from you, "Where are you from?" or "Wow, I've never heard a name like yours before. It's so beautiful," may seem innocuous, but it can come across as *You're different* or *You are an outsider.* Even if it's said in a friendly or complimentary way, the question can be more alienating than friendly. And for someone who experiences this frequently, it can be draining, discouraging, and even disheartening. There will always be differences between people, but don't use someone's outward appearance, name, or manner of speaking to assume that you know where they are from, what they understand, or what they might relate to. It's okay to ask appropriate questions and give compliments, but how you do it will determine whether or not it's polite.

PRIVILEGE can be and sound like many different things, but in conversation, it mostly comes across as a lack of awareness that you have benefited in a way others may not have. Lots of things that are out of our control can make our lives easier or harder—our health, gender, age, sexual orientation, race, religion, ability, class—and nearly anyone can make a statement of privilege and not realize it. Privilege can be assuming that everyone grew up in a financially comfortable family or went to college, when not everyone did. Or it might be the thought *Everyone wants to lose a few pounds after Christmas*, when not everyone does (either want to lose weight or celebrate Christmas). It may be an assumption of good health or circumstances. For example, saying "I did really well during the COVID-19 pandemic," might be true, but is insensitive to the many people who struggled or lost their homes, jobs, or even their loved ones.

Own your story. Understand what you bring to a conversation—both your unique perspective and your blind spots. You can always acknowledge where you are coming from and invite other perspectives: "From my perspective, as a fortysomething white author from Vermont, this is what I see going on, but I'd really like to hear how this looks from your point of view . . ." Remind yourself that you don't know anyone else's story, and try not to make assumptions about others' privilege. The easiest privilege to check is your own.

TYPES OF TALKERS

Emily carved out humorous caricatures of the "Types of Talkers" that we all encounter. What follows is our updated group of today's talkers. If you're dealing with one of these characters, appreciating their cartoonish nature and having patience is usually the most polite move.

MS. CEE SLESS would be so delightful if she took a breath and allowed others to participate. She starts by asking how you're enjoying your meal and before you can answer, she's told you her childhood history and where she'd like to be in five years. If only she would leave space for others to respond.

MX. DOOR SLAMMER (a great-grandchild of Mr. Door Slammer from Emily's 1922 edition) shuts down every attempt at conversation with curt answers and usually a bored or negative demeanor. Try as you might, you cannot draw them into polite small talk. No bait you dangle will result in a conversational catch. They would benefit from showing the slightest interest or willingness to participate.

MR. NOAH TALL truly *thinks* he knows it all. No matter *your* experience or expertise, you are nothing compared to him. Mr. Noah Tall has done it all, seen it all, and likely invented it all, too. The word *actually* precedes almost all of his comments. He cannot sit out and just listen to a conversation. While he might implode if he uses it, he desperately needs to learn the phrase "I don't know."

MRS. PRIVIE LEDGE can't see past the end of her nose. She doesn't realize that what she says paints a picture of someone who is oblivious. It must be very nice to live in her world, but it causes people to listen to her politely for a time and then leave, seeking a dose of reality and a broader perspective in their conversations. She would do well to listen to others' experiences in life and moderate her words accordingly.

MS. EXTRA EXAGGERATED is enthusiastic beyond belief. Everything is hyperbole, and as that fish she caught keeps getting bigger and bigger, she becomes phonier and phonier. She may be entertaining, but she is also exhausting. She doesn't need the "extra" she keeps on giving. Wildly flamboyant characters can be delightful, but Ms. Extra Exaggerated is too much. She ought to take it down a notch.

MX. DULLASA DOORKNOB may not mean to be dull, but they respond with only monotone *mmmm*s and *uh-huh*s, and when they finally venture into sentence territory, it's with something like, "The cheese . . . is soft," which, true as it might be, is not exactly riveting repartee. A bit of inflection could make such a difference.

MR. OVER LEE INTERESTED cares too much about what you're saying—almost more than you do. He asks too many questions about mundane details and is overly interested in how you feel about everything. Is it because he can't come up with topics of his own, or because he doesn't understand boundaries? We may never know, but please excuse us while we get some air. He would benefit from letting some things remain a mystery.

MRS. MIA CENTRIQUE is the sun and air. She is the star and we are all just members of her supporting cast to help her shine. She *never* asks, "How are you?" or responds with concern. Instead, she launches into how what you just said reminds her of something in *her* life. She is best taken in small doses by her friends and relatives. At work, she clears the break room quickly. If she would only ask a simple "What's new with you?" she could completely change the impression she gives.

DISENGAGING FROM AN
UNPLEASANT CONVERSATION

Despite the best intentions, sometimes a conversation can turn unpleasant, either because of gossip being spread, the tone taking a bad turn, or someone starting to say something to you or about others that you don't feel comfortable hearing. It's okay to "call it" in a conversation and admit that you don't wish to continue. You can also be clear that a topic isn't okay with you without it coming across as a judgment on others. To leave a casual conversation among a group at a party, you might calmly excuse yourself: "It's been great chatting with you. I'm going to keep making the rounds." You might even add, "Take care. Maybe we can chat more later," if it feels right. If you're talking one-on-one with someone, you might be more direct: "I'm going to excuse myself now." You don't have to apologize for wanting to move on from a conversation. (See Making Conversation, page 181, as well as Conversation at the Table, page 293, for how to handle racist or hate speech when entertaining.)

Another approach is to let someone (or the group) know that they've brought you into conversational territory you want to avoid: "Colt, I don't want to ruin a great story, but I have to admit I'm rather squeamish about this; could you table it until after dinner?" Here you're admitting what you don't want to talk about, rather than excusing yourself. It can help the other person understand what to avoid when speaking with you (at least in this moment) and allow for the conversation to continue but on a different topic. Setting boundaries is so important and can be kind and helpful for others, if done politely. There are many ways to deflect or redirect, and even admitting that you "don't want to go there" is okay. "How's recovery going?" "Oh, let's talk about *anything* else. It's good to get my mind off it." When we're setting social boundaries (especially with folks outside our innermost circles), doing so gently and with an easy tone can really help keep things from getting awkward.

There might be times when, rather than end the conversation, you transfer it to a better medium like from a text to a phone call. Ironically, while an awkward in-person conversation might get back on course with a follow-up phone call, a phone call gone wrong might need an in-person conversation to fix itself.

ENDING A CONVERSATION WELL

All conversations must come to an end, and ending one well is an art. Hanging up too soon, walking out without saying goodbye, or suddenly leaving an in-person group conversation can make others confused or lead to general awkwardness. Fortunately, in many of our day-to-day conversations, endings are clear and easy: we're leaving for work, we're at the register paying for a sandwich, the conference call is over and we can all hang up. We let the last thing be said and then say, "Goodbye," or "I'll see you later," or even "Good work, team." There are times when we have to make it clear that we need a conversation to end, whether we just want it to or we are in a rush. During these moments we want to lean on our magic words and use either a clear and firm tone or a friendly and apologetic one, depending on what is warranted. "Pardon me, Ms. Cee Sless, it's so great to see you. However, I'm in a rush and have to be on my way. I'm sorry I can't chat longer. Take care!" (Or, "Dude, great to see you, sorry but I gotta run. See ya!")

IN-PERSON CONVERSATIONS

We place a high value on in-person conversations. When someone is physically with us, we can connect with them in a way that we cannot via phone, video, or written words. While those methods of communication can be powerful, feeling another person in your presence, experiencing with all your senses what they are trying to communicate and how they are receiving you isn't just the most effective means of communication, it's also pretty incredible. Given that all our senses are engaged and there's so much to interpret and react to, it's important to take care with our in-person conversations.

CONVERSATIONS IN PASSING

We may have the briefest of interactions with store associates and people on the street, at sporting events or religious services, but without the most basic manners, rudeness can rear its ugly head. For instance, if you walk into a store and the sales associate stocking shelves near the entrance greets you with a friendly smile and says, "Hi, how are you today?" and you walk on by, you have just been rude. A simple, "Hi. I'm well, thank you" or "Good, thanks, 'n' you?" costs nothing and acknowledges their welcoming greeting. Even if you walk in while talking on your phone, a wave, smile, and eye contact would be more polite than breezing right on by.

While you are out and about in your neighborhood, at a local diner, in your building hall-way, or at work, you'll have a range of conversations in passing. Sometimes just giving a nod and saying the person's name or "Hi" will suffice. Or you might pass your neighbor on the sidewalk and say without slowing down, "Gorgeous day out!" and they could smile, wave, or say "Isn't it?" not really expecting you to answer, but happy for the brief, pleasant exchange. The important thing is to acknowledge or respond. Not doing so is rude.

CASUAL CONVERSATIONS

We have casual conversations all the time. And when we do, for the most part they are simple and pleasant. We might chat with a fellow traveler, a coworker, or the person next to us as we dine at the counter or bar. Or we might be shooting the breeze with a friend. What we say doesn't matter too much except to offer some points of connection; it's easy, Tier I–level conversation (see page 61). This is basic politeness at work. It's nice.

What you shouldn't do with in-person, casual conversations is reach too far too quickly. Emily compared conversation to fishing. You put out a little bait and see if someone takes it. If they don't bite, you try different bait or back off. Try once or twice, and if you get nothing, assume the person doesn't want to chat; leave your conversation at a pleasant greeting and that's it. Don't try to force a conversation that isn't happening, and likely doesn't *need* to happen.

To decline a casual conversation with someone you don't know, you can simply say, "It's nice to meet you. I'm going to read until we get to Boston," or "Nice to meet you. I'd like to eat quietly today," or "I don't intend to be rude, but I'd like to be by myself right now." (See On Airplanes, page 374, for details.)

IN-DEPTH CONVERSATIONS

Be it a business meeting or listening to your best friend discuss something deeply personal, in-depth conversations require our best selves: the very best listener within us and the very best responder. Any time we're having a serious conversation or one concerning a sensitive topic, our phones should be put down and out of sight or on silent. We should make eye contact. We should be focused on the person we are speaking with. Here are some tips to help.

- Avoid being distracted (by your phone, pets, kids/other people, the TV).

- Make eye contact (if possible).

- It's okay to ask questions, but do so thoughtfully. Ask yourself, *Is now the time to ask for these details?*

- Exercise patience. Let someone get through all or most of what they need to say before responding.

- Don't fidget.

- Offer your perspective rather than just giving it: "I could give you my thoughts if you think it might be helpful," or "I'm happy to share my story if you'd like to hear it." Or in a business context, "We'd be happy to reflect on this and come back with ideas next week."

APPARENT CONDITIONS

Some of us have or exhibit apparent conditions such as stutters, tics, trembling, different eating or breathing styles, or the many effects of PTSD. And many people have difficulty making or maintaining eye contact. If someone has an apparent condition and is comfortable discussing it, they will. If they don't bring it up, you shouldn't either. If you have sincere and thoughtful questions, they may be welcome; just remember to make sure the time and place is appropriate before asking them. Usually, it's best to do so once you've gotten to know someone better.

In the moment, and always when meeting someone for the first time, keep the focus on the conversation at hand. When it comes to conversation, you definitely want to avoid "hurrying things along" or "helping" someone you've just met. It's rarely as assistive as you might think. For instance, if the person you are speaking with has a stutter or isn't speaking fluently, don't guess their words for them or suggest they relax, thinking it's helpful. It's not. Instead, be patient and focus on the words as they come. If you miss something, ask the person to clarify; this is more polite and effective than pretending you understand when you don't.

DISTRACTING HABITS

Some habits can be distracting to those you are talking with, like tapping your pen, biting your nails, cracking your knuckles, twirling your hair, running your fingers through your beard or mustache, or bouncing your foot or leg. While it can be hard to interrupt a habitual action, finding more discreet outlets is best, if possible. For example, rather than bouncing your leg, try pressing your thumb and forefinger together; taking a deep breath is another. Frustratingly, we don't always notice these habits in ourselves. Not sure if you have any distracting habits? Ask a friend or partner; they may appreciate the opportunity to point something out.

CONVERSATIONS VIA PHONE

The word *hello* didn't take on its current usage until the late 1800s, when it was repurposed from an expression of surprise to a greeting when using what was then a brand-new technology: the telephone. Our phone capabilities have come a long way since Emily's day. Not only have we fully adjusted to having phones in our homes and talking on them frequently, but we've moved our phones (now mini computers) to our pockets and have added the complication of trying to use them while on the go. In fact, we've evolved so far that until the COVID-19 pandemic, when phone calls became lifelines for many people (as well as a great break from all the video calls), we were hearing that younger generations disliked reaching out via phone. Some were even afraid to receive or place a call, and avoided the phone entirely. Whether fearfully modern or frightfully quaint, conversations via phone have evolved, and good etiquette is still important.

TIME AND PLACE

Placing a call when it's not really a good time for you to talk, or answering the phone when you're in a noisy location or you're focused on something else isn't polite for the person on the other end. Answering a call while driving carries all kinds of risks, and safety ought to be prioritized over etiquette. It's never bad to start a call with a quick, "Is now a good time?" or, "Did I catch you at a good time?" just in case.

While younger generations may be phone shy when it comes to placing a call to a friend, it's still perfectly polite to do so. Let this be your encouragement: call people! The worst that can happen is it's not a good time and the person says so, or you leave a message. Those aren't terrible moments to live through. Many people rely solely on their cell phones for calls, so there's less worry about calling a house phone that might ring in multiple rooms at an undesirable hour. The general guideline for timing an unplanned call is between 9:00 a.m. and 9:00 p.m., and this is particularly important to observe with regard to landlines that might ring throughout a home. Outside of that (and perhaps depending on whether or not you know the person is a night owl), shoot someone a text first to see if they're available, or wait until a better time.

Where we choose to place and take calls matters as well. When dining with others is never the right time and place. During a party, when hanging out with a group, when meeting someone new (like your dad's new girlfriend): these are times when your focus—emergencies aside—should be on the people you are with. Avoid taking calls during these times, and fight the urge to excuse yourself to make a non-emergency call during such an occasion. That said, there are some cases where you might take a call when you're around others. Say you're hanging with your kids and partner, your brother calls, and it's an okay time to talk; you excuse yourself and step away to take the call so that you aren't disrupting the group or subjecting them to half a conversation.

While the phone is an amazing invention, and cell/smartphones even more so, there are times when written communication can enhance a phone call. Whether it's an emailed recipe, texted directions, or scheduling information, following up a phone call or additionally giving someone written information instead of just verbally can ensure everyone is on the same page, which is always a courteous thing to do.

VOLUME AND TONE

One of the very best tips for a pleasant call is to *smile*. The other person cannot see you, but they will *hear* your smile on the other end, and it really does make a difference. Since you can't use facial expressions or body language to help you communicate via phone, you want to check your volume and tone to have a successful call. Volume can be difficult to gauge, because if you're having trouble hearing someone, your natural response is to raise your own voice. This goes for whispers, too. You don't have to match the person on the other end when they speak loudly or whisper. Do be receptive, though, when someone says they are having trouble hearing you. Whether it's too quiet, too loud, or a bad connection, the exact cause might not be apparent right away. It might take a minute to figure it out. Be patient and try not to take it personally or get frustrated.

If you find yourself struggling to understand someone because of a bad connection or background noise, resist the urge to let your frustration show. Remember, you can always say nicely, "Let's try this again another time," or suggest disconnecting and restarting the call. When connection is the issue, it might be a one-sided decision: "Okay, I still can't hear you; if you can hear me, I'm going to hang up and call back."

BAD PHONE CALLS

Bad connections, dropped calls, conversations that take a turn: whatever the reason, a bad call is frustrating. Imagine being alive before the telephone! If a letter or an in-person encounter didn't give you all the information you needed, you were a long way from being able to do much about it quickly. Today, when a call drops or a frustrated person hangs up, repeated calls, texts, and emails can be sent to follow up—though whether or not they *should* be depends entirely on the situation and what's being said.

When technology is the problem, do your best to keep your frustration focused on the medium and not the person on the other end. If you frequently have issues connecting via phone, it's best to forewarn people and direct them to the most reliable way to reach you: "I don't get good reception at my house, so here's my landline just in case I don't respond promptly," or "I'll have to use audio FaceTime or Skype for the call. I can't get a cell signal and we don't have a landline." Another convenient way to head off a bad connection before it becomes annoying is to determine who should try to call the other person back: "I'm driving through a low-signal area so I'll call you once I get bars again. It might be a while if it drops."

When a call ends because it has become tense or even out of control, take the space you need to process it and then come back when you can to either apologize or try to continue the conversation. If you need time, ask for it. Switching to text is tempting and might even be the way to get the conversation going again, but don't rely on it to finish the fight or make your point. If possible, try to reconnect calmly in person or again on the phone.

SAYING GOODBYE

Saying goodbye on the phone is an important part of the call, as is hanging up. It may help to remember the old telephone tradition where the person who initiated the call is the one responsible for ending the call.

Our goodbyes can vary, "Okay, bye!" "Goodbye!" "Take care, talk soon." "I've gotta run, but this has been great!" or "It's been so lovely speaking with you. I really look forward to working together. Take care! Bye!" Whether long or short, the goodbye should happen. It closes the conversation. A goodbye that feels abrupt leaves the other party wondering, *Was it something I said or did?*

The opposite of awkwardly abrupt is the overly dragged-out goodbye. One version of this is when someone says they must go but then picks up another topic of conversation; the next thing you know, you've been on the phone another twenty minutes! Sometimes this is delightful, other times excruciating. If the latter, you may always say as politely as possible that you must go, but you'd love to discuss this more another time. "Viv, I hate to cut in, but I've got to get ready to head out. Could we pick it up again next time?" but be sure you don't introduce a new topic of your own. Finish with a goodbye.

The more annoying and less manageable version is when the other person wants you to hang up first (a trope usually reserved for the lovesick), or their goodbye consists of all the goodbyes and never really ends: "Okay, cheers, thanks so much, love you, really miss you, adios, so excited to talk again soon, this has been so nice and you are just the greatest, ciao, take care now, okay, bye, goodbye, bye-bye now, bye, bye, take care . . ." This is one time where it's okay to talk over someone, "Yes, so good. Can't wait till next time. Take care, bye!" *CLICK!* And you're out. No matter what, remember to actually disconnect or hit "End." While it might be easier to let the other person hang up for both of you, by not doing so, you risk a live mic situation.

VOICEMAIL

Lots of parents and grandparents today talk about being "trained" by their kids and grandkids not to leave voicemails because they are just ignored, and to instead send a text or expect a missed call to be returned. Time is precious, and while reading a message is often faster than listening to it, this trend seems to be born out of a me-centric attitude. If you're going to try to dictate how you receive messages from others, the polite version of "training" is to ask nicely. "Grandma, I love hearing from you but I don't often check voicemail, would you be willing to text me instead, please?" Another option, if you aren't going to listen to or respond to voicemails, is to shut off the service.

Some might not like listening to or leaving voicemails, but because they are still so commonplace, especially in business, it's more polite to leave voicemails and listen to them than it is to not. Assuming a missed call is enough to get a call back isn't smart. Lots of people won't return a missed call unless there is a voicemail (or text) asking them to. Many others won't return a missed call from an unknown number. It's better to leave a voicemail and not chance it. While it's usually best to respond in kind with a return phone call, under some circumstances (though certainly not in a work context or when just starting to date someone) you might reply with a text: *Got your message. We'd love to come over this afternoon! Anything we can bring?*

When you do leave a message, be clear and concise. State your name, number, the reason for the call, and a good time to call you back. Then state your name and phone number again (yes, even with caller ID, still state your number). Remember that many people are receiving voicemails transcribed as text, so having important information and contact details stated clearly can be useful. "Hi, Elliot. My name is Anna Post. My number is 802-888-9999. Alexia Bean gave me your number and said you might be interested in babysitting. I have two kids: Jasper, three, and Delphine, one. Please give me a call back any time after 5. Thanks for your time. Again, my name is Anna Post and my number is 802-888-9999. Thanks so much."

WORK CALLS

Since many people work from home these days, we often need to switch between our professional and personal roles. And while for many, work calls have become increasingly casual, professionalism is still deeply important. You'll want to have that polished version of your voice ready to go when you need it.

ANSWERING WORK CALLS

Isn't it such a relief when you call somewhere and the person answering is pleasant, and it's easy to tell you've reached the right place? That's what to aim for with incoming business calls. What you say will depend on your company and your role. "Hello, Acme Glass Company. This is Jeremy. How may I help you?" might sound like a mouthful even if it takes only two seconds to say, but it offers so much to the person calling. Not only do they know they've called the Acme Glass Company, they know they are speaking with Jeremy and he is willing to help. That would make any customer feel confident. And if Jeremy said instead, "Acme Glass Company, how may I direct your call?" we would know right away that he was the operator or receptionist and able to get us to where we needed to go.

For those who might not need to state a company name, answering with your name is also acceptable: "Hello, this is Arianna," or "Hello, this is Arianna Arroyos." This is particularly common for in-company calls and for those using a dedicated extension. However, if you can tell an outside number is calling in, it's still best to state a greeting, your company, and then your name: "Hello, Common Sense PR, Arianna speaking."

PLACING WORK CALLS AND LEAVING PROFESSIONAL MESSAGES

We know that placing calls may be daunting for some, but two things can make it easier: practice and preparation. No, you don't have to read a script, but it can help to think about the purpose of the call and what you need to say when the call is answered. First, identify yourself, then state who it is you are trying to reach and why: "Hi, this is Miles Jameson. I'm calling for Coco Turner. I have a meeting scheduled with her at 10:00."

Having an idea of what you need to say in a message if you need to leave one is another way to prep well before placing a call. Jot down notes if you need prompts. If you are sent to voicemail or need to leave a message with someone, be sure to include your name and callback number (better than spelling out your email address) and the reason for your call. In fact, giving your name and callback number twice is preferable. If you'd like to give a good time to reach you and it makes sense to, then do so. While it's technically preferable to be formal with anyone in business, more and more people are leaning on first names as a default, even in messages to someone they've never spoken to before. Judge whether or not to be formal or familiar based on your industry, company, and whom you are calling.

FOR A FORMAL MESSAGE "Hello, Ms. Turner, my name is Miles Jameson from US Mutual. We met at the SHRM convention last week, and I'm calling to set a time to discuss your training needs. Please give me a call back at 212-555-5656 when you are able, or I can try again on Friday. Again, this is Miles Jameson and my number is 212–555–5656. Many thanks, and best to you. Goodbye."

FOR A CASUAL MESSAGE "Hi, Coco, it's Miles from SHRM last week. Great speaking with you. Was hoping to set up a time to talk about training. Feel free to reach me at 212–555–5656, again that's 212-555-5656, or I'll try you again on Friday. Cheers till then! Bye."

CONFERENCE CALLS AND MEETINGS

Conference calls between three or more people have become a staple in the world of business. A well-managed and well-attended call is appreciated by all, especially your company. Here are some tips for a good conference call:

- If you are hosting the call, invite the participants well by being clear about the time (including time zones) and the meeting agenda.

- Make sure everyone has the correct call-in information, and resend it 15 minutes beforehand.

- Be sure you have the proper materials at hand before joining the call, even if it's just a notepad, pen, and glass of water.

- Begin with introductions, if necessary, and be sure to include or disclose everyone on the line (or in the room who can hear the call).

- Restate and follow the agenda for the meeting. Take questions and discuss topics when necessary, but also know when to table something for later. It's okay to say, "Good topic; let's set another time to discuss it," or "Good question; let me look into it and I'll get back to you."

- Identify yourself when you speak so that others who are not used to your voice will know it's you: "This is Carlos. I've got the numbers for that right here . . ."

- Be careful not to interrupt; wait for a pause or to be addressed to speak. You can always write something down so as not to lose a thought or question.

- Avoid multitasking and background noise. No eating unless you are very, very close business partners and have an understanding—and even then, never on a call with a client, vendor, supplier, or prospect. Also, tempting though it may be, avoid doing something else while you talk. The dishes you're washing can be heard, the traffic on your walk can be heard, the email you're typing can be heard. Yes, you might try muting yourself, but your delay or lack of reply or attention will be apparent. Stay focused on the call.

- If you use the mute button, be sure it is working before you rely on it.

- Close out the meeting well. Ask if anyone has any questions or thoughts that need sharing. Go over any follow-ups or takeaways that need reiterating and then close the meeting properly by saying thank you to everyone and goodbye before hanging up. Be sure you give the others a chance to say goodbye as well. Saying "Bye" with a quick click will not do for most conference calls; be sure you hear the others say goodbye before you hang up.

CONVERSATIONS VIA VIDEO

Conversations and meetings via video call were popular before the COVID-19 pandemic, but during it, they became a big part of our everyday lives. While there are many etiquette pointers for talking via video that may seem obvious—don't eat on a call, be aware of your background, make sure your mute button works, wear clothing—it's easy to slip up. Sometimes the errors are funny and forgivable, like a small child walking through the background wearing a cape and a boot on her head. But we've also seen how they can lead to disaster. Clearly, video call etiquette matters.

CALLING AND ANSWERING

If the point of the call is to see each other, then make an effort to present a decent view of yourself when you place or answer a video call. Having the camera aimed at the ceiling, the inside of a pocket, or up your nostrils (the list goes on) isn't necessarily rude, but it's not exactly polite either. Before you begin talking, take a moment to ensure the connection is clear and that you are both there. Avoid moving the camera constantly. It's best to take the call when you can aim the camera at your face, but if that's not possible, acknowledge it, say a quick, "Sorry, I can't join with video, but I can talk," or "Hang on one sec while I adjust."

SOCIAL VIDEO CALLS

People find all kinds of things to do together on video calls, from watching movies or TV to cooking and baking, doing schoolwork, playing games, going on walks, cleaning the closet, or sharing happy hours or smoke sessions. There's no shortage of reasons to hop on a video call with friends, family, and significant others. For social video calls, you can create your own experience based on whom you're talking to. You can always set an expectation at the start of the call that you only have a few minutes or that there might be disruptions. You won't treat all video calls the same, even short ones. Your best friend or sibling might get to see the laundry piles in the background, or not care about being left on your desk looking up at the ceiling. But when on with Grandpa for a holiday call, make sure you have a nice (or at least non-distracting) background and avoid walking around on the call, as it might be a bit disorienting.

Do be understanding if someone has to go or doesn't feel like being on video. Video calls can take a lot more energy than phone calls or texting, so don't take it personally if the person you'd like to chat with just isn't up for it.

GROUP CALLS

Group video calls between friends and family are a new type of gathering that more and more people are experiencing and there is definitely emerging etiquette around this new shared experience. If you want to get a group call going, offer to be the host, organize a time in advance, and send out a link for the call, or let everyone know you'll be the one to initiate it and loop everyone in. That's more effective than everyone agreeing to a call and no one taking charge. Small group calls of people who are close don't generally need anything in the way of programming, but larger gatherings, parties, or groups where not everyone knows one another generally do benefit from some sort of plan, or at least a designated person who can serve as a host. Otherwise, you risk twenty people in a video call party staring at each other, unsure of what to do or who should speak.

If joining a call, it's important to be on time. While being 15 minutes late to a dinner party is perfectly acceptable, 5 minutes is the grace period for video calls before people should really start without you. If you run into tech issues, use another form of communication to let folks know you're running late or having problems. For a small group of friends, a quick text alerting them that you'll be late is really helpful. The others might wait or start the call without you and have you join once you are able. For a party or "family Zoom holiday," a host shouldn't wait for one guest. Instead, start the conversation or festivities after the 5-minute grace period. If you're worried about a guest who might be struggling with the technology, try reaching out to them via phone, text, or email and help get them on the call.

If you're part of a small group of friends chatting, try to stay focused on the call. If you're going to be doing something like cooking, or anything with noise in the background, mute yourself until you're going to speak. For a small to medium-size group, it's fine to tap out of the call when you're ready. It's always nice to do so with something like, "Hey guys, I'm gonna pop off now. It's been great to see you both!" For a larger party or group, there's no need to issue a goodbye or wait for your goodbye to be returned before just hanging up (though you might type one into the chat feature).

CLASSES

When joining an online class or group via video, you'll want to be sure to participate well. (Think of your guest role; see A Good Guest, page 187.) Show up on time for the class, ready with everything you need. Treat your background like part of your attire and dress it (and yourself) appropriately. Rushing around for 5 minutes while the instructor or leader waits for you to get settled isn't considerate of the rest of the group. Get ready before you sign on.

Depending on the group, you might be automatically muted the whole time, with the instructor's screen pinned, shared, or spotlighted. In that case, follow along and use the chat if you need to communicate anything to the leader or group, or to participate. Usually, someone will unmute you at the end for questions or goodbyes.

If you're allowed to participate more, definitely do so! It enhances the group experience. Ask questions and make comments in the chat, or "raise your hand" to let the leader know you'd like a chance to speak or contribute. If it's an open conversation, treat it like an in-person conversation: jump in when you'd like, but make sure not to step on anyone's toes or talk over them.

Eating can sometimes be part of a class or group call, and it's best to remember that you're on camera doing it—and that means audio too! Please mute yourself if you are eating on camera while there is a presenter. If you're feeling a little unsure about eating on camera, try it out before your call by eating in front of a mirror or using a smartphone to record yourself. You'll quickly see if there's anything you should watch out for. All the basic table manners still apply: keep your mouth closed when there's food in it, take small bites, don't guzzle your drink, chew quietly, and use a napkin.

Remember, you can always mute yourself if you're eating something noisy such as chips. (For more about eating etiquette, see Chapter 5: Basic Table Manners.)

BUSINESS VIDEO CALLS

Just like an in-person meeting, a video meeting has host and guest roles to be played.

AS THE HOST, greet everyone as they join. Once the whole group is logged on, you can do another greeting, go over the format, expectations, and agenda, and away you go! It's important to pay attention to the attendees. Keep an eye not just on whether anyone is raising a hand, not responding, or looking distracted, but also on the group chat and any messages people might be trying to send to you during the meeting. Do your best to move through your agenda in a timely manner, remembering that you can also agree to follow up on something you don't know the answer to in the moment.

As long as it's appropriate for the nature of the meeting, it never hurts to smile, have an upbeat tone, and encourage those you're on the call with to participate. Video calls can often have a stale quality, and while you don't need to make a show of it (forcing a smile the whole time), keeping a friendly demeanor, looking into your camera, and having an active and engaged attitude can go a long way toward keeping your attendees' attention.

It is often up to the host or organizer to end the call. As with any good meeting, it's best to open it up at the end for any questions or thoughts, if appropriate. Give a warning if possible and try to finish on time. Remember, you can always agree to discuss a topic further at another time if needed. Make sure everyone has had a chance to say their goodbyes before you hang up or end the call. A message after the call thanking everyone for their participation and detailing any actions to be followed up on is thoughtful.

AS A PARTICIPANT, show up on time or even early in case you have connection issues, and get ready to be on camera. Bring whatever you need to the meeting. Don't think you need to bring anything? Bring a pen and notepad—or something to take notes on—so that it paints the visual image that you are ready to take a note if you need to. Be sure to pay attention to any requests the host has made about the agenda and format of the meeting. Keep your attention on the call. It's easy to let your attention slip, especially if the host isn't in screen-sharing mode but just talking. Try to look into the camera lens and avoid an angle that has you facing away from it, which gives the appearance that you are not "looking at" others on the call.

Do your best to be patient when trying to participate, or when dealing with spotty connections such as screen freezing. It can be irritating, but for most work video calls you can always find a way to bring up your point, add your thought, or ask a question, even if it doesn't happen in the moment. Take comfort in knowing that, as it will help you destress during a bad connection. Always say thank you before your goodbyes. You may leave once you've said your goodbyes to the group.

TIPS FOR BUSINESS VIDEO CALLS

The world of business is usually more formal than our social lives—even when working from home. And this is true with video calls as well. While these calls may be set up in advance or happen on the fly, they still require preparation, attention, management, follow-up, and of course, etiquette.

THINK LIKE A HOST. What is the agenda or goal? Who should attend? When? How long will the call be? What platform would be best? You might be asked to use a company's internal or preferred platform for the call, in which case you are still the host, but the company will issue the link for the scheduled call and any login information. Offer to help attendees set up and test their systems ahead of time.

TAKE CARE WITH TIME ZONES. Triple-check that everyone knows the correct time and date of the call. This includes the duration or end time information as well. When confirming the time, don't use "tomorrow"; based on when you send the message and when the recipient reads it, your "tomorrow" may not be the same.

MAKE SURE THE LINK OR LOGIN INFORMATION IS SENT TO ALL PARTICIPANTS. Keep your email or phone at the ready in case anyone has issues and tries to reach you just before or at the start of the call. If possible, share your backup plan for the call as well in case anything goes wrong. Pay attention to privacy settings that control how information is shared between attendees, for example email and contact information.

SPECIFY THE AGENDA AND CIRCULATE ANY NEEDED MATERIALS. Topics you want to cover and any necessary links or documents should be shared with the participants prior to the meeting. Also, give everyone a heads-up regarding the format. Will everyone be muted automatically? Will questions be taken at the end, or as they arise? Also confirm whether video is expected.

WEAR APPROPRIATE ATTIRE. The whole point of a video call is that you have an opportunity to be seen. Seize this opportunity and put your best self forward. Think about the purpose of the meeting, who will be on the call, and dress accordingly, or even better, one notch up.

A BAD VIDEO CALL

Whether it's because a connection has gone wonky, the call is dull, or the conversation has turned ugly, a bad video call is awkward. For technical difficulties, do your best to send a text, email, or other message to the host or organizer to let them know that you are having tech issues and will be delayed, need help, or will reschedule, depending on the problem.

When a social call is dull and no one is really talking anymore, it's okay to excuse yourself: "Well, everyone, this has been lovely, but I'm going to take off now. Love to you all!" If the conversation has turned heated or ugly and it's not going to be fixed or worked out in the moment, tapping out is a good idea. Rather than exit in a huff, try something like, "I think I've reached my limit, and it's best if I take some time to regroup. Let's talk again another time."

CONVERSATIONS VIA TEXT MESSAGE

Remember when we had to type ":)" into a text message to indicate a smile, and if the person didn't get it, it just looked like a typo? Oh, how far we've come! Our text-speak and emojis are now a language, love, and labor all their own. Hidden meanings, trends, shorthand, personalization:

it's almost endless, and it can be hard to keep up. While the tips that follow are focused on text messages, they can also apply to any messaging medium, from Slack channels to DMs and other message services.

GET THE RECIPIENTS RIGHT. The worst of the worst (and we have *all* done it) is to send a text to the wrong person. While occasionally funny, or great for a future dinner party story, no one loves experiencing these situations. Some people add nicknames to their contacts to help them avoid mistakes with autofill and voice commands. Whether you do or don't, double-checking before you hit "Send" should be a constant reminder in your head (or thumbs). Being the wrong recipient can also be funny or awkward: declarations of love and war seem to lose their oomph when sent to the wrong number. Do your best to make it clear (no matter how thickheaded the sender might be) that you are not the intended recipient. *Wrong number/person* is simplest. *I think you have the wrong number* is a dash more polite. While clearly entertaining, you don't have to keep responding after your initial text. If you are the one receiving a "wrong number" text, apologize for your error. "Oops."

SAY WHAT YOU MEAN. Using only emojis in your texts, saying *LOL* just because you don't know what to say, or continually replying with "K" or a thumbs-up emoji is immature. It's one thing if now isn't a good time to text and you want to give at least a response, or the simple answer really is *the* answer, but whenever possible, say what you mean and say it clearly (then add the fun stuff). When faced with a text you cannot decipher, it's okay to admit it: "Wait—I don't know that one; help me out. What is SMH? I haven't seen that before" (or just, "SMH???"). A quick Google search will usually illuminate the answer, but it might leave you 😳.

BE CLEAR IF NOW ISN'T A GOOD TIME. There are lots of reason why you might not want to get into a text conversation or respond right away: you're in the car, it's not a good time to text because you're with other people, or unable to focus on the content of the conversation. You can send a simple "Let's talk later" or use an auto-reply (*Now's not a good time. I'll get back to you as soon as I can*) or something simple (*jogging, can't type*) if we need to and it's both helpful and preferable to no response. That being said, it should also be understood that if someone isn't replying (or isn't replying in kind), they are likely busy and will respond when they can. Badgering someone for a reply isn't likely to help matters.

RESPOND PROMPTLY. This may mean different things to different people, and it's important to take note and honor expectations that develop (or change) in relationships. Your girlfriend might be used to getting quick replies, but you might have an understanding with your mom to give each other a couple days to respond. Some people expect a prompt response to every text; others think, *Oh, a message from Nic*, and then don't think about it again, sometimes for hours or even days. And thus an unanswered text can create awkwardness and uncomfortable impatience. So take care with how expectations develop in your communications. Pay attention to the content of a message as well. Every second an important text remains unanswered can make the sender wonder, *Did it go through? Why are they not responding?* We might even scroll up or check their social media to see if anything is amiss. Meanwhile, the recipient is often just busy, or is not a prolific texter. To begin with, we should trust that we rarely need to worry when a text isn't immediately replied to. That said, responding as promptly as possible, while not universally expected, will alleviate a great deal of anxiety. You can always reply, *Busy [Got it/Love ya/On my way . . .]. I'll get back to you later.*

PAY ATTENTION TO YOUR TYPING. Conversations with friends and family with whom we have a strong rapport can be fired off so rapidly that if anyone else were to read the thread, they'd be lost. This is definitely a sign of a close texting relationship. When we are texting with others, slowing down just a bit and allowing someone to finish typing when we see their "typing text" bubbles is akin to not interrupting (and just like interrupting, there are some times when you might need to do it). We can also use good texting etiquette by making sure we send one longer message instead of six short ones in reply.

SKIP THE SALUTATION. When texting you don't need to start with a greeting or sign your name. Text messages don't require opening greetings (although *Hi, Hello, Hey*, and many others are frequently used) or signatures unless you are unsure whether the recipient has stored your contact information, or you know they haven't because you're messaging them from a new number (or a number that's not yours, like if you're using a friend's phone because yours has died).

MAKING INTRODUCTIONS VIA TEXT

When introducing someone via text message, first ensure that both parties are okay with their information being shared. Then proceed to send a group text: *Anthony, I'd like you to meet Marc. Marc, this is Anthony. Hopefully you two can connect for the game, I'll leave you to it!* Marc and Anthony may then each say thank you and start a text between just the two of them to handle the details.

GROUP TEXTS

Group texts can be very useful and even fun, or they can be the worst. Many families have a group thread that never ends. Sending photos, making plans: members often turn off notifications on the thread because otherwise their phone would chime nonstop. Other times we are thrown into group threads we have no desire to be a part of. We may also find ourselves receiving a group text for a party invitation of some kind.

Realize you're giving out people's phone numbers when you send group texts to people who don't know each other or who you don't know for sure have one another's numbers. This can be helpful, for example when you're part of a bridal party or study group. Or it can be extremely annoying when it's just for funsies. While yes, you can shut off your notifications, there are times when, as each person responds, a new text thread is started that won't have the notifications turned off. This can quickly become burdensome and annoying. So make sure the group you're including in your group text will actually appreciate it. For group invitations, do your best to suggest that no one RSVPs to the group text:

> Taraleigh's Birthday Bash
> Backyard BBQ and floating on the lake!
> Friday, June 24th—Fun starts at 4 pm. BYOB, a suit, and a floaty!
> Please RSVP individually, not to the group. Thank you.

Remember that you are in control. If you don't like being part of group messages, turn off the notifications for the ones you get looped into, leave the group if possible, and figure out a different way to get the information or respond. If it's really a problem, let your friends or family who are the worst offenders know that you'd rather not receive or be part of group texts.

COMMUNICATIONS VIA EMAIL

After the telephone and fax machine, email was the next big change in our communications. For all the commotion it made in the 1990s when email became mainstream, it's still the preferred method of contact in business, and the way many families still keep in touch and organize holidays and events. Although many offices have exchanged their internal email threads for Slack and Teams channels, and friends now text and DM rather than email each other, email is still an essential part of both our professional and personal lives. People often keep their work and personal email accounts separate for good reason. Despite predictions, email did not replace letters or thank-you notes and it looks like text messages won't be replacing emails, which are here to stay. An email was originally meant to mimic a letter, and many people still use it this way, following the classic format below:

> *Greeting Person's Name,*
>
> *Followed by the body of the email in standard paragraph format.*
>
> *Closing,*
> *Your Name*
> *Contact information if necessary*

Today, few of us send email versions of letters to our friends and family. Instead, we use personal email to organize events and share news. This means that "proper" greetings are geared more to the type of recipient than a designated format. A group email might start with *Hey Fam!* or even just an event title (*New Year's Eve This Year!*), as opposed to a traditional salutation. That being said, there's nothing wrong with starting an email to your family or friends with *Dear Family and Friends*. Memes, jokes, and links to things are all great to share, and can often be sent without comment—or even a sign-off. Though until that type of email rapport is established, it isn't a bad idea to add a little context: *Laughed so hard over this one, had to share!—Jackie.* It should also be noted that unless asked a direct question or an RSVP is being requested, a recipient need not reply.

You can take advantage of the delay feature in your email program or platform in case you need to make an edit, fix a mistake, or adjust your tone before it's sent. If you read an email aloud before you send it, you may not need the delay feature. By reading it aloud, you'll be able to hear the tone and catch any errors either in your copy or meaning.

EMAIL GREETINGS

In most professional emails, starting with a greeting is polite. When initially emailing with someone, a formal greeting is a good choice. Once you start a back-and-forth thread, the formality usually drops to no names or greetings in subsequent emails, as the thread itself is mimicking a conversation. With close friends and family, we may feel comfortable using email almost like a text message and use no greetings at all. From formal to casual, the greetings we choose set the tone of the email. Often the best thing is to choose something that sounds like you, and how you would greet the recipient given the circumstances.

FORMAL	INFORMAL	CASUAL
Dear, To Whom It May Concern, Good Morning, Good Afternoon, Good Evening	*Hello, Good Morning, Good Afternoon, Good Evening, Greetings*	*Hi, Hey, Everyone,* [the person's name or initial(s): *Yasunori, Y*]

EMAIL CLOSINGS

Closings can be a bit trickier than greetings. For formal or first-interaction emails, definitely use a proper closing followed by your name. You might forgo closings for casual emails or work emails with those you communicate with daily, but still use your first name or initials to "sign off." One thing to watch out for is saying *thank you* or *thanks* preemptively. If your email asks for a favor or task to be done, it's best not to close with a *thank you,* as it assumes the answer is yes. Instead, you can close with, *Many thanks for any help or direction you can offer. Best,* [*Your Name*]. By making your thanks for the "help or direction," you are recognizing that the person you're asking might not be the person who ends up helping you. You also remove the thank you from the assumptive closing position, and make it a direct sentence at the end of the email before the close. Or you could say, *Thank you again,* if you've thanked them properly in the note. *Best* works for just about everyone, but it can sound a bit stiff when writing to someone you are close with (similar to signing an email to a close friend or family member with your full name). So speak it aloud and ask yourself, *Is that what I would say to this person?* Here are classic options for closing an email:

FORMAL	INFORMAL	CASUAL
Sincerely, Best regards, Kind regards, Yours truly, Gratefully yours, With high regard	*Best, All the best, Affectionately, Regards, Warm regards, Take care*	A dash followed by your name or initial, *XOXO, Best, Take care, Bye for now,*

Note that business closings should not include *Affectionately, Yours truly, xoxo, Love,* or anything else that strikes an intimate tone, unless you are incredibly close with the person and have clearly established a relationship that is both business and warrants *x*'s and *o*'s.

WORK EMAILS

Emailing for work is an entirely different ball game. When initially sent, work emails take on the format of a social letter, though with different contact information formatting than that used in a business letter. Once replies start going back and forth, it becomes more like a conversation. The subject line is important and should always be used intentionally. In business emailing there's courtesy in using a clear and concise subject line so that the recipient has an easier time quickly identifying what's inside, and a much better chance of finding it later if they need to.

> *Dear Ms. Ketchum,*
>
> *Thank you for giving me the week to think about your offer. I would like to formally accept.*
>
> *I am very grateful for the opportunity, and I look forward to hearing more about next steps. It has always been a dream to work for Ten Speed Press, and I am excited to be part of the team.*
>
> *Sincerely,*
> *Elizabeth Connolly*

While you might have a client or boss you always address as *Mx., Mr., Ms.,* or *Mrs.,* you are often welcome to start using the person's first name once you see it in their signature.

A reply to the above might look like the following, with just a tad less formality. The honorifics have been removed, and the *Dear* is made friendlier with a *Good Morning.* Note that the second word of a greeting should be capitalized, and when using *To Whom It May Concern,* you would always capitalize each word.

Good Morning Elizabeth,

We are thrilled to hear the news, and may I be the first to welcome you to Ten Speed Press. We were so impressed during your interview, and we cannot wait to see what you do with the job.

Would you like to have lunch together on your first day? There is a lovely spot around the corner from the office. My treat.

Best,
Kaitlin

Editorial Director, Ten Speed Press
she/her

159 Main Street
Emeryville, CA
879-404-5678

Now that both parties have done proper greetings and closings, the email thread can start to resemble a conversation rather than a letter. (Note that the stock signature Kaitlin uses can communicate any work contact information you'd like.)

That is such a kind offer. I would really enjoy that, thank you!

Thank you again,
Liz

Great. We'll pick a time on Monday once you have a handle on your day.

—K

INVITATIONS AND ANNOUNCEMENTS

Always remember that the main goal of an invitation is to *invite the guest,* and to do so with a level of formality appropriate for the event. Everything beyond that (for written invitations) should usually go on an insert or be sent or discussed separately.

For formal invitations, the hosts *request the pleasure of someone's company* for an event. Month, day of the month, year, and time of day are spelled out (without using *and*). Numbers in street addresses are spelled out up to twenty (*Eleven Oak Street*); after that, use numerals (*24 Oak Street*). No abbreviations are used, except for *Mr., Mrs., Ms., Mx., Miss, Jr.,* and *Sr.* If an RSVP (with or without a deadline date) is being used, it is left-aligned and placed at the bottom of the invitation. Traditionally, only black or white tie attire suggestions were included, but today it's not uncommon to see other attire designations as well. These are placed on or below the same line as the RSVP and are right-aligned. Formal invitations may be handwritten, printed, or done by a calligrapher.

Casual invitations come in so many forms: via text, email, phone, fill-in cards, digitally, or printed or handwritten. The format takes a more general tone: *Join us, Come celebrate,* or *You're invited!* Numerals and abbreviations are okay.

On the rare occasions when it is used, the "No gifts, please" line is placed under the RSVP and left-aligned.

Today, invitations to showers are typically sent digitally. Look for an invitation service that doesn't put the registry front and center but guides the guest to it, and that doesn't send or push advertisements on guests. For printed/handwritten shower invitations, include an insert listing the store(s) where the honoree is registered. Showers are the only invitations where it is appropriate to put registry information right on or with the invitation, as the event is specifically to "shower" the honoree with gifts. All other parties are not solely about gifts, and therefore registry information is included in an insert, or spread via word of mouth or when someone RSVPs and asks for gift ideas. (Note: For weddings, the wedding website is indicated on an insert included with the invitation, and guests will find the registry on the site.)

When cohosting, aside from defaulting to "Mom first," it doesn't really matter in which order the cohosts for any event are listed on an invitation. The important thing is to offer to include anyone who is participating as a host (remember, to be a host you don't all have to contribute in the same ways). You can also describe yourselves as a group (*the family of* or *the friends of*), or list the hosts alphabetically. (See When Cohosting, page 186, for more.)

ANNOUNCEMENTS

Announcements are sent *after* graduations, marriages, new additions to the family, or a new home. Companies send announcements for mergers, promotions, and new hires. Generally, these go to business associates, vendors, and clients and follow a similar structure to the examples in the Reference Guide on page 104. Announcements are not invitations; they come after the event. No announcement ever carries the obligation of sending a gift or a response. It is simply to announce the news! Remember to adjust for formality. See Invitations, below, for formality points to look out for and sample announcements on page 117.

_____ *are/is pleased to announce*
_____ *has* _____

on _____.

Please join us all in congratulating/welcoming _____.

When you are on the receiving end of an announcement, there is no obligation to buy a gift, or even to reach out at all. However, it's okay to do so. Not only is it thoughtful, but most announcements we receive inspire us to reach out with our congratulations. Sending a card, calling, or shooting someone a congratulatory text are all acceptable ways to respond when you receive an announcement.

POSTCARDS, NOTES, AND LETTERS

In Emily's day, handwritten notes, cards, and letters were *the* method of communication outside of in-person chats. They were sent frequently in both long and short forms. The mail was delivered twice a day in many areas, or notes were hand delivered. And although we've taken to calling it "snail mail," today, most letters will likely arrive within a few days, or possibly the next day if sent within the same area. Such quick "physical" service is quite remarkable in our online world.

Many people today have never written a thank-you note, let alone a letter, and might need to look up how to address a *real* letter. Why should anyone bother with handwritten notes? They take time, cost money, and require effort. But that is exactly why they are special. No matter how hard technology tries to replace them, handwritten letters, notes, and postcards delivered by mail are here to stay, and they can be very meaningful. To see someone's handwriting and know they took the time to sit down and write out this note means something to the recipient.

Emily's 1922 edition of *Etiquette* included extensive details on the style, size, and weight of the paper one ought to use for correspondence. While fewer of us have personal stationery today, it is worth noting that etiquette for letter writing has been some of the least modified advice over time. It is the foundation for so much of our current written communication in its digital forms. For those who love practicing this "ancient" craft, (in the old ways) personalized social stationery can inspire more card, note, and letter sending. (See A Stationery Wardrobe, page 118, for details.)

POSTCARDS

Postcards are delightful. There are so many options to choose from, not to mention the endless possibilities when making your own. A postcard is like a friendly wave from afar, a quick note to say hello—though if your writing is small you can say quite a lot! For this reason, and because it is not sent in an envelope, the content of the card should always be simple and something you wouldn't care if anyone read. While bad news or apologies might come to mind first as topics to avoid writing about on a postcard, postcards are also not recommended for thank-you notes. The recipient might not want their generosity known, and a postcard can be read by anyone along its way, making it less personal.

NOTES AND CARDS

Short notes are easy to write and a quick way to brighten someone's day—yes, even when it's a condolence note. Whether it's a printed card, your own personal stationery, or something homemade, keeping some note cards on hand is mighty useful. We send notes and cards for birthdays, invitations, congratulations, condolences, apologies, thanks, welcomes, farewells, and just to say hello. The only reason not to send a note is when it's an angry note; in that case, we suggest you have a conversation, when possible, instead. A note should always have a greeting, a body, and a signature. Some notes might look like a letter on a small card, while others will resemble something from the florist: *Just saying "Hi!"—Lemar*. (For sympathy and condolence notes, see Sympathy and Condolence Notes, page 235.)

STRUCTURE OF A NOTE OR CARD

Notes are less formal or structured than letters. The date goes on the upper right, the salutation is a line down on the left, the next line down starts the body, followed by a closing on the lower right and your signature or initials.

DATE

Salutation Name,

Whatever you'd like to say in the body of the note or card.

Closing,
Signature

TYPES OF NOTES

SOCIAL NOTE. A simple social note is usually just about saying a quick hello and wishing someone well. It can be sent on any type of flat or folded card, either with or without a pre-printed greeting. Since it is social and not usually formal, you may use any type of greeting you wish to write, including just the recipient's name or initials. That being said, the formal *Dear* is very common, even for casual notes. Tone the formality up or down by using someone's title and full name, full name, first name, nickname or initials. In Emily's day, the date could also appear in the lower left-hand corner of a social note, though this was not done for other types of notes and is rarely seen today.

THANK-YOU NOTE. For a note of thanks, try for a three-line minimum: an opener, the thank you, and a closing. You can add more, but keep the focus on your gratitude and wishing the other person well, rather than a full catch-up of how *you've* been. Send a thank-you note for gifts you haven't thanked someone for in person, meals someone has treated you to, special opportunities (like a job interview), and favors done for you, or because you just want to let someone know you appreciate them. (For more, see Thank-You Notes, page 213, and Sample Notes, page 106.)

BREAD AND BUTTER NOTE. This is a thank-you note for being someone's houseguest (also called a houseguest thank-you note), often accompanied by a gift if sent after the visit. It should be thoughtful and include details from the visit. If you gave a small gift at the time of the visit, the note on its own will suffice as a thank-you after the visit. (See also Sample Notes, page 106.)

CONGRATULATORY NOTE. A congratulatory note might be very similar to a social note in length and style but focuses on the achievement being celebrated. It can also be incredibly casual and brief, using only initials and a single congratulatory phrase (L, Congrats on the book! —M). Sometimes it's sent and other times it's given in person but often accompanies flowers or a gift. Whether an opening night of someone's performance or a note tucked into a lunch box on the first day of school, a congratulatory note is always a good idea. (See samples in the Reference Guide, page 108.)

APOLOGY NOTE. Formal but effective, an apology note focuses on the apology and making amends. It does not focus on reasons and excuses, no matter how tempting or fair. The point is to make sure the apology is clear, and that forgiveness is requested, not expected. (See Sample Notes, page 108, for a sample. Also see The Good Apology, page 66.)

LETTERS

The handwritten letter is a lost art for many. Notes, cards, and postcards are sent far more often than traditional letters. In fact, outside of summer camp and pen-pal letters, few social letters are ever sent. Half of Americans haven't sent or received a letter in the last 5 years. But they are not gone yet, thank goodness. A good letter is a beautiful thing. It's personal, it makes you feel connected to the person who wrote it, and who, may we ask, does not love receiving mail that is not a bill or piece of junk?

SOCIAL LETTERS

The social letter has the same structure as the social note but contains much more content. Letters might go on for pages, in which case you should number them. While it's okay to write on the front and back of a page, try to make sure your ink doesn't bleed through, making it hard to read. While it's best to write in such a way that the letter "sounds" like you, do filter yourself by using punctuation and proper spelling. Good spelling and grammar clarify communication, making it easier for the recipient to understand. Remember, the hope is that the recipient will enjoy reading your letter. Write about the weather, what you've been up to, what you are looking forward to or what interests you. Writing a letter is in many ways like carrying on half of a conversation without the other person present. Tier I (see page 61, The Three Tiers of Conversation) topics set a safe tone and are good places to focus. You might recount a story or joke you heard, but avoid getting too gossipy about other people. Always remember that once you send a letter, what happens to it (and who else might see it) is out of your hands.

DATE

Greeting Name,

    Body of the letter. For social letters, indent the start of the body and then proceed in traditional paragraph form.

To close the letter, you may choose whatever closing sounds appropriate for the nature of the relationship. Remember that you generally want to be friendly rather than formal. And finish it off by signing your name.

Closing,
Signature

BUSINESS LETTERS

A business letter has a more structured appearance than a social letter, and follows some old-school standards. If you aren't using company letterhead, write your company name at the top left followed by its address, with each line flush left. Two lines down, put the date. Two lines below that, put the recipient's name, then the recipient's title or department, followed by the recipient's company name and address, each on a separate line. The salutation begins two lines below the recipient's address. If it's a formal letter, use the recipient's title and last name; if it's a more familiar letter, you may use the person's first name. Always use *Dear* as the salutation.

    The body of the letter is not indented, and each paragraph is separated by a line space. The closing is left justified. Leave space below your closing to add your handwritten or digital signature. About two to four lines below that, print your name, then beneath it put your title or department, followed by your phone number. The last line should be your email address. (See Sample Business Letters, page 117, for a sample.)

THE ANGRY LETTER

Try to avoid sending an angry letter. While an excellent therapeutic exercise for calming yourself down and organizing thought, it is not the best method of handling your anger and frustration when shared with others. The letter could hang around long after the feeling that inspired it is gone. Be careful about leaving a record of your most angry moments. If you are upset, and need to communicate with the other person, consider calming down enough to be able to address the issue in person or over the phone. That said, the desire to send someone an angry letter is understandable. Even when sending the most common angry letter—to a politician or establishment—think carefully about what you want to say and how you say it. It might allow you to share your perspective in a smart, confident manner as opposed to an exaggerated, rage-filled one. Which kind of letter would you pay more attention to if you received it? Strong emotions are not necessarily bad and don't have to be hidden behind fake pleasantries, but if they aren't constructively channeled, they can overshadow your valid points and perspective. This is true not just with letters, but with any written communication.

ADDRESSING A LETTER, NOTE, CARD, OR INVITATION

In our ever more tech-heavy world, many people aren't used to addressing mail. Below is the basic format for addressing a standard letter or envelope sent within the United States.

Name of recipient	*Susan Iverson*	*Susan Iverson*
House number and street	*25 Crossroad St.*	*c/o The Emily Post Institute*
address	*Suite 2B*	*25 Crossroad St., Suite 2B*
(and apartment number)	*Waterbury, VT*	*Waterbury, VT 05676*
City, State Zip code	*05676*	

The suite or apartment number can go on the "second street line" just below the house number and street address, or follow the street address on line one, separated by a comma. If you need to send something "care of," or to a work address, then you would put "care of" or the company name on a second line below the name.

When writing to married people or those in long-established relationships who live together, put both their names on one line with the word 'and' between them. If their names are too long to fit on the first line together, put the second person's name on the next line, indented and beginning with the word *and*. Here are some samples of the various ways a married couple could be addressed with Mrs./Ms. Emily Post and her second husband, Mr. Chilval Russ. If the couple does not share the same last name, use their titles and full names:

Mrs. Emily Post and Mr. Chilval Russ

or

Mrs. Emily Post
    and Mr. Chilval Russ

If the couple does share a name, use their titles and shared last name:

Mr. and Mrs. Russ

If the woman of the couple uses her husband's full name:

Mr. and Mrs. Chival Russ

Note: *Any* of the examples above could also use the title *Ms.* if the woman holding that title wishes to, yes, even *Mr. and Ms. Chival Russ*. Unconventional as it may seem, it is an option. Or, you can use no titles:

Emily and Chival Russ (if they share a last name)

or

Emily Post and Chival Russ (if they don't share a last name)

Absent a ranking professional title, either name can go first except for the example *Mr. and Mrs. Russ* which is kept in that order. When using first names with a combined last name, it's fine to use either partner first. *Emily and Chival Russ* and *Chival and Emily Russ* are both correct if they share the last name.

Remember if you don't know how a couple chooses to use titles or if they share a last name, you can always ask. If you don't know *and* cannot ask, take your best guess as to a title and use given names with "and" to indicate marriage. *Ms. Emily Post and Mr. Chival Russ.* This is a good reminder to ask, when someone gets married, how they are handling last names and titles so that you do know the answer and then to write it down somewhere so you can refer to it when needed.

When writing to a group of people who live together but are not in a relationship, list each recipient's name on a separate line:

Jacqueline LeChevre
Sarah Diedrick
123 Church Street
San Antonio, TX 78212

You might be tempted to put *and Guest* on the name line for an event where a guest would be given a plus-one, but this is best left for an inner envelope or as a note attached to an invitation inviting the guest to bring a plus-one:

Outer envelope: *Mr. David Coward*

Inner envelope: *Mr. David Coward & Guest*

Or an included note: *Davey, we'd love for you to bring a guest if you'd like. Please let us know when you RSVP if someone will be joining you.*

STUFFING AN ENVELOPE

For letters, cards, notes, and invitations, you want to stuff the envelope so that when it is opened and the contents pulled out, it will naturally be positioned in a way that is easy to open the card or letter and read. Do not fold it up into a square when the envelope is long or fold a letter so many times that it opens like an accordion.

For letters, fold the bottom third of the letter up and make a crease, then fold the remaining top third down over the bottom third. Stuff the envelope so that the folded bottom edge goes into the envelope first and the top folded edge is at the top, facing the envelope opening (the back), not the front of the envelope. Seal it and you're good to go.

Cards and fold-over notes are stuffed so that the open edge is inserted first into the envelope, and the folded edge is at the top of the envelope opening. The card should be inserted so that the front of the card or note is facing the back of the envelope. This way when opened the card is facing the person opening the envelope.

If there are any enclosures, you may stack them with the letter or invitation, usually putting the enclosures on top of the invitation itself. This helps you ensure that nothing gets left behind in the envelope. Sometimes items are also tied together in a little bundle.

When a check or cash is given with a card or letter, it is usually placed within the folded card or letter to prevent it from being lost in the shuffle of opening the card. Placing the money inside the card also shields it from being seen through the envelope.

TRI-FOLD: FOLD BOTTOM THIRD UP, THEN TOP THIRD DOWN

FOLD 1

FOLD 2

OPEN EDGE FIRST

STACK ENCLOSURES WITH AN INVITATION

Invitation
Enclosure
Enclosure

CASH OR CHECK INSIDE LETTER OR CARD

EMILY POST'S ETIQUETTE

Note that an oversized envelope will likely need extra postage, as will an overstuffed one, which may even need different packaging.

COMMUNICATIONS VIA SOCIAL MEDIA

Social media has become a behemoth—to the point where a lot of people having joined in have now quit it altogether—and is how many like to communicate for both social and business purposes. Our profiles and accounts are filled with different versions of ourselves, as well as both lasting and fleeting moments in our lives. People from all over the world log into social media, and depending on what spaces you choose to participate in and how, you may be interacting with individuals of different viewpoints, cultures, and backgrounds. For this vast a space and experience, we aren't going to parse each potential interaction, but we do have a few key pointers for navigating your conversations on social media and in online threads. Conduct yourself with integrity and care for others, and you will be in good shape wherever your online journey takes you.

PUBLIC POSTS

Public posts are . . . public. In some cases, they might be permanent, either because you can't delete the post, or because someone might have seen it or copied and forwarded it before you managed to edit or delete it. It's also not always possible to delete the impression that something has created by taking it down. In some ways we've come to live with this and accept it. In other ways we are still so naïve. Be sure to share only what you would be comfortable having your employer, child, coach, neighbor, or parents see. This is not to say that you can't express yourself, but be smart and filter yourself well so that you can feel good about what you post. Using the same rules for online conduct as you do in person helps to keep these different areas of life in harmony with each other.

When it comes to social posts—as opposed to business posts—one big component of etiquette has to do with making sure you have people's permission before you post images of them or tag them. Be sure you know it's okay before you post pictures or personal information about others (especially photos of other people's children). While we can't control everything, many people really want to control what is seen of them online, which, from a politeness perspective, is their right. If you are upset by a post that's gone up, or don't want a certain photo or caption used, by all means reach out to the friend or family member who posted it. "Zephyr, I had a ton of fun Friday, but would you please take down the photo of me by the pool? I'm not comfortable with pics of me in a bathing suit being online—even among friends." "Of course, and thank you for letting me know!"

Sharing bad news and posting how you feel is acceptable, but many people choose to use social media platforms to post just their life highlights and positive thoughts. Think about the dosage of any type of post you make—positive or negative—and consider whether this is the version of yourself you want to present online or on that platform. Too much good news and you're boasting, too much bad news and you're a downer. Your digital presence is part of your overall image, and it's up to you to strike the balance that matches who you are.

When it comes to commenting on posts, there is no one polite way. Humor, sincerity, opinions, questions—these are all usually welcome when they treat the person who has posted with respect. Stay on topic, either adding or responding to what is said and participate in the online conversation as you would in person. Avoid hijacking someone's post by posting about your own life or issue in the comments. A post about your child's summer birthday party shouldn't result in your sister commenting on the post with a picture of her kids at Mardi Gras saying "and aren't Jackson's cousins krewe-cute in their costumes?!" That would be hijacking your post. It's okay to delete or moderate comments left on pages and posts that are yours or that you manage. You don't have to mention the deletion to the person, but there are times when it could be beneficial, like when setting boundaries about what types of photos you're comfortable with people sharing about you, or what type of language you're willing to entertain in comments on your page.

While we have the ability to say what we want, we don't have to all the time. Hitting the "Like" button instead of commenting with tons of emojis and exclamation points, or conversely ignoring instead of responding to a post that annoyed you are always options.

PRIVATE MESSAGES

A private or direct message (DM) sent on a social media platform shouldn't be considered as personal or direct as a text message. No matter the content of the message, there is no guarantee as to how quickly someone will check their social media account or respond to a DM. While most people will respond to each DM they get on their social accounts, it's not always possible, and you shouldn't expect it. No one is obligated to *heart* every story or mention they receive via DM—especially if it's something that expires after a period of time.

Today, some companies and individuals doing business may use social media accounts only as their connection to their markets and audience. But many companies utilize websites and brick and mortar locations as well as social media. Before you reach out via DM to a company or individual you'd like to do business with, be sure to see if they have already provided other contact information such as email or even a phone number on a website or google listing. These methods should be your first form of outreach when possible.

ONLINE COMMENT THREADS

Many online forums and comment threads have rules that users agree to when signing up for the platform, and users will be notified (or kicked out) if they break them. These rules make the space safe and keep the conversation focused. Therefore, it's important to understand and abide by the rules for any threads you participate in so that you can participate well. Use the tiers of conversation (see page 61) to guide your conversations online. Tier I? Go for it. Tier II? Proceed with caution and keep it positive. Tier III? Better not. Instead, find a different method of communication or a different audience.

For comment threads it's important to follow the conversation and be sure you're posting to the right name or section. Often threads allow for people to reply or respond directly to a person in addition to the original post. Be sure you're hitting reply to the right thing and addressing the person or post you wanted to.

Avoid engaging with trolls (people who seek to make their mark by being disruptive or contrary). Trolls are rude, and it's just not worth it. They are looking for attention with negative behavior, and the best option is not to give it to them. If you are going to clap back (respond with a comeback), be prepared to stop after you've said what you felt you needed to. Getting into a back and forth with someone who is only looking to get you going plays right into their game.

Count us in the camps of *if you don't have anything nice or constructive to say, don't comment,* and *"thank you"* is the best response to typo correction comments.

REFERENCE GUIDES

WHAT NOT TO SAY

There are many things that are said with good intentions, and yet when we stop to think about them, we realize they aren't good things to say. Here are few common examples, why they don't work, and what to say instead.

WHAT NOT TO SAY	WHAT TO SAY INSTEAD	WHY
"You look so good I almost didn't recognize you!"	"I'm so happy to see you again!" Or "It's so great to see you again!"	Outward appearance shouldn't be a first compliment and saying that someone is almost unrecognizable isn't a compliment. Save true compliments like "You look great!" for those you *know* appreciate hearing it.
"I know how you feel."	"I've been through a similar situation." Or "I can't say I know how you feel, but I can imagine that this is hard."	While well intentioned, the reality is that we can't fully know how another person feels. These alternatives help to avoid bulldozing someone's experience.
"Oh my gosh, your accent is adorable. Where are you from?" Or even worse, as a follow-up: "No, where are you *originally* from?"	"It's so nice to meet you." Or "Good afternoon." Or "Nice day, isn't it?"	Rather than guess about someone's past, ask a question about the present. If someone wants to tell you their history or background, they will.
"Oh, it'll work out. You just have to [stop looking, relax, try harder, think outside the box, try this diet]."	"We can't know the future, but I'm always hoping for good things for you." Or "How are you thinking you'll manage that?"	Meant as encouragement, telling someone they "just need to" is not polite. You don't actually know that this is what they need and cannot predict what will happen for someone else. Instead, express your hopes for good in this person's life. Or ask them for their perspective on handling the situation.
"Don't be so sensitive." "Don't take it personally."	"I'm sorry you're feeling this way about it." Or "Is there anything I can do to help?"	Conversations are personal much of the time, and while these phrases can be good advice when given to yourself, they can be completely unrealistic and even harmful when directed at others.

WHAT NOT TO SAY	WHAT TO SAY INSTEAD	WHY
"I can't believe you're single; you're so great!" Or "You must have been married before." Or "You must be with someone."	"I'm sure glad to have you in my life." or "Every day brings new opportunities."	Being "great" is not connected to why someone is or isn't single, and being independent is not a tragedy or mistake. These statements project your perspective onto their life.
"You know, she's well educated—she went to Swarthmore College . . ."	"She's really learned a lot in her life."	Our education comes from so many places. Connecting being well-educated only to college graduates or certain schools is elitist and limiting.
"Oh my gosh, you look so young!"	"You look fantastic!" Or "I'm so glad you're well!"	Focusing on youth as a goal is ageist and doesn't help society value aging—we all get older every minute. Saying someone looks fantastic, or saying, "I'm glad you are well," if the person is doing well, are better choices. That being said, if you know someone appreciates hearing compliments on their looks, by all means go for it with them. (It's been 15 seconds, you're older and wiser now.)
"I'll let you go now."	"I'm sorry, I've gone on too long; it's been great chatting with you."	Using phrases such as "I'll let you" or "I've kept you" when on the phone assume you're in control of the situation when it's actually a two-way street.
"I don't care."	"I don't have a preference."	"I don't care" suggests that something doesn't matter to you, whereas "I don't have a preference" suggests that the options may matter, but you are fine with whatever is chosen.
"I hate cilantro." Or "Cilantro is so gross/disgusting!"	"I don't care much for cilantro." "Cilantro is not my favorite."	*Hate* is a strong word, and strikes an unpleasant tone when used. And labeling something "gross" or "disgusting" when others may like or even love it isn't very considerate or respectful—even if to you it's honest. To put it simply: don't yuck someone else's yum.
"Let's do lunch." Or "Let's get together soon."	"Let's set up a time to have lunch, I'll text you tomorrow." Or "Would you like to have lunch together this week or next?"	While well intentioned, "Let's do . . ." isn't an actual invitation, it's a light suggestion. Either make a clear invitation or ask if the person would like to meet up for X and then list a more specific time frame than "soon."

HOW TO SAY IT

To deliver a phrase or question well, it's not just *what* you say but *how* you say it that makes an impact. Here are a few classics with both gracious options and casual options to fit your scenario.

PHRASE/QUESTION	SAY IT GRACIOUSLY	SAY IT CASUALLY
Declining	"Thank you for asking; I'm going to/have to decline/say no." "I do not/cannot, but thank you for asking."	"No, thank you." "No, but thank you."
Asking to repeat something	"I'm sorry/pardon me, I didn't catch that. Would you mind repeating it?"	"Sorry, say that again?" "Sorry, didn't catch that."
Asking to talk	"There's something I was hoping to talk with you about. Is now a good time?"	"Do you have a minute to talk?"
Declining to host a houseguest	"Unfortunately, that date won't work for us." (You can then suggest one that does if you'd like to.)	"No, I can't host then, I'm sorry." (Use for those you are closest to and have good rapport with.)
Asking to split the bill	"Thank you for inviting me out; I'd be happy to split the bill." "How about we split the bill when we go out on Friday?"	"Could we split the bill?"

SAMPLE NOTES

THANK-YOU NOTE (short)

1-28-22

Dear Chris and Betsy,

Thank you so much for the blueberry muffins! They have been such a treat in the mornings this week. I still think you make the very best! Thank you again for the lovely treat!

From,
Bridget

THANK-YOU NOTE (long)

January 28, 2022

Dear Peggy,

We hope this note finds you well. As we work on the new book we are reminded of the wonderful work you did to carry Emily Post through the 1990s and early 2000s. Each day we are grateful for the work that we do, and to us that is truly a gift—from you, from Emily, from the family. Thank you so much for all you have brought to this tradition and for always encouraging us each step of the way.

Much love,
Dan and Liz

THE SYMPATHY NOTE

October 12, 2022

Dear Lorraine,

I am so sorry to hear that you are not well. I want to be here for you in the ways that you need right now, whether that's finding laughter and silver linings or listening and being a shoulder to lean on. I hope these flowers cheer you up until I can be there in person. I will try you this weekend over the phone.

Much love,
Kim

THE CONDOLENCE NOTE

April 23, 2022

Dear Virginia,

I am so sorry to hear the news about Mac passing away. My heart aches for you and your family right now. When I picture Mac, I can't help but smile. That big grin, his wild bow ties, and the sparkle in his eye. What a treasured friend to have. And what a wonderful husband, uncle, brother, and son. I'm thinking of all of you at this time, and I will reach out to check in on you in the coming weeks. Right now, I hope you are surrounded by the love and support you need and that you are comforted by all the wonderful ways Mac was able to touch so many people's lives.

With sympathy and love,
Elizabeth

THE APOLOGY NOTE

March 18, 2022

Dear Naomi,

I am so sorry for not understanding what you were saying and for losing my temper. I was a guest in your home, and we are friends, and I should not have acted like that. I should have listened. I am sorry, and I hope you will forgive my words and actions. I do not intend to repeat them, ever.

All my best to you,
Reese

CONGRATULATORY NOTE (short)
(often sent or given before an event along with a gift or flowers)

J—

Good luck tonight! I'll be cheering you on, kid.

—L

CONGRATULATORY NOTE (long)

November 14th, 2022

Dear Christiana and Jesse,

Congratulations on the launch of your new business! It is so wonderful to see you two pursuing your ultimate dream. I couldn't be happier for you and I can't wait to see Airborne Arborists take off! Sky's the limit! Congratulations to you both!

Best,
Alonso

THE SIMPLE NOTE TO SAY "HI"

12-17-22

Jermaine and Caroline!

I just wanted to do something different and pop you a note in the mail. I hope all is well in your world and this little note finds you having the best day. I am doing great. I've started working weekends at Slim's on the boardwalk, which will be great for the summer tourist season. AND I booked a trip to a beach cottage for a week at the end of the summer! I can't wait! Please keep me posted on what's new with you, I'm dying to hear it all!

XOXO,
Georgie

TIPS FOR WORK EMAILS

Here are some basic business email tips for communicating well with others at work.

- Double-check the recipient(s) you are sending to.

- Include a subject line that is pertinent to the body of the email.

- Always use a salutation and closing for your first email to someone.

- Correct spelling, grammar, and punctuation are important.

- Be sure to include useful contact information in your signature line.

- Reply the same day when possible, or by the next business day.

- Use reply all only when all recipients need to see the exchange (be extra careful when responding that your message is for all the recipients).

- Start a new email thread if yours gets too long or changes subjects.

TIPS FOR VIDEO CALLS

Here are some basic tips to set you up well for a video call.

- Confirm date, time, and time zone.

- Check the link and connection before you begin.

- Wear appropriate clothing (including below the waist).

- Use a non-distracting background free of bright lights, mess, and private items.

- Choose an appropriate camera angle.

- Minimize loud background noise.

- Test your speakers and microphone.

- Remember to smile.

SAMPLE INVITATIONS

For the following invitation examples, we have included a variety of wording and structure, events, formality, hosts, honorees, gift and no-gift situations, and RSVP examples so that you can find the right combination for your invitations. When inviting locally, including the state is not necessary. The date and time can be on separate lines or together.

BIRTHDAY

ADULT'S BIRTHDAY

Adults often use formal invitations for big birthday years and "organize" a birthday party for the in-between years. (Not a rule by any means.) If you are hosting, remember that the formality of the invitation should match that of the event.

> *SHHHH . . . It's a surprise!*
> *Please join us to celebrate Raja's 40th!*
> *Friday, June 24th, at 7 p.m.*
> *84 Northwood Street, Apt. 3C*
> *Brooklyn*
>
> *RSVP by June 10th*   *Cocktail attire*
> *BibiMukherjee@gmail.com*   *requested*
> *No gifts, please*

CHILD'S BIRTHDAY

Children's birthday invitations will often be on fill-in cards or use simple wording, and the addressed envelope indicates whom it is intended for. If you want to include someone's siblings, write an extra note on the invitation, or put both names on the envelope.

> *Join us!*
> *Saturday, September 11th*
> *to celebrate*
> *Sunny's 3rd birthday*
> *from 3 p.m. to 5 p.m.*
>
> *17 Peach Tree Lane*
> *Ashville*
>
> *RSVP by September 9th*
> *Sunnysmom@gmail.com*

COMING-OF-AGE CELEBRATION

BAT/BAR MITZVAH

*Please share in our great joy
as our daughter Lindsay Ruth
[insert Hebrew name (optional)]
is called to the Torah as a Bat Mitzvah
Saturday, the twelfth of April
two thousand twenty-two
at nine o'clock in the morning*

*Congregation Rodelph Sholom
198 Fairview Boulevard*

*Montclair, New Jersey
Kiddush lunch reception to follow*

RSVP: Polly and Joshua Silverman

QUINCEAÑERA

*Cecilia Martinez
joyfully invites you to her
Quinceañera*

*Mass
11 am on Saturday, March 17
at St. Catherine of Siena Church
243 Oak Street,
Fort Worth*

*Quince Ball
7 p.m.
Colonial Country Club
4751 Riverside Drive
Fort Worth*

*RSVP by February 21st to
Victoria, VMA@gmail.com*

CHRISTENING

*Please join us
at the christening of
Thomas James Belisle III
on Sunday, June 26, 2022
at 11 a.m.
St. Andrews Church
345 Maple Street
Hudson Falls*

NAMING CEREMONY

*Please join our family
for the naming ceremony for our son
Rémi Michael Turner
on Saturday, July 16th
at 10 a.m.*

*222 Esplanade Ave.
New Orleans*

GRADUATION PARTY

SINGLE HONOREE

*Please join the family of
Brian Michael Hughes
in celebrating his
graduation from Pembrook High School
Sunday, June 12th, at 4 p.m.
55 Marden Drive
Kingsbury*

*RSVP: Sandra
334-142-8767*

MULTIPLE HONOREES

*Please join the Hughes, Sharif, and Patel families
in celebrating the graduation of
Brian Michael Hughes, Jr
Ahmed Joseph Sharif
and
Vijay Ritu Patel
Pembrook High School, Class of 2022
Sunday, June 12th, at 4 pm
55 Marden Drive
Kingsbury*

*RSVP
Sandra: 984-102-9067
Joseph: JSharif@gmail.com
Prythee: 342-344-9987*

DEBUTANTE BALL OR COTILLION

DEBUTANTE BALL

The Omaha Symphony Guild
requests the pleasure of your company
at the 50th annual
Omaha Symphony Debutante Ball
honoring
Debutantes and their Families
Sunday, the twenty-fifth of December
two thousand twenty-two
at six o'clock

Palace Ballroom
The Hilton Hotel
Omaha, Nebraska

Formal Attire

COTILLION

The Cotillion Committees of
the Opera Guild and the Louisville Guild
request the pleasure of your company at
a graduation dinner and dance
honoring
the 2022 Cotillion Class
the seventeenth of June
two thousand twenty-two
at six o'clock

West Ballroom
Louisville Holiday Center
Louisville, Kentucky

Formal Attire

HOUSEWARMING

Note that there is no RSVP because a response isn't expected for an open house party. An open house party is one of the few occasions where an end time is listed.

Please come warm our new home!
Saturday, August 20th, from noon until 6 p.m.
1810 Camel's Hump Road
Duxbury

ENGAGEMENT PARTY

This example is for a brunch, but engagement parties could be held at any typical party time.

Please join us for brunch
to celebrate the engagement of
Gillian Weeks
and
Jonathan Bulette
Sunday, January 16th at 11 a.m.
46 Highgate Road
Sheldon

RSVP: Jane Bulette
JB63@gmail.com

WEDDING

The following samples are just the tip of the iceberg when it comes to wedding invitations. For more detailed wedding invitation advice, including a myriad of hosting situations, please see our books *Wedding Etiquette*, 6th edition, and *Do I Have to Wear White?*, or visit emilypost.com.

FORMAL (WHEN PARENTS ARE HOSTING)

Mr. and Mrs. Allen Danes
request the honor of your presence
at the marriage of their daughter
Vanessa Elizabeth
to (and)
Evan Josiah Green
Saturday, the seventh of July
two thousand twenty-two
at four o'clock

Ridgewood Botanical Gardens
Tisdale, Virginia

(Add an RSVP line here if   *Black Tie Requested*
no reply card is used.)

INFORMAL (WHEN THE COUPLE IS HOSTING)

Robert Love and Lila Parker
request the pleasure of your company at
their marriage
September 22nd, 2022
at 4:30 p.m.

High Meadows
Menemsha, MA

(Add an RSVP if
no reply card is used.)

CASUAL (WHEN THE FAMILIES ARE HOSTING WITH THE COUPLE)

Together with our families,
Casey Collet and Felix Edgers
invite you to join in celebrating their marriage
Saturday, October 15th at noon
Callahan Park
Wilford, TX

(Add an RSVP if
no reply card is used.)

COCKTAIL PARTY

Cocktail parties often state an end time when not followed by dinner and sometimes include B.Y.O.B. (see A Note about B.Y.O., page 271, for more on this designation).

Please join us for cocktails
Thursday, May 14th, 6 to 8 pm
420 Pinkerton Street
Apt. 2B

RSVP: Luna 212-212-2121

DINNER PARTY

CASUAL

Few hosts use mailed invitations for casual dinner parties, but that doesn't mean you can't.

Please come for dinner
on Friday, April 20th
at 7 pm
34 Fuller Street
Edgartown

RSVP: Emily
233-659-1547

FORMAL

A formal dinner invitation is handwritten on your house stationery. If you are printing invitations, you would s ubstitute the invitee's name(s) with "your," and the guests are indicated by the names on the addressed envelope.

Mr. and Mrs. Chival Russ
request the pleasure of
Mr. and Mrs. Colin Bailey's
company at dinner
on Friday, the twenty-second of July
at seven o'clock
34 Fuller Street
Edgartown

RSVP: 233-659-1547

SHOWER

Of course you will specify the type of shower (wedding or new child). Showers are the only events where it's appropriate to put where a person or couple is registered on the invitation, because the point of the party is to give gifts.

The pleasure of your company is requested at
a baby shower for Jamie!
at 4 pm on Saturday, March 18th
435 Pioneer Road
Salt Lake City

RSVP: Melissa or Herb,
879-786-6617

Jamie and Jim are registered at
MountainFamilyLife.com

ANNIVERSARY PARTY

The pleasure of your company is requested
in celebrating the 50th wedding anniversary of
Mr. John Senning and Mrs. Lucinda Senning
Saturday, December 12th
at seven o'clock
The Equinox Hotel, West Ballroom
7 Splendid Lane
Ripton

RSVP: Joan Shultz,   *Black Tie*
JShultz@gmail.com

RETIREMENT PARTY

Add an RSVP (left-aligned) at the bottom if a head count is needed. And remember to put any attire information on the bottom and right-aligned.

Please join Ms. Jessica Chamberlain and staff
in celebrating the retirement of
Mx. Arlo Washington
Friday, November fifteenth
at seven o'clock

Bistro Margolese
3142 West Bleecker Street
Farmsdale

CELEBRATION OF LIFE OR PRIVATE MEMORIAL SERVICE

Please join the family of
Patricia Coward Kolbe
at a reception
to celebrate her life

Friday, September 16
6 to 8 p.m.
Edgartown Reading Room

RSVP:
Tricia Post: 565-128-7831
Sara Blum: VUSB@gmail.com

EMILY'S INVITATIONS

It's always fun to look back at Emily's world and let ourselves be inspired by its grace and formality. Here are some invitation samples from her 1922 edition of *Etiquette*:

THE GENERAL INVITATION BLANK

Mrs. Stevens

requests the pleasure of

Mr. and Mrs. Claude Rubenstein's

company at *lunch*

on *Saturday, February the 4th*

at *one* o'clock

Two Elm Place

THE DINNER BLANK

Mr. and Mrs. Huntington Jones

request the pleasure of

Mr. and Mrs. Claude Rubenstein's

company at dinner

on *Saturday, February the 4th*

at eight o'clock

at Two Thousand Fifth Avenue

FORMAL INVITATION

Always handwritten and on house stationery, which typically has the street address printed at the top.

350 PARK AVENUE

Mr. and Mrs. John Kindhart
request the pleasure of
Mr. and Mrs. Robert Gilding's
company at dinner
on Tuesday the sixth of December
at eight o'clock.

PUBLIC BALL

Note that the word *ball* appears only on public ball invitations, never private ones.

The Committee of the Greenwood Club
requests the pleasure of your company
at
The Sugarplum Ball
to be held in the Greenwood Clubhouse
on the evening of November the seventh
at ten o'clock.

For the benefit of
The Neighborhood Hospital.

Tickets five dollars

PRIVATE BALL

A private ball, whether held at home or at a venue, is structured as an "At Home" event.
The invitation is engraved in block or shaded block type.

Mr. and Mrs. Titherington de Puyster
At Home
On Monday the third of January
at ten o'clock
One East Fiftieth Street

The favor of an answer   Dancing
is requested

SAMPLE ANNOUNCEMENTS

Here are some sample announcements. Remember to use name and title structures that fit the formality of the occasion and, most important, the individuals they represent. If you don't know, ask. (See Invitations and Announcements, page 93 for more details.)

GRADUATION

Some institutions provide announcements, and the graduate's name can be written in. They are sent for high school, university, and graduate school, but not middle school. If a school has not provided one, here's a sample format:

> *George Daniel Flynn*
> *earned a*
> *Bachelor of Arts in History*
> *from the University of Pennsylvania*
> *on June 3rd, 2022*

A simpler version is to send something like a postcard with a photo of the graduate and the following text. Card companies have many designs to choose from:

> *Class of 2022*
> *Emily Hepburn [and degree, if any]*
> *June 22, 2022*
> *University of Vermont*

MARRIAGE

Remember that an announcement is not an invitation, it does not come with any obligation for the recipient to send a gift.

> *Mrs. Betsy and Mrs. Elenore Rhinald-Blakely*
> *are pleased to announce*
> *the marriage of their daughter*
> *Cecily Katherine*
> *to*
> *Evan Rickley Reynolds*
> *on Saturday, the twentieth of July,*
> *two thousand twenty-two*
> *[Or July 20, 2022 if using a more casual tone]*
> *Claremont, California*

NEW CHILD

> *Heather Gregorick*
> *is delighted to announce*
> *the birth of*
> *[Baby's first and middle names,*
> *or whole name if last name is different]*
> *August 10, 2022*
> *Weight [optional]*

For an adoption, you can use:

> *Mr. and Mrs. Tyler Blackwood*
> *announce the adoption of*
> *Simon Andreas*
> *born August 10th, 2019, Quito, Ecuador,*
> *who became a part of our family*
> *in September 2020*

NEW HOME

> *We've moved!*
>
> *Our new address is:*
> *Debbie and Joe Jarecki*
> *1425 Lake Street*
> *Charlotte, VT 05445*
> *802-444-8989*

[or date of move if in the future, and change the first line to read *"We're moving!"*]

A death is never announced via a mailed notice. (For more on death announcements, which are published or posted, see Spreading the News, page 227.)

A STATIONERY WARDROBE

A well-appointed "stationery wardrobe"—consisting of basic pieces such as cards, social cards, note sheets, letter sheets, blanks, and envelopes—should have you well set up for any correspondence. What matters is to include the pieces that meet *your* needs. Personal stationery will have your name, initials, monogram or family name, or crest engraved or printed on it. House stationery, which can be used by anyone living or staying at your address, will have the street address at the top. Type, color, and graphics options are infinite. More informal social stationery can use playful colors, fonts, patterns, and images. For formal styles, choose simple, clean lines and classic colors. Cards and sheets are paired with matching envelopes. A local stationer can be a great asset when making decisions.

CARDS

Blanks, which are personal fill-in cards, are ever so cool. A note card is the most typical kind, either folded over or flat. Having greeting cards, plain note cards to decorate, blanks, and postcards are all great ways to be ready when life warrants sending a card or invitation!

FOLD-OVER NOTES AND ENVELOPES

Style: Various

Purpose: Thanks, condolences, congratulations, special occasions

SOCIAL CARDS

Style: Engraved with name (centered). Any additional information written by hand

Purpose: Social exchanges, first meetings, special notes, reminders, included with gifts

Size: 3½ by 2 inches; 96-pound weight suggested

CORRESPONDENCE CARDS AND ENVELOPES

Style: Engraved with name, monogram, or family crest, and optional border

Purpose: Quick notes, follow-ups, thanks, invitations

Size: 4½ by 7 inches or 6⅜ by 4¼ inches; 96-pound weight suggested; pair with envelope

NOTE OR MONARCH SHEETS AND ENVELOPES

Style: Name and/or address suggested (centered at top)

Purpose: Social letters

Size: Note, 6⅜ by 8¼ inches or Monarch 7¼ by 10½ inches; 32-pound weight suggested; pair with envelope

FULL-PAGE LETTER PAPER AND ENVELOPES

Style: Name and/or address suggested (centered at the top)

Purpose: Personal business letters

Size: 8½ by 11 inches; 32-pound weight suggested; pair with envelope

PENS AND POSTAGE

Keeping pens you like to write with and a variety of postage with your stationery makes writing easier and getting notes and letters into the mail much more likely to happen.

FOLD-OVER NOTE
AND ENVELOPE

ANN ROBERTS
Text me for tennis!
414-978-1234

SOCIAL CARD

CORRESPONDENCE CARD
AND ENVELOPE

MONARCH SHEET
AND ENVELOPE

FULL-PAGE
LETTER PAPER
AND ENVELOPE

PENS AND
POSTAGE

SAMPLE SOCIAL LETTER

Friday, June 30, 2022

Dear Michael,

I hope you are enjoying summer camp this year. I went to the same camp when I was a kid, and we did so many fun things. I can't wait to hear about what you love the most. Have you gone on your first camp-out overnight yet?

Write to me any time, kiddo! I miss you and love you and can't wait to hear what your favorite activity is.

Have fun!
Aunt Carroll

SAMPLE BUSINESS LETTERS

ACME Gift Co. (your company and address, if not using letterhead)

456 Eddington Drive
Tucson, AZ

January 2, 2021 (the date)

Liz Miller, (recipient)
Marketing Manager (their title or department)

ACME Stationery Co. (their company name and address)
123 Main Street
Eugene, OR 10000

Dear Ms. Miller, (or if more personal, use Dear Liz,)

The body of the letter is left-aligned (not indented) and each paragraph is separated by a full line space.

The closing is left-aligned and stacked, as is the heading. The sender's full name, without title, should be printed below the closing and then a space reserved for an actual handwritten signature followed by the position of the sender and their company name, followed by the company address and telephone number.

Sincerely,
Jefferson O'Neill

Jefferson O'Neill
CEO
ACME Gift Co.
808-123-4567
ABigWig@AcmeGift.com

CHAPTER 4

Personal Appearance

"Clothes are to us what feathers and fur are to beasts and birds; they not only add to our appearance, but they *are* our appearance. How we look to others entirely depends upon what we wear and how we wear it; manners and speech are noted afterward, and character, last of all."

There is a great difference between the fashions and appearance expectations of Emily's day and today. Few of us wear top hats and formal gloves today, and although in Emily's day women had stopped wearing corsets and could bare their arms in public, she certainly didn't deal with side boob or anyone wearing things "ironically." Today, we believe it's important to wear what makes you feel confident and to respect the occasion when choosing your attire.

There may be only one way to chew (with your mouth closed), but there are many ways to express yourself and present the image you wish to portray in a given situation. However, this doesn't just happen—cultivating your personal appearance takes thought, time, and care. It goes beyond the classic images of balancing a book on one's head and crossing one's legs at the ankles. While good posture and deportment can help (and courses in these may be beneficial), we should all imagine the version of ourselves we'd like to present to the world and take steps to achieve it.

You are in control of your image. There are so many choices to make with regard to appearance, actions, and words and they all say something: *sophisticated, rugged, flamboyant, beautiful, smart, unkempt, relaxed, handsome, carefree.* How you portray yourself is up to you. You'll have different goals for different events in your life. Your inner *bohème* may dress you for a festival weekend, while your inner boss takes over when you head into work on Monday. The impressions we create get reflected back on us. What's the story you want to tell about yourself? What is the story you want others to tell about you? "Mitch looks a bit uptight, yeah?" "Oh, he just dresses that way, get him talking and he'll open right up."

WHY IT MATTERS

Whether we like it or not, our appearance matters; it impacts how others see us and often how we feel about ourselves. In our social lives, we may wear whatever we like—critics be damned—and experience fewer consequences, while in our work lives, others' impressions of how we present ourselves are often part of the job and should be taken into account. We want our character and work to be the focus, not our fashion choices or hygiene. If these things are distracting, it can be harder for people to focus on our words and actions. It's important to note that some appearance ideals are oppressive and unnecessary, such as banning certain hairstyles or requiring makeup. Many other style suggestions, however—like not wearing loud jewelry (like noisy bangle bracelets) or clothing that is ripped or stained—are meant to keep our appearance from becoming a distraction in certain situations.

How we present ourselves impacts our relationships and how we are received by others. Far from being simply superficial, your appearance is how others see you. They don't always have the benefit of knowing your thoughts, feelings, and intentions when they first interact with you. Making an effort, being intentional and aware, and taking pride in an image you're comfortable with is making an investment in yourself and your relationships. It says, *I know how to represent myself and I want to do it well,* which is a healthy and confident mindset to operate from.

SELF-ASSESSMENT

If etiquette is about how we interact with the world, it's good for us to understand not only who we are, but also how others see us. Honest, ongoing self-assessment is a critical skill for making choices about how we present ourselves. Hugely successful people regularly practice self-assessments to understand what others are seeing, and then use that to their benefit. Everyone is capable of doing this. Look at yourself, right as you are now, with no quick touch-ups and no past or future versions in your mind's eye. Follow these steps of self-assessment:

1. **BEFORE YOU START, COMMIT TO BEING KIND TO YOURSELF DURING THIS ASSESSMENT.** It's not about seeing where you've failed or what you dislike; it's about how you can emphasize what's best about your appearance and work on what could be improved. No negative self-talk here, okay? Respect yourself as you challenge yourself.

2. **PICK CONCRETE AREAS TO FOCUS ON.** Ask yourself specific questions about your choices in the following areas to get yourself thinking about what other people are likely to notice. There are no right or wrong answers.
    How is my appearance? grooming, hygiene, attire, accessories
    How are my actions? posture, gestures, eye contact/attention, nervous habits
    How do I speak my words? tone, speed, volume, pronunciation, inflection

3. **ACKNOWLEDGE THE DIFFERENT ASPECTS OF YOURSELF.** We are all complex. Sorting out which parts to share and when is an ongoing process. Who are you today, for yourself and for the different people in your life? Pay attention to how you shift your presentation, actions, appearance, and words as you change roles with different audiences at different times.

Now that you've reflected on who you are right now and in different scenarios, what do you feel good about? Which areas would you like to improve or change? Maintaining a good image is about consistency; improving your image will require a willingness to change. Big or small, think them through, and make choices that help present your best self to the world around you. You can always start with one improvement at a time and go from there. This process will build your confidence and put you more at ease as you interact with others.

APPEARANCE, ACTIONS, AND WORDS

Our overall image at any given time is made up of three things: our appearance, our actions, and our words. Together these form our outward persona and the version of ourselves that others interact with. Because these three elements affect the image others have of us, it's mighty important to pay attention to them and understand their potential influence. What we choose to project will be reflected back to us in the reactions and interactions we have with others. For example, if you don't smile easily but want to be seen as friendly, you'll have to use your words, tone, and body language to convey friendliness, since the action of smiling, which is easily understood by others as friendly, won't be as naturally accessible to you.

APPEARANCE

Our appearance (including hygiene) communicates to others that we are taking care of ourselves and that we are conscious of how we present ourselves to the world around us. Things to consider when it comes to your appearance include the cleanliness of your skin—especially hands and face; your hair—there are many options, but what matters is that it should be groomed in a way that isn't distracting and shows you take care with it; whether you are giving off a strong, neutral, or pleasant aroma; if your clothing reflects the occasion as well as your personal style—remember, the fit and condition also impacts your overall appearance; your accessories, such as makeup, jewelry, or wearable tech, which also create an impression; and finally, body art, when visible, can definitely create an impression, be sure yours says what you'd like it to.

A note on judging appearance: For all that we talk about how you present yourself will create an impression, it's never in good taste to judge someone else on their appearance. Mocking or negatively commenting on anyone's voice, actions, or appearance is a surefire way to make a lasting negative impression. These types of comments are so hurtful, they can do serious and lasting damage to relationships. This is equally true of subtler reactions such as eye rolls; silently judgmental, condescending, bemused, or shocked looks shot behind someone's back; or fake compliments—all of these are considered rude and are far from the behavior of Best Society. The appearance you should pay such attention to is your own.

ACTIONS

The actions we take, our posture, and our gestures all contribute to the impression people have of us. When your posture is upright and relaxed, you are approachable and look engaged but not intense. This makes it easier for others to talk to you and feel confident and at ease interacting with you. Hunching your shoulders and looking down, purposely avoiding eye contact, or crossing your arms will often give the impression that you are unapproachable, guarded, or unfriendly. Save these for times when you want to signal that you'd rather be left alone. If your body naturally assumes this posture, use your tone, words, and gestures to help convey approachability and friendliness.

Our gestures also contribute to the overall impression we give. Large, wild gestures can make someone seem vibrantly alive, wonderfully entertaining, or over-the-top and even distracting, depending on the circumstances. Pay attention to moderating your gestures the same way you would moderate your voice.

Facial expressions have a big impact on interactions with others. When our expression doesn't match our mood, we can unintentionally send the wrong signal to those around us. Have you ever been asked if you're okay when you're absolutely fine? Chances are something about your facial expression was indicating to others that they should ask the question. Take some time to observe your facial expressions—either by having a friend, roommate, or partner snap some candid pics or by paying attention to how your face feels as you experience different emotions (including relaxed, benign moments). You'll have a better sense of your personal range of expressions, which will help you connect more intentionally with others.

Habits like tapping your fingers, twirling your hair, biting your nails, or cracking your knuckles can give the impression that you are unaware, nervous, or preoccupied (see Distracting Habits, page 76). Finding ways to channel that energy can prevent others from being distracted by it and puts you back in control of your image.

WORDS

Your tone, speed, inflection, volume, and laughter all contribute to how you are heard and understood. When in doubt, it is usually a good idea to speak more softly and slowly. Practicing your "friendly," "concerned," and "caring" tones will help you access them more easily at moments when you may be tempted to use a less polite tone. Save your serious, angry, and even humorous tones for when they are truly needed—they will be more effective if they match the moment rather than become your default. Take care that filler words such as *like* and *um* don't disrupt your speech unintentionally. A pause, or breath, can replace them if you need to.

CONFIDENCE IS KEY

Confidence, not arrogance, is key to your personal appearance. No matter your size, shape, age, ability, or style, if you feel confident and comfortable in how you present yourself, you're well on your way to making a good impression on anyone you meet. Knowing what is expected and how you are meeting those expectations is one way to build confidence. Making choices that are true to yourself and express what you intend are another part of the confidence equation.

FOCAL POINT

We do want others to focus on us—our ideas, personality, and appearance—in positive ways. How we present ourselves will help to pinpoint that focus. It's good to be aware that sometimes others can become so focused on one aspect of our appearance—whether that thing is shocking, stunning, unique, or otherwise—that they cannot focus on the substance of what we are saying or doing. Think first about the purpose of your interaction and then dress accordingly. Are you presenting to a new client? Attending your niece's wedding? Going to a religious service with your in-laws? Hanging with your oldest friends? Going on a big night out? You won't likely wear the same thing to or behave the same way at each event, but in each case the attention you give your appearance matters both for you and others. By making intentional choices about our appearance, we can help direct what other people focus on. It's one way of taking control of our identity and the impression we make on the world around us.

HYGIENE AND GROOMING

Whether going *au naturel* or using a buffet of products, Ms. Hy Jeane believes in always keeping clean and hygienic as a first step to rocking her appearance. Washing your hands before eating, tending to your hair, and brushing your teeth are basic habits that speak to personal care, grooming, and hygiene. While what counts as hygienic and what grooming is required to meet that standard may change, there are always social rewards for meeting the benchmarks and norms of the day.

The occasions when you can get away with being dirty, messy, or gross and still be considered polite exist but are fairly limited. There is a difference between trying a new beard (fine) and trying a new beard that routinely collects food and liquids in it (gross). Or eating with your hands because the situation calls for it (fine), and eating with your hands when better/more appropriate options are available (gross). Should you have a hygiene concern, or haven't done a self-assessment in a while, giving a close friend permission to talk to you about these very personal things is well advised. In fact, the best way to get good feedback is not just to give someone ongoing permission to tell you what they notice, but find a friend you trust and ask specifically either about an area that you are concerned about or use the hygiene checklist (page 137) as a guide. People don't usually comment on these things (because they are trying to be polite), so inviting someone to do so specifically may be necessary if you want to get advice and make improvements. We all experience physical changes in life (a new workout routine, aging, a new diet, hormonal changes, dental work can even change how often food sticks in teeth) and you're not likely to smell your own breath or body odor or see new (and possibly unwanted) hair growth. It's smart and good to ask for help when you feel you need an outside perspective.

ATTIRE

In Emily's day, there were limited options and strict expectations about what to wear when. Today, we can run the gamut from wedding receptions that request casual cut-off jeans to events like the Met Gala in all its costumed "creative black tie" glory. Traditionally, you would put only *white tie* or *black tie* on an invitation. For everything else, it was expected that people knew how to dress for each event. Now we have so many types of events and styles of living that it's not as easy to tell what's expected by the invitation alone with no designation. Private parties, club events, school events, company events—all of these use attire designations to help guests understand how to dress (successfully) for an event. When creating an invitation, it's important to strike a balance between helpful and guiding versus bossy or unnecessary. On an invite to a beach party, *beach attire* is unnecessary. For an organization's charity event, on the other hand, it's definitely helpful to know when it's semiformal and not black tie or casual.

FORMAL ATTIRE

Mx. Monna Cull is always thrilled to attend a formal occasion. They see it as an opportunity to break out their very best, which is always a treat for them to wear. Most often we put on formal attire for weddings, galas, formal charity events, or performances where it is traditional, such as the opera, ballet, or opening night at a theater or Broadway performance. For formal wear, well fitted is usually the goal. If the garment is too small, short, or tight, or too large, long, or loose, it will look out of place. Aim for the midrange unless your persona supports an appropriately creative or festive look. While ornaments like sequins, sparkles, fringe, and tassels are fabulous, traditional formal wear finds ways to use these elements sparingly.

WHITE TIE is the most formal traditional attire, reserved and required for occasions like Mardi Gras balls, the Nobel Prize banquet, or a state dinner. Should you be fortunate enough to be invited to such an event, expect black jackets with tails and black trousers, wing-collared white shirts (fly or stud-front shirts are also options), white pique vests with matching bow ties, cuff links or stud sets, and black Oxford lace-ups. Top hats, scarves, gloves, and pocket squares may also be worn as accessories. Chesterfield coats, which are formal, dark-colored, knee-length coats with velvet collars, may also be worn as outerwear if the weather is cold. If you go to an incredibly formal event during the day, you wear a morning coat instead of white tie. (It's the same level of formality, but white tie is reserved for evening and morning coat for daytime.) For those not wearing tails, ball gowns and long formal dresses with formal shoes are the expected white tie options. On a rare occasion you might see their counterparts: formal pants and dress top or formal skirt and dress-top—but they must be very formal versions. With dresses, gloves (of varying lengths) and tiaras are other possible accessories.

BLACK TIE as we know it today was born in the social club of Tuxedo Park, New York (which Emily's father, Bruce Price, designed and where Emily lived for many years), and came of age in the social revolution of the late 1960s. Black tie is the next most formal dress option after 6:00 p.m. (except when asked to wear black tie to an afternoon wedding with an evening reception following it). Often worn only a few times in a person's lifetime (if ever), black tie can be found at a prom, wedding, or annual gala. Expect guests to wear tuxedos (see the Attire Guide, page 136, for details), evening and formal dresses or outfits, formal shoes, and jewelry. You could wear a very dark suit and a black necktie (particularly if *black tie* is listed as *optional*). White jacket tuxedos are an option for summer; they're thought of as more of a cocktail jacket for warm-weather outdoor events. If you want something different for a winter option, you could wear a velvet smoking jacket.

BLACK TIE CREATIVE (or sometimes *festive*) was born of the need to break the rules, and tuxedo wearers should feel okay going outside the traditional black-and-white color scheme. Elements of flair or fun can also be added. Play it up! This goes for gowns and formal two-piece sets too. The attire should still be formal black tie, but a bit splashier and more playful—perhaps a colorful bowtie and matching cummerbund.

SEMIFORMAL ATTIRE

Semiformal attire is a step up from dressy casual, but two or three steps below formal. Expect suits, jacket and tie with slacks, dress tops and dress pants, long dresses (typically a maxi dress instead of a gown), tea-length or cocktail (knee-length) dresses, or two-piece outfits. Here's where you can mix and match to set the right tone for the event. You might wear a long maxi dress in a casual jersey knit to your friends' beach wedding, or a jacket with corduroy pants and suede dress shoes to a new gallery opening. We see semiformal attire requested frequently on invitations; it's also when we see most of the "creative" attire labels on invitations, like "diamonds and denim" or "dressy Western," which are generally best used for specific events or when guests will truly understand them. Semiformal events can be everything from school dances, office holiday parties, charity events, art openings, and weddings to retirement parties and milestone birthdays and anniversaries.

Remember, you can easily remove a tie or tone down the jewelry if you feel overdressed. It's usually better to aim for more formal and take it down a notch than show up on the casual side and be underdressed.

BUSINESS ATTIRE

Your business dress code will vary depending on the industry you work in and the company you work for. There are many industries that are traditionally conservative in their work attire (like law and finance) and others (such as fashion) where the players are literally creating the styles of the day, and it would be a mistake to *not be of the moment*. Your work at a tattoo studio might give you a chance to proudly display and talk about your body art. Ask your company what their dress code is and what any confusing terms mean to feel confident you're meeting expectations. When in doubt, fall back on clean and classic items: a buttoned shirt of quality fabric, fitted well and in good condition, and a pair of slacks with simple, closed-toe shoes will work almost anywhere for anyone. Keep a simple, well-fitted jacket on hand to easily polish almost any look.

For business attire, open-toed shoes, shorts, short skirts or dresses, low-cut shirts or dresses, cut-out styles, and anything exposing a shoulder are typically avoided. Patterns and colors aren't necessarily muted, but they are not usually bright and bold either (unless you've cultivated a personal look based on loud patterns and colors).

DRESSY CASUAL

Dressy casual means the best of our casual wardrobes. Not all T-shirts, jeans, or sweaters are created equal. For dressy-casual events, choose nicer fabrics, newer items—rather than your old faves that are looking worn—and more flattering cuts. You may be in jeans and a sweater, but a bit more dressed up than how you might look when running errands or visiting friends. You might wear stylish shoes, jewelry, or other accessories to dress up an everyday outfit. How you style your hair and, if you wear it, apply makeup can also dress up a simple outfit. This is not the time for rips and tears, though it might be the time to wear some super-styled sneakers.

BUSINESS CASUAL

Business casual is a slightly dressed-down version of traditional business attire. For some companies this will be the everyday dress code, and you'll want to check with your employer regarding expectations. Other times, it's allowed periodically as a relaxing of the usual company dress code, for example, when a company has casual Fridays. You might not go so far as to wear shorts and sandals to the office, but a non-button-up shirt, polo shirt, or casual sweater might take the place of a button-up shirt and jacket, and loafers might replace lace-up shoes. Patterns and colors can be more expressive. Anything that's too revealing is still a no-go for work. You can always ask to be sure you're relaxing the dress code to the right level.

CASUAL

Casual attire today is a huge category covering everything from jeans and T-shirts to athleisure wear, shorts, skirts, tank or tube tops, flip-flops, and sneakers. The difference between casual and unkempt is fuzzy, but there is a line. Being clean with your casual is the difference. A clean tank top and pair of shorts can look great when you're freshly showered, or at least still clean from the day before. But a stained tank top, dirty hair, or body odor will take you out of casual and into the category of looking like you don't care or aren't taking care of yourself. We can dismiss the importance of appearance thinking, *I don't care how I look.* But when it comes to good etiquette and making choices that build relationships, people will respond to what they see. Being clean and presentable as a baseline for our appearance when interacting with others is worth aiming for.

A NOTE ABOUT "FESTIVE" ATTIRE

The designation *festive attire* conjures images of ugly Christmas sweaters; red, white, and blue on the Fourth of July; or glitz and sparkle on New Year's Eve. But *festive* can quickly cross into cultural appropriation if you aren't careful and aware. *Cultural appropriation* refers to the use of objects or elements from a particular culture in ways that reinforce stereotypes, don't respect their original purpose or meaning, and/or don't credit their source. It's generally not appropriate to wear items of clothing or iconography from cultures that aren't your own when attempting to "festivize" your look. Turning someone else's culture or identity into a costume is hurtful and in poor taste. When considering "festive" attire, always remember that you can be festive without being disrespectful or inappropriate.

THREE OCCASIONS WHEN
YOU MUST GET IT RIGHT

There are three situations when you really want to get your attire and appearance right: job interviews, when honoring others, and when attending religious ceremonies or entering a house of worship. There are of course clubs and restaurants with dress codes; sometimes they have clothing options for patrons to borrow if needed, and most will post their dress code on their website or tell you when you call to make a reservation.

JOB INTERVIEWS

Congratulations on the interview! This is one of those times when someone else's impression of you matters greatly. Other people are reading you for cues all the time, and nearly 70 percent of hiring managers surveyed by Career Builder noted that dressing inappropriately was the biggest turn-off when considering applicants. Jobs are important, and dressing for an interview is no less so.

It's a good idea to dress in accordance with the industry or position as best you can when interviewing—even if the job will be one you work from home. Consider the culture of the place you're applying to and the position you're applying for, and then dress one notch up from what you would expect your everyday wear to be. You can always call or email to ask, for example: "Before I come in, I wanted to know what the company's dress policy is." Or, "I know I will be working remotely for the company, but I was wondering if there is a preferred dress code." Sometimes you have already met your interviewer or you know the team you'd be applying to work on, and if this is the case, aim to wear something that matches what the interviewer will likely be wearing. Whether your interview is virtual or in person, you'll want to dress for it from head to toe. Make sure that you and your clothing are clean. Looking dressed and ready for the interview will certainly impress a potential boss, even via video.

HONORING OTHERS

When the occasion is to celebrate someone else's moment, be it a wedding, coming-of-age ceremony, memorial service, graduation, or other event, show your support by dressing in the proper attire. If the family is casual and T-shirts and shorts are the norm for big celebratory dinners, then T-shirts and shorts it is. But if your sister and her new fiancé are dreaming of a formal wedding, wearing formal attire is key to supporting them on their day. While you might have to step slightly out of your comfort zone, if you receive an attire request from the host or honoree for the event, it's best to participate—with gusto, if possible. Remember, the occasion is about the honoree(s), and this is not the time to call attention to yourself because your attire is out of sync with the event. You are the supporting cast, not the star . . . this time around at least.

RELIGIOUS AND OFFICIAL CEREMONIES

At religious ceremonies and in houses of worship, as well as during any official ceremonies, whether for the military or an organization you belong to, it's imperative to dress appropriately. Not doing so on these occasions can cause deep offense and, in some cases, prohibit your participation in or observance of the ceremony. If you are unsure of what to wear, your best bet is to lean conservative and be properly covered (especially your shoulders, chest, upper legs, and sometimes lower legs). In some spaces you may be asked to remove your shoes or wear a head covering. You can always call your host or the house of worship to ask what's appropriate. If you cannot be suitably attired, call your host in advance to inform them that you won't be able to attend, or ask if they have suggestions to help you attain the proper attire. If you know other guests, you might call them and ask if there is something you could borrow. It would be the height of rudeness to ignore the attire requirements. It's one thing if your host responds to your regrets or your question with "Please come as you are; it will be all right," but you should never assume this will be the case.

WEARING WHITE

Back in Emily's day, the summer season was bracketed by Memorial Day and Labor Day, and "society" flocked in droves from city town houses to seaside cottages or mountain cabins to escape the heat. City clothes were left behind in exchange for lighter, whiter summer outfits. Come fall and the return to the city, summer clothes were put away and darker city clothes were donned once more. It was an age when there was a dress code for practically every occasion, and the signal to mark the change between summer resort, camp, or beach clothes and the rest of the year was encapsulated in the dictum "No white after Labor Day." And it stuck.

Of course, today you can wear white after Labor Day, and it makes perfect sense to do so, especially in climates where September temperatures are hardly fall-like. It's more about fabric choice and whether the white is creamier (winter whites) or brighter in tone (summer whites). Even in the dead of winter in northern New England, the fashionable wear creamy-white wools, cashmeres, and down-filled parkas. The true rule is, always wear what's appropriate—for the weather, the season, and the occasion.

REMOVING HATS

Brimmed hats and the etiquette around them—especially for men—hearkens back to the age of knights, when visors were lifted so you could see if it was friend or foe beneath the helmet, and being able to make eye contact and recognize each other was important for one's safety. Today, hat etiquette is still about eye contact, letting your face be seen, and showing respect.

Anyone going indoors should remove their hat once they have reached their destination. If you're in a large building, the lobby and elevators often count as *outdoor spaces,* where hats are acceptable to leave on, but hallways, dining areas, rooms, and offices are considered *indoors,* and therefore hats are to be taken off.

Hats, including ballcaps, should *always* be removed at the table. Eating with others with your head shielded is not polite. Hats are also removed during introductions. The exception might be when dining or hanging out outdoors and the sun is an issue. Traditionally, women wearing fashion hats didn't follow the same rules of removing them because they were pinned to their hairdo and were an integral part of their outfit. Today, this is less likely the case, and we encourage people of all genders to remove hats when a wide brim or cap bill would shield your face during an introduction. If we are just passing by someone we know and want to acknowledge them, a tip of the hat's brim is all that's needed (see The Nod and the Hat Tip, page 19). You might leave a brimmed fashion hat on during a conversation, whether indoors or out.

When it comes to the casual ballcap we can't just say you remove your ballcap indoors because there are plenty of casual situations today where a ballcap is perfectly appropriate indoors—hanging with friends, at a bar watching the game (maybe even the bar at the clubhouse), even just around your own home for the day. While you may wear your hat indoors, it's important to be respectful when you are in someone else's home and you know they appreciate the old custom of always removing a hat inside. The best way to be polite about a ballcap is to remove it for dining and introductions, and when you are wearing it around others, make sure they can see your face, especially your eyes, when you speak.

Winter hats without brims (like beanies) do not need to be removed during an outdoor introduction. A hat with a brim should always be at least tipped when meeting someone new. Brims or no brims, hats are removed for the national anthem if they are not pinned to your head.

Chemo caps, hats, or scarves worn for any kind of temporary hair loss due to a treatment or condition never have to be removed. Nor do head coverings worn for religious purposes.

ON SUNGLASSES

Sunglasses can be a fashion statement, a favorite accessory, a health precaution, a security blanket, or quasi-jewelry. Unfortunately for interacting with others, they also cover our eyes. During conversation, and especially when being introduced, take your sunglasses off if you are able. Once you're inside, or when they are no longer needed to shield your eyes from the sun, check that they don't shield you from others. The courtesy is to take them off during introductions and in general if you are with others and don't need them. Whenever we can, we want people to be able to see our whole face and make eye contact if possible.

ON TIE KNOTS

Learning how to tie a tie (or a few different tie knots) is a life skill that can help you feel confident dressing for many different events in life, from formal functions to business scenarios and any time you might want to sharpen your look. The four knots that are great to know are the standard, the partial or half-Windsor, the Windsor, and the bow tie. Become familiar with these and you'll have nothing but options!

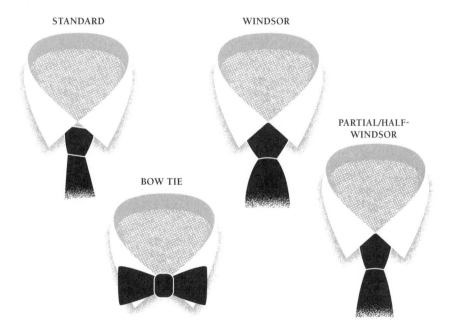

REFERENCE GUIDES

ATTIRE GUIDE

We dress our best by making sure the formality of our attire matches and respects the event we're attending. People of all genders can wear the following garb to events. Use this guide to determine what options are appropriate for the formality of event.

WHITE TIE	BLACK TIE	BLACK TIE CREATIVE/ FESTIVE	SEMI-FORMAL
White bow tie, black jacket with tails, matching trousers with a satin or braid stripe, plain front wing-collar French cuff shirt, stiff white vest, cuff links or studs, black or white braces, black socks, black formal (patent leather) pumps or black lace-up Oxfords	Black or midnight navy tuxedo jacket and trousers, wing- or regular-collar white formal shirt (fly or stud-front or pleated or bibbed front), black bow tie, braces or suspenders, vest (if you wear a vest, do not also wear a cummerbund), cuff links or studs, cummerbund (should match bow tie and lapel fabric), black socks, black formal (patent leather) pumps or black lace-up Oxfords	Same as black tie but with colors or elements added to spice it up a bit. For dresses and two-piece outfits it's the same as black tie but with more room to experiment with color, texture, and accessories	Suit and tie or jacket and slacks, buttoned shirt, belt, and dress shoes. Or more casual long dress (nicer than a casual maxi dress but more casual than a gown), formal cocktail at or below the knee; a dressy skirt and top or dressy top and pant outfit; and dress shoes
Or, a floor-length gown, possibly a *very* formal two-piece outfit, optional long gloves, formal shoes Rarely if ever would a dress pant and dress-top combo be worn for white tie	A white dinner jacket may be worn in the summer or in warm climates. Or floor-length gown (material and structure can be more casual than white tie but still usually very formal), a very formal cocktail dress—at or below the knee (no shorter), formal shoes		

BUSINESS	BUSINESS CASUAL	DRESSY CASUAL	CASUAL
Suit and tie, buttoned dress shirt, belt, dress shoes Dress slacks/trousers with dress top. Or more conservative dress or two-piece outfit (nothing too low cut, short, or luxurious in material or color); close-toed shoes if not in a fashion-forward industry	Suit (no tie) or seasonal coat with trousers, dress jeans (if allowed), button-down, polo, sweater, or open collar shirt, belt, socks, loafers or dress shoes Dress slacks/trousers with more casual top Dressy jeans and top or dress or skirt-and-top combo can run the gamut (nothing too short or low cut, even when casual); Ask first if open-toed shoes are okay	Jeans and sweater or casual buttoned shirt Dress pants and casual top Casual pants and dress top Dress or skirt-and-top combo that is comfortable; any shoes	Jeans, shorts, T-shirts, pullovers, hoodies, tank tops (as long as you're covered and clean, you're likely in good shape) Dress or skirt with any top (as long as you're not topless, you're good); any shoes

GROOMING AND HYGIENE CHECKLIST

- Hair clean and free of odor

- Face and body washed and smelling pleasant or free of odor

- Teeth brushed and flossed

- Hands washed, nails clean

- Facial hair intentionally groomed (don't forget ears, nose, and neck)

- Unwanted facial hair removed or kept in check

- Minimal scents for perfumes, colognes, and body sprays

Ask someone you trust to give you feedback on body and breath odor and errant or unwanted hair.

CHAPTER 5

Table Manners

"Elbows are universally seen on tables in restaurants, especially when people are lunching or dining at a small table of two or four, and it is impossible to make oneself heard above the music by one's table companions, and at the same time not be heard at other tables nearby, without leaning far forward . . . At home when there is no reason for leaning across the table, there is no reason for elbows . . . Elbows are *never* put on the table while one is eating. To sit with the left elbow propped on the table while eating with the right hand (unless one is all alone and ill), or to prop the right one on the table while lifting the fork or glass to the mouth, must be avoided."

Basic table manners are among the manners that change the least over time. Table manners are remarkably durable. The fork has been set on the left (save the oyster fork) for generations. Using your napkin to keep your face and hands clean while you dine is not new. And for as long as we've been writing about dining, opening your mouth while there is food in it is the definition of rude, whether you're at the table or not. Basic table manners can serve as a baseline minimum standard for civility, important in every culture around the world. We gather at the table not just for nourishment but also to enjoy food and each other's company. Table manners are the tools that let us do this without grossing each other out. And therein lies the most important advice about table manners: don't gross out others. Grossness is the litmus test for table manners.

Even when mastered, the fundamentally important skill of table manners can still be tricky. Difficult or never-before-eaten foods, high-pressure situations, all those utensils and courses . . . to cap it all off, we try to eat and talk without actually talking while we eat. It's wild! Yet when we are graceful and thoughtful with our manners at the table, we can be confident around others and are likely to come across as engaging, enjoyable company. Or maybe we are at a business luncheon, and because our table manners are smooth, the client's focus is entirely on our brilliant idea or perfect sales pitch.

Having polished and practiced table manners means we can dig into chicken wings or nachos or that giant burger casually but not disgustingly. We can of course relax our table manners at home when alone, and we can also pull out our best when on a date, at an awards dinner, or when impressing family. The quickest way to know if you have good or bad table manners—aside from someone telling you—is to use a mirror or record yourself eating and see if you'd like to dine with yourself.

For all the details and options there are when dining, table manners and the structure they provide are ultimately designed to make people feel comfortable and confident navigating a shared dining experience. Let's take a look at North American table manners.

TAKING A SEAT

You would think that sitting down wouldn't need much explanation. However, there are a few considerations. First, always sit at your host's invitation and never before. In a home, wait for your invitation to the table before taking your seat; at a restaurant, if it's not "seat yourself," wait for the host to bring you to the table. If you are serving yourself from a buffet at someone's home or at an event, you may sit down as soon as you've filled your plate. In the most formal of situations, everyone sits down simultaneously at the host's invitation. Your host might use place cards to assign each person a seat or, if place cards aren't set, you should ask: "Where would you like me to sit?" Take note, there is a tradition of standing for a lady when she approaches the table, or rising when she leaves. This custom is less common today, as most women will say something like, "Please, don't get up." While we see this tradition slowly disappearing, for those that would still like to practice it, we suggest taking gender out of it, and rising for anyone who approaches a table, or is going to leave it. Whenever possible you do still stand for introductions and more formal greeting.

HOLDING A CHAIR

If you are going to hold a chair for someone, ask first: "May I hold your chair?" or "May I get your chair for you?" Saying, "Here, let me get that for you" *assumes* the other person wants their chair held, which they might not. Ask the question rather than state the action. Holding a chair for a dining companion is something that, while traditionally discussed in relation to men helping women, does not need to be. A teen might hold her grandmother's chair. A young man might help a younger sibling. When done well, holding a chair for a romantic partner, to assist someone, or simply out of respect, is thoughtful.

To hold a chair, stand (if you aren't already) as the person approaches. Before they take hold of the chair, ask, "May I hold your chair?" (It's always "May I," not "Can I" or "Let me.") If they say, "Yes, please," stand to the left of their chair or behind it, and pull the chair back from the table about a foot (or more, if needed) allowing the person to get in front of their chair. As they sit, gently push the chair in behind them. Don't ram them at the knee, and definitely don't move too slowly; they might sit too quickly and catch the edge of the seat or, worse, fall. It sounds fraught, but it's quite easy and happens naturally in the moment.

Should the person say, "No, I'll get it, thank you," simply smile, give a nod, and sit back down. It might feel like a rejection, but, really, it's a sign of success. You did the right thing by asking. Even though the question was met with a "no," you achieved what you'd hoped: finding out what the other person preferred in the moment. That is the respectful thing when it comes to acts of chivalry.

Today, a point to remember regarding any chivalrous act is that the gesture is intended to both be helpful and show respect and awareness of another person. By offering to do something for someone, you leave them in control while at the same time honoring your desire to help. It's disrespectful not to honor someone's wishes when a chivalrous gesture is declined. If the act is unwelcome, then doing it would be offensive, which is definitely not the goal of good etiquette. Our gestures of respect might be different today from those of prior times, but they are still rooted in consideration for those around us and demonstrating respect.

NAVIGATING THE TABLE

The American table setting is well established. It might vary slightly from home to home and certainly in formality from occasion to occasion, but with some basic knowledge you should be able to set and navigate any place setting confidently.

THE STANDARDS

There are a few standards when it comes to the American place setting. The first is that you are provided with only the utensils you will need to use for the meal. The second is that each group of utensils will be placed in the order they are to be used, arranged from the outside of the setting in toward the plate. The third is that with the exception of the oyster fork, dessert fork, and dessert spoon, forks are always on the left and knives and spoons are always on the right, grouped together. Knives are placed next to the plate and spoons to the right of the knives. And, finally, the bread and butter plate is always on the top left and your drinks are always on the top right of the setting. (See Navigating Your Setting, page 173, for helpful ways to remember these standards.)

NAPKIN

As soon as you are seated, place your napkin in your lap. For many diners this is the moment the meal truly begins and it matters not whether the napkin is cloth or paper. Try to keep one side or area of your napkin clean so that if you do raise it to your mouth, you won't be showing a dirty napkin to everyone else or getting more mess on you. (For details about using linen napkins well, see Using Cloth Napkins, page 174.) Use your napkin as you need to throughout the meal, but avoid wadding it up in your fist and wiping your face as you would a child's. Instead, gather a small section of the napkin and dab or do a small wipe against a specific area. Should you have spilled a bit, you might first dab at your clothing or remove any food and then excuse yourself to the restroom to do damage control. Remember too that while your napkin is there to help keep you clean, if you are so messy (and it isn't because you're eating something messy like wings or whole crab) that you would basically coat a napkin with food smears, you might need a trip to the restroom to clean up. This is especially true when dining in someone's home and using their cloth or nice linen napkins.

If you have to leave the table, lay your napkin loosely or naturally folded to the left of your place setting, hiding any visible stains. You can use "LLL" to remember "Leaving Loosely Left." Do not be tempted to leave your napkin on the back of your chair, and especially not on the seat of your chair. If your napkin is messy, it could result in staining an upholstered dining chair or transferring the mess to your clothing when you return to your seat. While it may not happen every time, the chance is too great to risk. Despite what you may have heard, leaving your napkin on the back of your chair is not a signal that you are going to return to the table.

Typically, it's best never to pick up anything that has dropped onto the floor, and this includes your napkin. Bringing the floor up to the table is not considered hygienic or appealing to other diners. That being said, we live in a casual world where we are often dining with close friends and family in our homes. Under these circumstances and when you know it won't make others uncomfortable, go ahead and pick up your dropped napkin. If you are the one who would prefer not to use a dropped napkin, then simply get or ask your host for another. The more formal the occasion, the less you should feel inclined to pick up a dropped napkin. And when dining out, it's always acceptable to ask for a replacement of any dropped item.

If you're chewing something and realize you need to remove it, please do not put it in your napkin. Simply place it on the edge of your plate, covering the transfer action with your napkin. If this won't work for you, then it's truly best to excuse yourself to remove and dispose of the item. (See Removing Something from Your Mouth, page 168, for more on removing unwanted items.)

In Emily's day, there was much to be said about folding napkins and how many folds there should be based on the type of napkin and the meal it was being set for. Today, as long as the napkin looks clean and isn't taking up an absurd amount of space, it's fine to fold it however you wish. The folded end is always set closest to the plate, with the open end (if there is one) to the left. Folded and set this way, it's easy to use one hand to pick up and unfold your napkin all in one motion. However, other folding styles are just as lovely; think of the aesthetic of your setting and the formality of the meal to decide what fold to use. Occasionally, you will see a napkin placed in the center of the setting, usually on top of a charger or place plate and often in a napkin ring. While many restaurants place napkins in water glasses, we do not recommend it (too tippy!).

UTENSILS

Emily was responsible for encouraging that tables be set with only three courses' worth of utensils at a time, regardless of the number of courses planned. Beyond the ones set, other utensils were to be brought in per course as needed. This was a change from the seemingly endless courses— and utensils—presented in the Victorian era.

FORKS, used for piercing, holding, and scooping, are placed to the left of the setting in the order they are to be used, from the outside in. They can have three or four tines. The *dinner* or *entrée fork* is the largest. The *salad, first course,* or *luncheon fork* is smaller. There is also the *fish fork,* which often has a tine with a curved point to help pick out bones. This fork (along with the *luncheon* or *salad fork*) can also double as a *dessert fork.*

If salad is offered before the entrée, you'll see the salad fork set to the outside of the entrée fork. If served after, it is set inside or closer to the plate than the entrée fork. There are two fork placement exceptions: the *oyster fork* and the *dessert fork.* The oyster fork is very small. It has a curved bowl and three short tines, and is placed to the far right of the spoons. (While it's called an oyster fork, you see it used for small shellfish like mussels and shrimp as well.) The dessert fork, if it doesn't look like the fish fork, will be the size of a small, often wide-headed, salad fork. If placed out for the entire meal, it will be found at the top of the setting, above the plate, with its handle pointing left. Alternatively, it might be brought out with dessert.

KNIVES, used for cutting and sometimes pushing, are always placed directly to the right of the plate in the order of use and with their blades facing the plate. Margaret Visser, author of *The Rituals of Dinner,* goes into detail about how this is a less threatening placement than if the blades are facing outward, toward the other diners. The *entrée knife* is the largest; it may have a rounded or pointed tip. The *salad, first course,* or *luncheon knife* is usually smaller, with a rounded tip. The *fish knife* has a scalloped blade and a curved, pointed tip to pick out fine bones; the fat, flat blade slides nicely between the skin and the meat of the fish. The *butter knife,* small and with a rounded blade, is placed on the bread plate. If steak has been ordered or planned, a steak knife is used. Steak knives are large, with a pointed end and serrated blade, and might be offered by a host for any meat that requires a sturdier blade or precision cutting, regardless of whether it's served sliced or whole.

SPOONS, used for scooping, are found to the right of the knives. The *soup spoon* is largest and, hopefully, has a deep bowl. (A shallow soup spoon can often be frustrating.) The *dessert spoon,* if set out for the duration of the meal, is found above the plate and below the dessert fork, or in place of the dessert fork, its handle pointing right. If tea or coffee is being served, a *teaspoon* will be brought out with your cup and saucer. When serving demitasse (a small cup of espresso), a tiny *demitasse spoon* will be brought with the cup and saucer. If iced tea is served, you might be given a long *iced tea spoon* in your tall iced tea glass. Leave it in the glass, unless there is a saucer under the glass on which you can place the spoon. Alternatively, you could place the spoon on your bread plate, if you have one.

SPECIAL UTENSILS such as *escargot tongs* for holding snail shells, *grapefruit spoons* with serrated edges for citrus, lobster and crab *crackers* and *picks* are used for specific foods and either will be at your setting or will be brought out for the appropriate course. If hosting, place these items logically based on how they are used. Since escargot tongs would be held in the left hand, place them to the left of the forks. Crackers and picks might be placed at the top of the setting if it's crowded, or to the right of the knives and spoons.

PLATES AND BOWLS

For most meals we'll be dealing with just one plate, but it's helpful to know them all.

The **CHARGER** is a large plate that your other course plates will sit upon until the main course is served. Sometimes it's called a *place plate* because it holds the place of the entrée plate until the main course, when it is removed for the rest of the meal. The charger can act as a tray for the course before the main course, with both the course plate or bowl and the charger being removed at the same time. There are some times when the charger is simply used as decoration to help fill out the settings until the meal begins; in this case it is removed before the first course is served.

The **ENTRÉE PLATE** is the largest plate we eat from; most often our entire meal is served on it, or we are given an entrée plate at a buffet. Occasionally you'll be served the main dish on an entrée plate and side dishes on literal side dishes. Some entrées eaten with either a fork or spoon (or both) call for a *pasta bowl*, a broad shallow dish with higher sides than a standard plate (often used for pastas and dishes with either lots of sauce or thinner sauces or broths). A disadvantage to serving something that needs to be cut in a high-sided bowl is that it forces the diner to raise their elbows to cut their food, making for an awkward position and the potential to bump your neighbor. Avoid serving foods that need to be cut in a high-sided bowl. It should be noted that hosts (whether in a restaurant or home) should not serve meals in dishes that make it awkward for diners to eat. Do not sacrifice functionality and practicality for the sake of trend or aesthetic at the table.

The **SALAD, FIRST COURSE, LUNCHEON,** or **DESSERT PLATE** is a smaller plate placed on top of the charger, if it's being used, or directly on the table for a first course. Size can vary for all of these smaller plates. While some might be interchangeable, make sure the salad plate doesn't look too big if it's being used as a dessert plate.

A **SOUP BOWL** is usually large and can be deep or shallow. Cream soup or any broth containing pieces of vegetable or meat is eaten with a spoon. Broth-only soup may first be tasted with a spoon and then, if the bowl has two handles, held by the handles and sipped directly. (If you're being hosted, watch your host to see if they do this, and then follow suit, or use a spoon; if you are not being hosted, choose what's best based on the circumstances.)

The **DESSERT BOWL** is small, sometimes the size of a 1-cup measure. Or it can be shallow, perfect for pie and ice cream.

A **BREAD PLATE** is tiny, but it is not a saucer; it does not have a special lip or rise to hold a teacup as a saucer does. It looks just like a salad or entrée plate, but is much smaller in comparison. While you typically use it only for bread and butter, it can also double when dining out as a place to put any accumulated table mess from towelettes, sugar or seasoning packets, or creamer containers, until the server clears it away.

The **SAUCER** is meant only for holding a teacup. It is never used as a side dish, butter dish, or dessert dish—even in a pinch. The one exception is that it might be used under the small dish of a condiment to protect the table and hold the serving utensil. A bread plate could serve this function as well.

GLASSES GROUPED   GLASSES CASCADING

GLASSES

Glasses are always found to the upper right of the place setting and usually cascade out to the right of the setting at about a 45-degree angle off the tip of your largest knife going up and to the right. They are set in the order they will be used, from the outside in. If the table is a bit crowded, a host might have the glasses grouped instead of cascading down in a line (still at a 45-degree angle off the knife, but clustered together).

WATER GLASSES come in many shapes and sizes, but whether stemmed and footed like a goblet or straight sided, they are usually taller than a *rocks glass* or *tumbler,* which is typically shorter and wider. They are placed closest to the setting and they remain for the entire meal. Water may be sipped at any point during the meal.

ICED TEA GLASSES are very tall and slender, unless they are more goblet-shaped with a short stem and large bowl. When iced tea is served on a saucer, it allows for the spoon to be removed from the glass and can also prevent condensation from dripping down and collecting on the table or tablecloth.

PINT and **PILSNER** glasses are tall, 16-ounce glasses used for beer, hard ciders, water, and soft drinks. Pint glasses (not typically pilsner glasses) can be used as water glasses at the table, and you might be given one by a host if you ask for a nonalcoholic drink instead of wine. Pilsner glasses are used for beer; they look like a combination of a Champagne flute and a pint glass.

You may have two **WINEGLASSES**: the larger one for red wine and the smaller one for white. If you see two wineglasses, know that you're likely going to be offered more than one type of wine with the meal. A white wineglass can also be used for rosé and sparkling wine. Hold stemmed glasses by the stem, except for a red wineglass, which may also be held by the bowl in less formal situations.

CHAMPAGNE GLASSES are either *coupes* or *flutes*. The tall, narrow shape of the flute reduces the amount of liquid exposed to the air and will prevent the fizz from going flat, so it is often used for other sparkling beverages (like Prosecco or Cava) as well, though not hard ciders. The coupe is round and shallow; it's gorgeous in shape, but with more surface area exposed to the air, the bubbles dissolve faster. Don't feel you have to chug a coupe in order to enjoy the Champagne's effervescence, however. Never chug liquids at the table.

SHERRY GLASSES are very small and can also be used for many types of after-dinner drinks, from sherry to limoncello.

SHOT GLASSES are never set at the table, but might be brought out at the end of the meal for something like grappa or limoncello, or possibly a small amount of whiskey or scotch to sip on. (They are not used for shots at the table.) When they are brought out, they are set on a tray with the liquor bottle and glasses together.

A **BRANDY SNIFTER** is used for brandy, port, or other aromatic after-dinner drinks that like to breathe. It is not set for the whole meal, but brought out at the end.

The **COFFEE CUP** or **TEACUP** is a cup with a handle and a saucer, not a mug. It's more likely to be brought out when it is served than set out ahead of time, though some banquet services choose to set the coffee/teacup and saucer out for the entire meal.

COCKTAIL GLASSES won't usually be encountered at or brought to the table when dining in someone's home. *Tumblers*, *highballs*, *martini glasses*, or *beer glasses*, however, are more common to see at the table when dining out.

STEMLESS GLASSES are very popular, and come in different shapes for red, white, and sparkling wines. They are great because they lessen the chance for spillage, particularly at a crowded table. Hold stemless glasses for white or sparkling wine delicately, with your fingertips, so you don't warm up the wine.

EXTRAS

Below are some other items you might find at your place setting:

PLACE CARD. Often decorative and possibly in a cute or stylish holder, your place card has your name on it and indicates that you should, indeed, sit here. Not *there*. Here. It is the height of rudeness to move your place card to a different position.

SALT AND PEPPER. Sometimes you'll have your very own set of salt and pepper. If so, you'll notice that there is a set for everyone rather than just a pair for every four or six guests. Salt and pepper are typically passed together and kept together as a set at the table. Sometimes you'll see a salt well, where salt is served in a small dish with a little spoon. If the spoon is silver, you'll want to remember to not place it back in the salt, but alongside the well. The salt can ruin the silver if left on it too long.

FAVORS. At festive meals, you might find a little favor at the top of your setting. If it's a dessert item, like a chocolate or candies, wait to eat it until after the dessert has been served and eaten. If it's something fun like a popper, scratch ticket, or little toy, save playing with it for after the dessert has been eaten, or in the case of the poppers for when your host decides to start cracking them. You may also take these favors with you when you leave. If you don't want it, just leave it at the top of your setting.

WHEN TO BEGIN

When you are being hosted, there is only one rule: wait for everyone to be served and for your host to lift their fork as the signal that everyone else may, too. If your host directs you to begin before all have been served, then by all means begin! If there is no host, use your best judgment based on the number of people and the nature of the meal, or what you know about the people with whom you're dining. At Post family gatherings (going back even to Emily's dinner table), we always say, "Please begin while it's hot," with the idea that making a guest wait and letting their food get cold is completely unnecessary and even a bit inconsiderate. Remember to taste your food before you season it. Seasoning before tasting is very assumptive, as it can be perceived as a negative comment on the quality of the food, or worse, you could end up ruining a dish by overseasoning it.

Your day-to-day dining experiences will vary greatly, and so too will the answer to the question of when to begin. When you're with friends at a restaurant for a quick bite between classes or meetings, you're likely going to eat as soon as you sit or get your food, since time is limited.

And you might even leave before others are finished. When you're at someone's home for dinner, you may have to wait until everyone is seated and served and grace is said before you begin, depending on the household traditions. At an event with buffet service but with assigned seating, wait until at least three people at your table have sat down with their food before you begin. At a large banquet where you're flying solo and there is no assigned seating, you may choose to eat once you're seated, since you don't know if anyone else will be sitting with you.

If you're dining out with a large table of family members, they might say, "Start as soon you're served!" but if you wish you may decide to wait until everyone else has been served, or maybe just your end of the table.

SAYING GRACE AND MAKING TOASTS

Saying grace, offering a blessing, or taking a moment to reflect before we eat is very common, even if not everyone observes it at every meal. If you would like to participate in holding hands, speaking, or saying grace before a meal, you should feel confident in doing so (though do not chime in or follow up someone else's grace unless invited to speak). If people are offering their gratitude or intentions, take your turn as they go around the table, if you wish.

If you are the only one who would like to observe a moment before eating, it's perfectly acceptable to take a moment quietly for yourself at the start. Avoid imposing on others. Alternatively, if you do not wish to participate in grace, a blessing, or a pause for reflection, sit patiently while the rest of the table engages. It's important in this case to wait to begin eating until everyone is ready.

Toasts are often given at the start of a meal, but can happen at any point (although smack in the middle of a course is a little odd). The most common time to toast is once everyone is seated but before the meal begins. However, it's never inconsiderate to let folks tuck in for a bit, or even to wait for a moment between courses. Also common is during the transition into dessert or after dessert. You may toast with *any beverage* in your glass—just as long as it isn't empty! Ginger ale and sparkling cider make nice substitutions for Champagne, a very classic formal toasting drink. Water is also perfectly acceptable.

When you are offering a toast, stand if you can, raise your glass, and say what you wish. The very *best* toasts are short and, let's face it, often sentimental. In longer toasts you might tell a story or make a certain point. Always stay focused on the honoree or close to the point of the toast. Remember, people may be waiting to eat, so don't prolong it too much. At the end, raise your glass and say, "To _____!" (love, prosperity, Garret and Sue, family . . .) and then take a sip. Do not drain your glass. And definitely do not slam the glass down afterward.

If someone is toasting you, *do not drink to the toast.* Nod or smile in thanks. You may also offer a toast of thanks in return and drink to that. Or you may simply raise your glass in thanks after everyone has had a sip in your honor and then after this take a sip yourself. Many people mistakenly drink to a toast being offered to them. And even though it is technically wrong, rest assured that this is unlikely to be noticed today.

HOLDING UTENSILS

If we accept the idea that eating can be a difficult task, then an approach to doing it that is controlled, precise, and well tested is advisable. There is a difference between a fist clasped around a utensil plunged into a piece of food as though stabbed, and a precision grip used to maneuver the food with dexterity. Holding your utensils properly gives you control over both your implements and your food. Hold your knife in your dominant hand and your fork in your other hand. When used alone without a knife, your fork is held in your dominant hand. (See Using Utensils, page 150.)

When cutting, hold the fork tines down, with the handle in the palm of your hand. Close your middle, ring, and pinky fingers around the handle of the fork. Place your index finger on the back of the handle, just above where the head and handle join. Use your thumb to securely grasp the fork. Hold your knife the same way (with the blade down), but always in your more dominant hand, because it is the most dangerous utensil and you want full control over it.

When using a fork or spoon to scoop something, hold it in your dominant hand and adjust your grip so the tines or bowl are facing up. The handle rests on top of the perlicue of your hand (the curved space between your thumb and index finger). Your middle finger is under the neck of the spoon (where the bowl and handle join). Your index finger rests on top of this same spot and the thumb rests naturally on the side or top of the spoon's handle to balance. The ring and pinky fingers support the middle finger by resting under it. It's a similar grip to how many people hold a pen or pencil.

USING UTENSILS

CUTTING. For both *European (Continental)* and *American* dining styles, when cutting you hold your utensils the same way, with the knife in your dominant hand and the fork in your other hand. Use the fork to pin the item down and the knife to cut or slice it. Always keep your elbows in while cutting—you don't want to bump your neighbor, and having your elbows out (like they are wings) can look like you need to gain leverage on the food and is less elegant. One advantage of the grip suggested in Holding Utensils, page 149, is that it allows you to exert more precise pressure with your fork onto the item you're cutting. Don't press too hard, lest you send the item you're piercing skidding off the plate—and possibly into the lap of another diner. "I'm terribly sorry, could you please pass me back my chicken?" is not a sentence you want to have to utter at the table (nor would it be the thing to do). The side of your fork may also be used to cut or slice something when you are not using a knife, such as a soft lasagna or a scalloped potato dish.

It is refined table manners to always set your knife down in the resting position when you are not using it for cutting. For a right-handed diner, this would be the top right side of your plate, where it is out of your way.

AMERICAN-STYLE EATING. After you cut a piece of food, you lay your knife across the top right side of your plate, with the blade facing you. Then transfer your fork to your dominant hand, turned tines up, so you can eat the piece you just cut. When it's time to cut again, you then transfer your fork back to your other hand, tines down, and pick up your knife in your dominant hand. Generally, you keep your fork in your dominant hand to pierce or to scoop food when not cutting. To rest your utensils, leave your knife across the top of your plate with its handle to the right. Rest your fork with the handle at the four and the tines (up) pointing toward the ten. This tells a server you aren't finished yet. If your left hand is your dominant hand, the rest position for your utensils will be reversed.

CONTINENTAL (EUROPEAN)-STYLE EATING. Your knife remains in your dominant hand and your fork in the other, tines down, throughout the meal. You pierce each bite of food with your fork and bring it to your mouth, or, in the case of something like mashed potatoes, use your knife to push a small portion onto the back of your fork. To rest your utensils, in the Continental style, place the fork (tines up) and knife (each from your respective left and right hands) on the upper left and right sides of the plate with their handles facing out.

Either the American or Continental eating style may be used, and you might even choose to switch between the two during the same course in a hybridized style. While you should not switch styles when you are visiting Europe, at most American tables it would likely go unnoticed.

You can use your knife as a "pusher" to help transfer a bite onto your fork. This is a necessary move, like when using your knife to push a last bit of stuffing and mashed potatoes onto your fork as you finish Thanksgiving dinner. Should you need to pierce something round and roll-y, like a cherry tomato or olive, use your knife to brace the item and then pierce it carefully with your fork, going against the pressure of the knife to keep the item from rolling. Once pierced, a cherry tomato can be tamed by slicing it in half before eating it, ensuring that no seeds go squirting out of your lips. Never pierce anything with the tip of your knife. You also want to avoid gesturing with your utensils. Set them down to gesture with your hands in conversation.

The fork and spoon are both used for scooping. Scoop up and under the item and away from yourself. This helps prevent any sauce or oil splashes from hitting you. Don't scoop too big a bite. Getting into a balancing act with the food on your fork or spoon is rarely going to end well, especially if you rush to catch a falling bite.

Do not scrape or lick food off your utensils—and certainly not off the plate! If you want to get every last morsel of flavor and join the clean plate club, you can use a piece of bread to sop up the last of the sauce. Break off a piece, spear it with your fork, use it to soak up the last bits of deliciousness, and enjoy. Don't use your teeth on utensils; the sound can irritate fellow diners. Close your lips around the utensil when you remove it from your mouth to contain the yummy food you desire.

A rule that applies to both American and Continental dining styles is that once a utensil has been used, even if only to butter bread, place the utensil on a plate. Do not place it back down on the table surface.

FINISHED POSITION. When you are finished eating for a course, set your utensils down so that both the fork and knife handles are pointed at four o'clock and the fork tines (up) and knife tip point to ten o'clock. A spoon is placed on the right side of the underplate when finished. If there is no underplate, leave it in the bowl, handle positioned like a fork. This tells your server you are finished with the course and makes it easy for them to clear your plate.

AMERICAN
RESTING POSITION

EUROPEAN/CONTINENTAL
RESTING POSITION

FINISHED
POSITION

COURSES

Casual dining may consist of anywhere from one to three courses, whereas semiformal occasions can range from three to five courses and formal occasions could have anywhere from three to six courses served. Very few at-home dinners are six-course, gourmet meals these days—though some might like to attempt the challenge! (We salute you.) Whether you are dining out, at someone's home, or choosing a menu to serve, the following are the courses you may encounter.

HORS D'OEUVRES

Hors d'oeuvre is French for "out of the work," but translates to "outside the meal." It is generally a one- or two-bite item that's served prior to a meal. Hors d'oeuvres can be passed by a server or set for guests to serve themselves. That said, we've seen parties (especially cocktail parties) that have hors d'oeuvres only; in such cases, they tend to be enough to leave guests feeling sated. Here in the United States, we tend to serve hors d'oeuvres either passed or as a buffet.

For smaller parties, hors d'oeuvres are often served during the cocktail hour wherever guests are gathering. A host will typically serve a few hors d'oeuvres, but certainly could make just one offering—crudités or cheese and crackers, for example. (A small bowl of peanuts or potato chips doesn't really count as an hors d'oeuvre; think of those as little "nibbles.")

American hosts tend to extend the interpretation of hors d'oeuvres beyond one or two bites—platters of crudités, shrimp cocktail, satay or caprese skewers, chips of all kinds with dips, bowls of spiced and sugared nuts, cheese and charcuterie boards are all regularly seen in American living rooms and on kitchen islands, porches, and patios for guests to enjoy before dinner. Remember to use the cocktail napkins, picks, and discard dishes provided, and whatever you're eating, do not double dip. Not even by turning that carrot around.

AMUSE-BOUCHE

Amuse-bouche is French for "to amuse the mouth." It's like a tickle, or a little tease into the meal. It's a sexy little course, usually just one bite, and it's meant to delight, prepare, and leave you wanting more. It's normally saved for meals with four or more courses (it being the first) and is served at the table, unlike its close cousin, the hors d'oeuvre, which is served during the cocktail hour and sometimes as the main event. Often it is sent out by the chef, and not something you will choose or see on your bill. Typically, you see this course served at a high-end restaurant, not in someone's home.

APPETIZER

Sometimes called *antipasti,* sometimes the *starter* or *first course,* the appetizer is usually our first plated menu item. It can be heavy or light, hot or cold, but it should balance and work with the other courses. A lighter entrée would allow for a heavier first course, and vice versa. While soups and salads can be courses on their own, separate from an appetizer, many people choose to serve (or order) either dish as an appetizer. These small plates might also be anything from spring rolls with a dipping sauce to crostini with thick spreads or an assortment of meats, fruits, and cheeses. They might be eaten with the fingers in more casual settings, but for anything even remotely semiformal they will likely be eaten with a fork and knife or a spoon (or specialty utensils). When dining out, it's fine from an etiquette perspective to choose an appetizer as your entrée, but double-check with the waitstaff that it's okay to do so.

SOUP AND SALAD

No secret codes here—these courses are exactly as they sound. Soup is usually served early in the meal, as opposed to after an entrée, whereas salad can be eaten either before or after an entrée. You may find an etiquette fanatic or foodie who will debate the merits of the "French" style (salad after the entrée) versus the "American" style (salad before the entrée). It's a matter of personal preference. Our view is that salad is lovely, whether you eat it before or after the entrée.

FISH

The fish course is often skipped nowadays, which is a shame because there are so many wonderful fish dishes. A lighter protein, it used to regularly be served as its own course before a meat entrée. Today shellfish often ends up being served as an appetizer, such as oysters, shrimp cocktail, or clams casino. Of course, fish may be served as an entrée as well, though you should avoid serving it as both an appetizer or fish course *and* entrée unless there is a theme to the meal that would require it. Fish is often served with specialty utensils, whether crackers or picks or a fish fork and fish knife. A discard bowl should be provided for items like bones, heads, tails, or shells.

ENTRÉE

This is the one course you are definitely going to serve at your dinner party or likely order when you're dining out. Sometimes called the *main course,* this is the most filling course, and often consists of some type of meat or protein-heavy item served with one to two side dishes, or a one-pot dish (such as shepherd's pie). You may of course also serve no meat, or multiple proteins (like surf 'n' turf). Entrée portions can be smaller when numerous courses are served. If you're serving only the entrée course, be sure to make enough so that guests can get their fill.

COFFEE, DESSERT, AND AFTER-DINNER DRINKS

While you don't have to serve coffee and dessert together, they often pair nicely. Dessert might range from fruit or cookies to pies, cakes, tarts, truffles or chocolates, pastries, and all manner of puddings, trifles, and ice creams or sorbets. Anything that is either sweet or fresh is usually a wonderful cap to a meal.

Espresso, cappuccino, macchiato, regular drip coffee, decaf coffee, and tea or infusions are all options for after dinner. Though not traditionally served after dinner, tea is becoming a more common after-dinner option, especially herbal varieties. When serving coffee, be sure to include options such as sugar, sugar substitutes, cream, milk, and a nondairy milk such as cashew, almond, or oat milk. While this is often a more relaxed time, don't forget that table manners still matter, and taking care to not make a mess or take more than a reasonable share from the sugar or creamers offered is thoughtful. Sometimes, even when you plan to serve them separately, a guest might ask for coffee with their dessert if none is present.

After-dinner drinks, like port, sherry, and brandy, are always options to serve and can add a distinctive touch to a fine dinner party at home or evening out.

DRINKING PROPERLY

Drinking properly is simple, and we've being doing it—usually pretty well—since we were little, after being discouraged from blowing bubbles in our drinks or chugging, gulping, or guzzling them down—and certainly from ever spitting them out. Nor do we slurp or lick up the last drop, and we never upend our glass while throwing our head back. In short, anything you've seen at a college kegger (or a movie version of one) is not the way to behave in polite company, which is to say anywhere but a college kegger. Beverages are not there to wash your food down with haste: always chew and swallow and wipe your mouth with your napkin if necessary.

Mrs. Five O. Cloque-Sumware *sips* her drinks, be they hot or cold; she never guzzles them. When drinking from a straw, she avoids making loud noises when she reaches the end of her drink. She also resists the temptation to suck down her beverage in one long, slow draw, never letting the straw leave her lips. Instead, she takes smallish sips and engages in conversation in between. She knows it's not a race.

Unless you're at a backyard barbecue, tailgate party, clambake, seafood boil, or other casual outdoor party, it's best not to bring a bottle, can, or juice box to the table. Instead pour your drink into a glass or leave it behind and take what's being served with the meal.

When you're having cocktails in someone's home, always remember to look for a coaster or cocktail napkin to put under your drink when you set it down. If you don't see one, ask if the host has any.

When drinking coffee or tea from a cup with a handle (not a mug), whatever you do, *please* do not put your pinky out like a little flag. It is the biggest misconception in the world of etiquette that affectations like this are proper. (And no, you do not need your pinkie out to "balance the cup.") Hold the handle, tuck your fingers under, and you'll be fine.

PACING YOURSELF

Paying attention to the pace at which you eat while dining with others is considerate. This is not to suggest that you match your host or others at the table bite for bite. But showing basic consideration for your fellow diners means avoiding either wolfing your food down or eating so slowly that the other diners are left waiting (a long time) for you to finish before they can move on to the next course or finish the meal. Here are some tips for helping slow down or speed up your eating.

TO SLOW DOWN	TO SPEED UP
Chew and swallow each bite before preparing the next.	Prepare the next bite while you chew.
Take the time to talk between bites.	Eat while you listen to others talk.
Periodically set your utensils down.	Stop talking and focus on eating.

If you are trying to speed up your eating, avoid rushing. Overloading a forkful might clear your plate faster, but it's likely to be messier and harder for you to manage. You might finish more quickly, but it may push you past the point of being an appealing dining partner.

PARTICULAR MANNERS FOR PARTICULAR FOODS

There are many categories of food that require us to use our utensils in particular ways, or that have common pitfalls. Below are some of the classics.

BREAD AND BUTTER

Mr. Grayson Eleganz is adept at eating bread well at a meal. He knows it's okay to begin eating his bread when he's out to eat, after everyone's placed their order but before the food arrives. In someone's home he waits for his host to invite him to begin before tucking into his roll or asking for someone to "Please pass the bread basket." He breaks his bread with his fingers—never with a knife, and never rips straight from the roll or loaf with his teeth. No. He takes his roll or slice, holds it down near his plate, where crumbs will be contained, and tears off a small piece (or about one to three bites' worth). He is careful to serve himself using the butter knife that comes with the butter dish to place a pat on his bread plate, and then to switch to his own knife to butter his bread. Mr. Eleganz then takes his butter knife with a smattering of butter and, holding the bread against the plate, spreads a small amount on his bite-sized piece. Then he pops it in his mouth. He never makes a butter sandwich at the table with others, or breaks up the entire roll into bite-size pieces all at once.

This bread-breaking method works great for shared seasoned oil, too. By breaking off bite-size pieces and dipping them one at a time into the oil, nothing that touches your mouth goes back into the shared oil. You could also pour or spoon the seasoned oil for yourself onto your bread plate and use your own "well."

If there is a bread basket, take a roll and pass the basket to the right. Avoid picking out the piece you want by moving the rolls around. And definitely touch only the bread that you will be taking and eating.

If there is a whole loaf, it is often served with a napkin or cloth around one end. This is to hold the bread while either cutting or tearing off your share so that you don't put your hands on bread that others will eat. Try to take a small piece to start, and then if there's enough, take more. You want to make sure everyone has a decent slice of the loaf. It is acceptable to slice several pieces to make it easier for your dinner companions who take bread after you.

SALAD

Traditionally, the "rule" was to never cut your salad, because the metal on your knife was likely to react with the (often) vinegar-based dressing and ruin the knife. Today we rarely face this problem, so the rule no longer applies. It is okay to cut away—especially something like a wedge or whole-leaf romaine Caesar salad. Usually a salad needs only a few quick cuts to reduce the size of any large lettuce leaves, meat, or vegetables and make them manageable with a fork alone, or by using a knife as a pusher (see Using Utensils, page 150).

If you're dining out and you haven't been provided with a salad knife, it's okay to use your dinner knife for any items that are too big. If you're at a restaurant when you do this, you can always ask for another knife when it's time for the entrée. When dining at a host's home, for a more casual meal or dinner party, you might not be given a salad knife. In a casual setting, if any items are too big, it's okay to use your entrée knife to cut them and then set it on your bread plate when the salad course is cleared. Your host will either notice and give you a fresh knife, or let it be since they may not have a replacement to offer. For a more formal setting, a salad knife will usually be provided, but in the rare case it isn't and an item is too big, just leave it be and eat the rest of the dish.

When dressing your own salad at the table or buffet, it's fine to use the dressing liberally, but remember that wet lettuce leaves and thinly cut veggies can quickly get messy. Think about how easy it will be to manage the salad without getting messy before dressing it.

SOUP

From brothy wonders that heal our souls when we're sick to hearty, deeply flavored stews that are almost like a plate of food in a bowl and everything in between, soups can be tricky. There is the splashing and dripping, sure, but also how hot they are, how well you can keep them on your spoon, managing the chunks, or noodles, and of course the desire to slurp.

When taking a spoonful of your soup, scoop your spoon *away* from you. Then, gently touch the bottom of the bowl of the spoon to the far edge of the soup bowl to encourage any emerging drips to drop where they are contained, or hopefully just drip down the inside of the bowl. One of the biggest mistakes people make when eating soup is to eat it too quickly. That's often when the splashing and dripping occur. Go slowly and scoop away from yourself and you'll catch your drips.

If you want to get that final spoonful, it's all right to tip your bowl away from you slightly to scoop the last mouthful. Tipping away is important, so that if the bowl slips, it doesn't go right into your lap. Remember this phrase: *scoop away, drip away, tip away.*

Some soups will come with an accoutrement, like Vietnamese phō, which is often served with Thai basil, lime, bean sprouts, and a spicy sauce on the side, or the classic New England clam chowder, which is served with oyster crackers (croutons are another common soup addition). These extras are offered as suggestions, so feel free to add them as you like. Other soups might contain seafood shells that will be discarded either into a discard bowl or onto an underplate.

French onion soup, with its top of perfectly melted Gruyere cheese, might require you to stretch a small amount of cheese out from the bowl and cut it from the soup by using the edge of your spoon against the edge of your bowl, or you may need to use a knife for this maneuver. Winding the cheese around and around your spoon could get awfully comical (generally not our goal at the table and certainly not during a formal dining experience).

Typically, if a bowl of soup has handles, it can be picked up and sipped straight from the bowl. However, this is a fairly uncommon custom today in the United States. A miso soup bowl is an exception—it often has no handles and yet is sipped.

SANDWICHES

Sandwiches may be delicate and neat, served with tea, or messy and loaded with the works as we casually chow them down. Sandwiches—especially the latter kind—do not make for smart choices when at a business meal, unless the place you're dining at is known for its big messy sandwiches and that's the point of eating there.

Hold your sandwich not in the middle, but closer to the end you aren't biting from as you bring it to your mouth. This will help keep all the good bits inside and prevent them from squishing out the back edge. So will starting from the corners. Take one bite at a time, chew, and swallow. Gnashing two or three bites as you rip them away from the sandwich is not appealing.

Rather than tucking your napkin into your shirt collar, lean in over your plate when eating a sandwich—not down and hunched over it, but up over the plate. Depending on the company you are with, you might need to cut your sandwich into a manageable size before biting into it. An open-faced sandwich is always eaten with a fork and knife. It is perfectly fine to use the last bites of bread to soak up any sauces or spreads from the plate.

DIG-IN FOODS

While some sandwiches would certainly count as a meal we'd "dig into," the following foods require us to think beyond the traditional fork, knife, and spoon.

ON THE BONE

Some meats served on the bone, or "bone-in," are eaten by holding the item with your fingers when among friendly company, or at the suggestion of your host—or, of course, at a rib- or wing-type joint when gloves, bibs, and wet wipes might be provided. When you have not been given the go-ahead and the occasion is more formal, you will want to do your best to use your fork and knife to remove the meat from the bone and slice it. Bone-in items that are always eaten with a fork and knife include steaks (like a T-bone), pork chops, small poultry or fowl, and fish. Lamb chops and chicken legs are usually eaten with a fork and knife, but don't be surprised if your host suggests that you nibble the bone. This doesn't mean picking up the lamb chop and eating it from the bone to start with, but instead picking it up to nibble the last of the meat, which is too hard to reach with a fork and knife. But again, do this only if your host suggests it.

Fish might be presented to you whole and then taken away to be deboned, or it might be served for you to handle. At a restaurant, it's fine to ask your server to take it to the kitchen to prepare it for you. At home, most hosts will serve fillets or steaks rather than a whole fish to keep things simpler for guests. If you do happen to encounter a whole fish on your plate, you'll be given a fish knife and fork to make the job easier. Don't feel shy about asking your server for any tips for how to debone it.

To debone a fish, start by inserting your knife into the fish's back (near the head on the top of the spine) using your fork to hold the rest of the fish steady. As the blade enters the fish, feel for the spine and the rib bones connected to it—you'll be under the fillet but on top of these bones. Keep the blade on top of the rib bones, flat against them, and gently slice from the backbone down along the rest of the rib bone to the belly. Lift the fillet off the fish. Using your fork and knife, flip the fish over and repeat the procedure. Then use the edge of the fish knife to check for any small bones, especially around the belly area of the fillet, and remove them—this is where that little curved point on the knife and fork come in handy. Hopefully, there will be a side plate for the parts you won't be eating.

FROM THE SHELL

Shellfish, such as lobster, oysters, shrimp, crab, crawfish, clams, and mussels, might be served from the shell or have part of the shell still attached (think shrimp cocktail tails). Whether you're at a lobster, crawfish, or shrimp boil, crab fest, or clambake—or just your own dinner table—there are special tools to help you eat crustaceans.

Crackers help to break through tough shells like claws. This is a time when it's fine to wear a bib or use your napkin as one. We should note that at a formal occasion, you would never be asked to crack your own claws; you should be able to eat the shellfish presented with a fork, either a regular one or an oyster fork. Do your best not to launch pieces of shell and meat across the table, or frankly around the room, as you dig out the sweet meat. Picks help to get meat out from small areas like knuckles, legs, and claws.

At a seafood boil or bake, you're going to be encouraged to eat with your hands and get messy, dipping the meat in sauces or lemon butter and sucking the heads of things like crawfish, whereas at a restaurant or as a guest in someone's home, the goal is to get the meat out as easily and cleanly as possible. And to dip it (not drench it) in any sauces offered.

Use the oyster fork for clams, mussels, and oysters served at the table. You may have to use your fingers to gently hold the shell while you remove the meat with your fork. The idea is that you don't eat directly from the shell. The fish should be served in a way that makes it easy to eat with your utensil.

Do use the discard bowl provided for any shells. It helps keep the mess contained and leaves more room on your plate for the food you can eat.

THE CHARCUTERIE BOARD

Whether at home or out to eat, a charcuterie board is a delight. Meats, cheeses, nuts, fruits, crispy crackers, all textures and flavors of spreads—it's mouthwatering to think about the combinations, and everyone loves to pick and choose their favorites and try new things. Because a charcuterie board is usually shared when dining out and at more formal occasions, it's best to take a few items using the serving utensils provided, and put them on your plate. Pay attention to your portions, taking only your "fair share" or roughly thereabout. Take less at first; you can usually go back for more. For cheese that is unsliced, don't hold it down with one hand while slicing it with the other. Instead use a (clean) fork if you need to steady it. Meats and fruits may be cut if needed to make sharing them easier, or to allow everyone to have a bite of each item. Don't get too precious about the board. While the goal is to not touch anything you won't be eating, and to not take more than your share, you also don't want to be the person watching the board like a hawk ready to pounce if someone double dips or takes the last slice of Manchego cheese. Relax and enjoy.

FORK OR FINGERS?

There are plenty of foods that can be appropriately eaten with both a fork and your fingers, but it all depends on where, when, and how. Look for what utensils are set out; they could provide a clue as to how you might proceed. French fries served at a fast-food joint and eaten among family and friends can be eaten with your fingers and more than one at a time, and there's little reason to fret about drenching them in ketchup or vinegar. Whereas fries served as part of *steak frites,* where there is juice from the steak and likely a little demi-glace or mayonnaise, are best eaten with a fork and knife, usually cutting the fries to make them more manageable. Poutine and chili cheese or gravy fries are also best eaten with a fork. Pizza is usually a finger food in America, but you might find in some restaurants that you feel more comfortable tackling a flatbread or a deep-dish pizza with a fork and knife. If it's at all a step above casual, consider a fork and knife. This is also true for a pizza with a very thin crust, especially when eating near the center of the pie, which may simply be too floppy to pick up by hand. Barbecued chicken at a barbecue or cookout and when served on the bone is eaten with the fingers, but when served at a more formal dinner table or in a restaurant that is even the slightest step up from super casual, it should be eaten with a fork.

Some foods you'll start with your fingers and then switch to a fork, like when eating tacos at the table. You'll use your hands for the taco but your fork for all the items that have spilled onto your plate.

There are plenty of times when we are choosing from a harvest table, buffet, or platter of hors d'oeuvres, and we use our fingers and go back for more. It's so important to be hygienic in these cases. Touch only the food you intend to eat, and if serving utensils are provided, use them. Double dipping (which includes dipping one end, then the other), picking something up and then setting it back down on the tray or platter, and not using a serving utensil are all habits to avoid. Take the food closest to you when possible, and avoid reaching over shared platters or dishes if you can. Note: If serving utensils aren't provided, ask for some.

DESSERT FORK OR SPOON?

There are times when you will be given both a dessert fork and a spoon, and it's up to you which you use for what. Hosts, take note: this is why it's nice to offer both when serving something like cake or pie with ice cream.

Anything that requires more of a bite gets a fork, and anything liquid, pudding-like, or that melts in your mouth is likely better handled with a spoon. Pick the utensil that works best for you.

There are a few times when you'd use two utensils at the same time during a dessert course. For example, poached pears are served with a spoon and fork, which you use by holding the pear with the fork and using the spoon to scoop out bite-size pieces. Being offered uncooked fruit is rare, but a potential time when you might see a dessert fork and knife. It takes some practice, but you can quarter and core (and the very skilled can skin) stone fruits or apples or pears well with utensils.

When dining out, someone will often make a suggestion to share dessert. This is best done with close friends and family and avoided at business meals. Like sharing any communal dish, use your own fork or spoon, and eat out of the side closest to you. Take a portion reasonable to the number of people sharing. If you aren't as intimate a group, ask for separate plates and divide up the dessert.

COFFEE AND TEA

The rituals for drinking coffee and tea are old and refined and vary by culture and personal taste. The science and lore behind the serving and enjoying of these beverages could fill a whole book. There are also some relatively common expectations that are worth considering.

The casual version of coffee and tea is sitting with a friend in your kitchen, drinking from mugs. If your host hasn't offered them, it's fine to ask for lemon, sweeteners, or a milk that you might like to add.

For coffee or tea offered after a meal or during a party, your host should provide all the above options. If you don't see a milk or sweetener alternative, it's fine to ask about it, but remember that this isn't a restaurant setting; you are not placing an order. Prepare your coffee or tea as you would like using the teaspoon or demitasse spoon provided (avoid hitting the inside of your cup with the spoon when stirring, as it is noisy and unnecessary), and set it down on the saucer when not stirring.

You shouldn't have to worry about empty sweetener packets or creamer cups at someone's home, but when dining out at casual restaurants, these are problematic. Where on earth do you put them? They are essentially table garbage. When dining out at casual restaurants, the easiest thing to do is to set the trash on the side of your saucer. But many restaurants use only mugs. If you don't have a plate of finished food to place the garbage on, do your best to make a neat little pile of the items. If you've been served a tea bag, once it's finished steeping, remove it (avoid squeezing it out) and set it on a saucer or a small plate your waiter or host should have provided. If they haven't provided anything, ask for something to set the tea bag on. A spoon is a poor solution, as often there is more liquid left in the tea bag than the spoon can hold.

While no drinks should be guzzled or gulped, tea and coffee in particular are meant to be sipped. Not only are they hot, but draining one's teacup has never been appealing to watch. Hold the teacup or coffee cup by its handle, not cupped from underneath or with your pinky sticking out.

If you're having afternoon tea or a tea service and are treated to tea with cakes, sandwiches, or other nibbles, it's fine to help yourself to what you've been offered. Remember not to overload your plate; you can always go back for more.

PASSING AND SERVING YOURSELF AT THE TABLE

In the 1922 edition of *Etiquette,* Emily noted that "Dishes are *never* passed from hand to hand at a dinner, not even at the smallest and most informal one. Sometimes people pass salted nuts to each other, or an extra sweet from a dish near by [sic], but not circling the table." Today, while individual food items are still not passed hand to hand around the table, dishes are often passed when dining "family style" because few of us have staff or servers to do it for us. (Some households avoid the issue—and a cluttered table—by using a buffet style of service even for casual family meals.) It is easier to pass dishes in one direction, as it prevents a diner from ending up with dishes coming at them from both sides. For many right-handed diners (the majority at any given table), it's easier if dishes are passed from the left to the right. The person passing the dish is in a good position to hold the dish for the person receiving it, if that's helpful, or to place it on the next person's left or simply pass it to them if it's light enough for them to hold and serve themselves at the same time. A thoughtful dinner companion will always offer to hold a dish for someone else.

Passing from the left to the right allows for you to reach across your body with your right hand to serve yourself (rather than using your left arm, which would end up in a tight spot between the dish, being held for you to your left, and your body). While this practice does favor the right-handed, passing to the right also follows the "leave left, retrieve right" standard. (See Entertaining at Home, page 292.)

When taking a serving, it's best to estimate how many people still need to serve themselves and what an even portion might look like. It's a guess that happens in milliseconds. Note that the size of the serving implement you have might not be the same as the size portion you should take. Start small, and if you'd like more, ask if there is enough for seconds after everyone has had a chance to serve themselves.

If you do not care for an item, we suggest that you take a "no thank you" portion. This is a small amount—only a bite or two—that allows you to try the item. If you don't care for it, you haven't wasted a lot of it, and if it turns out to be prepared in a way you do like, then you can be excited to finally enjoy Brussels sprouts, salmon, mushrooms, or whatever it is. (It should be noted that this advice does not apply to items you may be allergic to or are prevented from eating due to dietary restrictions.)

THE DEAL BREAKER

The number-one dining deal breaker, the one thing that first dates, businesspeople, and mothers-in-law anywhere will tell you they will write someone off for, isn't an outburst or even swearing at the table. It's chewing with your mouth open or talking with your mouth full. Showing or—even worse—showering people with the food that you are masticating is absolutely gross, and the number-one rule of dining is to not gross out others at the table.

This rule cannot be stated enough: if you are physically able to close your lips and still be able to breathe while chewing, then it is an absolute must. If someone tries to talk to you while your mouth is full, signal with your index finger that you'll be just a moment while you chew and swallow. In more casual settings, you might cover your mouth with your hand or napkin and say (carefully, without releasing any food), "One sec," or "Pardon me."

THINGS NOT TO DO
AT THE TABLE

There are *lots* of things we shouldn't do at the table. Here are some of the most common table manners mistakes and how to avoid them.

INTERRUPTING SOMEONE DURING TABLE CONVERSATION. At the very most, issue an "Excuse me" if you need to cut into the conversation or if the two who are speaking are unaware that they have left no room for anyone else to participate. Otherwise, it's likely that whatever it is you'd like to say can wait. The dinner table is not the place to fight for a piece of the conversational pie.

IGNORING SOMEONE ON YOUR LEFT OR RIGHT (OR FRANKLY, ANYONE AROUND YOU). Often this happens because we are so engrossed in conversation that we literally forget. In Emily's day, a classic point of dinner party etiquette was for a hostess to "turn the table," which meant that she stopped speaking to the person on her right (usually the guest of honor) and turned her attention to the person on her left. All the ladies, like dominoes, would then follow suit, turning to speak with the person on their left instead of on their right. While Emily's era allowed for everyone to spend equal time talking to those on their right and left, we appreciate a less structured table experience today. Make it a point to share your attention with all those around you.

SHOUTING ACROSS THE TABLE. Interruptions and outbursts can draw you the kind of attention that is best avoided. Don't talk over people across a conversation or raise your voice too loudly (remember indoor voices?). This might happen from time to time when the table is long and the conversation boisterous—for example, to call someone's attention to a part of your conversation or to engage them ever so briefly for fun—but only in very friendly company and certainly never for an extended conversation. At a restaurant, try to keep your voice to a level where people at the next table won't hear the details of your conversation. (See Body Language, Vocal Tone, and Volume, page 59.)

SEASONING YOUR FOOD WITHOUT TASTING IT FIRST. You should always taste your food first before seasoning it. If you season first, you could not only ruin the dish by overseasoning it, but you may also insult the chef whether at a restaurant or in someone's home.

REACHING. You should never need to reach for anything at the table. Instead, if something is not directly in front of you or within half an arm's length, you should ask for it to be passed to you. No one wants an arm—especially an elbow—in their face during the meal.

PASSING GAS. No matter which exit it takes, gas happens—but not at the table. Should you feel an emission coming on, excuse yourself to the restroom or the hall and, even though we are sure you will do your best to stifle the sound, try your best to be out of earshot. A belch that rattles the chandelier is impressive indeed, but is better suited for summer camp hijinks than at even a casual American table.

ANYTHING TO DO WITH A DEVICE OR HEADPHONES. Be it a tablet, smartphone, or gaming console, it is absolutely not invited to the table, whether you are talking on it or checking the score. If your host has thoughtfully said something like, "Snap your Insta pics now and then let's put phones away for the meal," you may certainly take your picture and then turn your phone to silent and stow it. But you should never bring a phone or other device to the table without the host's invitation or unless it is needed as a communication aid.

BRINGING UP NEGATIVE NEWS. Your bad test results, your brother's breakup, other negative news—these are likely important things to talk about, but not at the table. Many people physically struggle to eat when difficult, negative, or sad topics are brought up. We come together to enjoy a meal. It's important to give people the time and space to eat and save difficult, sad, or negative topics for another time when they can get the attention they deserve. For some this could be when the meal is complete even if you're still at the table. This is similar to the traditional rule of business topics being saved for the host to raise after the main course is complete.

GROOMING. Brushing your hair or beard (with an actual brush or just your fingers), grooming pets, picking your teeth, putting on makeup—none of these should happen at the table. If you need to freshen up, do so *before* you sit down. If you need to refresh yourself, excuse yourself from the table and take care of what you need to elsewhere. The only makeup that has been deemed appropriate to apply at the table is lipstick, and that is only if you can apply it discreetly without using a mirror (and certainly without using a knife blade as a mirror substitute).

LEAVING A MESS. In general, try to keep things neat. It's not a crime to spill a drop of something or have a small piece of food slide off your plate, but your place at the table shouldn't look sloppy or careless.

THE "CLEAN PLATE" CLUB

There are many traditions that teach you to always leave a bite, as an empty plate signals that your host should keep serving you more. Other customs tout the opposite: that you must clean your plate of every bit of food served or it's a waste or a possible insult to the host. Unless you need to follow a particular culture's dining practices, do your best to eat your fill and don't worry if it's not every bite. Also, don't try to mix or mash the food around your plate to make it look like you ate more than you did. There's no need to play with your food this way; as long as you try everything served (allergies or restrictions aside), you should be in good stead.

EXCUSING YOURSELF
FROM THE TABLE

If you need to excuse yourself from the table, either during the meal or at the end, the goal is neither to sneak away nor to make a production of your departure, but to quietly and politely take your leave. To whomever you are speaking say, "Please excuse me. I'll be right back," or "Please excuse me for a moment." You do not need to give a reason. In fact, more often than not, you shouldn't. No one needs to know that you need the restroom or, worse, why. Excusing yourself for a phone call should be done only if there is an emergency or if you are coordinating with someone who has yet to arrive.

If you're excusing yourself because of food that you need to remove from your mouth, an oncoming coughing fit or sneeze, or another bodily function and you can't speak, raise your index finger in a "wait just a moment" gesture as you take your leave. You can apologize for the unexpected departure when you return, and explain if you wish. "Sorry about that. I had a dry spot in my throat that caused quite a cough." However, in general, an in-depth explanation isn't necessary—and might be something people appreciate you keeping to yourself.

FIXING MISHAPS

Plenty of things can happen unexpectedly at the table. Sometimes we have time to fix them before others are aware. Other times we have to excuse ourselves to help manage the damage. The following are some classic table mishaps.

SOMETHING STUCK IN YOUR TEETH

If you have something stuck in your teeth, it is awfully kind for others to tell you discreetly if you haven't yet figured it out yourself. Either way, once you realize there's something there, if a quick and discreet working with your tongue behind closed lips doesn't dislodge it, excuse yourself from the table to handle it. Your napkin can make a handy visual shield if you can do quick and discreet work at the table. Do not take a sip of water and swish it around your mouth or try to use your fingernail or toothpick to dislodge it at the table.

Should you spot the proverbial spinach in someone else's teeth, it is very kind to indicate it to them. Catch their eye when they aren't talking and motion ever so slightly to your teeth. There's no need to create a comedic scene in an effort to get someone's attention. If your mission fails after a few attempts, there's not much else you can do to help from afar. When close enough for a discreetly quiet comment or when with close friends or family, you can just tell them: "Jenna, you've got something in your teeth." They can then respond, "Oh, thanks. I'll go take care of it," (if in a formal situation) or, "Oh thanks, where?" (if among casual friends).

TOO HOT: SAFETY FIRST

When something is too hot, it can not only be surprising but damaging to your mouth and throat. Try to avoid this situation to start with by taking a tiny bite or sip to test the temperature of hot food or beverages. If you do happen to take a bite or sip that is scalding hot, and a cold drink or covering your mouth with your napkin and letting some air in won't help, spit it out in as contained a fashion as possible, preferably into the bowl or cup it just came from. If you make a mess, you can excuse yourself to clean up and then apologize for any disruption once you return.

THE PROVERBIAL FLY IN THE SOUP

Whether it's that pesky little fly, a hair, or some other item in your food, when dining out it's easy enough to have a server take care of it and bring you something new. But when in someone's home and at their table, it can feel a bit more awkward. A good host would want to know, and a good guest would not want to embarrass a host. If you feel comfortable simply removing the item with your fork or spoon and setting it on the side of your dish, then do so. If you cannot bring yourself to continue eating (maybe after finding half a worm in your salad), stop, and if your host notices and asks if something is wrong, you may say with a light and relaxed tone, "I must confess there was a little surprise in my salad." You'll likely be met with a "Oh, I'm so sorry! Here, let me fix you another plate." If among friends you know wouldn't be embarrassed, it is fine to mention it quietly rather than waiting, especially if you are seated right next to the host: "Alice, would it be possible to get a different serving of this? I seem to have a swimmer in my soup." "Oh goodness, my apologies. Yes, one minute!" Most hosts will want to know, but alerting them with tact and kindness will smooth the moment for everyone.

For something more alarming like a glass shard or a raw piece of poultry, get your host or server's attention as quickly as possible to let them know what you have found. Safety really does come first, and if such things are on people's plates or in other dishes, they could have truly serious consequences. This is another time when safety supersedes any embarrassment that might be caused.

REMOVING SOMETHING FROM YOUR MOUTH

There's an old rule that says, "It comes out the way it went in," meaning if it entered your mouth on a fork, it should leave your mouth on a fork. If you ate it with your fingers, then it can be removed with your fingers. It's actually easier than it sounds to edge something such as a pit from your lips back onto your fork and set it down on your plate. You may also hold your napkin up in one hand as a shield as you quickly and discreetly use your other hand to remove the item and set it to the side of your plate. Never stow it in your napkin.

If you bite into an olive that still has a pit or take a bite of crab bisque that contains a piece of shell and you need to remove the item, the most important thing is to do it discreetly. (No one wants to see you pull or spit things out of your mouth.) If it's a gristly piece of meat or something that would look most unappealing on the edge of your plate, then you must excuse yourself. For less gross-looking items, like a large seed, pit, shell, or bone, you can use either your fingers or the fork method.

COUGHS, SNEEZES, OR BURPS

As mentioned above, coughs, sneezes, burps, and the like should be avoided at the table. As soon as you feel one coming on that can't be stifled, it's best to excuse yourself. Small burps that you can pass silently and without a large exhale can often be managed at the table by simply covering your mouth with your napkin, or hand, and saying, "Excuse me" if someone notices. But occasionally a sneeze will be so sudden you can't leave the table in time. In this case, turn completely (180 degrees) away from the table and try to sneeze into your elbow rather than your napkin, which someone else has to handle after you, be it your host or a server. When you're in a crowded setting, do your best to minimize the impact on others. You may need to excuse yourself anyway to go clean yourself up.

SPILLING AND DROPPING THINGS

No matter how gracious you are, that doesn't guarantee that you (or others) will always be graceful. Spilling anything is always a table fail, but it happens, and we shouldn't get bent out of shape about it. It's one thing if scalding-hot tea, coffee, or soup has been spilled on you. That is a safety-first situation, always. But drinks get knocked over or sloshed a bit if they are set down hard. Sauces and dressings drip and dribble even in the steadiest hands. Between conversation and good food, it's easy for crumbs and other bits to fall off the side of your plate. Not every meal will be neat and tidy, but that's not a permission slip to make a mess.

Do your best to serve yourself and eat neatly. Move slowly. While you might use your napkin to quickly dab at a small drop or spot, leave it to your host or the restaurant to help with bigger spills. Small drips and dribbles are expected. Never dab someone else without first asking if it's all right to do so. Do apologize immediately for any large spills that you cause. ("I am so sorry!") Privately, away from the table, you can offer to your host (if you are able) to help clean or replace any ruined items.

Typically when dining with others you would not handle items that have touched the floor. If something drops, leave it until after the meal or until you can let a server know that you dropped it. They will then replace it. When you're with family or friends, you might choose to pick up a dropped napkin. At a casual gathering you could certainly pick up a dropped fork or knife and then wash it and your hands before returning to the table. But it's kind for a host to offer to take care of it when you're in a dinner party setting. The more formal the occasion, the more likely it is that you should leave the dropped item alone and make do without, or ask someone to get you a replacement.

USING SOMEONE ELSE'S PLACE SETTING ITEMS

This rarely happens, and guides like the "b" and "d" rules (see Navigating Your Setting, page 173) can help prevent it, but mistakenly taking something from someone else's setting can be rather embarrassing. Occasionally, at a table crowded with glassware and utensils galore, you might take someone else's fork, or drink, coffee cup, or bread. If this happens, apologize for the mistake and offer to swap—if yours is unused—or get them a fresh glass, roll, fork, or whatever the item is. "I'm so sorry, I don't know where my head is. Let me find you a fresh bread plate."

ENDING A MEAL

Typically at family dinners and dinner parties with our nearest and dearest, and even at events like weddings, we rely on our hosts to excuse us from the table by indicating that the meal is over: "Thank you all for a lovely meal. I have coffee and cookies for us in the living room/by the fire/ in the den." It's best not to try to leave or depart before this. Hosts take note: your guests may be waiting for this cue.

If you're in a pickle, you may always excuse yourself from just about any situation. "I'm terribly sorry, but I must excuse myself for the evening. This has been lovely and I'm sorry to have to leave."

When dining out, everyone waits for the bill to be settled before leaving the table. For more casual dining (say out to a weekday lunch), a quick check-in with your pal as to whether they are "ready to go?" is all it takes to kick an exit into gear. A favorite and important part of the wind-down ritual is offering gratitude. Giving thanks for the time spent together over a meal, whether to the cook, the host, the guests, or your companions, is a wonderful way to end a meal and leaves everyone feeling good. "Thank you so much for [joining me/a lovely meal/getting together]; this has been [lovely/great/awesome]."

REFERENCE GUIDES

TABLE SETTING DIAGRAM

Use this diagram to help navigate your table setting. More casual meals will feature fewer utensils and glasses, and likely not include a charger plate at all. Not all utensils need to be set, you may choose to have some brought out with a course to save tablespace.

1. Bread plate & butter knife	6. Sherry glass	11. Charger
2. Dessert fork	7. Wineglass	12. Entrée knife
3. Dessert spoon	8. Napkin	13. Salad & appetizer knife
4. Water glass	9. Salad & appetizer fork	14. Oyster fork
5. Champagne glass	10. Entrée fork	

HOW TO HOLD UTENSILS

CUTTING

Handle rests in palm gripped by middle, ring, and pinky fingers. Tines or blade down. Index finger along back of handle. Thumb rests along the side to secure the grip.

SCOOPING

Tines or bowl face up. Handle rests on web between thumb and index finger. Middle finger holds the neck of the handle from below. Index finger holds from the top and the thumb secures the grip from the side.

WHERE TO PLACE UTENSILS

RESTING AMERICAN

If resting your silverware but not yet finished with your meal, the knife is placed across the top of the plate. Its handle to the right at about the 1 on a clock face and its tip at about the 11. The fork is placed with its handle to the right at about the 4, and its tines up, pointing toward the 10. The spoon rests in the bowl with its handle to the right, just like the fork.

RESTING CONTINENTAL/ EUROPEAN

For the Continental or European resting position, the fork should be placed along the left side of the plate with the handle pointing at the 7 or 8 if the plate was a clock face, and the tines (up) at 10 or 11. Never let the handles rest on the table. The knife is set on the right with the handle pointing at the 4 or 5 and the blade tip at the 1 or 2. The spoon rests in the bowl with its handle to the right, just like the fork.

FINISHED AMERICAN AND CONTINENTAL/EUROPEAN

The fork (tines up) and knife are placed together, with the handles pointing at the 4 if the plate was a clock face. The tines and blade tip will point toward the 10. Never let the handles rest on the table. The spoon is placed on the right side of the underplate when finished. If there is no underplate, leave it in the bowl, handle positioned like a fork.

NAVIGATING YOUR SETTING

Here are some great memory aids to help you remember your place setting, and how to use the utensils in it.

BREAD AND DRINKS

Make a circle with your thumb and forefinger, allowing the other three fingers to stand up straight. Left = *b* (bread). Right = *d* (drinks).

BMW

Bread, Meal, Water to remember that bread goes on the left, the meal in the middle, and water on the right.

FORKS

Read your setting like the word *FORKS*. First on the left is F = forks, O = plate, because a plate looks like an *O*, R = right of plate, K = knives, S = spoons.

OUTSIDE IN

You eat from the outside in per utensil grouping. As each course is cleared, the relevant utensils are also taken away, leaving you with only what is needed for the rest of the meal.

USING A CLOTH NAPKIN

In casual settings or when using paper napkins, you might not worry about napkin niceties; however, for semiformal or formal dining, use your napkin as follows: open the napkin halfway (you'll have either a triangle or rectangle) and place the folded edge against your waist with the open end draped evenly over your leg(s). Use the inside of the open end of the napkin to clean your hands or face. This will both keep food off your clothes and allow for a clean napkin facing others if you dab your mouth. Remember that even though a host should expect a napkin to get used, do not cover someone's entire cloth napkin in food smears. If your mess is that great at a meal, excuse yourself to the restroom to clean up a bit.

SAMPLE TOASTS

SHORT AND SIMPLE	GRATITUDE-BASED	TO THE HAPPY COUPLE	TO AN ACCOMPLISHMENT
"To health and happiness!"	"A toast to our host and chef, who has created such an amazing meal and who has not only filled our bellies but also warmed our hearts."	"To Elena and Pete, may you treasure the big moments and celebrations in life, as well as the everyday mundane details, for together they create the beautiful life we know you'll share."	"I'd like to ask that we raise a glass to the team tonight. Everyone has worked so hard, and we wouldn't be standing here confidently, ready to launch, if it hadn't been for everyone's incredible efforts. Cheers!"

Remember: Embarrassment is never in good taste. This isn't a roast, and humor is rarely executed well in a toast, so when in doubt, stick to simple and sentimental. (See Saying Grace and Making Toasts, page 148, for more details.)

BUFFET TIPS

- Wait to be invited to serve yourself from the buffet, especially at weddings.

- Always use the provided serving utensils.

- Don't assume the serving utensil suggests the size portion you should take.

- Take a small amount to start; you can always go back.

- Keep the buffet neat: serve yourself from what's nearest to you and avoid spills.

- Come back for extras such as drinks if your hands are full.

- Always take a fresh plate when you go back to a buffet for more.

CHAPTER 6

Hosts & Guests

"The ideal guest is an equally ideal hostess; the principle
of both is the same. A ready smile, a quick sympathy, a
happy outlook, consideration for others . . ."

We often describe the relationship between host and guest as a dance. This host-guest dance has been going on for thousands of years, and involves two of the most basic lessons in hospitality: how to behave as a guest and how to make someone feel welcome as a host. When we allow empathy, consideration, and graciousness to guide us, the dance looks beautiful and everyone leaves with a smile on their face.

The ultimate goal of any gathering, be it a casual hang or a formal evening event, is that the host provides and cares for their guests' well-being and that the guests enjoy, participate in, and appreciate their host's efforts. Members of Best Society, like Emily's Mrs. Kindhart, wouldn't grimace at gluey mashed potatoes or think, *I wouldn't do it this way*. Instead, she would compliment other aspects of the meal ("this beef is so tender!") and enjoy the rest of the dinner as best she could. Today, we would think of Mrs. Kindhart as a chill-but-classy, plan-well-but-go-with-the-flow type. She praises her friends for what they do well, both in execution and intention. She focuses not on differences in entertaining style, but on the positive aspects she and her friends and acquaintances bring to their roles. It's a wonderful spirit to aim for.

We take on these roles outside the home too. When a client visits our office or workplace, they are the guest. When we visit a client, we are the guest. When we take someone out to a meal and are treating them, we are the host; when they treat us, we are the guest. We can plan to take on these roles long in advance or jump into them in the spur of the moment. Even our virtual lives have host and guest roles for online meetings and gatherings. Whatever the situation, take the time to think about what role you're playing and the most considerate way to play it.

A GOOD HOST

Mr. Heeza Goodhost creates comfortable and entertaining experiences for his guests. These are two simple goals to aim for. He is also enthusiastic about hosting. He isn't over the top, but his friends and family can tell he is thrilled they came and that he really prepared for their visit. He doesn't see hosting as burdensome or anxiety inducing—it's fun! (Maybe not the cleaning ahead of time, or having to track down RSVPs, but Mr. Goodhost generally likes to be a host.) He does his best to help his guests out when he can, such as by providing his Wi-Fi password, or accommodating a dietary restriction. He's also smart about his smart speaker, and turns off reminders and alerts so they don't blare out during a party. He knows how to redirect his guests when necessary and is confident saying no to things he cannot accommodate. With a strong sense of what he's comfortable providing and what his guests enjoy, Mr. Goodhost is the kind of host people always hope for an invitation from. And if they can't say yes, they hope for a raincheck. We might not all be great at throwing large or intricate gatherings, but everyone has it in them to be a Mr. Goodhost.

INVITING WELL

A good host issues a good invitation. Through its formality, delivery, and content, a good invitation is easy for a guest to understand and respond to (see Invitations and Announcements on page 93 or the Sample Invitations on page 110 for specific invitation wording).

For a host to invite well, they must communicate the basics: *who* is being invited to *what* and *by whom, why* there is an event, and *when* and *where* it will be held. Whether the invitation is sent via mail, phone, text, email, social media, carrier pigeon, or in person, an RSVP is helpful. RSVP stands for *répondez s'il vous plaît,* French for "please respond." An RSVP request usually provides the name of the person to RSVP to and the preferred method of contact. You may also add a deadline if needed. (For examples, see Sample Invitations, page 110.) Indicating either *regrets only* or *acceptances only* often causes more confusion than is necessary. We suggest you avoid using these phrases.

It's also important for your invitation to be consistent with the event you throw, as it sets the tone. A formal invitation suggests a formal event and formal attire. If your invitation implies jacket and tie but you open the door wearing jeans and a casual shirt, you aren't creating consistency for your guests or helping them know what to expect, and that can be uncomfortable—and is a breach of good hosting etiquette. For casual invitations, be clear with your language. There is a difference between suggesting you meet up with someone for lunch (not hosting) and treating them to lunch (hosting). Be clear in how you describe the event itself. "Please come for dinner on Friday night" implies that you are providing the meal, while, "Let's do dinner Friday" is more vague and could mean a number of things. "Potluck at my house, Friday" lets people know they will be expected to bring a dish if they say yes.

When a guest does RSVP, this is a true host-guest dance moment, for each has a role in making the dance go smoothly and easily for the other. Sometimes a simple "Yes, we are coming," or "Sorry, we can't make it," completes these opening dance steps (cha-cha-cha). While a guest who has an accessibility need, dietary restriction, food or pet allergy, or other accommodation is likely used to raising it when they RSVP, the good host move is to proactively check in about any necessary accommodations that would help make a guest more comfortable or even able to attend. While you may know your guests, remember not to make assumptions. Let's say you want to invite your friend Rachel to your annual party; she uses a wheelchair and you're concerned about accessibility. Don't overthink it. Send the invitation. If you don't issue it, you lose out on the chance for her to come altogether. If you've requested an RSVP, she'll connect with you then and you can discuss the accessibility of your home and options to accommodate her. If there is no way to make it work, at least she knows you wanted her there and didn't just assume she couldn't come. Or worse that you just didn't want to "deal with" possible accommodations—a hurt that no host should impart on any guest. For food allergies or restrictions, a guest might offer to bring a dish that meets their needs, or you as the host might make the meal so that it suits their needs. Either way is polite, but checking in as the host makes it easier on the guest. If something comes up that you can't adjust for as a host, be clear about what you can and cannot do so that your guest can make a good decision. "Oh dear, Julianna, I'm so sorry, we have both cats and dogs; I'm not confident I can get the house pet hair–free by dinner Friday."

It should be noted that a host does not post or display the guest list to any formalized event. While an invitation via a social media platform may automatically display a guest list (and even more cringeworthy, who is attending or not) when sending out a digital invitation you shouldn't display the guest list if it can be avoided. Guests should come to a party because they want to attend, not because others are going or not. If safety is a concern regarding the presence of certain guests, a host and guest can work that out privately.

CONSIDERING YOUR GUESTS' ENJOYMENT

There's a lot to consider when it comes to pairing your vision for your gathering with your guests' enjoyment. As a host, your guest list does not have to include all your friends for every gathering. Use your knowledge of your guests to your advantage when considering the gathering you're host-ing and whom to invite. A good host will strike a balance, aiming for all guests to find something enjoyable at the event, whether it's the food, the company, the atmosphere, the purpose, or all of the above! There should always be options for different ways to participate, and no one should ever force someone to join in the entertainment. "Danny, why aren't you dancing?!" is better said, "Danny, want to come dance?!"

When you host a gathering that has a guest of honor, you want to put the honoree's wishes as a top priority—within reason of course, some things you truly might not be able to do. While you want your guests to have a good time, as you plan let the honoree's preferences come first. For example, while some guests grumble about playing games or watching gift openings at a shower (and maybe you've even heard some of those on your guest list make such comments), if the honoree has requested these games, you should honor their request.

A good host will pay attention throughout their gathering, stirring conversation if it starts to wane and checking in on guests—especially at a more mix 'n' mingle–style event as opposed to a sit-down dinner—to see that everyone is having a good time, or has enough to eat and drink. That is, without smothering them! While it may sound counter to the advice of taking care of your guests, a good host also does not overdo it. To ask if folks are all right every 5 minutes is too much and will make you look nervous or anxious. Instead, a few check-ins throughout the entire night is fine. Remember, one of the best ways to ensure your guests are relaxed is for you to be relaxed and enjoying the party too.

LEADING THE WAY

A good host leads the way for their guests—not by dictating and micromanaging, but by staying engaged with guests, gently guiding them, and going with the flow when necessary. If an extra guest shows up, something breaks, or something goes unserved . . . these things happen! Worse, though, is when a host doesn't really show up for their party. They may be there physically, but guests have been left to pour their own drinks, introduce themselves, entertain each other, or make their way to the table for dinner on their own. Not ideal at all. Here are some ways to lead your guests as a good host.

THE RIGHT ATTITUDE

Your mood will set the tone. If you are positive, warm, and lighthearted, like Mr. Goodhost and Mrs. Kindhart, your guests will feel it, and the occasion, no matter how formal, will also reflect this atmosphere. But if you are tightly wound, fretting about the timing of food or what was supposed to be this way but is that, your guests will feel your anxiety and disappointment. And while it might not ruin their night, it will shift their focus from having a great time to wondering how you are doing.

WELCOMING GUESTS

You should always aim to greet your guests as they arrive. Be ready at the door and help them with outerwear, bags, or other items. A good host will set up their entryway so it's easy for guests to remove their outerwear and, if they need to, their shoes. If you plan to ask guests to remove their shoes (which 35 percent of American hosts do), it's kind to leave house slippers or disposable slippers at the door for them to use, or better yet to invite your guests to bring "indoor" shoes for the gathering. (We recommend not asking guests to remove their shoes for anything more formal than a casual occasion at home.)

MAKING INTRODUCTIONS

One of the simplest and most effective ways to be a good host is to make introductions when necessary. No guest expects to have their host by their side all night long. However, most guests do appreciate an introduction or two. And a good host does this almost without thinking. It's often the first thing they do after taking someone's coat and offering them a beverage. "Tina, this is Chase. We play ball at the park on Sundays. Chase, this is Tina. She works with me in the design department." Or, in more casual situations: "Everybody, this is Zach, from my yoga class. Please introduce yourselves! Zach, can I fix you something to drink?"

MAKING CONVERSATION

Whenever possible, a good host makes introductions with a little tidbit of information about each person so the conversation can carry on without the host. Don't just offer any random fact; pick topics likely to ignite a conversational spark between the guests. The art of easily moving between guests, checking in, spreading good cheer, and seeding conversation is where Mr. Goodhost shines. (See Making Introductions, page 18, or The Three Tiers of Conversation, page 61.)

MAKING GOOD TRANSITIONS

A good host knows how to move a party or event along, paying attention to their agenda for the entertainment and food and the vibe of the party. A "cocktail hour" is so named because it's meant to last roughly an hour. A four-hour cocktail hour followed by dinner is not what most American guests will be expecting. Likewise, shutting down a cocktail hour as soon as the last guest arrives (twenty minutes into the evening) doesn't give that last guest a chance to settle into the gathering. Gauge the room. Are guests having a good time? Are there still refreshments to be consumed, or have you run out? Not everything has to be done to the minute. A good host balances transitions so they make sense not only according to their original plan but also with how the party is unfolding.

Clearly announcing to guests that dinner is ready, or that it's time for the gift opening, a game, or other entertainment is a host's duty and one you should embrace as the ringleader you are! Use your own style, but do make an effort to lead, because your guests will be looking to you for these transitional cues. This includes leaving the table, and saying goodbye or good night. If your guests have not budged and it's at least an hour since you've all left the table, or the meal has been deemed complete, it's fine to let guests know you're going to be shutting the party down. "This has been so lovely," you might announce, "however, I'm going to have to call it a night." (See Say Good Night, Gracie on page 200 for more.)

DEALING WITH MISHAPS

As a good host you want to handle mishaps such as spills, breaks, or disruptions without embarrassing your guests or losing the focus of the party, which is usually about having a good time. If a plate breaks, red wine spills on the white couch, or the toilet clogs, you'll want to quickly attend to the matter without calling too much attention to it. Do not shame a guest in front of others, though you might make a mental note not to invite someone again (a decision usually made only for very serious offenses), or invite that guest for only certain types of parties from now on. As a good host, grieve away from your guests if a cherished item has been broken or stained. You definitely don't want to curse in anger at what horrible luck you have or what a buffoon the guest was to make the error. Never. The key to any good host's management of a mishap is not embarrassing a guest, whether or not that guest seems remorseful.

Reassure your guest that accidents happen and there is no need to cry over spilled milk (or wine, or anything else). If any repair is to be done and the guest offers to reimburse you for the expense, you may certainly accept if you wish. If you don't want to, then chalk it up to the cost of entertaining. If, for example, a guest at a party knocks over a vase, the host might say something like, "You know, that was a gift from my ex-husband, and I have been looking for a way to get rid of it." (Okay, maybe leave out the knock to the ex, but still, a bit of humor can help.) A good host will never say to a guest, "You owe me for that." Instead, always leave it to the guest to offer to pay for a repair or replacement. And a good host would never think that any offer wasn't enough.

Now, a smart host will also make sure that anything expensive or special is put out of potential harm's way before the event, especially when children (or pets) are coming. The same is true for any table linens, dishware, silverware, glassware, or crystal that you worry might become stained, scratched, chipped, or broken. Don't use it if you can't lose it.

HOW TO HANDLE DE-RANGEMENTS

No matter how well a host might plan, arrangements can unfortunately be "de-ranged." As a general rule, we suggest that hosts have a backup plan (see Backup Plans, page 199). If the oven breaks, grab your take-out menus. If guests are late, set the dinner to warm and make an additional pitcher of mixed drinks. If extra guests arrive, switch from buffet to plated meals to make sure there's enough for everyone. If the toilet clogs and it's the only one and you can't unclog it, well you're . . . out of luck. But you can still handle it with grace: "My friends, we have lost our bathroom for the evening." Then either move the party elsewhere or send folks home with the meal to go. Remember, when combined with a sense of humor and the reassurance that this is *not* the end of the world, a host can navigate any mishap well.

THE UNEXPECTED GUEST

You might find yourself spontaneously hosting at the end of a night out, or when a friend knocks on your door because they were in the neighborhood. It's in these moments when we can lean on circumstances and experience to help us relax the rules. There is a dance in that as well. While a gracious host might apologize for a messy living room, a kind guest will follow gracefully in step and not be bothered that their host wasn't ready for their surprise visit: "I'm so sorry for the mess; please come in." "Thank you and no worries at all; I know you weren't expecting me."

While it may be the last thing you needed, unexpected guests should always be made to feel welcome. And though it would have been nice to get a heads-up text or call prior to their arrival, if you aren't graced with that, you want to make sure your brain switches from thinking, *Oh snickers!* to actually saying to your new guests, "The more, the merrier! Welcome, come on in!"

Employ the "family hold-back" technique, meaning family members (or anyone close enough to the host to help) take smaller portions to stretch the food for the extra guest(s). If you are serving something like an individual roasted quail for each person (bravo, you!), break them apart, giving light and dark meat to each guest, and cry later about your presentation dreams going *poof* when the extra guest arrived. Take comfort in knowing that you can host your tiny bird dinner again another time. Next time, make a couple of extra servings of everything so you are prepared if anyone springs an extra guest on you (or the dog jumps on the counter).

There is also a version of the unexpected guest that is absolutely delightful, and that is when someone happens to drop by right around mealtime and the host asks the unexpected visitor to join in. It can be such a wonderful surprise for the guest (and take note: it's okay to join if you're being invited to!). There are even traditions of welcoming an unexpected guest (especially around certain holidays), where a symbolic spare place is set at the table. All the same advice applies here: make your guest welcome, reapportion the food if necessary, and get ready to enjoy a good time.

THE LATE GUEST

If you get word that a guest is going to be late, you may decide to wait for them or choose to move ahead. As the host, it is up to you. Once your guest arrives, it's kind to offer to catch them up on the meal. Either a full plate of the previous courses or the current course is best. Unless they say, "Oh no, I'll just join you all for dessert," do not *punish* a late guest, especially if this is a frequent problem, by not serving them any of the courses they missed. Even though your guest may have made you uncomfortable, it's important to take the etiquette high road and make your guest comfortable. Switch your thinking from *They're late!* to *I'm glad they were able to make it at all.*

THE LAST-MINUTE CANCELLATION

Nothing is more of a bummer to a host than a last-minute cancellation. There is nothing to do but say, "I'm so sorry that you cannot make it. You will be missed, but I look forward to seeing you soon." Rather than get steamed up or down in the dumps, focus on the guests who *could* make it and how great a time you'll have together. Guests, take note: don't be the person who cancels at the last minute. It is the peak of rudeness and should be avoided. Obviously emergencies, a babysitter cancelling at the last minute, or a sudden stomach issue are reasonable excuses, but they are among the few.

WHEN DISASTER STRIKES

Many of us have experienced the personal devastation when a large event (especially a wedding) must be canceled or rearranged due to a catastrophe. The COVID-19 pandemic and its effect on weddings is the clearest example, but other natural disasters and unavoidable circumstances have derailed many a big plan. There are two options for a host here: one is to postpone, which aims to have nearly the same party—all the guests are still invited—but with other elements changed, like the location or date. The new plan is then presented either with or soon after the announcement of the postponement. The second option is to cancel the event. Not every party can be rescheduled. Never uninvite some guests and keep others—instead cancel the entire event as planned and re-plan a new event with new invitations. If you do this—canceling rather than postponing—you have the option of changing any element you wish (or can): the guest list, venue, date, style, menu, etc.

The main objective is to communicate with your guests. If your guest list is a close group of fifteen, you might choose to call them to tell them they are invited to a new event instead of resending printed or handwritten invitations. Many people will understand if a big wedding guest list must be reduced to just immediate family—especially if newly instituted capacity limits or other mandated restrictions are the reason—but it's still best to cancel and then reissue new invitations to the smaller group. Be ready to answer questions and help your guests as best you can. Below are some example notifications for a canceled or postponed event:

CANCELLATION

Due to the pandemic, we are canceling our wedding on July 27th.
We apologize for any inconvenience this may cause. Our hope is to celebrate in
some way once we can all gather together again safely.

Stewart & Paola

POSTPONEMENT

The wedding of Paola Azevedo and Stewart Phillips
is postponed until further notice.
We apologize for any inconvenience this may cause.
We hope to celebrate with you all together once it's safe.

Stewart & Paola

If you are postponing your event and know the new date, you can add it to the note (*. . . is rescheduled for July 28, 2023*), followed by the time and location.

DIFFICULT GUESTS

Mr. Goodhost and Mrs. Kindhart are not afraid to handle difficult guests. They know that if a guest behaves badly, that's on the guest, not the host. (Unless further difficulty arises from you not doing anything about the difficult guest—then it's on you.) If the difficulty is a generally sulky or bad attitude, it's best to ignore it. Check in privately that nothing serious is going on, and if not, carry on with the rest of the party as best you can. Here are some examples of how to handle more egregious behavior from guests.

OFFENSIVE BEHAVIOR

Social accountability is important. While it's okay for the host to ignore bad behavior (a messy eater, someone who frequently interrupts others) as an act of graciousness toward the person who is doing it, bad behavior can rise to a level where it gives offense. When it does, a host can feel confident addressing it directly for the sake of everyone who is impacted. Truly offensive behaviors include aggression toward others, racist remarks or other hateful language, unwelcome advances, misogyny, and bullying. It's not okay to let these things slide, and as the host in a social situation, you have the most authority to handle them. It's a misconception that it's polite to be silent about something that offensive. Safety comes first. Always. If someone's behavior is making you or another person feel unsafe, it must be addressed and the offender asked to leave. If a guest is behaving offensively, making others feel uncomfortable or offended but not unsafe, it is still important for you to speak with them. If you can, address it in the moment: "Helen, I'm going to take this moment to redirect the conversation. Let's talk about . . ." Or perhaps you pull someone away first "Larry, come help me with this" and then address it once you're at a distance from other guests "Dude, stop hitting on Beth. Not the time or place." As the host, if you decide to say something in the moment, take charge swiftly and be clear.

Along with talking to the offender, another option is to follow up with anyone who was directly offended so you can issue apologies or address what occurred, as necessary. "Beth, I'm so sorry about Larry's behavior last night. I want you to know I spoke with him and told him I wasn't okay with it. I also wanted to check in with you about it."

OVERINDULGENCE

If you choose to serve your guests alcohol or cannabis (where the latter is legal), it's important to determine your liability. This isn't to avoid being a responsible host; it's so you know the stakes. Many homeowners insurance policies and state laws list the homeowner as liable for an inebriated guest. To complicate matters, a guest who has overindulged might not be aware that they've gone too far. As the host, it's important for you to see that they remain safe until sober. While it could be socially uncomfortable to address this issue with an inebriated guest, be prepared to do so.

Often this means removing the alcohol or cannabis and offering the guest water and a place to rest. If time and water don't help, don't just put your guest in a cab and send them off into the night. That puts the onus of dealing with them on the driver and doesn't guarantee they will get home safely. Instead, ensure your guest makes it home yourself, or invite them to "sleep it off" on your couch or in your guest room: "Isabel, I'm concerned about sending you out the door. Please let me fix up a bed for you." You should always check in on a guest who has chosen to stay with you until they are sober again. Even if they are resting, there is reason for concern until someone is truly sober and awake.

WHEN COHOSTING

Communication is the key to successful cohosting. Whether you're asking someone to cohost or being asked, make sure to clarify exactly what the request is so there is no confusion before agreeing. After you say, "Let's do it!" sit down with your cohost to discuss the event's dates, guest list, budget, and responsibilities. Divide the duties, taking advantage of each person's abilities, skills, and interests. Remember to consider your roles during the party as well, such as greeting guests, serving and replenishing refreshments, and guiding guests through the gathering (it doesn't have to be an even fifty-fifty split—even when it comes to the costs).

For those entertaining as a couple, consider yourselves default cohosts, equally responsible for the hosting duties. This might not be true if you're inviting your bestie over for afternoon iced tea or to watch the game, but it is when you're throwing a gathering together (a hint: both of your names are on the invitation). When the party's over, don't forget to kick back and celebrate a job well done together. Thank your cohost for their efforts. Note that in roommate situations, roommates are not automatically cohosts when one person in the house hosts others. While they should always be courteous of other roommates' guests and should take care of any personal belongings and help tidy up, they are not obligated to actually host.

HOSTING VS. ORGANIZING

When you host, you are responsible for organizing *and funding* the gathering. When you organize (or suggest) a get-together, you are helping to coordinate, but the expectation is that everyone will contribute or take care of themselves. The classic example is a birthday party at a restaurant with friends. If you are hosting, you would take care of the invitations, the cost of the meal, and anything else associated with the event. If you are organizing, you would reach out more casually and ask people if they want to participate by spelling out the details: *Hey! Looking to organize a b-day dinner for Alicia. We could pay for our own, plus split the birthday girl's meal or split the total, next Friday at Honey Road. Here's the link. Let me know if you can make it!* Remember to be clear with your language so others know the plan you're proposing. When you're hosting, your invitation says it all. Here's a sample hosting invitation:

HOSTING

*Please join us for cocktails
to celebrate Anisha's birthday
on January 24th, at 6 o'clock
at the Broadmore,
821 Funsie Lane*

*RSVP Dylan (Dylan@bestcousin.com)   No gifts, please
or Stella Grace (SG@bestcousin.com)*

When you're organizing, you can text, call, or email to let friends and family (aka the guests) know what the plan is and how they can participate. Here's a sample organizing via email, text, or phone call:

ORGANIZING

Hey everyone! We are organizing a little meetup to celebrate Anisha's birthday, thinking cocktails at the Broadmoor (821 Funsie Lane). We will be there between 6:00 and 9:00 p.m. Feel free to swing by!

BIDDING YOUR GUESTS GOODBYE

All good things must come to an end, and that includes your incredible gathering. A good host says goodbye well, whether it's to a brief drop-in visitor, guests from a well-executed formal dinner party, or your bestie who was visiting for a long weekend. Understanding when a guest says they must take their leave, Mr. Goodhost would reply, "Oh, it has been so wonderful having you here; thank you for coming!" and then promptly escort his guest to the door, checking to make sure they have all their belongings and accepting any thanks graciously. Mr. Goodhost also knows that his guests will be watching him for clues as to when the gathering is over. He does not fret as the party continues on, knowing it's up to him to watch for yawns or lags in conversation and insert a grateful but conclusive "This has been such a wonderful time; I'm so glad you could make it. I do hope we'll be able to do this again soon." (In other words, the party's over!) For more on saying goodnight, see Say Goodnight, Gracie in the Reference Guide, page 200. For how to help someone with their coat, please see Hosting the Classic Dinner Party, page 289.

A GOOD GUEST

Mx. Alwaysa Goodguest is a host's dream. They respond promptly to invitations, whether casual or formal. When appropriate, they always offer to bring something. They show up on time with anything they had promised to bring, and without anything extra that could be an imposition. Mx. Goodguest is adept at participating during any gathering: talking with other guests, oohing and aahing over gifts opened, joining appropriately in any entertainment like dancing or games. They never take advantage of or try to stretch a host's generosity. Mx. Goodguest knows to offer help at casual and informal events (but knows not to offer help during formal gatherings) and will happily return to enjoying the party if their offer is declined. They always compliment the host on whatever is going well or is excellently done. Mx. Goodguest senses when the party is winding down and does not depart a moment before. When the time does come, they say, "This has been so wonderful, but I believe I have to be heading home" to their host before heading to the door, and before they depart, they thank their host for a most wonderful time. They are a dream to entertain. We all have it in us to be a Mx. Alwaysa Goodguest. (For information on being a houseguest, please see As a Houseguest, page 371.)

RESPONDING TO INVITATIONS

No matter what form an invitation takes, a good guest responds promptly (usually within a day or two). For most formal events, you'll have plenty of lead time to figure out if you're available and able to attend. A good guest will respond as soon as they know for sure, and *always* on or before the RSVP date listed.

The RSVP is not a guideline—it's a deadline. When you see one listed, your host has included it to ensure they can plan well for the party. Ignoring it or making your own adjustments to it is not helpful or polite. Instead, always respond in the manner requested and by the date listed if one has been given. If the manner is not specified, match the medium: a call for a phone call, a text for a text, and so on. You do not have to wait for the response date to respond. If you have an answer as soon as the invitation arrives, go ahead and issue your response. If there isn't an RSVP date, a good guest will reach out quickly either with their answer or to ask when an answer is needed. A considerate guest never waits to RSVP in the hopes that a better invitation will come along.

While Emily Post's Mrs. Worldly had an A-plus social secretary who handled issuing invitations and organizing guest lists and responses, very few of us today enjoy such a luxury. Instead, as good guests we are our own A-plus social secretaries. We must remember the invitations we receive and make notes or reminders to ourselves to reply to them promptly. Technology can be very useful here.

When it comes to RSVPing via social media, squash the urge to hit the "Maybe" option. It's just a stalling tactic. You could just as easily write to your friend, *Hey, saw your invite. I won't know if I can come until next week, but I hope to be there!* Okay, so that may not be as simple as hitting the "Maybe" button, but it's easy enough and far more useful to your host.

If you're responding to a digital invitation and there is a visible guest list, resist the temptation to review the list before responding—it's the digital version of asking a host who else is invited. No one should be judging whether they will attend an event based on who else is going. You should decide about an event based on whether you want to go and are able to go.

To delay a response to an impromptu invitation, you can say, "Oh, that sounds fun. Let me get back to you by Wednesday." And then follow through on the follow-up. Try not to restructure your invitations from friends by saying, for example, "That sounds nice, but would you be willing to come to my place instead?" You can do this once in a while, sure, but friends who do this frequently aren't being considerate of those inviting them.

When you do RSVP, that is the time to mention any accommodations you might need to ask a host about. You can offer to bring a dish to meet your dietary needs, inquire about gifts that might be part of the event, or ask about accessibility, kids, pets, or anything else that is truly important for you to know. Always be prepared to accept what your host suggests in response to your question, knowing that if it doesn't meet your needs, you can easily decline the invitation. "Oh, I'm sorry to hear that. Unfortunately, that means we won't be able to come this time, but we appreciate the invitation."

MAKING AN ENTRANCE

Arrive on time. Punctuality is polite. While socially there is a standard 15-minute grace period, beyond that your host has no obligation to wait for you, and if you are going to be late (beyond that 15-minute grace period) it's important to reach out and let your host know so that they can adjust on their end if needed. Showing up on time is important, but a good guest will make sure not to show up early for an event—as it creates an awkward situation for a host to have to try to host while they do party prep. If you arrive early, rather than wait right out front, take a short walk, go for a drive, or run an errand—anything to avoid hovering outside the entrance or going in early.

It's thoughtful to wipe your shoes on any welcome mats and for less formal occasions to ask your host if their home is "shoes on" or "shoes off". While 65 percent of Americans say they don't ask guests to remove their shoes, for a casual get-together many people will ask for shoes to be removed especially when it's muddy or wet outside. It's okay to ask to leave your shoes on if you need to for accessibility or health reasons. Bringing a pair of "indoor shoes" can be a good idea. If you've brought a hosting gift, now is a good time to give it to your host—they may or may not choose to open it in the moment.

Just as a host's tone can set the mood, a guest's enthusiasm or good spirit can help contribute to a party's atmosphere. So, be sure to arrive with bells on!

PARTICIPATING WELL

Participating well can involve a number of things: responding to the invitation, arriving on time, enjoying the food and drinks offered, engaging in the conversation and entertainment. When it comes to bringing things, one way to participate well is to bring the item you've been asked to bring. You may very well bake a better pie than the side dish your host requested, but is the point to show off your pie or to help your host with their request? Let the host lead, and be supportive of their efforts or requests. (If your host asks you to prepare something you are not capable of making, it's of course okay to speak up!)

A good guest does not try to micromanage the event, and will offer possible suggestions in ways that allow a host to easily turn down the offer. "If it would be helpful, I could also bring a cheese board." "Thank you for offering; however, I'm all set on hors d'oeuvres. Just the side dish will be great!" A good guest participates to the best of their ability when warranted by bringing food, oohing and aahing, dancing, playing games, or just joining in the conversation. They think about what their host is trying to achieve and jump in to help make it happen (without taking over).

In some situations, such as a formal dinner party, it would not be proper for a guest to help out with the event (offering to pass hors d'oeuvres, clear plates, or wash up). For most casual and even semiformal events, on the other hand, especially if you're close with the host, offering to help pass items, serve, or clean up is always appreciated, even if you are turned down. If the host says, "I'm all right, thanks," a good guest goes back to enjoying the gathering and the host-guest dance goes on.

BEING RESPECTFUL

A good guest is respectful of the space they are in, their host, and the other guests. They show this not just by participating, but in what they *don't* do. A good guest doesn't arrive late, show up with an extra guest unannounced, sulk during games or activities, complain to other guests about what could be better, snoop, spend the whole time absorbed in their phone, or ditch out early. A good guest doesn't try to change the agenda of the party or make it fit their desires.

A good guest respects their host's privacy and boundaries. In an office or a home, taking care as a visitor is a sign of consideration. Resist the urge to peek behind closed doors, and stay out of cabinets and drawers. Never look through or around someone's desk. Phones and computers are very personal devices; keep your hands off them and your eyes to yourself unless you are invited to view them. This also applies to any remote controls for a TV, stereo, smart speaker, or fireplace. When it comes to Wi-Fi or internet access, it's perfectly okay to ask if you can join someone's personal network ("Mind if I hop on your Wi-Fi while I'm here?"), but be understanding if they decline your request. And recognize that asking implies you'll be needing your phone and internet connection while you're hanging out or attending this gathering.

A good guest will also not put their own relationship issues (safety aside) on a host to deal with. They would never ask their host to uninvite someone on their behalf. If you and your ex are both in the same social circle, it's up to you two to manage your behavior well at events where you are both invited, or decide between you who goes if you can't both be there and keep things civil. The same is true for frenemies and family rifts.

DON'T BE MR. CLUELESS

Mr. Clueless is the guest who leans too far into the host's accommodation offer. "Do you have any food restrictions or anything I should know for Friday night?" "No, but I would like to bring my son. If you could set him up in a bedroom, with his own meal—he won't eat anything but chicken nuggets—that would be great." Toes have definitely been stepped on here in the host-guest dance. It's okay to decline when a guest takes it too far. "I'm sorry, I won't be able to accommodate that, but if you and Janine find a sitter, let me know; I'd love for you to join us."

Mr. Clueless really is a terrible guest; he thinks that a host should always accommodate his every need and thinks nothing of how a host might feel or what they have planned. If he thinks your party would be better with "the game" on, he's going to find a way to turn the game on. If he thinks the dish needs more salt, he puts it on the entire platter not just his own portion. He doesn't realize that his jokes aren't getting laughs and he thinks it's okay to talk about anything, anytime. Mr. Clueless is not a good guest.

TAKING RESPONSIBILITY

Accidents happen, things get broken or damaged, we say the wrong thing, or use the wrong tone. However, all of us are capable of reflecting on our behavior in such a moment or during an event. Should you do or say something you regret, or feel uneasy about, it's best to take responsibility and touch base with the people affected to help repair any damage you've done. This might mean offering to pay for a broken, stained, or otherwise ruined item that needs to be cleaned or replaced; or mean apologizing for your words, tone, or demeanor that weren't helpful, kind, or respectful. "I'm so sorry I wasn't a very good guest yesterday, and I wanted you to know that I felt bad about it and also what a great job you did hosting everyone." We all get things wrong from time to time and some things truly are accidents, but *how* we repair the situation is what will turn an embarrassing regret into a moment of learning and acceptance.

EXPRESSING GRATITUDE

Mx. Alwaysa Goodguest always says thank you for a wonderful time when departing. They never ghost their host, even at an open-house party where guests come and go. They always find their host, express their gratitude, and leave without lingering too long on the doorstep. ("Marisol, thank you so much for a wonderful evening. I can't wait to make that recipe! The pie was delicious. Thank you again!") Mx. Goodguest also follows up after the event (usually within 48 hours) with another sincere thank-you for a wonderful time. Whether your thank-you is by phone, text, email, or handwritten note matters only if you know it matters to the host. If you don't know, let the formality of the event and your closeness to the host determine the appropriate method.

(Though it's worth pointing out that a handwritten thank-you note is almost always appreciated and never goes out of style.)

Why two thank-yous? You don't have to issue the second one, but this is an opportunity that is fantastic to take advantage of (particularly if someone you don't know very well has taken the time to prepare a meal for you). While the doorway goodbye is a perfect chance to express your appreciation and is absolutely appropriate and covers your polite thank-you, the follow-up thank-you provides a moment to reflect a bit more on just how much effort your host put into the gathering and how glad you were to have attended. It's pretty amazing that people choose to clean their homes and spend time, money, and effort to provide us guests with refreshment and a good time. The extra recognition is guaranteed to be appreciated, even if your host isn't looking for it.

RECIPROCATION

Typically (and traditionally), a social invitation is supposed to be reciprocated. You invite me to dinner at your house, and I invite you to dinner at mine. It's a longstanding piece of Emily Post advice that cocktail parties provide an easy way for a host to reciprocate a number of invitations at once. You might have had dinner hosted by others on five different occasions over the last six weeks, and you can return all those invitations with a cocktail party for those who hosted you—so long as you genuinely think they would make for a good guest list together.

Not all invitations are going to warrant a reciprocal invitation in kind—weddings, for instance. And there are plenty of friendships where you always gather at so-and-so's house because it works the best and they love entertaining. While this person may love to host, don't forget to say thank you for all the hosting they do for your group. Overall, though, when it comes to your social life, try to make an active effort to host your friends in return. Don't worry if your budget or home or cooking skill isn't the same as theirs. Focus on the hospitality you can provide to someone who has recently shown some hospitality to you.

This practice can extend to your casual hangouts as well. The friend who only accepts invitations and never issues them may make others wonder, *Does he really want to get together, or is it just convenient that I offered him something to do?*

In your social life you're likely to play the role of guest more often than the role of host, but try to have some give and take, back and forth, and balance in playing your roles of host and guest. Making an effort to reciprocate and host those who have had you as a guest is good etiquette.

ATTENDING SPECIFIC EVENTS

For the most part, our duties as a guest are the same for each party. But there are a few specific times when it's important to think a bit more about the event we are attending and how to participate well.

AS A PLUS-ONE

If you are a "plus-one" at an event, you are the guest of a guest. Joining someone at an event they have been invited to can be both exciting and daunting. It can feel like you don't belong, but you can trust that you have been invited by extension and are very welcome. Lucky you!

GET ALL THE DETAILS. You need to make sure you can really commit to the event before you say yes, so get all the details: where, when, the purpose of the event, and of course attire and any related expenses.

IS A PLUS-ONE A "DATE" DATE? Joining someone at a wedding or even a ball didn't use to be thought of as a solely romantic or romance-seeking opportunity, and we're trying to get back to that today. A plus-one can be your friend; they don't have to be a romantic interest. So if a friend or relative asks you to be their plus-one, it's okay to say yes. There is no expectation that a plus-one to an event is meant for a romantic date. (Note: If you are the guest who has been given a plus-one, you may ask anyone you know to be your companion for the event.)

COMMIT AND STAY COMMITTED. While you are a "plus-one" and not directly invited, it's still important to honor your commitment if you say yes. Ditching someone at the last minute is not polite, to either the person bringing you or the host.

GIFT OR CONTRIBUTION? If the event is a wedding, where gifts are traditional, it's a good idea for both the invited guest and the plus-one to sign the card for the gift. A plus-one to a charity event, however, is not obligated to donate unless they wish to. How gifts or contributions are handled is a personal decision between the two of you; often it will make more sense for the guest who was directly invited to be the one covering this cost.

SAY THANK YOU. Thank the host if you get a chance to meet them at the event. And definitely thank the guest who invited you to the event, both as you leave and text, call, or email them again the next day to express your gratitude with a bit more reflection.

AS A WEDDING GUEST

As a wedding guest, it's important to dot your *i*'s and cross your *t*'s. Usually the host and others are managing the largest, most complex party they will ever throw (and if not, it's often the most meaningful event they'll ever host) and making it easy for your hosts is kind.

RSVP. It's *very* important to RSVP properly as a directly invited wedding guest. Use the RSVP link or reply card provided, or for a more casual wedding, you may be asked to RSVP via email, an RSVP link, or by phone. It is especially important to RSVP to a wedding by, if not before, the RSVP date. If there is no date, be sure to respond ASAP, and never later than 2 weeks before the wedding. If you have been given the option of a plus-one, it's polite to let your host know the name of the person you are bringing. Under no circumstances should you bring anyone who was not included in the invitation. Leave the kids at home if they weren't explicitly invited or fly solo if you haven't been extended a plus-one.

USE THE WEDDING WEBSITE. This is intended to give you all the information you could possibly need about the wedding. Explore each page so you can see what your host (or hosts) is trying to communicate about the formality, style, colors, their personal story, their registry, accommodations, directions, venue policies, and travel info. It will all be there ready for you. Going to the website first is more considerate than directly asking the host or the couple, even if it's a good friend, as they will often be inundated with other details and questions while planning the event.

GET A GIFT. Currently, wedding invitations still come with the obligation of giving a gift to the couple, regardless of whether or not you attend (see Thinking Forward, page 391, for more thoughts on this). The wedding registry offers great gift options to choose from. You don't have to purchase a gift from the registry; however, it can be useful even just to look at to get a sense of the couple's style and needs. You should always stick to your budget when buying a wedding gift. Quality handmade or sentimental items and gifts not purchased from the registry can also be options. Remember that even if you've already given a shower or engagement gift, a wedding gift is still expected. Many people budget accordingly, even planning for a smaller shower gift and a bigger gift for the wedding itself.

PARTICIPATE WELL. While it's expected for a guest to participate well, a wedding is truly about the two people getting married, and the focus should remain there. You might want to "get this party started!" but unless your host is looking to you to get people on the dance floor, you want to rein in your inner party animal and take your cues from the couple and other guests. Engage, but don't steal the show.

SAY THANK YOU. It is imperative to speak with the couple at a wedding (and if they aren't the hosts, then to also speak to the hosts for a moment) to tell them what a wonderful wedding it is, and thank them for including you. If there is one, the receiving line is often the perfect place to do this—it's actually the purpose of the receiving line, to connect guests and hosts at a big event. Since you won't know if there's going to be a receiving line, it's smart to pay attention to the invitation and take note of who is issuing it. If it isn't obvious who the hosts are when you're at the wedding, it's fine to ask. Then seek out the hosts to express your appreciation.

AS A GUEST OF HONOR

It's an honor to be a guest of honor. It can be one of the most satisfying things in life to be acknowledged by others, especially loved ones. Most of us will experience this at our childhood birthday parties. Our friends, family, or co-workers may also celebrate us at a birthday, graduation, meaningful achievement, shower or pre-wedding party, when we are welcoming a new child, or for an anniversary or retirement. When we are a guest of honor, the experience can run the gamut from uplifting and encouraging to overwhelming and embarrassing. (Hosts take note: be sure the person you are honoring is truly comfortable being celebrated. While most people think it's a good thing, there are some who are uncomfortable with it. Always check first when you can.) As the guest of honor at any event, know that it is okay to accept your position. It's okay to allow others to tell you how much you've meant to them, how great your accomplishments are, and/or how excited people are for you.

BE GRACIOUS. Talk with each guest and spend time thanking them for supporting you. "Gene, thank you so much for coming. This whole night has really warmed my heart."

OPENING GIFTS. If the party is a shower, then the point of it is to give gifts to the guest of honor, so you should expect to receive and open gifts. You'll want to be sure to connect warmly and graciously with those who gave gifts (see Receiving Gifts Well, page 204). If the event is more about honoring you for an achievement (such as a retirement, anniversary, or graduation), gifts from individuals may be opened later. However, if there is only one gift being presented to you from the group organizing the event or the host (like a watch for a retirement gift), then of course you should open it in the moment. Gifts can also be opened later for parties where they aren't expected, like an adult's birthday or possibly an engagement party—events where gifts are sometimes given and sometimes aren't. (For gift openings at children's birthday parties, please see Receiving Gifts Well, page 204, and Children's Birthday Party, page 305.)

THANK YOUR HOST. Aside from thanking each guest personally, you will also want to thank any hosts who have thrown a party in your honor. Usually a small gift and/or note is appropriate.

Dear Yo,

Thank you so much for hosting my shower! It was such a wonderful time, and I felt so very supported and cared for by all my friends and family. Thank you for all the detail you put into the menu and the decorations—it was more than I could have dreamed of. I can't wait for you to meet the little one! Thank you again for everything.

> *Much love,*
> *Tae*

AT BUSINESS EVENTS

Whether you're an employee or a plus-one (see As a Plus-One, page 193), when business is the purpose of the event, even if it's a celebration and not a mix-and-mingle or a specific work function, being at your best is key. This is not the time for your inner party animal to come out, and if you choose to drink alcohol, we strongly encourage you to stick to one drink just in case.

RSVP. The RSVP is just as important for a business event as for any other event. Do not skip it. Some business invitations will be more like social invitations, inviting you to a party or dinner, and you're usually asked to RSVP. Other events, like trainings or opportunities your company sets up, will be ones you're asked to register for. Don't miss an invitation just because it comes in the form of an email at work. And don't forget your social obligation to respond. Think of this registration like an RSVP and don't forget to sign up if you are going.

GET IT RIGHT. Show up on time and in the proper attire. Remember that you can usually take an outfit down a notch, but it's harder to dress up something casual in the moment. If you're bringing a plus-one, make sure to tell them what attire is appropriate.

ENGAGE. At any business event, you will be expected to engage. Whether it's an internal company party, a client's or prospective client's event, or a networking event, you are there to make connections and participate. Dance, use the photo booth, enjoy the buffet, laugh at the roast, sing karaoke, commit to meeting three new people or learning something new about folks you already know, engage in small talk—these are all ways to participate well. If you're the date of a guest to a business event, talk with them about what they hope to accomplish during the event and help them do so. Be sure to give your date a chance to shine or engage; this doesn't mean you should stay silent, but avoid dominating the conversation or leaving anyone out.

SAY THANK YOU. Often work events go underappreciated. Be sure to send a note or email to the host or organizer thanking them for a great event. If you are the guest of a guest, you can say thank you to the host or organizer if you meet them at the event, but your date will take care of thank-yous as the person more directly connected to the occasion. Be sure to thank the guest who invited you.

REFERENCE GUIDES

SAMPLE SCRIPTS

Here are some common situations that involve the host-guest dance and sample scripts for them. Of course, you'll want to adjust the language to fit your particular circumstance.

SITUATION	HOST SAYS	GUEST RESPONDS
Saying no to guests who want to bring pets to a gathering	"I love Woofy, but tonight it's just the humans, thank you for asking."	"Okay, thanks for letting me know."
	"Oh, good question. I'm going to say no for this visit."	"Good to know, we're looking forward to it.
Planning dates for a houseguest's visit	"Let me check and get back to you."	"That'd be awesome; let me know as soon as you can."
	"We can't do the 21st and 22nd, but we could host from the 16th to the 20th."	"Thanks for letting me know what works for you; I'll check with Calvin."
	"Those dates don't work for me, but let's try to find something that does."	"Oh bummer, thanks for letting me know. And yes, let's find something that works."
Setting boundaries nicely	"Help yourself to anything in the fridge except the chocolate cake, which is for tomorrow's picnic."	"Okay, thank you, and thanks for the heads-up on the cake!"
	"The downstairs bath isn't working; please feel free to use the upstairs one."	"Got it, Mr. Sutherland, thank you for letting me know."
	"In this house, we don't jump on the couch."	"Okay, sorry about that."
Accommodating food allergies and restrictions	"I'm so glad you can come. Do you have any allergies, restrictions, or major dislikes?"	"I'm looking forward to it. Thanks for asking; I'm good with anything." Or, "I'm looking forward to it. Thanks for asking; I'm vegetarian. I can bring a dish if that would be helpful."
	"Thank you for telling me. I'd be happy to have you bring a dish that works for you."	
	"I'm so glad you mentioned it. I'd be happy to make sure the meal works for you."	"Oh thank you, that's awesome!"

GOOD HOST TIPS

A good host:

- Invites clearly

- Is ready to entertain whether the gathering is planned ahead or impromptu

- Leads the way in conversation and entertainment

- Spends time with their guests

- Leads guests through transitions during the event

- Handles mishaps with ease and humor

- Always thanks their guests for coming

GOOD GUEST TIPS

A good guest:

- RSVPs on time

- Arrives on time

- Participates positively in the gathering

- Doesn't take advantage of the host's generosity

- Offers to help (and respects declined offers)

- Doesn't leave too early or stay too late

- Always says thank you to their host

DEALING WITH THE UNEXPECTED

SITUATION	RESPONSE
For a late guest	Wait the obligatory 15 minutes, then feel free to begin. Help the late guest join in once they arrive.
For an extra guest	Welcome them kindly and do your best behind the scenes to accommodate them. Add a place setting and reapportion the meal, serving yourself less if necessary. Whatever you do, don't say: "Oh, I didn't realize you were coming too," even if it's followed by "the more the merrier!" If you were upset by it, weigh whether or not mentioning it after the party will fix anything for future gatherings you invite this guest to before you say something.
If something spills, breaks, or is ruined	Stay calm. Safety first: make sure no one is burned and that any shards of a broken item are cleaned up thoroughly. If stains are a concern, do what you can to get the item either removed and soaking or treated in place. Spend as little time as you can on all of this. Reassure the (likely sorry) guest that accidents happen. You can decide later to take them up on any offers of help, but don't ask them to pay. It's best to remove or not use anything that is important to you before an event.
For offensive remarks or behavior	Stop it in its tracks: either interrupt the person to redirect the conversation—"Jim, I'm not comfortable talking about that, I'd like to hear about X"—or ask to speak to them privately and then tell them that the remark or attempt at a "joke" was offensive and unwelcome. Be sure to apologize privately to your guests about the incident later.
If a guest has had too much to drink	Cut off their alcohol and take away their car keys. Offer them a place to sleep for the night, food, and water, or drive them home yourself. Don't just get a cab for them or shoo them out the door.
If a guest brings cannabis and you're not comfortable with it	With legalization becoming more prevalent, your guest might not think to ask you first before breaking it out. If you aren't comfortable with marijuana in your home, take your guest aside. "Jerry, I'd appreciate it if you'd save the pot for another time."
If there's not enough food	Rather than serving buffet- or family-style, plate the meal. Do what you can to serve the most to your guests and take the smallest portions for yourself and the rest of your family. (We call this FHB: "Family Hold Back")
If there's a dinner disaster	Congrats—you're a real-life sitcom classic! Laugh, because really, what else can you do? Order takeout, make PB&Js (or spaghetti with garlic and Parmesan), or ask the group if they want to move to the restaurant down the block. You can always try another time for that perfect meal.

SAY GOOD NIGHT, GRACIE

Good on you—you've thrown such a great party that your guests don't want to leave! But it's time to wrap it up. It's okay to politely usher your guests out through subtle or maybe not-so-subtle (but still good-humored) hints. Start at the top of this list to get things going, then work your way through it if you have to.

- Close down the bar and start putting food away.

- Turn the music down or off. And turn the lights up.

- Start cleaning up. Or for the formal parties call for the valet to start bringing cars around.

- Comment on your day tomorrow, how tired you are, and what a great time you've had.

- Be direct. Stand up and say, "Wow, look at the time! It's gotten so late! Time to call it a night, I've got yoga (a meeting, a class) first thing tomorrow."

- If the above hasn't moved your guests on from your home, you may just have to wave your little white flag and head to bed saying, "Hit the lights and lock up on your way out. I'm off to bed!"

AS A WEDDING HOST

Here are a few of the most important and broad-based things a wedding host should think about. For an entire rundown of wedding planning, please refer to our book *Emily Post's Wedding Etiquette*, 6th Edition. (For simple sample wedding invitations, please see the Sample Invitations, page 110; for wedding guest information, see As a Wedding Guest, page 194.)

After the engagement has been announced, an engaged couple and/or wedding host should consider the following:

- A meeting of the two families, if possible

- A rough idea of the date and style (season, formality)

- Which elements are musts and which can be flexible (lean into flexibility whenever possible)

- Exactly who is contributing and who is hosting (they may not be the same people); anyone contributing should be offered the position of host on the invitation

- A realistic budget, discussed candidly and respectfully. All expectations for contributions should be stated before the offer is accepted

- The venue(s) for the ceremony and reception. Securing a venue is the second most important thing after determining the budget, as many are booked up years in advance

- Vendors: look carefully at their contracts, and always remember to be polite when working with vendors and wedding coordinators; they do this for a living and deserve your respect

  - Caterer
  - Musicians/DJ
  - Florist
  - Photographer/videographer
  - Transportation
  - Hair stylist/makeup artist

- Your crew: attendants, ring bearers, flower girls, officiant, anyone giving readings

- The guest list. You'll want a spreadsheet for home addresses, email addresses, and phone numbers

- Invitations (printed or handwritten) should be mailed 6 to 8 weeks before the wedding. Work backward from your date using this timeline to determine when they need to be prepped, proofed, and printed, addressed, and assembled—remember a destination wedding might require invitations to be sent even earlier so guests can plan travel

- Attire for all participants

- The wedding website, which should include all details about the wedding, including your registry

- Setting up a registry and keeping track of gifts and thank-you notes as gifts arrive

- Details of the ceremony and reception, such as seating arrangements, the receiving line (if doing one), and whether you'll have a plated, family-style, or buffet meal

- Thank-you gifts for the hosts or cohosts and the attendants

CHAPTER 7

Gift Giving

"Dear Uncle Arthur:

I know I oughtn't to have opened it until Christmas, but I couldn't resist the look of the package, and then putting it on at once! So I am all dressed up in your beautiful chain. It is one of the loveliest things I have ever seen and I certainly am lucky to have it given to me! Thank you a thousand—and then more—times for it.

Rosalie."

Emily had little advice on general gift giving in the 1922 edition of *Etiquette*—her gift advice often fell under a more specific event like a wedding. It was demonstrated through examples about gift exchanges like the thank-you note on the opposite page, which illustrates the delightful impact a gift can have and how to say thank you for it. Today we ask questions about when gifts are expected versus when they are not, and how to handle asking for gifts you actually want versus things you won't use or don't believe in. The family who is avoiding plastic, for example, needs to find a balance between politely communicating their wishes and graciously accepting gifts they might not keep—which is perfectly okay. Much of the etiquette around gifts today comes from helping to manage desires and expectations of both the person giving the gift and the person receiving it, so that the exchange can feel good to both parties. While there are times when a gift is clearly inappropriate or shows absolutely no thought on the part of the giver, if we get too bogged down in our heads about a gift that misses the mark, we'll miss out on appreciating the spirit of generosity coming from the person who gave it to us. By finding ways to give and accept gifts graciously (both when we do and don't love the gift), we participate well in the experience and can embrace it with confidence.

THE SPIRIT OF GENEROSITY

The spirit of generosity is a beautiful sentiment that makes gift giving so special: I want to *give to you*. It truly is this "thought" that counts the most. Gifts are best offered freely, with no expectation of receiving anything in return; that is what makes them gifts. It doesn't need to be a special occasion for you to feel inspired to give; the spirit comes from a place of caring, of wanting someone else to benefit, of wanting to surprise and delight. When a gift lands well it feels so good! The person giving the gift is pleased they made someone smile, and the person receiving it is pleased they were thought of. Remember, too, your time and attention can also be gifts worth giving. Whether expressed in a physical form, or through an act or words, the fact that we have (and act upon) a desire to give is amazing, and good etiquette tries to celebrate this by acknowledging other people's generosity toward us. It's important to take care with the gifts we are given. One way to honor the spirit of generosity when you are given a gift is to focus on that gift (or favor, or kindness) and express your gratitude to the person who gave it to you. Find confidence in knowing that appreciating this gift, favor, or kindness is the polite thing to do—that, in fact, the perfect way to accept the generosity bestowed upon you is with a "Thank you."

RECEIVING GIFTS WELL

There is something so magical about a gift, whether it's wrapped in shiny paper with lots of bows, or with newspaper and kitchen twine, or even just wrapped in good intentions. The moment we are presented with a gift, the exchange comes alive with excitement and expectations, and you have a role to play. Good etiquette guides us to play this role well and be considerate of the situation we're in and the others involved. More often than not, we like the item we've received and it's easy to say "Thank you!" with true enthusiasm. There are, however, many reasons why you might be disappointed or confused by a gift. Finding gifts that people will go wild for is a combination of thoughtfulness *and* luck. This means there will likely be moments in our lives when we give gifts that receive a welcoming thanks but not an over-the-top reaction and times when we will be given something that slightly misses the mark or that we don't want or understand.

As long as the gift is not offensive or hurtful, there are plenty of ways to comment on other aspects of an off-the-mark gift while expressing your gratitude, whether it's for the thought and effort that went into it, or the gift's color, shape, size, or intended usage. Complimenting and commenting on a gift when you receive it is a great way to connect with the giver. But sometimes you don't have the words, and rather than forcing a lie that you might get caught in later, you can simply say, "Oh, thank you so much." You don't have to fawn over the gift and say how much you love it if you don't. You don't even have to come up with one polite thing to say about it. You can simply say, "Thank you." There are also times when a gift that flops can be appreciated when received with good humor—sometimes the flop can make the gift a memorable moment. "Trey once filled my room with Stargazer lilies, only to learn I was quite allergic! I was an itchy mess but love that it's one of our early dating memories."

Sometimes we are receiving gifts as a guest of honor. When we are, it doesn't hurt to have a practiced "excited-gift-opening-face" that is easily accessible. It's an "ooh, thank you!" expression. You don't want to fake it, and you don't need to be overly excited, especially if it's not "you" to be so. But throwing in a sincere "wow" doesn't hurt, either. And when all this is done well, it can make the giver and anyone watching feel good.

Many people feel guilty if they receive a gift and don't have one to offer in return. But a polite gift exchange isn't "Here's a gift for you" and "Here's a gift for you right back!" There are many occasions when we don't expect a gift in return when we give one—for example, at a birthday party or wedding, or when accepting a hosting gift. The polite exchange is a gift and a thank-you: "Here's a gift for you!" "Oh, thank you so much, Philip!" That is where you want to keep the focus as a recipient. We shouldn't let a feeling of awkwardness about not having a gift to offer in return interrupt our expression of gratitude.

There are times—like certain holidays—when gift exchanges are common. These scenarios can tend to make us focus on the reciprocity aspect of the exchange rather than the gift we've been given. If you find yourself being given a gift, and you don't have one in return, keep your focus on the gift you've been given instead of on your lack of a gift to give. Saying, "Oh, I'll have to get you something, too!" or "Your gift is still on its way," to buy yourself time is completely unnecessary. It removes the focus from the gift you've just been given and the generosity of the other person and places it on your lack of a gift in return. Focus on the gift and the spirit of generosity in which it was given—it really is the polite thing to do. You can always get someone a gift for the occasion and give it to them later on—no excuses needed.

THREE GUIDELINES
FOR GIFT-GIVING

There are three very important things to consider when giving gifts.

1. **STICK TO YOUR BUDGET.** A gift should always be within your budget, because that allows you to feel comfortable or good about giving it. Anyone who says you have to spend a certain amount for a gift to be worthy is selling something. Don't buy it. It's easier and better to feel genuinely good about giving gifts you can afford. (And no gracious friend or family member is going to expect you to overextend yourself financially in order to give them a gift.)

2. **YOU SHOULD FEEL COMFORTABLE GIVING IT.** Gift-giving is a personal choice and ultimately, it's up to you. Lists and registries are helpful guides intended to make life easier for others by offering inspiration and preventing duplicate gifts. If someone's wish list contains items you don't feel comfortable with, you should not feel forced to give them. They are meant as helpful suggestions and are not intended to limit you. Instead, find something that works for you.

3. **HAVE THE RECIPIENT IN MIND.** It *is* the thought that counts, and a gift that clearly had the recipient in mind will be well received. This one may seem obvious, but sometimes our gift giving gets so rote that we forget there's a person on the other end. This is an opportunity to do right by them. Golfers love golf balls. Coffee aficionados love coffee. The gift may not seem impressive to you, but it will be to *them*. A thoughtful gift is a tangible display of consideration for the person you're giving to. Keep the recipient in mind and keep it simple, and you'll likely do fine.

GIFTING MONEY

Gifting money has a reputation for being inappropriate and impersonal, when in fact this is far from the case. While there may have been a time when some found the idea a bit gauche, there are many traditions of gifting money, such as the gifting of cash or a check for a wedding, which has long been acceptable. Gifts of money for other special occasions such as a bar or bat mitzvah are common. Gift cards are so popular that they are often given for birthdays, graduations, teacher appreciation days, and many other occasions. Gift registries today have so many funding options for ways to gift money it's dizzying. We have accepted the truth that while material gifts are great, cash is certainly practical and appreciated. There are times when no check could compare to the personalized, handmade, unique, or thoughtful item that has been given to you. And there are other times when having the flexibility to get what you want or need is like a gift on top of a gift!

As everyone has different budgets, it's hard to say there is a *correct* amount for a cash gift, but there is a sense that the gift should match the relationship and the moment. Even though no one should ever look a cash gift horse in the mouth, certain amounts can be a little odd, depending on who is giving cash to whom and more importantly, how. A $10 bill in a thirtieth birthday card from Grandma? Sweet! A $10 bill handed over with a "Here, happy birthday," from a friend at your thirtieth birthday party? That could seem a little strange.

If the person you're giving to has a registry and there's a funding option, by all means use that easy system. You can always send a card as well. If you aren't giving your cash gift electronically, then it's often best to give a check so it can be replaced if lost. This isn't to say that cash isn't fun to give, and it's perfectly acceptable to do so. Sometimes tying a bow around a rolled-up check or stack of crisp bills is a nice touch, though many people will give cash or a check in a card. Whether gifting money by cash, check, or transfer, a card or note is always a must. It helps to personalize a gift: *Miguel and Steve, congratulations! Hope this helps welcome the new one—can't wait to meet her! Love, Uncle Tito.*

Since many people will exchange money on apps like Venmo or through a PayPal account, it's easy to think, *Why even do a registry or wish list—I should just give everyone my Venmo handle.* While that can seem convenient, sending guests your Venmo account handle for a wedding or other party is a little like saying, "Here, toss your money in my personal bank account." We all know that's where it's going, but it's a little uncouth. Also, if it's the *only* option you give people, if they aren't familiar with how to do it or don't have an account for that app, that could be a barrier for them. Giving multiple options to engage is always a good idea when gifts are expected.

REGISTRIES

Registries were created to help guests give during two particular events in life: weddings (and wedding showers) and showers to welcome a new child. That's it. Showers are specifically built around giving gifts, and that's why it's perfectly okay to include on a shower invitation where a person or couple is registered (*Bill and Maureen are registered at ABC store*). If it's a digital invitation, a registry link is included. While tons of websites have wish lists that can be shared among those who exchange gifts with each other frequently, these are different from registries and the courtesy is to wait to be asked before offering them to people.

For a wedding, you would never include registry information or even *No gifts, please* on the wedding invitation, even on an insert. Instead, include the wedding website on an insert enclosed with the invitation. Guests will find all kinds of helpful information, including the registry, or a statement of intention that the couple would prefer not to receive gifts, on the wedding website. It's okay to set up more than one registry: for cash contributions to a specific fund (like for a honeymoon or new house), donations to various charities, or for different stores. It's always good to have variety both in the types of gifts you're asking for and their price ranges so that no one feels priced out of using your registry. Registries also offer an easy way to keep track of gifts and to make a thank-you note list. Remember, a registry is a guide, not a checklist—there is no etiquette rule that says a registry must be bought out.

You should take care with your registry and the event it is created for. Its purpose is to help you get set up either in your marriage (where gifts are couple-focused) or to welcome a new child. While you might have desires for certain items, try to keep the gifts on the registry connected to the goal of the event.

Some people wonder about doing a registry for a housewarming or birthday. These are both parties where gifts *may* be given, but they are not 100 percent expected, as they are for weddings and showers. And sure, children's birthdays are pretty classic gift-giving events, but it's not the *sole* purpose of the party the way gift giving is for a shower. Nor is a birthday as monumental an occasion in life as a wedding, where gifts are traditionally expected. Adults rarely expect gifts at their birthday parties. For birthdays, graduations, housewarmings, anniversaries, and retirements, guests may ask when they RSVP about gifts and a host can share gift ideas, but a registry should not be used.

Housewarmings are traditionally thrown to literally "warm" a new home with the *presence* of family, friends, and new neighbors so the space doesn't feel so unfamiliar. It's a lovely sentiment and tradition. It doesn't matter what type of home you move into or how many times you have a new place to warm. If people do bring gifts, typically they are in the range of baked goods, houseplants, or freshly cut flowers in a vase—simple and sometimes consumable. Contrary to what some think, housewarmings are not about getting gifts and stocking your new place (or bar).

CREATIVE GIFT REQUESTS

Creative gift requests, like for donated items, one big-ticket item only, or no plastic can be great or awkward, depending on how they are communicated. Many people try to limit the number of material things coming into their homes or want to avoid gender-stereotyped gifts for children such as tea sets for girls and toy trucks for boys. (As a child, Emily was given a tea set, which she smashed to bits because what she really wanted was a toy truck—not exactly polite, but we love this story about her). Sometimes these requests are made for religious, political, or environmental reasons; other times it's a personal choice. These things are important to people, and while it's okay to indicate boundaries and preferences, when it comes to the generosity of others, you really don't want to manage it too much for the gift giver.

Gift requests like "Fivers" (giving kids a $5 bill instead of a gift with the goal being to use the "fives" they receive to get one gift), "No Gifts," are all convenient for sure, but gifting directions like these also limit the experience kids get in learning about gift exchanges: picking something out, wrapping it, presenting it, and handling the gift opening well socially. When making requests for specific types of gifts, we recommend that you (a) don't put the request on the invitation (which takes the invite from being about inviting the other children to being about micromanaging the gifts); and (b) suggest the idea when parents RSVP, if they ask about gifts: "Oh, I'm so glad Kiley will be able to come!" "She's really excited! What might Layla like this year?" "We've been suggesting either a book because she loves to read or participating in a fiver gift." Suggesting your gift goal with one or two other gift ideas can be helpful and allow the parent and child giving the gift to make the choice. (For more on birthday parties for kids, please see Children's Birthday Party, page 305.) It may mean a few people will choose a gift outside of your suggestions, but you'll still be closer to your goals than saying nothing, and you'll be polite and considerate toward your guests.

Traditionally, the only gift information you would put on a birthday invitation is *No gifts, please*. Anything else should be conveyed to the guest if they ask directly for ideas, or via word of mouth.

GIFTS FOR HOSTS

In her 1930s radio program *The Right Thing to Do*, Emily answered a question about bringing a gift for a host by saying that it was equivalent to a bribe or payment for hospitality, and would be quite rude. Since then, the host, hostess, or "hosting" (as we prefer to say) gift has ironically become an American tradition. Some guests swear by it and some hosts expect it (even though no one should), while many don't worry about it at all.

It is relatively customary on your first visit to someone's home—either the home of a new acquaintance, or the new home of someone you already know—to bring a small gift. It's supposed to be a simple kindness. It is not a direct offering of thanks for the invitation, but it has a bit of that feel to it. Some say it's about honoring the effort your host has made. Others say it's so you aren't a complete burden. For this reason, many don't worry about bringing a hosting gift when they attend a potluck event. Let us reassure you: your presence and good behavior are not a burden to your host—they've literally requested your company!

Flowers in a vase (or even a mason jar) or a small houseplant are always lovely and make for classic hosting gifts. Other typical hosting gifts include (but are in no way limited to) specialty treats like candies, chocolates, gourmet nuts, jams or jellies, the classic bottle of wine (if your host drinks wine) or its contemporary sister (in states where cannabis is legalized), "the joint to share." Other gift ideas include small entertaining items like bowls, serving utensils (think small spreading knives with cute handles), or cocktail items like coasters or barware. Candles and fancy soaps may sound like clichés, but they are often welcome. If you think of your friend, their style, and their (literal) taste, you will likely pick something great.

A host does not have to use the hosting gift that is brought or enjoy it with the person who brought it. While they certainly may if they wish, it is a gift for the host who may choose what they do with it. Sometimes a hosting gift is set aside and opened later when the host has more time (making a thank-you note necessary). For casual friends, a text, or better yet, a phone call are both appropriate follow-ups. If a host can open something when they are given it, they should be gracious and of course say, "Thank you so much!"

Friends who regularly host each other at their homes don't usually bring a hosting gift each time. This doesn't mean that they can't bring something, but it might be more sporadic for those who socialize frequently with one another. During holidays, friends who gather regularly often decide to bring something special over in addition to their good cheer.

When you are a houseguest, it's customary to give your host a gift as a thank-you for having you for an overnight or extended stay. Houseguest gifts can range from houseplants, housewares, or entertaining pieces to special-interest items (if you know the host's hobbies or interests), specialty foods, a dinner out or a dinner in (cooked and cleaned up by you). This last one is often reserved for close friends or family who would consider your cooking for them to be a gift. You may either bring your gift with you or send it afterward. If you bring a gift, don't forget to send a thank-you note as well after you've left. If you send a gift, send your thank-you note along with it! For more on houseguest gifts, please see the Reference Guide, page 216, and As a Houseguest, page 373.

GROUP GIFTS

Group gifts are both a godsend and a potential quagmire. Being able to contribute a small amount to help get someone a big gift is wonderful—when it's done well. Pooled resources can allow you to give a gift beyond what may have been possible on your own. Group gifts without foresight or a thoughtful approach, on the other hand, can lead to frustration, regrets, and often one person not getting properly reimbursed. Here are a few steps to help you navigate a group gift well:

1. Think first about what you'd like to accomplish. Is the point to have an even split, to have people contribute what they can, or to find enough people to purchase a certain item?

2. Raise the question to the group members in a way that allows people to decline privately if they want or need to, and that gives them a chance to ask questions. Contacting people privately or blind copying them in an email can be a smart way to make the initial ask.

3. Once everyone is on board with the gift, be clear about who is managing which parts of the process.

4. Ensure that everyone who participates gets to sign the card, or is acknowledged as having been part of the gift.

5. Everyone should feel comfortable giving the gift.

6. Pay up. If you're part of a group gift, you must pay your share or reimburse the person coordinating it as soon as humanly possible (if not earlier!).

There is no etiquette rule that says each person has to pay the same amount, or that the person coordinating the gift doesn't have to pay as much because they are doing the legwork. And there is definitely no rule that says that just because someone didn't contribute, their name should be left off the card. Some people worry a lot about who is *getting credit* for a gift, which moves the focus from the gift being given and the receiver being delighted to how great the people who got the gift are. That is the wrong thing to focus on.

There are a couple of other things to consider when giving a group gift at work. Typically bosses and managers or higher-ups will give gifts to their employees or direct reports equitably. Should employees feel inspired to give a gift up the ladder, it would be best done as a group gift so they don't look like they are trying to gain favor. There are some exceptions for very close business relationships, usually with much smaller teams or companies or long-established working relationships. If you're going to do this type of personal gift exchange, try to keep the exchange private and discreet. For group gifts, there should also not be a "price of admission" to participate in congratulating or thanking a boss, and everyone on a team or staff should be included on a card, whether they were able to contribute or not (unless they specifically asked to not be included).

If you are asked to participate in a group gift, be sure you're clear about what's expected of you and that you can meet the expectations before you say yes. Remember though, just because a group gift is happening doesn't mean you have to participate or explain your reasons for declining.

REGIFTING

Regifting can be one of the biggest sources of awkward moments and hurt feelings when it comes to gift giving. We've heard horror stories of date- and monogram-engraved items being regifted to people who did not celebrate the date or have the monogram. We've heard about cards saying, "Happy Birthday, Donna!" being left in gift bags for Talia, and of books being given with an inscription to the wrong person. And of course, about partially used or broken items showing up in the gift pile, leaving the recipient in the quite awkward position of having to say, "Thank you for the [*cough* used] towels." Though the very worst might be when a gift is regifted to the person who originally gave it (*gasp!*). It happens, and it is *really* bad etiquette.

We want to help people regift well, because regifted gifts can be phenomenal! Sentimental or cherished items being passed down, unused items finding homes and purpose, the environmental benefits of not contributing to more demand for new stuff, and the fact that it fits almost everyone's budget. There are lots of great reasons to regift! Here are four general guidelines to help you regift thoughtfully:

1. The item should be something you think the recipient would *actually* want.

2. The item should be in its original packaging, not opened or torn (unless it's an heirloom). And it should certainly have any and all accessories or manuals with it. Look out for an enclosed gift receipt or other information that may indicate the item is being regifted and remove it.

3. It cannot be something unique, home/handmade, or personalized.

4. The feelings of both the person you're giving to and the person who gifted it to you should be taken into account. How would they each feel if they knew the item was being regifted?

The very best way to regift is not only to keep these four guidelines in mind, but to be open about it: "Carolyn, now this isn't a brand-new bracelet, but it's one that I have loved for years and I thought you might really like it." Or "Someone gave me the newest edition of Emily Post's *Etiquette,* and I already have it. It's so useful, and I really thought you'd love it. I just had to regift it to you!"

A DONATION HAS BEEN MADE IN YOUR NAME

Gifts of donations, whether they are options on registries or given in lieu of flowers, are an excellent way to make a gift reach beyond the recipient. Because we don't all support the same causes, you want to be tactful in what you choose. Make sure the cause is something *the recipient* supports. Since there won't be a physical gift for your recipient to unwrap, usually the organization will send an image or confirmation that you can print out and place in an envelope or card.

If you are setting up charity options for a registry, choose a few so that your guests have a variety. Consider a range of organizations: local and national, secular and religious, political and nonpolitical, humanitarian efforts, the arts, and so on. And if you receive a donation in your name, even though you're not getting a physical gift, it's still important to write a handwritten thank-you note if you haven't had the chance to thank the giver in person.

THE IN-PERSON THANK-YOU

Expressing gratitude for gifts is an essential part of the gifting experience. When we skip it, people's feelings get hurt, or they wonder if their gifts were received or appreciated. Not expressing our thanks breaches the principles of consideration, respect, and honesty.

The in-person thank-you is without a doubt the *ultimate* thank-you. It is the expression of thanks with the greatest potential to convey your gratitude. With your voice, body language, and full attention, you can say directly to the giver that you are grateful for their generosity. They can witness your gratitude in real time as you express it. While you may resent feeling pressured to say thank you, especially if you're not excited about the particular thing you received, it's a great minimum etiquette standard to hold yourself to. Although a video call or voicemail can come close, nothing else—not even a handwritten note—can surpass this expression of appreciation. An in-person thank you is both the most personal and impactful form of gratitude you can offer.

THANK-YOU NOTES

There is a certain magic to a thank-you note. The act of writing one is an expression of our gratitude—a physical creation made in response to how you feel about the gift and the generosity of the giver. Receiving a thank-you note can be a moment of such satisfaction and surprise, even if it's traditionally expected. Used for generations, thank-you notes are a symbol of etiquette at its best. True as that is, many might groan inwardly at the thought of writing thank-you notes, as if it's some kind of chore. Let us offer a different perspective and inspire you to get excited about sending your gratitude. Think of a thank-you note as an opportunity, not an obligation. It's an opportunity to develop a skill, make a connection, express your gratitude, and make a good and lasting impression on someone who was generous toward you.

Gratitude can be expressed in so many ways. If you know that a friend or family member would rather get a thank-you phone call, email, text, or video call/message from you (or your children), then by all means, do that! But when you can, take the opportunity (especially when teaching kids) to write a note.

For some of us, writing legibly is difficult, but don't let that deter you. Handwriting is very personal; even when it's messy, it's unique to you. Good or bad, it creates a personal connection when someone reads something you took the time to write by hand. It isn't just a deletable digital message in a standardized font. It came from the hand of the sender, who took the time to think about it, write it out, address it, get a stamp, and send it. Effort and thought went into extending their appreciation. It's a great tool to use, and it feels great to do it!

A good thank-you note greets the recipient, thanks them, and wishes them well. A *great* thank-you note goes into a little more detail. Both are completely acceptable. (You can also follow this format for any written, voice, or video message thank-you.) Try to keep the focus of the note on the person you are sending it to and what you are grateful for. If you wish to catch up, you can, but it's also nice to keep the focus just on the gratitude. You can always send a second note to catch up, making for one happy mailbox.

Send your note as soon as possible after you've opened a gift. It's never too late to say thank you—even if it's been years. You can also send a message to let someone know a gift arrived, and then a thank-you note once you've opened it: "Package arrived today; will wait to open until my birthday." Or send a quick text or email to say thanks and let someone know a note is coming. "Package arrived today—thank you so much for the teas (note coming in mail)!" You should send a thank-you note for a thank-you gift:

5/19/22

Lucy,
What a wonderful surprise I found Saturday on my doorstep—thank you so much for the lovely flowers! It was such a joy to host you, can't wait for the next time. You are the best!

—Shawn

But it's not necessary to send a thank-you note for a thank-you note. If it was, the cycle would never end! (See Sample Notes, page 106, for sample thank-you notes.)

TEACHING KIDS TO WRITE THANK-YOU NOTES

Teaching children the importance of showing appreciation for gifts with a thank-you note is a reminder of the importance of gratitude and a living example of how traditions renew themselves with each new generation. When we teach this common courtesy to our kids at a young age, we make it easier than ever for them to access this skill and have it become part of their gift-receiving experience. The good news is, it's never too late. We can learn and embrace how to write a thank-you note at any age. There are ways to participate in and teach writing thank-you notes at every developmental stage of childhood:

- The littlest tykes (toddlers 2 to 3 years old), can watch the note being written by a parent. It's important to do this with them. They can participate by scrawling a mark on the card, adding stickers, or drawing a picture.

- Toddlers, and kids who cannot yet write, might help compose the message. Ask them what they want to say to personalize the note. Having the gift present when you assist them with the note can help them remember what they liked about a gift.

- Those with early writing skills can use phonetic spelling and creative name signing to start taking a more active role in writing their notes. Decorations are of course still welcome, and a fun way to make an activity out of writing thank-you notes. They might even assist with putting on the stamp. (Super exciting!)

- When your child can write well, you can focus on how to compose a proper note, aiming for good spelling and punctuation and following the classic thank-you note formats (see Sample Notes, page 106). Choosing personal stationery (or decorating blank cards) and picking the pen can be personal elements that give your child some ownership over how they present themselves. Trying out different closings is another way a child can develop their social writing voice.

- Encourage your older child to take care of addressing and stamping the envelope and putting the note in the mail. Once your kids are old enough and have spent a few years receiving your timely reminders, hopefully this practiced skill will have become an ingrained habit, and they will actually notice opportunities to send someone a thank-you note without considering it a burden.

REFERENCE GUIDE

GIFT GUIDE

We have many opportunities to give gifts, but not everything requires the same level of gift, or even a gift at all; sometimes a card is just right. Here are the most common gift-giving situations we run into and some ideas for what to give. Don't forget that experiences—tickets to the theater, concert, or a museum, for example—can also make amazing gifts.

THINKING OF YOU	This kind of gift is almost always welcome and can be truly anything that inspires you to give to someone.
CHILD'S BIRTHDAY	Ask the parents about the child's hobbies and interests. Otherwise, go with something non-gendered and age appropriate. You can always give a gift receipt or send a link for a return.
ADULT'S BIRTHDAY	Usually a card is more than enough. Flowers and favorite consumables (gourmet food items, wine/top-shelf liquor, cannabis), small décor items, or framed pictures are great go-tos. Avoid anything too personal and don't expect gifts to be opened immediately, especially if not all guests brought them.
ANY SHOWER	You can use the registry to find a gift, contribute to a group gift, or use it as inspiration to then go "off registry" and get something that inspires you. If you decline a shower invitation, you don't need to send a gift unless you'd like to.
COMING-OF-AGE PARTY	Check with cultural customs, but most gifts are something that is commemorative or more adult in nature, like a desk or vanity set, fancy pen, or engraved picture frame instead of toys or clothing. Cash is often acceptable and for some celebrations, like bar or bat mitzvahs, it's traditional. Cards are always appropriate. Ask the host for ideas.
HOUSE-WARMING	A card, flowers, consumables, or other hosting-style gifts are all appropriate. Houseplants, coffee-table books, vases, candles, and linens (coasters, napkins) are all welcome. Think something small.
RETIREMENT	Traditionally, guests don't bring gifts, but a gift may be given from the company or employer. Cards are welcome.
ANNIVERSARY	Traditionally, guests don't bring gifts for other people's anniversaries. Cards are welcome.
HOLIDAY	Homemade and consumable gifts. Small handmade items like something handknit or embroidered, or other quality crafts. For bigger gift exchanges, aim for recipient's interests and remember that what's boring to you might be awesome to them.
GRADUATION	Ask the graduate or their parent or sibling for ideas. Classic gifts are "professional" items, like a briefcase, pen, journal, organizer, or classic etiquette book. Anything commemorative is nice (a piece of jewelry, a pin, hair clip, cufflinks, a tie or tie clip), or something related to a favorite hobby or sport.

HOSTING GIFTS Consider consumables like flavored oils, specialty spices, decadent gourmet treats (watch for allergies), Vermont maple syrup, or preserved goods of any kind. Alternatively, small home goods like candles, small bowls, wood products such as salad bowls or cutting boards, coasters, napkin rings, a small vase with flowers, a spreading knife, place cards, table décor.

HOUSEGUEST GIFTS Classic gifts include potted plants or garden bulbs; entertaining items (candles, trays, platters, large bowls); a picture frame with a photo from a trip or a meaningful picture; personalized items, like a cornhole set with the family name on it or napkin rings with the family initial; dinner out, or groceries to cook for your hosts, if appropriate.

BIRTHDAY GEMSTONES

Jewelry for all genders can make for a memorable and sentimental gift, especially when connected to someone's birthday. Here are the birthstones for each month.

JANUARY	FEBRUARY	MARCH	APRIL
Garnet	Amethyst	Aquamarine	Diamond
MAY	**JUNE**	**JULY**	**AUGUST**
Emerald	Pearl	Ruby	Peridot
SEPTEMBER	**OCTOBER**	**NOVEMBER**	**DECEMBER**
Sapphire	Opal	Topaz	Turquoise

ANNIVERSARY GIFTS

For items that are now illegal or endangered (such as ivory or coral) or that don't fit your lifestyle (such as leather or silk), simply choose an alternative.

YEAR	TRADITIONAL (ALTERNATIVE)	YEAR	TRADITIONAL (ALTERNATIVE)
1	Paper/plastic (clock)	14	Ivory (stone)
2	Calico/cotton	15	Crystal/glass (watches)
3	Leather (faux leather)	20	China (platinum)
4	Fruit/flowers (silk)	25	Silver
5	Wood	30	Pearl
6	Iron	35	Coral (jade)
7	Copper/wool	40	Ruby
8	Electronic appliance	45	Sapphire
9	Pottery	50	Gold
10	Tin/aluminum (diamond)	55	Emerald
11	Steel (fashion accessories)	60	Diamond
12	Table or bed linens	70	Diamond
13	Lace	75	Diamond

SAMPLE GIFT AND THANK-YOU NOTE LEDGER

There are many events in our lives where it helps to keep track of the gifts we've received and who they were from. This ledger is great for showers, birthdays, and even gift-giving holidays to help you stay organized and write your thank-you notes well.

DATE RECEIVED	GIFT	GIVEN BY	ADDRESS	STORE/ WEBSITE	T.Y. NOTE SENT

CHAPTER 8

Hard Times

"At no time does solemnity so possess our souls as when we stand deserted at the brink of darkness into which our loved one has gone. And the last place in the world where we would look for comfort at such a time is in the seeming artificiality of etiquette; yet it is in the moment of deepest sorrow that etiquette performs its most vital and real service.

All set rules for social observance have for their object the smoothing of personal contracts, and in nothing is smoothness so necessary as in observing the solemn rites accorded our dead."

In Emily's era, mourning was a highly ritualized time with strict codes about what to wear, how you were addressed, when you could go out, even what you could talk about—all designed to help someone through their deepest grief. While different cultures and religions have varying rituals and expectations around death and grief, etiquette can help us through some of our most difficult times, providing a structure to lean on for what to say and how to act when we are truly at a loss.

Death is not the only hardship we face. An illness, injury, recovery, divorce or a serious breakup, physical or financial life adjustment—all are times when even the strongest of us need someone to care and to acknowledge our situation, and even the kindest of us don't always know what to say. Traditions and standards can be a guide both for those who are struggling and those who want to help.

SHARING TOUGH NEWS

While news about a separation or divorce, financial upset, or medical issue or condition might not be shared right away, deaths and accidents are events that are important to share the news about quickly. You want the people who are affected to know as soon as possible and in the most personal way. If you are delivering the news, whenever possible speak to someone in person. For serious situations, consider sending a friend or family member to deliver the news if you can't. If you or someone else cannot be there in person, a phone call is still preferable to a video call, text, or email. Leaving a voicemail with serious news should be avoided, if possible. Instead, ask the person to call you back right away and use a calm but serious tone. "Tyler, I have some sad news to share. Please call me back as soon as you have time to talk." If you aren't with the person at the time the news is delivered, it's best to make sure they aren't driving or in a place where their reaction might be difficult for them to handle.

If you can find your own words to deliver difficult news and you have the ability or time to process it with the person, that's wonderful, but you might not have that ability, and that's okay, too. Here are two sample conversations, one in which the focus of the shared news shifts to not being able to discuss it, and the other in which offers of support or more explanation follow.

"Monica, is now an okay time? I've got some sad news."
"Oh no . . . yes, now is fine. What's going on?"
"Dev and I miscarried this weekend."
"Oh my gosh, Vanessa, I'm so sorry!"
"Thank you. I'm not really ready to talk about it, but I wanted to make sure
    my friends know."
"I understand."

"Thanks for understanding."

"Please, give my love to Dev and tell him I'm so sorry."

Or:

"Willa, is now a good time to talk? I've got some sad news."

"Oh no! Yes, now is fine. What's going on?"

"Ricky died last night. It was a heart attack and no one saw it coming."

"Oh Kevin, I'm so sorry."

"I know how close you two were, and I wanted you to know. If you want to come over and be with me and the family, we're in shock, but you're one of us and we didn't want you to be alone after finding out."

"I just can't believe it. Thank you for letting me know. I'm so sad to hear this. And thank you—yes, I think coming over would be good."

One other thing to consider is letting those you reach out to know whether it's okay for them to share the news and how. "Toby has asked that we not share the diagnosis beyond his immediate circle, so if you could please keep the news to yourself for now, it would be best."

WHAT TO SAY

Acknowledging a hardship can have a profound effect on the person going through it. Have confidence that it is appropriate to acknowledge hardship and offer your sympathy or condolences. If you hesitate, think, *They just need to hear that I'm sorry for their sorrow.* Appropriate phrases include "I'm so sorry." "I'm sorry you're going through this." "I'm so sorry this happened to you." "I'm sorry to hear the news." "I'd like to offer you my condolences. I was very sorry to hear about . . ." "My deepest condolences. I was really fond of Rita. She always had a joke for me on our coffee break."

You can keep it short and sweet, or you can expand on the emotion if it's the right time and place—meaning you and the other person have the time to talk and they don't appear to be wincing or going quiet after your first "I'm so sorry." Do try to be very aware and observant of the person you're speaking with and how they seem to be handling the conversation. One of the best things you can do is to mirror their language. If they say "lost" instead of "died," go with "lost" when you speak about what's just happened. (For sample scripts, see the Reference Guide What to Say, page 240.)

WHAT NOT TO SAY

There are also lots of things you shouldn't say to someone who is going through hardship. Predicting what will happen in the future, claiming the divine willed it, or assigning someone responsibility for those left behind is not helpful during the grieving process and should be avoided. While it might be tempting to try to find the silver lining in the loss or consider it a lesson, that's often the last thing someone who is trying to process their grief needs to hear. If the person struggling is leading the conversation in that direction, it might be appropriate to offer mild comments in a similar vein. You can always affirm what someone is saying by being an attentive listener. But to use such statements in your effort to console is not the way to go.

The kinds of things you shouldn't say include: "It was God's will." "He's in a better place now." "It's a blessing in disguise." "It was time." "You're the head of the house now." "You better take care of your [sibling/parent/grandparent] now." "She'll be back up and at it in no time." "I recovered from it quickly; they will too." "Oh, that sounds bad; that won't ever heal right." or "Your life isn't over—you just have to look for the silver lining." The only way some of these statements would be appropriate is if the bereaved says, "He's in a better place now," and you say, "Yes, he is," or "May that be a comfort." Or if a family member or friend of a person who has been ill says, "We are really looking at the silver lining in all of this," and you respond, "That's wonderful."

WHAT TO DO

One of the very best things you can do for someone who is struggling is to show them you care. You might not be able to loan them money to reopen their restaurant, provide counseling to fix their marriage, or bring their loved one back, but you can engage and follow through with your words and offers to help. In doing so, you can help create a community that sustains them through their hardship. Cooking meals (the most traditional offering), helping them out with chores or babysitting, offering rides, running errands, paying visits, even being ready to talk on the phone: all can be ways to help someone feel supported who is grieving or struggling.

It's best to make specific offers of help, rather than simply offering help in general: "Hey, Amelia, would it help if I took the kids to the drive-in sometime this week?" or "I'm heading to the store tomorrow; I'd be happy to get your groceries for you. Is there anything you need from . . . ?" Offering to take a walk or have a chat over tea, or even help with the gardening or chores are all appropriate. Just make the offer something that is easy for the person to say yes or no to. Saying, "Hey, I'd love to help. Just let me know what you need," while well intentioned, puts the burden on the person grieving to figure out what might be good and imagine what you can offer and then request it of you. Making a specific suggestion allows them to simply react to it with a "yes" or "no", and then if they think of something better, they can suggest it.

Don't feel bad if your offer of help isn't accepted. What matters is that you sincerely offered something you could commit to doing. It's okay to continue to offer to help even if you are refused. Use your best judgment to not hound or annoy the person you want to help, and don't take their refusal personally. Also, be sure not to make an offer you can't commit to. The last thing someone who is suffering needs is for their loved ones or community members to disappoint them by not following through on their offers of help or support.

Sometimes people from the community organize help, such as a meal train, where a different person will be responsible for bringing meals to the impacted person or family regularly for a period of time. The volunteers will drop off their meals, and there is no obligation on the recipient to entertain them or even answer the door. This can be incredibly helpful and kind, and joining in this support can be a good way to help. Some communities send money. Knowing how expensive medical bills and end-of-life rituals and services can be, and also how hard times can hit you from all angles, it's not uncommon to find a check or some cash included in a condolence or sympathy note. (When and if this is appropriate will depend on the situation and the customs of your community.) If you're sending a donation with your note, it's fine to acknowledge it: *Please use the enclosed to help during this difficult time.* If you're on the receiving end, you most definitely want to mention the support in your acknowledgment and express your gratitude as well: *It was incredibly generous of you to include a check with your sympathy note. We are most grateful to you for it. Thank you.*

Listening is the very best thing you can do for anyone who is struggling or grieving, or when speaking with someone at a memorial service. Whether you are providing a welcome distraction, a shoulder to cry on, or someone to bark at (to an extent), allowing someone who is struggling to be wherever they are with it, expressing whatever they need to, is a true gift.

VISITING

Visiting those who are experiencing hard times is both essential and requires a delicate approach. You always want to make sure the visit is welcome and that you won't be unnecessarily taxing anyone. But it's equally important to look for opportunities to visit, pay your respects, and support those who are experiencing hardship. Whether it's dropping off soup when a family is hit hard by the flu, having regular dinners with a friend after a divorce or breakup, holding someone's hand through a tough chemo treatment, or offering comfort by paying your respects at a shiva or wake, it really matters to show up for people who are feeling down. Different scenarios warrant different approaches.

For more formalized situations like a shiva, wake, or viewing, newspaper announcements and word of mouth usually indicate when the family is hosting visiting hours.

For hard times that don't have a specific event or opportunity for people to gather and express their condolences, you want to make sure you are making an effort to reach out by offering to visit or help. Send a text (*Hey, checking in to see how you're doing and if a walk this weekend would interest you?*) or give the person a call ("Hey, how are you doing? I'd love to cook you dinner this week if that sounds good. Is there a good night for you?"). Avoid making your offer via a public social media post, comment, or DM/PM. These types of messages should be delivered as personally and directly as possible. Don't be disheartened if your offers are declined—just offering shows you care. Giving the person some time and space between offers is thoughtful, and if a handful of offers have been declined, it's okay to restrict your support to well wishes and a listening ear if needed.

VISITING AT THE HOSPITAL

Hospital visits are largely dictated by the hospital's visiting policy for the patient's ward. If you aren't an immediate family member, it's advisable and nice to call the hospital to check visiting hours and procedures, as well as the family to ask about preferences and convenience: "Jin, I was hoping to come up and sit with Eliza for a bit. Would this afternoon's visiting hours be an okay time?" If you don't hear back, you can always show up, but be prepared to leave if it's not a good time—this is something you should be ready for no matter when you visit. One of the nice things about this is that by calling the hospital and getting their visiting information first, you don't place extra burden on a family member of the person you are visiting, who is likely dealing with a lot.

Bringing flowers in a vase is kind. Specialty foods can be a great comfort, but it depends on whether the patient is allowed to have such items. A promise for that favorite cake once they get the A-OK from their doctor is usually a better bet. You should also avoid bringing in food for yourself to eat that the patient cannot; exposing them to the smell of a forbidden Philly cheesesteak or the sight of an off-limits treat after they've eaten only hospital food just isn't thoughtful. There are plenty of times when this won't be an issue, but it's considerate to ask first before eating during a hospital visit.

When you visit, be prepared to sit, talk, read, play games or do puzzles, watch something, or listen to a show or podcast together. Keep your antenna up for cues that a patient is tiring. Be prepared to take your leave; it's nice to allow the person to rest as soon as they might need to.

If you or a family member have been staying in the hospital, a communal gift such as lunch, some type of shared fruit basket or tray of treats, or a thank-you note for the staff who took care of you or your family member is thoughtful after you've left. If it's a very long stay, you might consider doing something nice for the staff while you're there, but the traditional time is once you're discharged. Note: Tips are not expected during a hospital stay.

VISITING THE ILL AT HOME

When visiting someone who is ill or recovering at home, you may have to lean on whoever is with them to schedule your visits and know the expectations for a visit. A spouse or caregiver will know the best times and the most engaging activities. Listen to their suggestions. If someone says, "He really just likes to be read to," then break out your reading glasses and go for it.

Bringing something over like flowers or food is thoughtful, but might not be necessary for each visit. Bring items that don't require much of the recipient (or the caregiver), such as flowers already in a vase, food that's ready to eat or stores well, games, books, or audio or video content.

While offering to plump a pillow or get a glass of water for the person is often welcome, this is definitely not the time to offer your point of view on the patient's recovery or management plan, or how x, y, or z could be done better or be slightly adjusted by their caregivers. It's one thing if you've been asked for your opinion or expertise, but outside of that, try not to come in and manage the situation when visiting.

It's important not to visit when you might have a cold or illness yourself. While you might really want to be there, put the recovery of the person you wish to visit ahead of your desire to connect with and support them, and stay home until you are well. When bringing children to visit, consider whether they are in the right state to be good visitors. Prepare them well for your visit and try to schedule it accordingly. If they are rambunctious, try to reschedule for another time.

CONSIDER THE CAREGIVER

Remember to always be considerate of caregivers during your visit. Whether a caregiver is a volunteer, hired professional, or someone close to the person who is ill, injured, or recovering, it's important to recognize that they are closely involved in what's going on, including your visit. Being respectful of their suggestions and courteous with them will go a long way toward having a smooth visit during a difficult time. It's kind to bring them something or include them in your offerings. Food, baked goods, books, special interest, or self-care items might all be welcome, and flowers are of course always a cheerful choice. While many people are happy to do it, caregiving can also be emotionally and physically exhausting. Being respectful and considerate of caregivers is the height of good etiquette.

If the caregiver offers you refreshment, it's fine to say yes, but don't feel you have to. Also avoid asking too much of the caregiver. They are doing a lot of work physically, mentally, and emotionally. Asking them for a cup of this, a plate of that, for lotion after washing your hands—it's just not the right time. Make do with what is readily available, and pay attention and participate in the ways they suggest.

VISITING VIA VIDEO CALLS

We learned all too well during the COVID-19 pandemic just how incredible (and also how dissatisfying) video calls are with a loved one who is suffering or recovering. When visiting in person is not possible for whatever reason, a video call can help us and our loved ones to feel connected. The following make for successful calls:

1. Prearranging a good time for the call

2. A good connection or signal on your end so you aren't wasting the facility staff's or an ill loved one's time and energy on a problematic connection

3. Holding your camera still, not jostling it or walking around with it, both of which can be disorienting for the person on the other end, especially if they aren't in top form

4. Saying important, meaningful, or caring things upfront or as soon as you do have a good connection and their attention

5. Letting the person you are "visiting with" decide when the call is over

It's nice to give your loved one as much time and attention as you possibly can. Do be respectful if the call is short or they don't have the energy to speak for long, and say goodbye gracefully.

VISITING THE BEREAVED

The first year without a longtime companion or a close family member like a parent, child, sibling, or best friend is often the hardest. It's the year during which we notice the differences and feel the lack; everything feels like a comparison or connection to what was. Having loved ones check in and help make plans to celebrate holidays and events together can make a big difference to the bereaved. Some people may still want time and space to grieve on their own, which should be respected. But it's also okay—and often kind—to keep checking on them to let them know you are there when they are ready to get together again. Visiting those who have lost someone isn't just something we do during a formal ceremony like shiva, or in the weeks following a death—it's something we continue to do as caring community or family members.

When you visit, your behavior and voice should match the tone of the household. If everyone is quietly gathering in the living room, don't try to start an animated or jovial conversation with your brother-in-law about the Texans' big loss last night. While your brain might have space for and even crave these other topics as a distraction, if the rest of the company is showing signs of a solemn and quiet mood, then it's respectful and considerate to match that.

Sometimes it can be tempting to try to cheer people up, but that isn't always the point. Now is a time for grief. It's the hugs, the planning of normal things like a meal together, and just being with loved ones that can matter most, not trying to convert frowns to smiles. Now, if a good rousing conversation about the deceased gets started as people tell stories and remember the good times, that's perfectly appropriate. But to break a somber setting by cracking a joke or telling a story would not be. On the flip side, when you aren't attending a memorial or remembrance-style gathering, it might not be the right time to revisit your grief if people seem to be well and their spirits are good. Balance how you express your own feelings with the cues you are getting from the bereaved.

While customs may vary both regionally and culturally, you don't have to bring anything with you when visiting the bereaved, but it will likely not be wrong to bring something if it feels right to you. This could be the classic casserole, or pie, or something sentimental like photographs of the deceased you want to share or give to the family. Flowers, once again, are also an option. Some folks might also bring a donation, either to help with the funeral costs or to help the family during this hard time.

GRIEVING A LOST PREGNANCY

One kind of loss that has been swept under the rug for far too long is when someone is grieving the loss of a pregnancy. No matter what stage of pregnancy, or how long someone has wanted to bring a baby into their life (whether by personally getting pregnant, or experiencing pregnancy through a partner, adoption, or surrogacy), or even if they weren't sure they wanted to be a parent, the loss is real. For some this loss is experienced along with hormonal changes that can affect feelings dramatically. No matter the circumstances, it can be complicated and extremely hard.

This is why many people prefer to avoid the subject and pretend that while it's sad, it's too private to discuss. But in truth, this is why we must do our best to be there for our family, friends, or colleagues—if they have included us when they experience this. If you have not been directly told about the loss of a pregnancy, it's best not to bring it up.

Finding words of support can be tough, but keeping them simple and clear and of course compassionate will help. "I'm so sorry for your loss." "How are you doing? Would you like to talk today?" "I'm here for you, however you need." You absolutely want to avoid saying things such as "Next time it'll happen," or "This just wasn't your time." While these statements are intended to be encouraging, they end up not feeling supportive. It's better to focus on the moment and let the future unfold as it will.

Keep checking in. This kind of sadness may last for a long time even if the person conceives again. The polite thing to do is to follow their lead as they move forward.

Also, do not assume that the partners of the people who miscarry are excluded from this grief. Far from it. Not every pregnancy results in a live birth, and any parent could be affected. One mistake we often make when speaking about the subject is assuming that only the person who was pregnant needs support. All parents who experience this loss need support.

DEATH AND FUNERALS

We'd like to start by saying, if you are reading this section because you have lost someone, we are very sorry for your loss. We hope you are surrounded by comfort and support at this time.

There is no one way to process a loss. Celebrating joyously, mourning sorrowfully, being quiet and reserved, shouting out the deceased's name to mark their existence—all are appropriate to help the living grieve. You might do one, none, or all of these; you might mourn with many people surrounding you, or you may find peace in solitude. What matters is that we acknowledge and grieve a loved one's death, and that the community is aware that a member has passed.

In America, we observe death in many different ways. Homegoings, funerals, memorial services, shivas, second lines, cremation ceremonies, drive-through viewings, and sharing or spreading ashes are all common ways we honor someone's passing. Some observances might contain multiple elements, like a funeral followed by a memorial service later or in another location. If a service is publicly listed, anyone may go and you should always feel encouraged to attend if you'd like to. We might think we are not close enough, or did not mean enough to the deceased, and should leave those closer with them to their privacy. This is rarely the case, unless it's been specified. Communities grieve together. Paying your respects and participating is an act of compassion both for yourself and for all those grieving the loss. You don't have to give a speech or write in the memorial book, but always feel welcome to participate if the service is publicly listed. Should the service not be public, sending a note or signing the online guest book are other ways to participate.

SPREADING THE NEWS

It's important to notify the deceased's closest loved ones, especially immediate and chosen family and any close colleagues, of the sad news. It's best to tell people directly or over the phone and not via text message or voicemail, and never through social media. Before you share the news, make sure the person is in a safe space and not driving. Once the deceased's family, closest friends, and colleagues have been notified, it's thoughtful to reach out to the religious community of the deceased and any groups they may have participated in, such as a garden club, community center, or regularly attended class. It's appropriate to post a message on their social media profiles particularly once an obituary has been made public so that those who follow or interact with them there will know the news.

OBITUARIES

After the deceased's family, friends, and workplace have been directly notified, a public announcement is made. Placing an obituary in the paper is a long-honored tradition. A beautiful thing about publicly announcing deaths is that you never know whom the deceased might have impacted that no one else knew about. By announcing their death in the paper, perhaps with a photograph as well, people in the community whom the deceased may have known but not socialized with get a chance to hear the news and mourn as well.

Traditionally, the notice will start with where the deceased most recently lived, and sometimes will include phrases such as "died unexpectedly" or "following a long illness" and the date of death. The obituary then summarizes the deceased person's life in chronological order, starting with where they were born and to whom, and including anything notable about their childhood, the places they lived, where they worked, and any community involvement. At the very end, it will say, "[S/he/they are] is survived by . . ." and list the spouse, children, and extended family, if any. If someone was married multiple times or has children from multiple partnerships, it will start with the current or most recent one and then work backward. As the list of family members can be extensive, after the immediate family it may say "and extended family." If the deceased is not survived by anyone, no mention of family is made other than the deceased's parentage. The obituary will also list where the service is and if it is open to the public. It may also mention where to send flowers or donations.

A nice thing to include in an obituary is a small gesture that members of the community can do to honor the deceased. It might be: *Join us Sunday, May 17, at 5 p.m. Pacific Time from wherever you are. We will drink a toast and say, "Skol!" It will warm our hearts to know you're honoring Alfred too.* Or you might ask that on the deceased's birthday everyone wear something blue. Whatever it is, it should have a connection to the deceased and be something easy for most people to participate in. This can be a way for those who might not feel comfortable writing or attending a service to join in and feel like they've properly honored the death of a friend or acquaintance.

While this might seem like an awful lot to include in an obituary, especially information from the deceased's early days, it's important to have it, as it helps those who may have forgotten or not recognized a name (which may have changed) to realize that they do, in fact, know the deceased. And as not everyone will come to the service, an obituary can help people spread the word. (For an example obituary, see Sample Obituary, page 239.)

MAKING ARRANGEMENTS

Making arrangements takes many forms. There are decisions to be made about a number of different things, from where the final resting place of the body or ashes will be, to how the body may be handled or transported to events and gatherings that celebrate and mourn this life lost. You might make the arrangements for a loved one's celebration of life, or you might be asked to do so for a friend or family member who cannot handle the task while they're mourning. In either case, there are a lot of things to organize and decide. It is best to find your most patient self and let it run the show.

Once everyone close to the deceased has been informed, you can start working on arrangements. Most people will work with a specialist at some point, whether to plan a full service or to handle the body.

Find out if the deceased had any specific wishes about their end-of-life ritual, and also check in with immediate family members about their wishes. They may give different opinions or ideas, but that's okay. It's important information. Early on, decisions have to be made around handling the body and where it will end up. If you're working with a funeral director, they can often help to determine what's possible with regard to things like green burials (which have the least environmental impact) home burials, bathing the body, preparing it a certain way, or even, in some cultures, spending time with the body before burial or cremation. There are laws in many states that govern how this process is managed, and these will dictate some of the choices available at this time.

Decisions also have to be made around a service, whether it's a memorial service (without a body) or a funeral (where the body is usually present in some form). When talking to a service director, we highly recommend that you gather the information, review it carefully, and take it home or give yourself time to decide. It's also okay to ask questions. The director is there to guide you through the process, or at least tell you what their process is. You can always meet with multiple funeral directors (you don't have to choose the first one you meet with), and it's okay to say no after you've met with someone. This is your service for your loved one. It can be done in whatever way the family feels is right (as long as it's legal).

While public gatherings allow communities to come together, there are times when private ceremonies or gatherings will be part of celebrating a life. Open gatherings are announced in the paper and allow for anyone who reads them and knows the deceased to come and participate. This can be a wonderful way to witness the community of people a loved one has touched. That being said, they are not always possible.

Typically, the decision about whether to bury or cremate the body will help determine some of the other points of order in the service or ceremony. If there is going to be a casket, then either pallbearers or honorary pallbearers will be required. Pallbearers usually consist of six to eight of the deceased's closest friends, mentors, or colleagues. They may be of any gender. While the family typically walks behind the casket, some family members may also act as pallbearers. Usually at least one pallbearer will be a funeral staff member to help ensure things go smoothly.

Honorary pallbearers are selected when a funeral service enlists its own staff to carry the casket, or when the casket is on a "church truck" (a wheeled cart for the casket) and needs to be guided by only one person. In this case, the honorary pallbearers either walk next to the casket with their hands on it, or they walk behind it. These protocols will vary depending on the situation. The funeral director will discuss with you all the options and rules for carrying the casket. (For example, family or friends will often not be allowed to carry a casket on stairs, as it's an insurance liability.)

You'll work with the service leader, funeral home, or religious venue to create a program for the service for distribution (see Sample Program, page 239). Note that many people will want to hang on to their program as a keepsake.

Flowers, pictures, and an outfit (for the burial or possibly even for the cremation) will need to be chosen. For a green burial you will decide if the body will be covered or not and whether or not a simple biodegradable casket will be used. You will also want to think about the tone and music for the service. Eulogists and readers should be selected quickly so they have time to prepare and practice. Typically, you wouldn't choose more than three eulogists. Note that not everyone will say yes or feel comfortable speaking, and it's best to respect this.

Memory boxes can be set up during the service for attendees to leave their memories and stories about the deceased for the family. These are a wonderful tradition, and in a time when many people aren't certain, or even aware, of the custom of sending condolence notes and letters, it encourages and allows for their memories to be shared and preserved. Be sure to leave paper and pens nearby so that those who haven't thought to bring a remembrance can write one on the spot. Gathering comments from social profiles to be printed and displayed on a memory table or given to the family is another way to share memories.

You will also need to decide if there is to be a reception with light refreshments for those who have come to pay their respects. Some communities will do this automatically, with a potluck or reception organized by the congregation. For others, it's not set in stone. While a reception isn't mandatory, it is a nice way to meet and greet those from the community who would like to pay their respects. Sharing food and drink with others is nourishing and healing, and often helps us remember the good times, even during the difficult ones.

There is no one right way to celebrate a life. The biggest goal is to make sure that you feel you've included the rituals and traditions that the deceased would have appreciated and that the bereaved are comfortable with. Remember outside of any directives the deceased has indicated, a service is very much so for those living to process their grief and celebrate a life lost.

As the coordinator, you'll likely hear a lot of opinions. It can be hard to listen to them all without feeling overwhelmed. One helpful tip is to cultivate some PNRs (positive noncommittal responses), such as, "I'm hearing you. Let me find out more and get back to you," "That's an idea, let me think about it," "Thank you! I will add that to the list of things to look into," or "Thank you for sharing that; it helps me see more options."

Flowers left over from the service and reception are often donated to a local hospital or other space that appreciates the cheer. If the venue doesn't do this automatically, engage a couple of friends to deliver them.

EULOGISTS AND READERS

It's a great honor to be invited to be a eulogist or give a reading at someone's service, but not everyone is comfortable with giving one. Ask people who were close to the deceased and can speak to different aspects of their life and know how to keep it appropriate for a broad audience. Make it easy for those who are hesitant to turn the request down: "Phyllis, you've known our mother since girlhood. Would you be willing to give one of the eulogies at her service next week?" "It would be an honor," or "I'm so honored that you asked, but I must respectfully decline."

You don't want to offer too much guidance on what the eulogists should say; however, a rough estimation of length or possibly a time limit can help. Make sure everyone knows in what order they are speaking. Sometimes those speaking will consult each other so as not to repeat too many of the same qualities or stories about the deceased in similar ways. For secular readings, anything inspirational or that has a connection to the deceased would be a good choice as long as it's not too lengthy. Religious readings may be specific to the religious service and not something you have a choice about. If asked to read, a reading may be assigned to you, or you may be offered a choice of readings.

ATTENDING A FUNERAL OR MEMORIAL

There may be more than one event associated with end-of-life celebrations and rituals—for example, there may be a wake, a funeral service, a burial, and a reception all for one person. If the family is holding both a funeral and memorial service, you could go to either or both. Sometimes a belated memorial service is held when someone has loved ones or spent time living in multiple places; for example, someone who lives in the north in the summer and the south for the winter. Take note that there is no body at a memorial service, whereas at a funeral and wake the body is usually present. A lot of time, effort, thought, and emotion have been put into planning the service and ensuring there is room for all to grieve the loss. Honoring that is incredibly respectful and can be healing. It's easy to think of ourselves as more removed, or not worthy of comfort and community because someone else is closer to the deceased or grieving more deeply than we are. Do not minimize your loss in this way. Attending end-of-life events is a way for us to process, participate, and both give and receive the comfort an entire community needs and has to offer during this time.

If you're attending a reception after a service, you'll want to read the room. Some celebration-of-life gatherings are parties with dancing, music, and food to keep everyone in good spirits. Other times, they're quiet events where the family stands in a receiving line, and tables of small bites and beverages are offered. You mingle for a bit, and then get in line to pay your respects. Introduce yourself to the family members in the receiving line whom you don't know and let each of them know what the deceased meant to you and that you are sorry for their loss. Then take your leave, or you can continue to mingle with the other mourners.

If you're attending a type of ceremony you've never been to before, do your best to research the customs and appropriate attendee participation and attire so you can contribute to the event and not be a distraction. A variety of end-of-life services can be organized by funeral directors. You can ask them about these directly, or some funeral services will list common service customs (attire, ceremonies, offerings) on their website. Information on religious services can usually be found online as well. You might also talk to a friend, spiritual advisor, or family member who is involved or is familiar with the appropriate customs and traditions. Sometimes, once you arrive, you can find helpful information in the program itself so you know what to do while you're there. We hope to see more funeral directors post programs on the funeral service website ahead of time so that potential attendees can get a sense of what to expect and how to participate.

Sometimes a service will provide an opportunity for anyone who would like to say something to speak up. While you should feel free to speak from the heart, it's also thoughtful after a long service to keep your remarks concise to allow time for as many people as possible to offer their remembrances. Ask yourself whom you are speaking for and to right now.

The only time you wouldn't try to attend or participate in an end-of-life service or ceremony is if the religious customs do not allow it, or if you read or hear that the event is private. Should you find out that someone you loved and cared about will be celebrated privately and you aren't included, it's best not to ask. Do send a condolence note, and try instead to find a time and place to honor the deceased and your relationship to them. You will be told directly if you are invited to a private event.

IN LIEU OF

While it's traditional to send flowers to the service location or the family's home, many families prefer that you show your generosity in other ways. "In lieu of" often refers to giving something instead of flowers, but although flowers may be off the table, food and offers of help are still welcome. Donations in honor of the deceased to their favorite charities are typical; usually a few are chosen so that family, friends, and colleagues have options, which may also include college funds or family support. It would also not be "bad etiquette" if you did send flowers only to learn later that the family had an "in lieu of" request.

VIRTUAL SERVICES

Virtual services allow mourners to pay their respects while still maintaining appropriate social distancing (such as during the COVID-19 pandemic), or in case of mobility issues. Virtual services are likely going to continue since they allow many people to participate in or attend a service who would otherwise not be able to. Unless the family has requested otherwise, these are typically events you would stream only and not participate in as a virtual guest. At a smaller virtual ceremony among family and very close friends, you might be invited to share stories, sing, pray, and comfort each other. When circumstances prevent people from being there in person, sometimes a reading or eulogy can be conducted via video. A livestream might also be set up, or a recording of the event might be posted afterward.

If you are the organizer for a virtual service, sometimes the facility handling the memorial service will offer to handle it and help you create and send out links. Other times it's on you to set up a virtual option. If so, it is essential to send out the link and password to anyone who needs it. This might require tracking down a lot of emails, but it's worth the effort.

If it's a service that's open to all, posting the link publicly is thoughtful, though do be mindful of any limits on how many people can join the stream. Put someone tech savvy in charge. Make sure any maximum limits or "waiting rooms" have been removed (if appropriate), or that you are prepared to deal with them. Resending the link out an hour or two before the event is helpful. You can include the program information, and also give directions such as *We're going to unmute microphones during songs, and we hope you'll sing from wherever you are,* or *While everyone will stay muted for the service, we ask that you leave comments or participate through the chat feature.* For those who might have trouble with this technology, always offer to help or deputize someone as "tech support."

As the host or organizer, remember to thank everyone who came to the virtual service. You can close out the open chat with a thank-you, or you can speak directly to folks to say thank you and let them know that your thoughts are with them as well. It's always best to end a virtual service with something like this rather than just closing the stream abruptly.

HONORARIUMS

An honorarium is payment given to those (usually spiritual leaders or musicians) who officially perform a service during a memorial or funeral. Customs can vary when it comes to honorariums, and it's best to check with the funeral director or the person performing the service (or their office) to see if there is a suggested amount. These can range from $100 to $300 or higher. After the service, either you or the funeral director or coordinator would give a check or cash to the person who performed the service and separately to any musicians who played during it. The check or cash should be accompanied by a thank-you note.

If there are musicians during the service or reception, consult ahead of time with whoever hired them as to whether they request an honorarium. Again, present it to them after they finish, and preferably with a note of thanks.

EXPRESSING SYMPATHY

Whether it's through a condolence note, in person, or via phone, video, or even a text message, we typically say, "I'm so sorry" to sympathize with those who are going through hard times. If we bump into someone at a store or gathering who is experiencing a loss or hardship, we might not be sure if an expression of sympathy will be welcomed. More often than not, it's best to say something rather than not acknowledge the loss at all, especially if it's the first time you're seeing the person or if you have not yet had the chance to send a note or give a call.

Depending on what type of hardship someone is facing, you might also choose not to say anything about it. A lost job is indeed tragic, but it's not quite the same as a lost life. Not to acknowledge the latter would be ignoring the giant elephant in the room, whereas mentioning the lost job might identify an elephant someone wants to ignore or at least have some space from. Elephants do take up a lot of room, after all.

EXPRESSING SYMPATHY IN PERSON

AT A SERVICE OR MEMORIAL. Sometimes the receiving line at a service or reception will be the first time we have a chance to say anything to the bereaved. While this can cause a minor moment of panic for some, trust your heart to guide you and say, at the very least, "I'm so sorry about your wife," or "I'm thinking of you." You could always add, "Your wife was such a wonderful woman. I will miss her."

While it's okay to have a conversation about the deceased with any member of their inner circle at a service or reception, it's also very important not to take too much of their time. This is a time to share in their grief, but you want to make sure you are leaving them time to meet with everyone who has come to pay their respects.

WHEN OUT AND ABOUT. There are many people whom we might run into before we have a chance to sit down and write a proper sympathy note. Expressing sympathy in person can be as simple as saying, "Mary, I heard the news about Carla, and I am so sorry" the next time you run into Mary. If, in the very rare chance that you catch Mary in a moment when she really did not want to be comforted, immediately offer a sincere apology ("I'm sorry, I didn't mean to upset you and I have. Take care.") and then let them be. Do not try to force acceptance of your apology or carry on about how sorry you are. Just apologize and move on.

SYMPATHY AND CONDOLENCE NOTES

Condolence notes are sent only when a death occurs. Sympathy notes can be sent for both hard times and also when a death occurs. Sending your condolences to those who are grieving is actually a very meaningful part of the grieving process for both parties. Being able to reach out and say, *Your loved one meant something to me, too, and they will be missed* is deeply human. When your loved one has passed, receiving word of how loved someone close to you was, how appreciated they were, is comforting. Hearing stories about a person you cherished can be like finding proof and permanence when life just proved itself so fragile and fleeting. Even when you did not personally know the deceased, offering your condolences to someone you know who is grieving is appropriate and thoughtful.

There are some things to consider when writing a condolence letter, but first and foremost, write it from the heart. Write what you want to say. You can simply say how sorry you were to hear the news and that you hope the bereaved is comforted at this time. If you have a memory of the person that would highlight some of their good qualities, you may certainly include it. It will be welcome. If you had more of a connection with the bereaved, you can make that the personal point of the note.

For a sympathy note, keep the focus on the affected person and your good wishes for them. It's okay to address the news itself, for example, "I am so sorry to hear you broke your leg." But avoid assuming you know how they feel by saying things like, "That must be awful for you," or "You must be devastated." Instead try "I hope your recovery goes smoothly for you." (See Sample Notes, page 107.)

ONLINE CONDOLENCES

Often, newspapers and funeral homes will have an online remembrance "guest book" or other designated space for readers to leave condolences for the bereaved. Look for a designated link or space right after the obituary. The family may or may not respond, and they shouldn't be expected to, though you can usually trust that they will read all of the comments. The family might choose to post a message to all who offered their sympathies either in the publication where the announcement was made or on the funeral home's website.

While people are free to post what they wish, a family might decide to take down a post if it includes either an incorrect statement about the deceased or references private matters. Though they are often personal in tone, remember that these are public communications. If there is a personal message you really want to make sure the family receives, it's best to use a more direct method, such as a note or phone call.

CONDOLENCE AND SYMPATHY TEXTS, SOCIAL POSTS, AND MESSAGES

While we might think it's inelegant or awkward to talk about death via text or direct message (DM), or to post about it online, people do. For the outer rings of a person's social orbit, it is not uncommon to find word of their passing spreading via text, social media posts, and messages. Many people have online friends and contacts that they never see in person, and taking care with how the news is shared in this space is important.

Unless they are following explicit instructions from the deceased, family and friends should refrain from posting anything from someone's profile after they are gone. The obvious confusion this can sow can be avoided by exercising simple discipline. There are a lot of things to consider in managing someone's digital presence after they have passed away. Some profiles are taken down, while others are left up as memorials to the person; if this is the case for you, consider posting the person's obituary or a message with a link to the obituary to their feed to make news of their passing clear and help spread the word. Beware of any "auto-posting" features or letting the deceased's friends or family post for the account, which could confuse or upset the deceased's social media contacts. Someone should also moderate the account if possible to keep any comments appropriate.

SYMPATHY FOR DIVORCE

Divorce can be very tricky socially. Feelings around divorce can range from relief and even jubilation to deep sadness or anger. While a divorced person's nearest and dearest will usually know exactly how they feel about the situation, many friends and acquaintances won't know if sympathies are even needed. If someone tells you they are getting divorced and you don't know how they feel about it, instead of "I'm so sorry," one of the best things you can say is "Divorce can be hard. How are you doing?" This will help you quickly determine where the person is, and you can then support them more appropriately.

Often those closest to the couple will be riding the emotional waves of the relationship throughout the process. It can be hard to keep up sometimes. Do your best not to villainize either party. And avoid trying to push or suggest the right decision for a friend. Good default statements are "I'm here for you, whatever you end up deciding," "I think it's really great that you're thinking about all of these things," or "How are you feeling about it?" Follow the lead of the person going through it. This doesn't mean *not* giving your opinion, but it does mean recognizing that you aren't the one going through the divorce, even if you've been a support or a witness through it.

It's especially important to be careful what you say around children whose parents are separated or divorcing. Cheering the news or making negative comments is unnecessary. Remember that you never want to disparage a parent in front of a child.

If you're the person getting divorced, when you do start telling those beyond your inner circle, it's best to be as simple and clear about it as possible. Certainly tell your own truth, but good etiquette would suggest that the less you ask acquaintances to celebrate the divorce having happened or trash-talk your former partner with you, the less likely you are to make the person you're speaking with uncomfortable.

ACKNOWLEDGING CONDOLENCES

From an etiquette standpoint, the ideal would be for everyone who took the time to send a note of condolence to receive a reply, thus completing the "conversation" and properly acknowledging (in kind) the condolences and sympathy offered. The idea is not to leave something so kind and personal unanswered. While you might think it's cruel (even perverse) to expect those who are in mourning to express their gratitude through an acknowledgment note, especially in some cases when they might be arriving by the hundreds, this can be a particularly helpful way to move through grief. While writing acknowledgment notes won't erase your sadness, many people say that the act of reading condolence notes and hearing how their loved one was appreciated, or sensing the true sympathy and support offered them during such a sad time can be truly transformative, and that taking the time to write back and connect with the sender was more uplifting than they expected. Do your best to reply to each note that is sent to you. Here is a sample response to a gesture of condolence:

2-22-23

Dear Jill and Patrick,

Thank you both for the lovely casserole and the kind note you dropped off Saturday evening. We're sorry we could not accept a visit, but it lifted our spirits so much to know you had been here. It feels really good to hear your words about Giuseppe. We miss him so much.

We will enjoy the casserole and look forward to seeing you all soon.

Many thanks,
Chelsea, Luca, and Liza

If you have hundreds of notes to reply to, which does happen, or you are really too far into your grief to be able to rise to the task, you may enlist family or the very closest of friends, though usually just family, to help write acknowledgments on your behalf. Such a response would look like this:

10-12-22

Dear Mr. and Mrs. Chang,

On behalf of my mother, Alicia Faulk, I would like to thank you for the kind condolence note that you sent regarding my father's passing. We miss him dearly, and your words have truly helped during our time of sorrow. We are wishing you the very best.

My sincerest gratitude,
Gertrude Faulk

REFERENCE GUIDES

MEETING WITH A FUNERAL DIRECTOR

While most people meet with a funeral director, there are many different people within the field of end-of-life services who may help or assist you in different ways. Here are some things to consider as you work with end-of-life specialists:

- First check to see if the deceased has any directives about how they will be laid to rest and the type of service that might accompany it.

- Speak with the immediate family ahead of time so you have an idea of what the family is looking for. It's okay if ideas differ; a director can usually help.

- Find out what the legal obligations and requirements are for handling the body and any forms that need to be filled out or filed.

- Ask *any* question you may have. About *anything*. This is about you and your family processing a loss. No question is inappropriate. Your request might not be possible, but it's always okay to ask.

- It's okay to call ahead to get pricing or any other information, before meeting with someone.

- Remember, a director can't decide for you, but is there to help you make decisions. You can always take your time or come back again. There is usually not a rush.

- You can always say, "Thank you, but I'm going to keep looking."

SAMPLE OBITUARY

Elliot James Strand, 76, died peacefully, surrounded by family, on August 31, 2022. He was born September 9, 1946, in Danville, Kentucky, to Wilma and Ned Strand. Elliot spent his childhood and adolescence in Danville and attended Centre College. After graduating with a degree in molecular biology, Elliot went on to travel the world while working for a biotech firm. He lived in Singapore, Tokyo, Jaipur, and Paris. It was in Paris that he met and married Sabine Moreau. Together, they moved back to the States, settling in Atlanta, Georgia. Elliot was a member of the local Rotary Club, was an avid fisherman, and spent much time volunteering for his local V.A., where he worked closely one-on-one with its members. Elliot is survived by his wife, Sabine Moreau Strand; their children, Jennifer Strand Miele and her husband Antonio, Caroline Strand-Biggs and her wife Margaret, and Elliot James Strand, Junior; and his granddaughter, Rebecca Sabine Strand. A celebration of life service will be held at the Atlanta Rotary Club, 124 Peachtree Ave., from 4:00 to 6:00 p.m. on Sunday, September 4th. If you are unable to join us for the service, please join us in saying Elliot's favorite expression, "Always look to the light," from wherever you are at 5:00 p.m. Eastern Time on his birthday, September 9th.

SAMPLE PROGRAM

FRONT	INSIDE LEFT SIDE

A memorial service in honor of
Trey Jackson Thompson
[Image of the person or sometimes a religious or cultural symbol]
[Name of service venue]
[Address of service venue]
	A memorial service in honor of
	Trey Jackson Thompson
	December 30, 1955—April 12, 2022
	April 17, 2022
	
	PRELUDE *Performed by Lizzie Allen*
	OPENING REMARKS *Rev. Richard Wyndell*
	CALL TO WORSHIP
	HYMN NO. 525: "HERE I AM, LORD"
	PRAYER
	READINGS
	   Psalm 121 *Mr. Elan Thompson*
	   1 Corinthians 13:1–3 *Miss Madison Thompson*
	   Tribute *Mrs. Elizabeth Thompson*
	   "Shout to the Lord" *performed by Eli Barrett*
	   The Apostles' Creed *Rev. Richard Wyndell*

INSIDE RIGHT SIDE	**BACK**
Prayers or lyrics to hymns Benediction Postlude	Either the obituary or a poem, piece of writing, quote, prayer, or lyrics to a song. Or: Visitation with the family will follow in the parish hall next door. Service Participants: The Reverend Richard Wyndell, Pastor The Reverend Michaela Lynnfield, Assistant Pastor Eli Barrett, organist and soloist

WHAT TO SAY/WHAT NOT TO SAY

WHAT TO SAY	WHAT NOT TO SAY
"I am so sorry."	"You/We were expecting this."
"I was so sorry to hear about John, how are you doing?"	"It was time."
	"This has been a long time coming."
"I'll give you a call Thursday to check in and see how I can help."	"Call me if you need anything. Happy to do whatever!"
"I'll call you Thursday to check in about helping with meals and driving the kids."	"Let me know what I can do."
"I am wishing you all the love, comfort, and support you need right now."	"You'll have to step up and be the man of the house now."
"I'll be thinking of you."	"Chin up, brave face."
"I am so sorry for your loss. I know how much you were looking forward to this, how are you doing?"	"It just wasn't meant to be."
	"You can always adopt."
"How are you doing? Would you like to talk?"	"You have to be patient, it will happen."

WHAT TO DO

- Write a condolence or sympathy note.

- Contribute a donation to a suggested charity or fund, send flowers, drop off food or join a meal train, or participate in a commemoration (like wearing blue on the deceased's birthday or toasting them at a particular time). It might be wearing a ribbon or a team color for an injured teammate or community member.

- Offer a specific type of help—for example, bringing a meal or starting a meal train for someone; offering to come clean the house or help with the kids.

- Offer to call or visit at a specific time.

- Pay attention to and respect any caregivers who are assisting.

- Keep reaching out.

- If someone has died, share a story or memory with their loved ones.

- Give yourself a hug, too, especially if you are in mourning as well.

SAMPLE CONDOLENCE NOTES

May 24, 2023

Dear Sierra, Graham, Lynx, and Jackson,

We are so sorry to hear of Greg's passing. It has been so wonderful to get to know him and all of you over the past ten years living on Birchwood Lane as neighbors. Greg always had a smile for us as we passed him working in the yard. And we are so grateful for that day he caught our dog Bella before she bolted into the street. He will be remembered and missed dearly. We are thinking of you all at this time and sending you much love and support.

We'll check in to see if we can help with the kids, errands, and chores in the coming months.

With our deepest sympathies,
Joan and Wyatt Silver

June 3, 2021

Dear Richard,

It is with great sadness that I offer my condolences to you. Martin was one of the most accomplished men I have had the pleasure of knowing and calling a colleague. He will be dearly missed, and I am wishing you and your children much comfort at this time.

With sympathy,
Abigale

SAMPLE SYMPATHY NOTE FOR RECOVERABLE CONDITIONS

7-8-22

Dear Arya,

I was so sorry to hear about your leg. I'm wishing you the speediest recovery, and I can't wait to get back out dancing! Chair dancing till then—I'll make you a mix!

Love you lots,
Delphine

SAMPLE SYMPATHY NOTE FOR A TERMINAL CONDITION

11-12-23

Dear Tillie,

I am so sorry to hear that you are not well and will be staying in the hospital. We have arranged for fresh flowers to come weekly to brighten your room. And I will be sure to call regularly until we can come visit. Kamal and I are wishing you much comfort right now. We have you in our thoughts always.

Much love,
Alka

CHAPTER 9

Life at Home

"Just as no chain is stronger than its weakest link,
no manners can be expected to stand a strain
beyond their daily test at home."

One could easily say that what happens behind closed doors is certainly not ours to judge, and we should just keep our noses out of it. However, at home, many of us live with others, whether roommates, a partner, a spouse, or other family members, and just as our behavior impacts those we encounter in our social and work lives, it also affects those with whom we live. In fact, home is often where we need to take the most care, even if (and maybe because) it is the place where we relax the most.

We have an impression of what a happy home feels like: it's welcoming in appearance and attitude. This doesn't mean perfect paint or flooring, or a warm plate of cookies offered to you upon arrival. It means clean and cared for enough that those who live there and those who visit will be unquestionably comfortable. It's a place that respects all those who live there by meeting their needs.

A home should feel safe. A place where we can feel a sense of trust with those around us. It's not a place for perfection, but neither is it a place where we can drop civility and standards altogether. We might put our feet up on the coffee table, but we don't walk all over those we live with, dictating this and disrespecting that. We also don't want to relax our manners at home so much that our roommates, partner, or family feel like we don't care about them. At home, those we live with deserve our respect and consideration, our magic words, and our efforts to find what works best for everyone—this is just as important at home as it is in our work or social lives. The specific behaviors, expectations, and customs will vary from home to home, but for each, the home is a place where you, and those you live with, get to decide what you are comfortable with and capable of committing to.

THE THREE C's

One set of basics that seems to help smooth out the bumps, whether or not you are related to those in your home, is what we call "The Three C's"—communication, compromise, and commitment.

COMMUNICATION

It's crucial that you and those you live with maintain good communication habits around house-hold issues. Start by identifying your own perspective. Next, create space in your mind to hear others' experiences and perspectives. Then, set a time to talk. Creating a regular or recurring family or house meeting can help to facilitate good communication.

First, you want to establish some basic house rules, like no food outside the kitchen, shoes on or off inside, guidelines for inviting guests, who does what chores when, and so on.

Establishing these things means talking about them, not just assuming someone will wash their dishes right away or vacuum once a week. Once these rules are in place and understood, when things go wrong, you can talk about what's not working—which is better than letting it fester. When issues arise, the important thing is to *hear* the other person's perspective and try to find out if there's a better way to honor it. For example, you might text your roommates: *Hey guys, I'd love to have a house meeting Friday about the state of the kitchen and how we can make it work so it's not a mess.* Or you might say to your partner, "Honey, I'd love to have a chat about how we're handling household chores; is now a good time?"

It's important to hear each person's thoughts. While kids might not get to decide what chores they do, including them in age-appropriate ways not only shows them respect but also helps them build listening and participation skills. When listening to each person, it might become clear that one might not think the issue is a big deal, while another is really upset by it. "The TV is too loud." "But I can barely hear it." The point is to identify the issue, allow everyone's opinion to be heard, and find a better way to tackle the problem together. "Can we turn it down and use subtitles?" or "Mom and I can go talk in the kitchen instead." Another example, your roommate may need to do the dishes, but if establishing the original house rule didn't work the first time, telling them to just do the dishes isn't likely to motivate them a second time. You might suggest a time when you can all do the dishes together, or the roommate loses kitchen privileges until they can scrub a pot. The point is, don't just air your frustration; talk about doing something differently. Work at it instead of complaining about it.

COMPROMISE

Compromise is about coming up with solutions that the household can reasonably commit to. Think about the problem and the best way to motivate the people involved to commit to a solution that is reasonable. This is also a great time to bring your most gracious and creative self, the version of you that says, "Yes, I can." It's very easy if you're frustrated with a household issue to dive straight into righteous mode—no matter how deserved it might be—and try to get people who are failing at keeping up their end of house responsibilities or standards to change or "be better." It can also be easy to dig in your heels and declare there is no problem or that no solution but yours is going to solve the problem. But remember, compromise can sometimes be offering to help someone, or reexamining your own expectations, or being willing to try something just to see if it works. "Would it make it easier to all have dinner together if planned to start a half hour later?" Whether it's assigning tasks, doing chores together, allowing for reminders, or identifying consequences, it's important for everyone to communicate and be willing to compromise.

COMMITMENT

Commitment is the make-it-or-break-it moment when we put our compromise into action. Either our efforts work and we see good outcomes, or we see the pitfalls and can reassess. It might take a few tries for people to remember to do something. It's not just children who need to repeat an action multiple times before it becomes a habit: *Oh, that's right—no shoes!* or *I gotta wash this right now.* If you have a good attitude and make a real effort, you're likely to see a difference. Good etiquette takes practice, particularly at home. The challenge to be consistent, to be willing to try something again and again until you don't have to try anymore, is as important to the people we live with every day as it is anywhere else.

If the commitment you made doesn't stick, wash, rinse, and repeat the process. Go back to the first *C*—communication—and start talking about what didn't work and how to move forward.

AT-HOME COURTESIES

In her day, Emily never had to tackle such issues as mobile devices at the table, or a roommate who leaves their wet clothes in the washer too long, or how to handle limited broadband among multiple people in one house. But she, and the tradition she established, did address the impact that the introduction of telephones (and later, television) had on the domestic sanctuary of the home—inventions that would influence hosting, mealtimes, and sibling amiability for generations to come. Home life today is a little different from what we were used to even twenty-five years ago. Video calls, headphones, virtual classwork, working from home, smart speakers: all impact how we interact on the home front. Yet at the heart of so many issues we face today lie some very basic at-home manners that have persisted for decades.

ACKNOWLEDGING EACH OTHER

Greeting one another at home is just as important as when we are out and about. As soon as you see someone, if you aren't going to disturb them, greet them. It's polite to make sure that an acknowledgment is made fairly quickly upon noticing each other when at home. Whoever sees the other person first should really make the effort to say "Hi." This is particularly true the first time you see someone during the day: "Good morning!" After the first greetings of the day, you don't need to keep greeting one another. But if you haven't seen someone in a few hours or so, the next time you pass them in the house you might say "hey" again. And of course, always respond when someone greets you.

Who should greet whom when you enter a room? Some people learn that if you are the one entering, it is up to you to speak first and announce your presence to those already in the room. Others learn that if you are in a space, you should notice when someone enters and acknowledge them with a greeting. Originally, gentlemen were required to take notice and stand when a lady entered their presence. Today what matters is that neither residents nor visitors feel ignored in your home. That said, if your sister is on the couch reading a book and you are only passing through, it seems silly for either of you to extend little formalities such as "Hey" or "Whatcha up to?" That would be an unnecessary interruption.

Take note: many will still try to honor a person's seniority; for example, a younger person will often approach and address an older person with a particular title or other form of address as a sign of respect.

RESPECTING PEOPLE'S SPACE AND THINGS

There are also the obvious considerations when it comes to sharing space at home. In any living situation, closed doors should be respected. Only enter where and when you are invited. Respect an individual's need for privacy when bathing, dressing, using the bathroom, or hosting guests. These are all times and places where you want to knock first rather than just enter any room you need or want to be in. It's also important to not just hang around and intrude on another person's time with their friends or alone time. Your wife might love your company but still want to chill with her friends without you around the whole time. Same with kids: while they may need supervision, give them appropriate space to play and host on their own, too.

Other people's personal property should be respected as *theirs*, along with any rules they might have about it. Never take or use something without asking permission first. This applies to partners and parents as well as roommates, kids, and guests. Unfortunately, borrowing something without asking permission first, or damaging an item, are often frequent points of contention. Remember to take responsibility by offering to make amends if you have done something wrong or, worse, damaged something, whether it's a football that hit the favorite vase from Grandma or a younger sibling who got caught raiding someone's closet. The mistake may have been made, but taking ownership and apologizing shows respect.

For things that are shared—such as remotes, TVs, ovens, microwaves, Wi-Fi, or serving dishes—try to keep the item or resource available to everyone or share it equitably. Pay attention to people's usage patterns regarding an item or resource (*Dad always listens to the news before dinner*), and don't monopolize it. If you need something at a certain time, give people a heads-up and remind them ahead of time so no one is surprised when you "need it now." For more immediate situations, follow the "first come, first served" rule and then do your best to take turns or share.

With roommates, it's especially important to remember that while this is your home, you are likely sitting on, cooking with, or possibly wearing someone else's item—someone not related to you, who might not be in your life for more than a short period of time. Be careful. Red wine drunk carelessly on a light-colored couch, knives used in ways that can chip, rust, or dull them, platters or glasses scratched with abrasive sponges or cleaners—it's easy to ruin other people's things without realizing it. That's why it's important to listen to our housemates, think first, and be reasonably open to correction or take responsibility for a replacement or repair. Try to be the type of person who doesn't need reminders about caring for other people's things.

DEVICE DECORUM

Our preoccupation with our devices has wreaked havoc on our social skills at home. Have you ever tried to get a 4-year-old's (or 45-year-old's) attention while they are watching videos on a tablet? Nearly impossible. Or how many times have you caught yourself not quite listening to your roommate or spouse because you're scrolling through your email, news app, texts, or Instagram feed? And you didn't even realize you had picked up your phone! When it comes to devices at home, it is not polite to do the following:

- Focus on a device when you're supposed to be spending time together with others, even if that's watching a movie together.

- Answer a call—either video or audio, headphones in or out—and proceed to stay in a room with others present while you chat on your call. Take it into another room.

- When eating together, it's better to ignore your phone entirely (no talking, texting, browsing, or scrolling) during the meal.

- Wear headphones and ignore someone who is trying to get your attention. This is especially true when working from home, a situation where you'll want to set up guidelines for how to engage with someone wearing headphones. A tap on the shoulder, a wave of a hand, a knock on the door, a flick of the lights: all might be options.

- Put a call on speaker or listen to music or a podcast, TV show, or movie (or anything else for that matter) while walking around or through rooms or areas that others are in. Either use headphones or take your phone off speaker while you're passing through.

- Use someone's device without their permission or take a peek at something they didn't intend to show you (however benign). Snooping in any form has always been rude.

SMART SPEAKERS AND HOME AI

Today's home management often involves a "smart" system, including such things as speakers, thermostats, lights, or possibly a security camera and door system. We use our smart speakers to keep lists, order supplies, run timers and schedules, get reminders to feed the chickens or cue up personal encouragements. Via an app or voice command, we can turn on the oven, let people into our homes, check in when we aren't there, and confuse the living daylights out of the dog. It's all about convenience and ease in managing the things that help our homes run smoothly—and it often means a disruptive voice command in one way or another. As an overall rule: smart systems, speakers, and AI should be assets helping life, not interruptions or distractions from it.

SPEAKING TO A VIRTUAL ASSISTANT

Consider the tone you set with yourself and those around you when you speak to a voice-activated device. Even if the system doesn't feel emotions, the way we all behave when interacting with these devices has implications for both the way we feel and the environments we create. You can certainly choose to bark commands to your smart speaker and revel (if that's what does it for you) in the response you get, no matter how you sound. But we think it's best to use this device to help hone politeness in our speech rather than allow it to devolve. Here are some tips to make speaking to your AI device more pleasant:

- Consider others present before making a request of your assistant.

- Say "please" and "thank you" because it is excellent practice, and may even leave you feeling good—not to mention it sets a great example if you have kids in the house, and also sounds more pleasant when others might hear you. Taking a commanding or demanding tone with your device could make you sound pompous or arrogant and can create bad habits.

- Wait until after you're finished speaking with someone to make a request of your assistant. Breaking off mid-sentence to add tortillas to your shopping list isn't very considerate to the people you are with, even if in your mind it's quick and simple.

- Don't activate a device when others are speaking. It can be tempting to ask your smart speaker to settle a debate at the dinner table, but unless the whole group wants the answer, avoid the urge to interrupt the moment with your "quick question."

- Avoid shouting when others are present. Instead, speak clearly so you don't have to repeat yourself and move closer to the mic if you need to.

- Rather than change the vibe in the room by switching channels or turning the music on or off, consult with others first. If you and your roommates are listening to music via the speaker and you decide you want to hear the latest episode of the *Awesome Etiquette* podcast, don't just ask the assistant to change it for you. Ask those in the room if they're cool with it. If they aren't, go somewhere else or plug in your headphones and listen from a personal device.

- Don't mess with other people's routines, reminders, calendars, or settings on their smart speaker or AI device. If you do so accidentally, definitely inform the person and be sure to apologize for the mistake. While you might just be turning the volume down in the evening, it might mess with your roommate's alarm setting in the morning.

WHEN TO INFORM GUESTS

There is particular etiquette to follow for hosts and guests when it comes to privacy and new technologies. Telling guests about your smart devices and security systems can require a bit of a balance. You might not tell every person who comes over for a dinner party or a play date that you've got a smart speaker with a live microphone or a home security system that might record them (unless they will need to engage with it to get up the driveway or into the house, such as an intercom at a gate). You should let anyone who is staying over, or staying on their own in your house (like a house sitter), or working in your house regularly (like a babysitter) know about the systems being used. These are thoughtful and respectful times to give someone a heads-up. You might even turn off certain microphones and cameras as a courtesy for certain guests or so you don't feel compelled to disclose that they are in use.

SHUTTING IT OFF

When you are hosting, don't forget to shut off any regular reminders. You don't want, "Logan, you are awesome. Way to go making good choices today. Don't forget to tidy up and get in some meditation before bed. You rock!" to go off at 8:30 p.m. when your guests are just finishing dessert. While you could probably laugh off any potential embarrassment for yourself, you might startle the heck out of your guests. Shutting off the speaker for the house sitter while you're away is also thoughtful and considerate. Consider checking in periodically with those you live with that your digital assistant isn't interfering with their daily peace and quiet. A reminder to yourself to "take out the trash" might sound like a frustrated call-out to your partner who also forgets the task.

ROOMMATES

Choosing to live with others, either to better afford a place or because you enjoy their company, opens you up to all kinds of etiquette issues. Balancing cleanliness, routines, food, guests, and noise takes a lot of good etiquette skills and a ton of communication, whether you are living with someone you just met or a longtime friend (or even a partner). While most of the following is geared toward roommates who may be meeting for the first time, for those who are already acquaintances or even friends, the tips and suggestions can be useful to run through to help ensure everyone has a happy home life together.

THE MOST AWFUL ROOMMATE

We can easily pull together a picture of the most awful roommate, and many of us have either lived with or been this person at one time or another. We call her Ms. Rem Arkably-Awful. She is completely oblivious of her impact on others. She might have heard you discuss your daily schedules, sharing food, and chores, but not only did she not listen, she doesn't care. And she most certainly doesn't adhere to any agreed-upon household rules. Chore wheel, *shmore* wheel! Ms. Rem Arkably-Awful leaves a trail everywhere she goes (of crumbs, discarded items, clothes . . .), and always, *always* finishes the one item of yours in the pantry that you had been dreaming about eating on your way home from work. She talks loudly on her phone and occupies the only bathroom for hours at a time. And she has undoubtedly left the toilet paper roll bare (or replaced it going the wrong way) or, worse yet, left a note on the plunger that says, *Sorry. Good luck!* And that's if you're lucky. Ms. Rem Arkably-Awful never lifts a finger and is never around the week the rent or any bills are due. She brings guests over at all hours and has no regard for anyone sleeping, though she will utter irritable grunts and grumbles from the couch if you disrupt her nap during a football game or *Real Housewives* marathon. Ms. Rem Arkably-Awful always forces those around her to move or adjust for her; she is the center of the universe after all, and the rest of us don't matter. If you give her an ultimatum, she is happy to leave and set up her throne elsewhere—after sticking you with a hefty cleaning bill and moving-out damages. Remarkably awful, indeed.

THE MOST WONDERFUL ROOMMATE

In contrast to Ms. Rem Arkably-Awful, Mr. D. Lightful is a truly delightful dude. While he may be the very best of housemates to live with, he is not perfect. In fact, it is his normal fallibility that makes us like Mr. D. Lightful so much. He is human and he knows it, but he tries hard. Ahhh, to find comfort in common faults.

Mr. D. Lightful is always aware of his surroundings and his impact on them. He is the best at asking first. He pays his rent and bills on time and offers to help manage some of the other bills as well, so the burden doesn't fall on just one person. He would never use a mug or anything else that he knew was special to a roommate. As a most wonderful roommate, Mr. D. Lightful knows how to strike a balance between spending time in the home and outside it. He knows how beneficial it is to air out a home of its people, not just its dust. He remembers others' schedules and does his best to work around them when possible. Mr. D. Lightful commits to and follows through on agreements about things like cleaning chores, storing and labeling food, and guest visits.

He always says "Hi" brightly when he first sees you, but he doesn't feel the need to have a detailed chat every time you cross paths at home. Mr. D. Lightful participates in house events, be they meetings, parties, or consoling a sad roommate. He picks up on subtle cues, like maybe when a movie would be best watched by you and your date and not the whole house. He does not leave his items strewn about the common areas. Mr. D. Lightful pitches in when extra effort is needed, such as shoveling a walkway or doing some deep cleaning. He is the one whose presence you will miss when he has moved on, like Mary Poppins, to another lucky home.

CHOOSING TO LIVE TOGETHER

When choosing to live with someone, whether you are inviting someone into your home, hoping to secure a room in someone else's home, or selecting someone to find a place with, or even thinking about living with a partner or best friend, there are many things you'll want to touch base on and sort out before signing a lease.

ROOMMATE CONSIDERATIONS

There are a lot of things to think about when it comes to considering roommates. The following considerations aren't about right or wrong answers; they are about ensuring you talk about or consider these types of things before you agree to move in so you'll have a better shot at a positive living situation from the start. Whether you know your future roommate or are interviewing potential candidates you've never met before, the following are some important topics to cover.

DAILY SCHEDULES AND ROUTINES. For some, it might not matter to have a roommate come home at midnight and start their "off time" from work cooking, cleaning, socializing, and so on, until the wee hours, and then sleep through the morning before heading to work in the afternoon. For others, it would be the pits. Being realistic about the type of person you can live with means considering not just their personality but also their schedule and routine and how it fits with yours.

ROMANTIC OR SEX LIFE. Romantic partners of any kind are going to impact other housemates. It might seem forward to ask about this when you've just met someone, but a person's partner could end up being an "extra" roommate. Even if they aren't in a committed relationship, their dating or sex life could impact you. You can broach the subject by asking, "Are you in a relationship or dating, and if so, how do you see handling that with a roommate?" Whether it's politely ignoring what goes bump in the night, setting rules for one-night stands, or setting boundaries around a significant other who is over all the time, make sure to think about what you feel comfortable with and communicate it. (Obviously this might not need discussing if you're moving in with your partner and no other roommates.)

ADULT SUBSTANCES. Regardless of whether you abstain, smoke or vape cigarettes or pot, or drink alcohol, being honest and open about what you can and cannot live with or how you partake in substances is important. Be up-front if you haven't been asked: "I smoke pot frequently. Will that work for you, or are you looking for a smoke-free living situation?" or, "I don't drink and prefer not to be around alcohol. Is it possible for the house to be alcohol-free?" (See Smoking and Vaping, opposite.)

DEAL-BREAKER ISSUES. If you're a vegan who can't live with anyone who uses animal products, of course you're going to disclose this. It's fine to have deal-breaker issues. We all need to be comfortable in our homes. When choosing roommates, this sometimes means setting very firm boundaries. Some of the substance and romantic partner topics above could be deal-breakers for a lot of people. The goal from an etiquette standpoint is to state your boundary without judging the other person. "I'd like to be up-front: I'm a pretty strict vegan, and I need to live in a house with no animal products. It doesn't matter to me what someone else eats outside our house, but are you okay with keeping a vegan home?"

PETS. Whether or not pets of any kind are welcome is important to figure out up front, to be fair to the animal, to the roommates who have signed a lease, and to the landlord/owner who is setting the rules about their property. Be sure you understand extra fees, whether roommates are willing to help out, and how pet problems will be handled before agreeing to live with pets. (See Roommates and Pets, page 265, for a list of things to think about before saying yes to a pet.)

CONVERSATIONS ABOUT MONEY AND BILLS, RENT, AND AGREEMENTS. Money issues can be hard for people to talk about. Conversations about money should be open and honest and handled with tact. State up front either the full range of fees to live in a place or your budget if you're going to look for a place together. Starting off clearly will get you going on the right foot. Understanding what's expected and knowing the terms of any contract you might sign are important, as it will establish a baseline if you encounter issues later on.

SETTING BOUNDARIES

It's good to set some standards for living together right from the start, and then to set a date to check back in about them. Boundaries can be anything from "Don't leave any laundry in the washer or dryer," or "No toothpaste left on the sink," to "Don't enter my room without permission," and "No shared food." While you don't want to overwhelm each other with a litany of don'ts, it's also important to feel confident speaking up about what will really bother you or what is truly appreciated. There's a big difference between demanding what you want or need and asking or informing someone of a boundary you want or need to set. For example, "Never go into my room" can be softened in tone while remaining strong in message if reworded to "I care about privacy when it comes to my room. Especially if I'm out, I'd appreciate you not going in." It's so hard to predict everything you need to think about ahead of time, so it can be helpful to continue your conversations around boundaries with your roommates.

SMOKING AND VAPING

There are some specific things to consider around smoking and vaping. The first is to decide exactly what is allowed where. Many homes are cigarette smoke–free these days, and many similarly also choose not to allow tobacco vaping. Pay attention in outdoor spaces as well; your wafting smoke or vape can really impact your own home or a neighbor's. For cannabis consumers, some people are more tolerant about indoor smoking or vaping, but many others are not. Whatever rules work for you, be sure that as a household you all know the expectations and are willing to live by them and communicate them to your guests. Fans, air filters, or ventilation systems are great when you can use them. But be careful about adding more aroma to the mix, such as incense, to cover any smoke or vape odor. It rarely masks the smell and often just adds to it, making the situation even worse. Always use ashtrays. Butts and roaches should not be discarded on doorsteps or driveways. Always use an appropriate receptacle or offer one to your guests.

PARTING WELL

It can be difficult to broach the subject of parting ways with a roommate. Most of the time, a lease ending is an easy enough out. Even if you would have liked the brief smug satisfaction of telling off Ms. Rem Arkably-Awful for how horrible she was to live with, resist the urge. If you can wait it out, do so and then move on gracefully. It can be so tempting to want to hash it all out before it's over, but ask yourself, *Is it truly worth it?*

Whether you're going to be the one staying or going, speaking face-to-face is always best (as long as it's safe) to let the person know. "After giving it some thought, I think it's time for me to move on to a new living situation." Whether you are friends or "just roommates," and no matter if you're asking someone to leave or you'll be the one going, offer up a time frame that is fair and makes sense given the scenario. Together, you should settle up any bills, rent payments, security deposits, or personal reimbursements that may be outstanding. If money is an issue, obviously this might not happen, or you might set up a repayment schedule.

When you're the one leaving, it's considerate to leave your space in good condition for whoever is taking your place. Remove all garbage, give it a good going-over with a vacuum and duster, wipe down surfaces, and air it out if you can. Whether you're frustrated, sad, or elated by the fact that you're leaving, taking care to leave your place satisfactory is taking the high road, and that's good etiquette.

FAMILIES

Families are all unique. Your family's way of living together is probably somewhat different from that of your peers, neighbors, friends, and extended family, even if you live in the same neighborhood, worship at the same place, frequent the same restaurants, and belong to the same social groups. There is no one way to live under a roof politely with your loved ones—there are many different ways. While many aspects of roommate life can apply to a family home or to couples living together, here are some topics to think about when trying to embrace good etiquette in your family life.

THE FAMILY DINNER TABLE

From Emily Post to Martha Stewart, family dinner table protocol conjures iconic images of wholesome, quality time spent together around a meal. While our ideal might look like a neat and tidy table with two parents and two kids, people celebrate the family dinner table in numerous ways today with many different versions of family, from classic to elaborate Sunday brunch or suppers to casual weekend lunches that turn into lazy afternoons with our nearest and dearest. We enjoy dinner on the road at a fast-food joint or at a diner after a hockey win (or loss). And we delight in the opportunity to occasionally gather at a special spot to celebrate with a meal. Whether we are in our own homes, with extended family, or dining out as a family, we want to take the time to both learn and practice our table manners together. (See Chapter 5: Table Manners for more on specific dining manners.) Traditional manners for the family dinner may include the following:

- Arriving at the table ready for the meal (this might mean dressed nicely with combed hair and washed hands, or it might simply mean showing up on time)

- Removing your hat before coming to the table

- Not using devices at the table, in fact, avoid even bringing them to the table. (This advice used to be "No answering the house phone during dinner," and that still applies)

- Waiting until everyone is ready to begin (or applying the household rule if it's different)

- Participating in the conversation and keeping it positive. This is not the time to be tattling on siblings or bringing up negative news. But it is a time for sharing positive thoughts on the day, having fun discussions and debates, hearing about what everyone is up to, and even what you might be looking forward to tomorrow or later in the week

- Trying the food you are served, even if it's not your favorite meal. Having a taste to see if you care for something is a great thing to practice in the comfort of your own home or at a family dinner out

- Saying "May I please be excused?" if you have to use the bathroom

- Waiting until everyone is finished to get up and help clean up from the meal

HOUSE RULES

House rules are helpful for families. However, explaining your house rules or expectations to those visiting your home can be tricky. But even little kids know that the rules can vary from house to house. If you have a rule or expectation that you need to communicate to a guest, you have a few options for what to say to be clear. "No shoes" is short and simple. But *how* you offer the direction makes the difference to being polite. Phrasing a house rule as a request—with a friendly tone—rather than an instruction is thoughtful and leaves room for someone to respond in a way you might not have thought of. For example: "If you don't mind, can you remove your shoes? We're a shoe-free home." While most will say, "Sure, of course," you might have someone reply, "I have to leave mine on for balance, but I'd be happy to clean them off—would that be all right?"

If a young child who is visiting is misbehaving or breaking your house rules—such as jumping on furniture, going into rooms they shouldn't, or pulling the cat's tail—it is okay as a host for you to correct them. "Maven, in this house we do not stand on chairs. If you'd like something from high up, come find me and I'll get it for you." Explaining that "this is something we don't do in this house" and ushering the child to a different space, maybe to play with others or return to their parent, is perfectly fine. That is as far as you should ever go correcting a child you are not responsible for. Yelling at or scolding them is out of the question from an etiquette standpoint. Any discipline should be left to a child's parent or guardian.

MULTIGENERATIONAL HOMES

Negotiation is often a big part of living in a multigenerational home. If three generations are present under one roof, it can put one set of adults in the middle, as they will be both child and parent to someone in the home. Whether this is a welcome or imposed arrangement, it can also be one of the most rewarding times in life, and one that people are often grateful for since they get to spend so much time with other generations of their family.

While everyone in this situation is family, it's important to remember that those who own or rent the home, cover the expenses, and manage the running of the household are usually in more of a decision-making position, even if they might not be the most senior members of the family. It's good to be clear with all parties about what is expected and how time together and apart can be managed well so that everyone feels both included and independent at home. "Mom, is now a good time? I was hoping to talk with you about how we do family dinners, I'm looking to switch things up a bit."

This is not always an easy task. While you aren't going to use the roommate considerations list (page 251) before starting this arrangement, do take the time to talk. Come up with similar topics to discuss and create some understanding and boundaries around things like the purpose of the arrangement, nursing or childcare, food, chores, time spent together, financial responsibilities, and guests and visitors. Extra effort often has to be put into accommodating the different perspectives that different generations may have, especially around traditional manners like mealtimes, greetings, and keeping things tidy, and newer manners like appropriate use of cell phones and smart devices.

WORKING FROM HOME

While it has long been the norm in certain industries and jobs, working from home has become much more common since the COVID-19 pandemic began in 2020. In fact, it's estimated that by 2025, 22 percent of Americans will work from home. Office courtesies and workplace culture have always been important, and now for many they have come into the home. It isn't just jobs that are being done at home—students of all ages are engaging more with remote learning. Balancing work or student life with home life is a challenge even though there are many benefits. While each person and each home will end up with its own M.O. and rhythm for what works and what doesn't, establishing some basic courtesies for sharing your home with your roommates, partner, or family can help smooth the way and keep you focused on getting your job or schoolwork done.

When it comes to multiple members of a household working or studying from home, the very first piece of etiquette advice is to communicate. The second piece of advice is to communicate frequently. (The third piece is to then remind people about what you've already communicated.) You are responsible for knowing and communicating your scheduling needs in advance to those you live with. Following that, there is often a need to compromise. There's a lot to consider. One thing that can help overall is to be patient and try not to place any pressure from your work on the people you're trying to organize and schedule around at home.

PRIVACY. Work can involve confidential or sensitive information, and keeping it private and protected is key. While it may just be your family who is around, confidential is confidential. Do not leave client or company personnel files or private information out and exposed to others. And remember that while your household may be able to hear only your side of a phone conversation, it too should be kept private and out of earshot from those not involved with the work.

COURTESY IN REQUESTS. When carving out privacy and quiet for work time, make *requests* of the people you live with rather than demands. This means always saying "please" (sincerely, without attitude) and communicating with patience and kindness in your voice rather than frustration and shortness. Instead of "Can you *please* be quiet, I'm working!" try, "Hey, Don, it's getting a little loud for me to concentrate. I need to ask for quiet again, please." A simple, kind request often gets respected.

DEFINING YOUR WORKSPACE. If possible, clearly define a workspace for yourself at home. Whether you've always worked from home or are adjusting to a new situation, setting up a workspace—even if it gets packed up and tucked away once work hours are over—will help you and others in your home balance your work and home life both mentally and physically.

RESPECTING BANDWIDTH. Upload and download times can be heavily impacted by limited Wi-Fi bandwidth or slow internet speeds, affecting everything done online from streaming video, calls, gaming, browsing, and even sending emails. Discussing the night before what people's internet and computer needs are for the next work or school day can help you all prioritize what is needed by whom and when. You might have "no streaming or gaming" policies when someone has a virtual class or meeting to attend. Or, people who are able may volunteer to go work elsewhere (like a café) when possible to help balance everyone's needs.

TAKE IT ELSEWHERE. When a phone call or video call does come in (or is scheduled to), depending on where you are at home, you may need to excuse yourself to let someone take a call privately, or you may need to exit a room and find a place to take the call behind a closed door so that you aren't disturbing anyone else as they try to work in a shared space.

NEIGHBORS

A good neighbor relationship can be one of the most comforting aspects of home and social life—someone just next door, or right around the corner, who knows you, looks out for you, and whom you, too, can offer care or support to, or even just share a friendly chat or wave with. Feeling like you are well situated in a functional community provides a level of social security that can be foundational in life. Regrettably, we can't say this always happens. There are many who dislike their neighbors for reasons warranted (or not). And while you certainly cannot prevent or control someone else's words or actions, you can control your own. Finding ways to be a good neighbor—even if that means leaving someone alone—is good etiquette.

NEW NEIGHBORS

Never hesitate to welcome a new neighbor. Obviously wait until they are not in the middle of moving a heavy couch or appliance (unless you want to offer to help), but you should absolutely feel confident going over, knocking on the door (so scary sometimes, but often worth the anxiety), and saying, "Hi, I'm Libby. I live across the hall. I just wanted to introduce myself and say, welcome to the building." You might choose to bring over some baked treats or a houseplant, but you can also do this empty-handed. It is not rude at all. It is not a bad idea though to bring a note or card that you can leave if the person doesn't answer their door. If you want to leave your contact information, you certainly may, but only if you wish to and feel safe doing so. It can be both a blessing and a curse to have a direct line to your neighbors.

When you are the new neighbor, there isn't any etiquette that says you must wait for those who already live in the neighborhood to come and greet you. You can certainly pop on over when you move in to say hello and introduce yourself. (See the Self-Introduction, page 29.) While you don't typically bring over any treats or flowers when you introduce yourself as the new kid on the block (though you certainly could, it isn't customary), you might bring your contact information if you're comfortable sharing it. Since you aren't trying to welcome someone, but more to introduce yourself, don't worry about leaving a note if your neighbor isn't home. You can simply try to catch them another time.

In rural neighborhoods, you might not know you have a new neighbor until your child tells you there's a new kid in class and they live nearby. You can either drop off a note or flowers or go up to the house and introduce yourself. If you do leave something and don't get the chance to speak, leave your address or phone number so the new neighbor knows where to find you or where to send a thank-you note or text. For neighbors in a building, you might meet in an elevator, in the parking lot, or at the mailbox. You might be tempted to start off the conversation with "Did you just move in?" or "Are you the new person in 4F?" This is fairly polite (if a bit presumptive), but can be embarrassing if it turns out the person has been a neighbor for many years. If you aren't 100 percent sure they are new neighbors, you might try "Hello," or "Good morning. I haven't bumped into you before. My name is Hans Buetow, and I live in 7G."

After you've made your initial introduction, you'll have to decide how well you want to try to get to know your new neighbors. The key word here is *try*. There's no guarantee a neighbor will want to become friends. But that doesn't mean they won't be friendly or nice. That introduction you've just made is the perfect way to start.

If your new neighbor wasn't home and you left a note, remember that if you haven't actually met in person, they might not know that it was you who left the note. Don't expect a big thank-you the next time you see them. You can certainly say "Hi" and ask if they got your note (or treats). They will likely say, "Oh, that was you? So thoughtful, thank you! I'm Ryan Newbury and my roommate is Phillipe Boucher." (Last names may or may not be given.) Do your best to remember names, but don't be too hard on yourself if you forget. You can always ask when you bump into your neighbor again: "I'm sorry, I have completely forgotten your name. Do you mind telling me again?" Any polite person will offer their name up right away—life is not an episode of *Seinfeld*.

THE GREAT NEXT-DOOR NEIGHBOR

Mx. Ohso Neighborly strikes a balance; they are neither overly friendly and eager to merge their lives with their neighbors to become bosom buddies, nor cold or standoffish, a mystery behind the curtains. They pay attention to and respect the vibe they are getting. As a great neighbor, Mx. Neighborly is willing to listen or help if they have the time and always exercises patience in responding to complaints or frustrations. In fact, they are the type of person who offers you an opening to discuss any potentially problematic issues by saying something like "Hey, Aiden, I just wanted to check in. I know half of my tree leaves end up in your yard. I'm happy to come over and take care of them if it's an issue at all." Dreamy.

Mx. Ohso Neighborly abides by the community rules if there are any, and if there aren't, by a general sense of responsibility to the community. They bring their recycling, trash, and compost bins in after collection. And they acknowledge those who pass by with a friendly smile, or at least a polite nod. Mx. Neighborly makes sure that no items of theirs are left in a communal hallway or stairwell, or on the sidewalk, causing inconvenience for others who may be walking or wheeling by. They don't leave trash or debris lying about. Their garden or lawn, if they have one, isn't overtaking a neighbor's yard. While we might not succeed every day, as long as we are aware of our neighbors and treat them with consideration, respect, and honesty, we are off to a good start. (See Consideration, Respect, and Honesty, page 7.) Mx. Neighborly also knows that dropping off a treat from time to time doesn't hurt either, especially if their neighbor has done them a favor like shoveling their walkway—they just make sure to avoid alcohol or anything that features well-known allergens such as peanuts, at least until you know your neighbor better.

Mx. Ohso Neighborly, would you be mine? Could you be mine? Please, won't you be my neighbor?

GOOD COMMUNICATION

Whether it's construction or a party, when you're going to have "something" going on at your house that will impact your neighbors, it's best to warn them. When it's something like construction, you'll want to remember that remodels and builds can take much longer than anticipated. Communicating clearly with your neighbors about how long crews will be working at your place and when timelines get extended is thoughtful. If it's really bad, like when noise from a project is supposed to last a day, but instead takes a week or longer, you might even consider trying to smooth things over with an offer for a dinner out, or maybe lending them your noise-canceling headphones. At the very least, a batch of cookies might help take the sting out of hearing that the hammering will be going on for weeks.

When throwing parties at home, your neighbors are often affected. Of course, you must comply with any noise ordinances and parking or building regulations for visitors. But even when operating within these expectations, we want to let our neighbors know ahead of time if we are throwing a gathering that will impact them. A sleepover for fifteen 11-year-old girls in your backyard deserves a heads-up, as does your son's wedding afterparty held in your downtown loft.

Whether you leave a note, send a text or email, tell someone in person, or make a phone call does not matter. What matters is that you let your neighbors know in advance whenever they are likely to be impacted by noise or activity at your home or in the area.

NEIGHBORS HELPING NEIGHBORS

Neighbors often either offer or ask for help from one another. Sometimes this will be in the form of a request to quiet down or to practice the tuba only before 9:00 p.m. Other times, it is expressed by borrowing items, watching your house or pets while you're away, or offering to help with yard work or home projects. It's a special thing to have neighbors who feel confident asking for and offering small favors of and to one another. Here are a few ways to make sure that favors and help don't go unappreciated.

HELP OUT ONLY WHEN YOU TRULY CAN. If you're going to be stressed or strapped by offering or agreeing to help, it's probably best to decline. "Normally I would say yes to babysitting last minute, but I really have to work on my term paper tonight," or "I wish I could help, but I can't this time. I'm sorry."

WHEN YOU CAN SAY YES, DO. Commit wholeheartedly and be clear about what you can offer or how an item should be used and returned to you. "I'm happy to let you borrow our steam mop. I'll need it back by Friday though. I should let you know, it does require distilled water, and nothing should get added to it, like essential oils or bleach; otherwise it can clog up the water chamber."

ASK CLEARLY FOR WHAT YOU NEED AND BE PREPARED TO TAKE NO FOR AN ANSWER. Instead of "Hey, can I borrow your air mattress while my cousin is here?" try "Hey, would you be willing to lend me your air mattress? I would need it for 2 weeks while my cousin is staying with us over the holidays." Then be sure to take good care of it and return it before anyone would think to ask.

ALWAYS EXPRESS YOUR GRATITUDE. While most small favors (like borrowing a tool) don't need full thank-you notes, you absolutely should express your appreciation for the favor. Saying thank you in person or via text is fine if you've borrowed lawn equipment, standard tools, or kitchen gadgets and then returned it to the lender without seeing them. For larger favors, a thank-you note is key. It's also kind to think of other ways to show your appreciation. When your neighbor Mr. Plow always clears your driveway after those of his customers, leaving him a note and some banana bread within a few days of the favor is a great way to say thank you and do something kind in return. It's not needed for a polite exchange—just the thank-you is—but the baked good or other kindness is a great way to keep the good vibes going.

LOANING AND BORROWING

Loaning and borrowing items can get especially sticky between neighbors. Some folks go so far as to keep track with a log or app, listing whom they've loaned items to and the expected return date. This isn't a bad idea if you're in the habit of loaning things out and luck doesn't seem to return them to you.

When you loan an item or borrow it, the best thing to do is establish how long it can be used for, in what ways it may be used, and in what condition it should be returned. Obviously, if you're borrowing a rake, you're just going to borrow the darn rake. But other items might require a bit more instruction, or there may be requests about not using it in certain ways. If you are the one asking, listen to the person who owns the item. Don't dismiss their worry or concern. Remember, *they* are doing *you* a favor.

Items should of course be returned at the time and in the condition discussed. The pot should be scrubbed and cleaned, the drill returned with its bits, the book without dog-eared pages or penciled-in notes, and so on.

Don't make someone have to ask for their item back. Do your utmost to stick to the plan you've agreed to. If you find yourself needing the item longer, then by all means communicate that to the owner in the form of a question, not a demand. "Mx. Neighborly, may I continue to use your power washer this week? I didn't quite finish everything. I was hoping to get to it over the weekend." "Why certainly, Mr. Rogers."

ADDRESSING AN ISSUE

Issues with neighbors are never fun. This person is close by but, in all likelihood, they are not as close to you as your family or housemates. As long as your neighbor isn't violating a town ordinance of some kind, any solutions you propose to almost any issue is a request, not something that can be demanded. Starting off with a demand isn't the polite way to go. One must start addressing an issue by first addressing one's own state of mind. Are you seething mad about something? Has a dog ruined your garden bed, or is music being blared at 2:00 a.m.? Either of these could send anyone reeling and wanting to deliver a message, but possibly not in the politest or most effective of ways.

We've heard it all, from an overgrown lawn or garbage cans left out too long to noise of all kinds. Issues run the gamut from harmlessly annoying to problematic, dangerous, and potentially illegal. And they usually require us to address the issue with people. So, one place to start after you've taken three deep breaths is with a self-check.

DO I HAVE STANDING TO ADDRESS THIS ISSUE? Is it a violation of the lease or homeowners' agreement, or is it just annoying to me (which doesn't make it unworthy of voicing a request)? You might not even need to show that you have standing, but knowing whether you do or not can help in how you choose to ask. "Niah, it's so cool that you're on the dance team. I was wondering if you might be willing to put a 10:00 p.m. cap on practicing your routines? My bedroom is right below."

THINK ABOUT WHAT YOU WANT AND THE MOST POLITE WAY YOU CAN GET IT. Ask first. Express your perspective or experience without judgment, along with a recognition of your neighbor and a desire to hear their perspective. "Laura, is now a good time to chat briefly? I have something I wanted to talk with you about. There's what looks like a wild vine growing in the back corner of your garden. It's gotten so big it's changed the amount of sun my tomato plants get. If it isn't a beloved plant, I'm wondering if you would be willing to trim it back?"

LISTEN AND BE PATIENT. Be ready for a range of responses. Your neighbor may offer a perspective you hadn't considered or that makes you see things differently. Depending on what you are asking, the answer might be a simple "no" and you may have to accept that. You also might find that they just didn't realize that what they were doing was negatively impacting you and can be corrected easily. On the flip side, it might take a moment for them to absorb what you've said or come up with a solution that works. They might even be defensive, and giving them space to process your request might be necessary. It's never fun and can sometimes even seem petty or retaliatory, but don't be surprised if you get some requests, criticism, or questions coming back at you. Some people will use your request as an opportunity to air their own stored-up grievances. While it's better if they do that separately from this problem, if they don't, be patient and listen. Maybe you'll both be happier in the end with just a few adjustments.

COMPROMISE. Do your best to harness that second *C* from the Three *C*'s. For many things, the answer will be straightforward, but for others you might have to get creative or be willing to compromise to get what you want most.

IT COULD BE YOU. Addressing an issue might also mean taking responsibility for something. If a neighbor approaches you with an issue, do your best to listen. If you feel defensive or caught off guard, it's okay to ask for some time to think and give a thoughtful reply. Here is an example from Emily's 1922 edition:

> *Dear Mrs. Neighbor:*
>
> *My gardener has just told me that our chickens got into your flower beds, and did a great deal of damage.*
>
> *The chicken netting is being built higher at this moment and they will not be able to damage anything again. I shall, of course, send Patrick to put in shrubs to replace those broken, although I know that ones newly planted cannot compensate for those you have lost, and I can only ask you to accept my contrite apologies.*
>
> *Always sincerely yours,*
> *Katherine de Puyster Eminent*

GETTING OUTSIDE HELP. Sometimes it's not possible to reach an accord and the answer might be that you should address the issue with the resident coordinator, building manager, landlord, or home association board instead of directly with your neighbor. Avoid personal attacks and stay focused on the facts of the problem or issue as you describe or work through what has gone wrong.

VISITING NEIGHBORS

When you're the one dropping by, try to bring your casual positive self and good social spirit, but prepare yourself for the possibility that it might not be a good time. Even if it seems like your neighbor is not doing anything in particular, "nothing" time can be quite precious and needed. It is incredibly important to respect this, and if your drop-by is declined, to say sincerely, "Some other time then! Take care!"

If it is a good time for a visit, remember that you are dropping in on someone, so while they might offer you water or tea and a nice place to sit while you talk, beyond that they are not obligated to fix you food or entertain you. This visit is light and casual and highly interruptible. (For more on drop-by visits, see The Drop-by Visit, page 270.)

HANDLING DIFFICULT NEIGHBORS

While having a problem with a neighbor is often easily addressed once you find a calm way to broach the topic, a problem with a truly difficult neighbor won't likely be solved so simply or quickly. It can be easy to get caught up in the "she did, he did, they did" of it all. This rarely solves problems and, in many cases, can escalate them. Using the same calm approach that you would with any neighbor, as long as you are safe, muster your most gracious self and try to find cracks in their armor that can let good moments in. Offer them a smile. Do them a favor. If you can't get along, you can always choose to disengage. It's hard to sustain a feud or argue with someone who won't argue back.

Difficult neighbors can also be those who use property security, a Homeowner's Association, or the local police as a form of harassment. No person of Best Society does this to anyone. These types of authorities are meant for true violations and serious situations that require their intervention, and should only be used for such.

CELEBRATING WITH NEIGHBORS

It's common to wonder whether to include longtime neighbors at life events like new child showers, big anniversary parties, weddings, and graduations. It really depends on how close you have been with them over the years. Generally, it is not expected. If they have seen you and/or your children go through life and have always been pleasant and friendly, even if you've never once dined together, inviting them is certainly a welcoming gesture, and may be an opportunity to continue to grow the relationship. This is especially true if the event is held at home. Whether it's a casual invite or a formal one, making the offer is kind indeed, even if it's not required.

While it's lovely to consider inviting a neighbor when you are the host, as a neighbor you should never expect that you will be a guest. It is also true that not all neighbors become friends or extend these types of invitations.

Life is better together. While we can all appreciate the loveable, grumpy curmudgeon-next-door-type, it's good to be neighborly. Join in celebrating neighborhood events such as block parties, annual picnics, trick-or-treating, or town-specific events, like parades and farmers' markets if and when you can. Good neighbors can create good communities.

REFERENCE GUIDES

NEW ROOMMATE CHECKLIST

Be sure to cover these topics when meeting or interviewing a potential roommate; even if it's someone you already know, these are good subjects to consider and discuss:

- ☐ Daily schedules and routines

- ☐ Romantic or sex life

- ☐ Substances: tobacco, cannabis, alcohol, or other drugs

- ☐ Deal-breaker issues: accessibility, allergies, religious requirements, or diets

- ☐ Visitors to the house

- ☐ Expected chores

- ☐ Bills, rent, and lease agreements/understandings

- ☐ Pets

ROOMMATES AND PETS

We love our pets and we want the people we live with to love (or at least respect) them too. Our pets can fill our lives with love, but with that love comes responsibility. When it comes to living with your pets and other people well, here are some key points to think and talk about:

- How friendly or aggressive the pet is.

- How pet care will be handled: litter or cage cleaning, dog walks or attention, feeding.

- Handling messes or damage the pet makes on floors, carpets, or even furniture, or if personal items are ruined.

- Mitigating the impact of pet hair, which can be significant, affecting not only cleanliness but also comfort for any guests who visit.

- Care for the pet when the pet's person is at work or goes on vacation.

- Any pet deposit, or impact on shared security deposit?

- Pet noise, whether or not the pet's person is at home.

- What's appropriate for the non-pet-owner to do when it comes to handling the pet if the pet's person isn't there?

TIPS FOR WORKING WELL FROM HOME

- Define your workspace so that you know your designated zone.

- Avoid moving out of your zone and into others' work or living areas.

- If your space doubles as the dining table or living room, be sure to put all work away in your off hours.

- Communicate your schedule and compromise to balance broadband usage and the need for quiet or privacy.

- Be as flexible as possible with your schedule and others' household or work needs.

TIPS FOR BEING A GOOD NEIGHBOR

- Introduce yourself—it's never too late and it's always a good move. "Hi, I'm Becca, I've lived next door a while and thought I should introduce myself."

- Take care with the exterior of your home. Whether that means keeping shoes neat or out of a hallway, or bringing garbage or recycling bins in after collection, you want to be aware of how the outside of your home impacts your neighbors.

- Communicate when noise, parking, or people could be an issue, like when you are having work done on your home or are going to throw a larger party.

- Listen when others mention problems or concerns that involve you. Take your time and respond thoughtfully.

- Broach any issues you have with your neighbors carefully and with a considerate tone, remembering that asking and requesting are different (and more polite) than telling or demanding.

- Engage in small niceties like saying hello or giving a wave when you see your neighbor.

SAMPLE SCRIPTS FOR NEIGHBORS

Introducing yourself	"Hi, I'm Anwesha Greene. I just moved in next door and wanted to introduce myself." As a follow-up: "Here's my contact information if you need to get a hold of me."
Asking for help or borrowing something	"I'm looking for help moving a new couch in on Saturday when it's delivered. Would you be able and willing? I completely understand if you can't, or simply don't want to."
	"Terrance, I don't know if you lend it out, but I was wondering if I might be able to borrow your chainsaw this weekend?"
Making a request for change	"I was hoping to talk with you about the fence between our yards. Is now a good time?"
Declining a visit	"Now's not a great time, but let me check in with you later."
	"I work from home, so I can't do daytime visits, but would you be up for a walk after work?"
	"Now's not a great time, but thank you for coming by."
Pets	"We're so excited to have our new pup! If the barking gets to be too much or you ever see him doing something he shouldn't, like peeing on a flower bed, please don't hesitate to tell us and we'll work on correcting it."
Noise	"Andrew, I was wondering if I could ask that you save the loud lawn work until after 8 a.m. on the weekends? It would be great to get just another hour of sleep if I could."
	"Andrew, I just wanted to give you a heads up that we're having some remodeling done over the next few weeks, and apologize for any noise."
Party Prep	"Hi Nicole, we're throwing a graduation party for Fox on Saturday, if you're free, please come by! But I did want to give you a heads up if you saw a crowd at our house."

CHAPTER 10

Entertaining at Home

"The little dinner is thought by most people to be the very pleasantest social function there is. It is always informal, of course, and intimate conversation is possible, since strangers are seldom, or at least very carefully, included. For younger people, or others who do not find great satisfaction in conversation, the dinner of eight and two tables of bridge afterward has no rival in popularity. The formal dinner is liked by most people now and then (and for those who don't especially like it, it is at least salutary as a spine stiffening exercise), but for night after night, season after season, the little dinner is to social activity what the roast course is to the meal."

Nothing evokes a more classic or detailed image of etiquette than the thought of a host entertaining at home. From dreaming about Downton Abbey–esque affairs to picturing the stereotypical 1950s American housewife organizing a dinner party, to the reality of today's breezy casual hangouts, we relish entertaining. From old traditions that honor the passerby with a hot meal or a place to sleep, to trying our darndest to re-create a hotel or resort atmosphere for our houseguests, hospitality is an American tradition. When the lockdowns and mandates of 2020 prevented us from gathering together we felt that loss; in fact we were stunned by it. Sharing our homes with friends and family (and even sometimes colleagues) is not only good for us, it's important to us. Whether your style is casual or formal, whether you host easy hangouts or full-on dinner parties, we hope to encourage and inspire you to invite people to your home, take on the role of host with confidence, and take part in the traditions of hospitality and entertaining at home that we hold so dear. (To explore the qualities of a good host, please see A Good Host, page 177; for specific entertaining-at-home occasions, please read on.)

CASUAL ENTERTAINING

We are ever so grateful for casual gatherings at home. Whether planned or impromptu, they afford us the opportunity to be flexible and relaxed with our guests. Here are a few specific etiquette points that can help them go smoothly:

1. Invite well.

2. Make it easy for guests to attend.

3. Provide some type of refreshment.

Beyond that, let your imagination (or laziness) lead the way.

Inviting people well casually is as simple as saying, "Hey, feel free to come over. I'm home all day," or "Beer and burgers at our place today. Come by any time after four." Whether spoken, texted, or group chatted, spread the word in whichever way makes it easy (and likely) for guests to respond. "I'm around all day," "Text if you're in our end of town," "Stop by if you end up having time": these are all friendly invitations, but passive. It's good to remember that guests often need a little reassurance that they really are welcome. Invite clearly and follow up.

Small offerings, rather than large spreads, are fine for casual hangs. A beverage is customary, and a little bowl of nuts, chips or crackers with a spread or cheese, or some sliced-up fruit are perfect options. For what seems like a small offering, these items often end up being quite nice. One or two things is plenty for this level of entertaining, though this doesn't preclude you from offering more if you want to. The following three casual entertaining scenarios occur frequently, and all come with their own considerations for a host.

THE DROP-BY VISIT

The drop-by visit is totally unannounced. It's a knock at the door with the hope that you'll have time to visit for a bit, not just talk on the doorstep. It is entirely up to you whether or not you invite a drop-by visitor to come in. Drawing the shades and ignoring the doorbell, tempting though it might be, isn't very polite. If someone is going to be kind enough to interrupt your day, you should at least decline them directly. "Now's not the best time"—it's likely true, and the other person should have no expectation that this drop-by will result in a visit. You can always suggest a better time.

The last-minute nature of the visit does not demand that you go above and beyond to entertain. No need to whip up a full breakfast when an offer of coffee will do. Do your best to offer your guest a clean space to sit and enjoy their company for a bit. A gracious host might apologize for a mess, and in turn a kind guest will not be bothered that their host wasn't ready for a surprise visit: "I'm so sorry for the mess; please come in." "Thank you and no worries at all; I know you weren't expecting me."

When you're ready to part, thank them for stopping by or let them know (tactfully of course) that you're ready to get back to your day: "This has been so nice! I can't believe it's already 1:30 though; I have to get back to my day. Thank you for stopping by!" A good guest will pick up the cue and take their leave.

THE IMPROMPTU GET-TOGETHER

The impromptu gathering is a Post family favorite. You might be out adventuring with friends and then decide to do dinner at your place. Or be having a quiet morning, when a phone call leads to a spontaneous invitation to come on over for lunch! You throw together what you can on the fly, and the result is like a pop-up party.

After the invitation is posed and your guests say yes, planning is often a group effort where either host or guest can make suggestions. You may have everything you need to get things going or it might be a coordinated effort. People often say things such as, "Well, if you have the burger meat, we can bring over buns, condiments, and a salad," or "We'll order and pay for the pizza, could you pick it up on your way over like last time?"

As a host, it's nice to give your guests flexibility with an impromptu gathering. Obviously, people might not be able to drop everything, or they may need to check in with someone or "do just one thing" before they are really free to join. Have an attitude of "get here when you can" and "we'll make it work," and you're sure to have a great time! (See The Well-Stocked Host, page 316, for a list of items to have on hand.) Ending an impromptu gathering can be the same as ending either a classic dinner party or a drop-by visit (see The Drop-By Visit, opposite page).

THE GOOD HANG

A good hang is a casual get-together that doesn't necessarily revolve around a meal. It often emerges out of casual at-home plans that become an open invitation to those in your social circle. After hearing a friend once comment, "You know, she puts on a good hang," we adopted the term. It means the host can casually entertain well, letting guests know that there will be a space and some hanging out happening, and you're welcome to join. Without a set meal, there isn't a formal structure to this gathering. Everyone's got what they need, but the host isn't "working" this party.

A good hang begins with a well-issued invitation, whether in advance or last minute. It's a clear invitation stating who's invited to what, where, and when (sometimes including an end time) and what to bring, if anything. "Pool's open! We'll be puttering around the yard and garden but feel free to bring snacks and drinks and enjoy the pool!" As the host, you spruce up the areas that friends will gather in (straighten up the cushions and clear the coffee table, but you might not need to full-on clean) and shut the door to any rooms that shouldn't be entered.

To host a good hang, it's nice to have some refreshments to offer your guests. But because of how casual this is, it might be a "help yourself to the fridge" situation, or guests may bring their own drinks and snacks. If you're feeling it, you might prepare a few things: mix up a pitcher, whip up some dip, and set out some chips. Any and all are options, but be sure to communicate when you tell people to come over. "Hey! I made chili for watching the game today."

Whether you chat, watch the game, put on music, hang around a pool or on a porch, make sure you check in on your guests, "Everybody have what they need?" You might not be fluttering about refilling glasses but you should at least check in. Since this is a casual get-together, guests might suggest things, too . . . see what unfolds! Whether the gathering just peters out as friends take their leave, or you have to call it because it's time for you to move on to the next part of your day or evening, always thank your friends for coming over.

A NOTE ABOUT B.Y.O.

B.Y.O. (Bring Your Own) is a designation for hosts to use on a casual invitation to let guests know if they are expected to bring something specifically for their own consumption. Most common is "B.Y.O.B." ("Bring Your Own Bottle," typically alcohol), but we're fans of interpreting the second *B* as *Beverage*. The designation is a familiar-enough concept in casual entertaining that it's not seen as rude. B.Y.O. can be turned into many things. For years a favorite family event was an annual backyard lobster boil with—you guessed it—B.Y.O.L. on the invitation: Bring Your Own Lobster.

Guests participate in bringing the specified item only if they choose to enjoy it at the party. If you're going to have cocktails, bring what you'd like to drink. If you're going to eat a lobster, bring it with you. If you're not, there should be enough other elements at the party to enjoy. While this designation is intended for you to bring what you like to the party for your own enjoyment, it's okay to offer to share with other guests if the item is easily shared. B.Y.O. parties are not meant to stock a host's bar (or lobster tank). Guests may take their B.Y.O. item with them when they leave if it hasn't been finished. And a host should always remind a guest of this before they leave. "Oh, don't forget the rest of your wine before you go!" In some states you may want or need to cork the bottle and mark a line for how full the bottle was when corked, in order to transport an opened bottle of alcohol home.

A NOTE ABOUT POTLUCKS

The potluck is a great way for hosts to enjoy a full and fabulous meal with guests and create a community vibe around a gathering. Typically, a host will provide a main course and allow guests to bring items they are confident in either making or purchasing to fill out the meal.

It's best when a host has an idea of the menu but doesn't ask for specific recipes or for super specific dishes to be brought. So rather than say, "I'd love you to bring a tomato and cheese torte and please use this Ina Garten recipe" or "Please bring a Caesar salad," a host would say, "I'm still looking for guests to bring either salads or side dishes. We're having chili as the main course if that helps you think of ideas for either." Guests might ask for more specific guidance, and then it's perfectly fine to suggest what you think would be best.

While a host doesn't have to offer that guests bring home any leftovers from the dish they brought, it's awfully kind to do so if there's more than a serving left of the dish. If a guest isn't bringing the remainder of a dish home, or there's none left, it's kind for a host to do their best to clean the container and send it home with the person who brought it. If a guest encourages you to hang on to a container and get it to them later, that's fine, just label it with their name so you remember whose it is—and then of course remember to return it.

THE CLASSIC DINNER PARTY

We have arrived at the pinnacle of entertaining etiquette. Readers, we'd like to invite you to the Dinner Party. The classic dinner party is such an accomplishment: a beautiful mix of hospitality, graciousness, and enjoyment. When done well, it balances creativity, organization, time management, and practicality—all elements of good etiquette. Done poorly, it can result in a frustrating, embarrassing, or (sometimes) wonderfully humorous catastrophe of an evening (that you will likely never forget). While some might be daunted by the responsibility of hosting a dinner party, never fear—you can do this, and do it well!

HOW DINNER IS GIVEN IN A GREAT HOUSE

In the 1922 edition of *Etiquette,* Emily describes how a dinner is given at Mrs. Worldly's house. It's a peek into how a well-established household (i.e., its lady and her staff) would handle the details. As we quickly learn, it's a well-oiled machine:

> When Mrs. Worldly gives a dinner, it means no effort on her part whatsoever beyond deciding upon the date and the principal guests who are to form the nucleus; every further detail is left to her subordinates—even to the completion of her list of guests. For instance, she decides that she will have an older dinner, and in finding that the tenth is available for herself, she tells her secretary to send out invitations for that date. She does not have especial cards engraved but uses the dinner blank described in the chapter on Invitations. She then looks through her "dinner list" and orders her secretary to invite the Oldworlds, the Eminents, the Learneds, the Wellborns, The Highbrows, and the Onceweres. She also picks out three or four additional names to be substituted for those who regret. Then turning to the "younger married" list she searches for a few suitable but "amusing" or good–looking ones to give life to her dinner which might otherwise be heavy. But her favorites do not seem appropriate. It will not do to ask the Bobo Gildings, not because of the difference in age but because Lucy Gilding smokes like a furnace and is miserable unless she can play bridge for high stakes, and, just as soon as she can bolt through dinner, sit at a card table; while Mrs. Highbrow and Mrs. Oncewere quite possibly disapprove of women's smoking and are surely horrified at "gambling." The Smartlings won't do either, for the same reason, nor the Gaylies. She can't ask the Newell Riches either, because Mrs. Oldworld and Mrs. Wellborn both dislike vulgarity too much to find compensation in qualities which are merely amusing. So she ends by adding her own friends the Kindharts and the Normans, who "go" with everyone, and a few somewhat younger people, and approves her secretary's suggestions as to additional names if those first invited should "regret."
>
> The list being settled, Mrs. Worldly's own work is done. She sends word to her cook that there will be twenty four on the tenth; the menu will be submitted to her later, which she will probably merely glance at and send back. She never sees or thinks about her table, which is in the butler's province.

On the morning of the dinner her secretary brings her the place cards, (the name of each person expected, written on a separate card) and she puts them in the order in which they are to be placed on the table, very much as though playing solitaire. Starting with her own card at one end and her husband's at the other, she first places the lady of honor on his right, the second in importance on his left. Then on either side of herself, she puts the two most important gentlemen. The others she fits in between, trying to seat side by side those congenial to each other.

When the cards are arranged, the secretary attends to putting the name of the lady who sits on each gentleman's right in the envelope addressed to him. She then picks up the place cards still stacked in their proper sequence, and takes them to the butler who will put them in the order arranged on the table after it is set.

Fifteen minutes before the dinner hour, Mrs. Worldly is already standing in her drawing–room. She has no personal responsibility other than that of being host-ess. The whole machinery of equipment and service runs seemingly by itself. It does not matter whether she knows what the menu is. Her cook is more than capable of attending to it. That the table shall be perfect is merely the every–day duty of the butler. She knows without looking that one of the chauffeurs is on the sidewalk; that footmen are in the hall; that her own maid is in the ladies' dressing–room, and the valet in that of the gentlemen; and that her butler is just outside the door near which she is standing.

DINNER PARTIES TODAY

Giving a dinner was such a *thing* in Emily's day. For her, dinner in a great house often included staff, evening dresses, guests who were "good-looking," and backup guest lists in case people RSVP'd "No." As four people's work at a minimum (the cook, butler, maid, and social secretary) was based on the decisions the host and guests made about the dinner, it mattered that things be kept orderly and the numbers unchanged if possible. While it's interesting and even fun to peek into the world of the grandest homes, in the homes of America today, we've both relaxed and evolved a bit—while we still plan our guest list, prepare a menu and our space, and entertain our guests once they are here, few people make guest lists that have backup plans and substitutes. Even fewer of us have a butler, or a social secretary to deliver the place cards (in seating order) to the butler, and we wouldn't (or at least shouldn't) invite guests because they are "good-looking." But we do still think about and attend to our guests' comfort and do our best to bring together people who would enjoy each other's company. No matter what size your dinner party will be, or how grand your home, we'd like to think that many of us would instead emulate Emily's clas-sic character Mrs. Kindhart, who knows all the ins and outs of social behavior and executes her host and guest roles as the true "kind heart" that she is. She is thoughtful with her dinner party planning so as to create a wonderful experience for all.

PLANNING THE CLASSIC DINNER PARTY

A good host, even one for whom entertaining is old hat, plans their parties. Maybe not with an old-school party journal or a killer Pinterest board, but they think about how they want to execute an evening hosting their friends (or in some cases their business associates). A dinner party is not an impromptu affair. It's not "we'll just whip something up," or make a last-minute call to the Mieles to "just do pizza." The classic dinner party is a planned event, and should be treated as such, whether it's takeout (i.e., "purchase and present"—not served out of containers) and two dear friends around a tableclothed card table in a studio apartment, or a group of twelve, dressed up and sitting down to a six-course catered meal on a penthouse patio. Invitations should be clear and followed up on. Plans should be kept, except in the most extreme situations. This is not to scare anyone off, but to show the difference between dinner with friends (or the "Little Dinner," as Emily called it) and a *dinner party*.

SIZE

It matters. Determining just how many guests you can comfortably host in your home is key. We're guessing you can make a good judgment about how many people could easily sit around your table. Whether it's an actual dining-room table or a dressed-up card table in the living room, it's important to seat your guests properly at a table for a dinner party. Remember, too, that while you might be able to fit twelve on the patio or in the yard, if you can't fit that many inside should the weather turn, you will need to adjust your numbers accordingly.

The size of your party might also be decided based on the menu you choose to serve. If you're going decadent, you might have a smaller guest list to help meet your budget or be able to handle the meal prep and service without hiring staff. Or, if you plan to serve something simple but delicious and you have the room, you might have many friends join you for the evening. Whether or not you enlist help to execute your party may also dictate how many people you can comfortably host. (See Plan Your Menu, page 281, for more on planning a menu for a dinner party.) Thoughtfully choosing the size of your dinner party will make a difference to not only the amount of work you do planning it but the feel of the party as well.

FORMALITY

However formal you choose to be, you want to create consistency in your guests' experience. While you can get away with serving up five-star food wearing jeans and flip-flops, you can't suggest a formal evening and then serve Stouffers out of plastic trays (not that we don't love their mac 'n' cheese, but still . . .). While people like to play with comfort foods for fancy parties, it's one thing to have a single element juxtaposing everything else, but too many mash-ups and your party will be mush. Try to maintain a consistent level of formality between the invitation, the atmosphere and décor, the attire, the food and any music or entertainment. Let's look at what different levels of formality in dinner parties look like from a planning perspective:

FORMAL DINNER PARTIES. Invitations are printed or handwritten, and mailed or hand delivered. You typically hire staff for the evening, either professionals or someone you know (such as a neighborhood college student or a friend, if your party isn't for friends). At least three courses are served. Guests should not be asked to bring a dish, and they are not expected to offer to do so. Guests dress up for the event in more formal attire (suits and dresses most likely, though variations are possible), and shoes are not removed. A formal evening is more structured. Guests won't be offering to help you out by passing hors d'oeuvres or fixing drinks (as they shouldn't at a formal party). Place cards should be used to indicate seating arrangements, and your highest-quality dinnerware should be used, or tableware can be rented for the evening.

INFORMAL (SEMIFORMAL) DINNER PARTIES. Informal spans a range, from dressy casual events to almost fully formal occasions. It's a broad category, so think about what you hope to accomplish and make sure your invitations, menu, décor, and attire are consistent in delivering the message you want to convey to your guests. Invitations are printed and mailed or possibly sent digitally. You might enlist hired help or a cohost, but either way, you likely have someone helping you execute the evening. Typically, at least three courses are served with coffee afterward. This is not a potluck affair. If it's the formal side of semiformal, attire will be suits and dresses; if it's the casual side of semiformal, it will be dressy casual (a jacket, nice slacks, and dress shirt; a skirt-top combo or a casual dress; think special date attire). The evening is more flexible than that of a formal dinner party, but guests should not offer or be asked to help in the kitchen, with coats, or with anything else. Place cards may or may not be used, and the dinnerware could be either your special-occasion dishes and utensils or your everyday ware (however, do make sure it matches, or if it's mismatched, that it looks intentional).

CASUAL DINNER PARTIES. Invitations are usually sent digitally or by phone. A casual handwritten, fill-in, or dinner blank card might be used, but it's less likely. Attire is usually dressy casual, like nice jeans or other pants with a buttoned shirt and sweater or good top, or a casual dress or skirt. (See Dressy Casual attire, page 130). This gathering is more flexible than a semiformal gathering. Guests might offer to help you in the kitchen or in clearing items from the cocktail hour, though you might prefer to take care of this yourself. It's not likely to be a potluck (though potluck dinner parties do happen!), but a good friend might offer to bring a dish and you might say yes—remember, this is a casual dinner party, not a casual dinner with friends. Place cards may or may not be used, and the dinnerware can be your everyday ware (however, do make sure it matches, or again, if it's mismatched, that it looks intentional). There is space for you to host a casual dinner party that is still a step up from your own everyday casual entertaining style. For instance, instead of having a large potluck where everyone finds a seat where they can around the living room, dining room, or kitchen, you instead set a nice table, coordinate with guests on one or two dishes and serve buffet-style, and offer a defined meal together at the table. If you can feel the difference, your company will too.

DATE AND TIME

Dinner parties are, of course, held in the evening at dinner time. The standard is a cocktail hour starting between 6:00 and 7:00 p.m., with dinner served between 7:00 and 8:00 p.m. Occasionally, an early dinner party is thrown, usually on a Saturday or Sunday, where cocktails might start as early as 5:00 p.m. and dinner might start as early as 6:00 p.m. However, these early dinners are not usually served on weeknights, since many people don't get out of work until 5:00 or 6:00. Hosts and guests alike couldn't get home, dressed, and be prepared for dinner comfortably in time.

When considering the date, you might base it solely on your schedule, or the date could be tied to a special day. If you want to get a bit tactical, think about your guests and what you know of their schedules as you plan. What do you do if only one or two guests RSVP "yes" to your dinner? You have two options: Have the dinner for the two that accepted or postpone the event (if possible) to a date when more guests can attend. Either is okay. While it may feel like a disappointment, you can try for a larger dinner party another time. The real key is to communicate with everyone. In this case, graciously—and enthusiastically—going with the flow is a mark of Best Society. And remember, to guard against unavailable guests, send the invitations early to ensure more people haven't already booked that evening.

THE GUEST LIST

Deciding whom to invite is a defining moment for a host in the planning of a great party. The choice might be obvious, like when reciprocating for others who have hosted you, or inviting everyone from a group or family. Or there might be room for the host to choose more freely. In "How Dinner Is Given in a Great House" (page 273) Emily's character Mrs. Worldly would be characterized as shallow by today's standards for her guest list musings (inviting people because they were "good-looking" or not inviting someone because someone else would be "horrified" by them). For all that she details, the lesson we can take away is that to think about your guest's preferences and personalities is key to creating the dinner party you intend to provide. You might think, *Oh, she's so smart and fun and loves to talk—she'd be a great person to include! Or Grant and Kevin just got back from the Grand Canyon; now's the perfect time to have them over with Jerome and Celia, whom we camp with each summer.* A mellow and quietly contented table of friends can be just as wonderful as a raucously spirited group, unafraid to break into song at the table. Of course, you don't need to divide your friends so stereotypically, but be mindful of creating a guest list that will get along well and fit the mood you want to create for your gathering. The guest list should function like a good recipe, where different ingredients come together to make something great. You could host any amicable group casually or formally. And for your friends who really prefer one-on-one gatherings, consider inviting them to a small dinner party for just you two.

INVITATIONS

While we would love it if mailed dinner party invitations were a regular occurrence, the truth is that most casual dinner-party invitations among friends are done via text or phone call or sometimes even email. For anything more than a casual dinner with friends, print or write the invitations or create digital ones. Keep the language simple and clear. The more formal the invitation (printed, engraved or embossed stationery, calligraphy, mailed or hand delivered, formal use of date and time, etc . . .), the more formal your guests will expect the evening to be. It should be noted that digital invitations rarely truly strike a formal tone.

In Emily's day, the host (or their house secretary, if they had one) would issue invitations using the "blank" in their stationery set. This was like a personal fill-in-the-blank invitation card. On the left below, you'll see a general blank that can be used for any occasion, and on the right is a filled-in dinner blank. Take note that this blank template is specifically for dinners. You might choose to get a blank from a stationer that does not specify the meal, so you may use it more broadly. If you use a general blank, you should write in the meal by hand (for example: *dinner*) on the line after "company at."

GENERAL BLANK FOR ANY OCCASION **FILLED-OUT DINNER BLANK**

Elaine Charendoff
requests the pleasure of
_____
company at _____
on _____
at _____o'clock
1267 Ashbury Lane
Charlotte

Elaine Charendoff
requests the pleasure of
Mr. Peter Post and Mrs. Patricia Post's
company at dinner
on *Saturday, the 27th of May*
at seven o'clock
1267 Ashbury Lane
Charlotte
RSVP by Friday, May 19th
802-564-2123

Note that's not a mistake you see in the name above; many women today prefer to use the Mrs. title with their own first name and married last name rather than as "Mr. and Mrs. Husband's Full Name." (See Proper Use of Titles, page 93; Invitations, page 110; and Sample Invitations, page 93, and their corresponding reference guides for more detailed information.)

Below is an example of the structure and language for a dinner-party invitation that works for informal and some formal dinners at home. The difference in formality would be in its form and how it's delivered.

> *Please come for dinner*
> *on Saturday, May 27th*
> *at 7 o'clock*
> *1276 Ashbury Lane*
> *Charlotte*
>
> *RSVP: May 25th*
> *Elaine Charendoff*
> *802-564-2123*

If you're hosting a dinner party but keeping it casual, you might text or email the following:

Please join me for an Italian dinner party at my house, Saturday,
May 27th at 7:00 p.m. Please bring nothing but your wonderful self!
RSVP by Thursday, May 25th; text/call 802-564-2123.

If the invitation were to read, *Dinner at my place, Saturday, May 27th at 7pm—let me know if you can make it!* you might have stepped too far into the casual realm. Not only are your guests less likely to RSVP, but they may not understand that this is a true dinner party. It's wonderful to want to sound casual and breezy, but even for an informal dinner party (remember, that's a step up from casual), it doesn't communicate well to your guests the type of evening they are being invited to attend. (For more on the difference between formal and casual invitations, see Invitations, page 93. For more on proper use of names and titles, please see Social Titles on page 45.)

FOLLOWING UP ON RSVPs

After your RSVP date, it's essential to follow up with guests who haven't given you a response. You should never come across as badgering or annoying, which can easily happen when you've got preparations to make and people are essentially ignoring your thoughtful invitation. But put aside that venting voice and instead reach out the day after your RSVP date with a friendly call or text saying something like *Hi Teresa! I'm following up on the dinner party invitation for Saturday at my place. Will you and Elijah be able to make it?* Some guests may say they still need time, in which case it's best to be gracious and reply, *Of course—talk to Elijah and if you could let me know by Wednesday I can then tell the caterer the headcount.*

If you're still not getting a solid answer from your guest after a few attempts, leave them a message like *Hi Teresa—I know you haven't given an answer yet, but I'm going to count you in until I hear otherwise. Really hoping you can make it!* At worst, you will have extra food and need to adjust your beautifully set table at the last minute. At best, you've chosen to prepare in an inclusive way instead of an exclusive way. It's easy when someone isn't cooperating to want to punish them: *You're not responding in a timely manner, so you don't get to come to my awesome dinner party!* But you cannot uninvite a guest. By preparing for your guest, even without knowing if they will show, you stay true to your invitation and to the principles of etiquette.

PLAN YOUR COUNTDOWN

When it comes to planning your dinner party preparations (prepping your prep), a real Mr. Goodhost will sit down a few days to as much as 2 weeks ahead of the party and time out what needs to be accomplished, starting with the party's start time and working backward:

6:00 P.M. *Guests arrive, cocktail hour begins. Cheers!*

5:45 P.M. *Home and host are prepped and ready to welcome guests. (Time for a deep breath, a drink or puff, and a moment to appreciate all you've accomplished so far.)*

5:30–5:45 P.M. *Set out hors d'oeuvres, put out garnishes for cocktails at the bar, and fluff pillows one last time if needed. Check on any meal prep to make sure it is cooking, warming, or cooling appropriately.*

4:30–5:30 P.M. *Get yourself ready. Shower, dress, and clean up the bathroom you've used if it is to be used by others.*

1:30–4:30 P.M. *Meal prep: begin preparing or cooking anything you can make ahead of time.*

12:30–1:30 P.M. *Set the table and set up your bar area.*

11:00 A.M.—12:30 P.M. *Clean: put away clutter, dust/wipe down surfaces, vacuum, touch up the bathrooms, empty garbage bins, close doors to rooms that shouldn't be entered.*

9:30–11:00 A.M. *Pick up groceries and any decorations.*

NIGHT BEFORE OR 8:30–9:00 A.M. *Make to-do list.*

Obviously, your own list will reflect your personal pacing and needs, but work backward from the party's start time and go through absolutely everything you need to do to get ready with bells on! This is the part that can often foil a first-time dinner-party host: assuming you'll need half an hour to clean your house, when really you need an hour or two. Or thinking the shopping will take only an hour, and then having to go to extra stores because an item was sold out.

Move some tasks to a day or two before, like ironing your linens or polishing or dusting off any flatware or dinnerware. Do a big cleanup two days before, so that you only have to do a light touchup the day of, shortening your cleaning time. Shop for and prep whatever food you can earlier in the week so that it's easier to cook the day of. Allowing yourself an extra half hour or hour in any area of prep isn't a bad idea—except when it comes to the cooking. If you start something too early, it might be mush or dried out by the time it makes it to the plate. Starting it too late will mean you're juggling guests and dinner. Not a disaster, but something to be mindful about.

PLAN YOUR MENU

Experimentation, creativity, and the increased accessibility of global cuisine have given us such a rich world of food to play with. Coming up with a menu that's not only cohesive but that you can also execute well is a mark of a good host. Select a menu that allows you to host your party and still serve a properly prepared meal to your guests. For less experienced hosts or those hosting alone, this might mean making dishes that can sit well, or that can be mostly cooked ahead of time and then be finished off quickly just before the service without compromising the quality. The best menu selections are those that you feel confident in executing and that will allow you to host your guests while you do so.

Choosing drinks and hors d'oeuvres for your cocktail hour and courses for your menu depends on how formal your party is, how much you can handle, and what you want your guests to experience. Remember, it is perfectly okay not to serve alcohol to your guests, and even if you do, you should always offer nonalcoholic options as well. Two-course meals (entrée and dessert) often show up at casual dinners. Three-course menus (appetizer, dinner, and dessert) can be for any formality level. Four-course menus fall on the more formal side of semiformal. A formal dinner party menu can have anywhere from three to six courses, and is likely to require help in the kitchen and for service. Five- and six-course menus are rarely if ever found at a casual or semiformal at-home dinner party. Pick and choose what works for you and the type of evening you're hoping to have. If this is your first time hosting a dinner party, start with something simple, like a two-course meal. As you gain confidence and experience, you might plan more challenging or elaborate menus. Here we have Emily's course list from 1922 and, next to it, today's version:

1. Hors d'oeuvres	1. Amuse-bouche/small appetizer
2. Soup	2. Starter/antipasto/soup
3. Fish	3. Entrée
4. Roast	4. Salad (may come before entrée)
5. Salad	5. Cheese
6. Dessert	6. Dessert
7. Coffee	7. Coffee and/or after-dinner drinks (port, liqueur, digestif)

You'll notice the names are a little different and that today sometimes we'll serve coffee with dessert, or sometimes we'll serve it in the den or living room after dinner. A cheese course might precede the meal, be a course during the meal, or a cheese and fruit course may also be offered in place of dessert.

SERVING STYLE

Once you've decided the type and formality of your party along with the menu, you can determine which service style will be optimal for your dinner party.

PLATED. A plated meal means that each course is plated (the food is arranged on the plate) in the kitchen and individual plates are brought out and presented to guests (much like in a restaurant). For larger tables, this is best done when you have enlisted help for the evening, or if you have a cohost. This style is more common with formal dining at home, but is easily executed for small dinners that are informal or casual.

BUFFET. The food is arranged on platters and in large serving bowls, and the dishes with their serving utensils are set out in a line (together they literally make the buffet). Typically plates are stacked at the start of the buffet, and napkins and utensils are set at the table. When it is very casual and tables aren't set or guests aren't eating at a table (instead, eating on laps), napkins and utensils are set at the end of the buffet so that guests aren't trying to hold them along with the plate as they serve themselves. The buffet is a standard in the Post family. While you might see a buffet for a formal dinner, a plated meal is more common.

FAMILY STYLE. "Family style" means that all the dishes for the meal are set at the table and passed around by the guests, who serve themselves. This is best for casual and sometimes informal or holiday meals. It is not done for formal occasions. Someone might play the role of carving the meat for the meal by standing, carving, and filling a platter that is then passed family-style.

SERVING GUESTS AT THE TABLE. Serving guests tableside is typically reserved for formal meals; however, a host of a small informal dinner party might be able to pull it off, and certainly could with a little help from a cohost. Platters and dishes are presented to each guest, with the person serving standing to the guest's left. At tight tables this is not a good idea. A server should stand close enough that a guest doesn't risk spilling or dripping the food as they transfer it to their plate, but not so close that a guest will have no room to move as they serve themselves. For informal and casual meals, a host might also choose to serve a dessert from the table, such as a pie. With the pie and plates in front of them, they slice the pie, plate it, and pass it down the table to their right. And yes, this results in desserts going all the way round the table.

SEATING CHARTS AND GUESTS OF HONOR

As a host, it's up to you to arrange and seat your guests. And you will want to do this ahead of time rather than in the moment. Whether or not you have place cards, have a seating chart in mind. Generally, hosts are seated at the heads of the table. If there are any guests of honor, the first guest of honor is seated to the right of a host. The second guest of honor is seated to the left of the host. From there, a host may mix and mingle their guests as they wish. Traditionally, boy-girl order and keeping couples (except for newly engaged couples) apart were the rules to follow. Today, we still try to keep couples (and close family) apart—they likely see each other all the time, so they should be spread out and mixed in with guests they might not get to chat with as often—but boy-girl order is no longer necessary and, in many cases, may not be appropriate or inclusive of the guests attending.

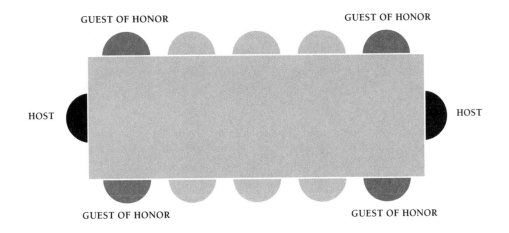

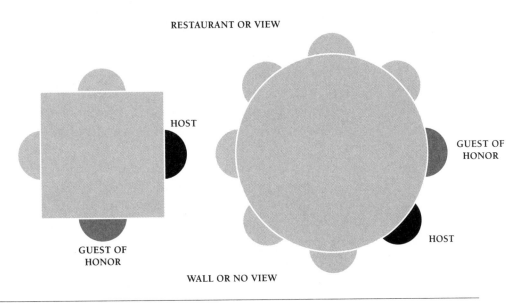

Once the hosts and any guests of honor have been taken into account, you can have some fun: pair guests next to those they may find interesting. Note that placing two talkers next to each other might not work, because no one will be listening. In the same way, placing two people with strongly opposing views right next to one another is more likely to stir discord than discussion than if they are seated farther apart.

While we have mentioned guests of honor, when there isn't one, a guest shouldn't assume that not being seated in those places means they are somehow lesser than the guests who are seated there. When there is no guest of honor, the seats to the right and left of the host (and their cohost if there is one) are simply seats around the table.

SETTING THE DINNER PARTY TABLE

To set a beautiful table is an art. It's an expression, a moment, an intention, a mood, a fantasy. It's a tradition. While we don't get so creative with our tablescapes as to disrupt the practicality of utensil placement (you will never hear us suggest stacking the fork, knife, and spoon above the plate with the glass on the left and the bread plate below it—no), experimenting with decorations and styles can not only be fun but also help you cultivate a hosting style and gain experience that will take you far in being a confident host. So get creative, try things out, throw dinner parties often, and figure out what works best for you at your table!

For many hosts, this is a point of pride: a beautifully laid table ready and waiting for guests to enjoy its ambiance. Entire competitions, books, Instagram accounts, and courses focus on setting the table and tablescapes. For your dinner party, you'll consider the spacing and placing of guests, what utensils and tableware you'll need, and what kind of décor you'd like to add.

Start with your linens, then set each setting, and then place any décor (keeping space of course if dishes are to be served at the table family-style). The main rule for setting any table is to set only the utensils you will use for each course, and to set them in the order they will be used (per utensil grouping), working from the outside in toward the plate. The menu will dictate the utensils used and their placement. You may credit Emily Post with suggesting you place a maximum of three courses' worth of any type of utensils at a setting at a time. Anything necessary beyond that is brought out with the specific course. Sometimes the dessert utensils break this "rule" and are set on the table (at the top of the setting); other times they follow the rule and are presented with dessert. (See Utensils, page 142, for more about individual utensils and where they are placed on the table.)

For most, this will mean dinnerware consisting of first-course utensils, entrée utensils, dessert utensils, water glasses, wineglasses, bread plates and butter knives, place cards, a centerpiece, candlesticks, and salt and pepper shakers. At a dinner party, condiments or sprinkled items like Parmesan cheese are always placed in dishes, bowls, pots, and jars with serving utensils, with an underplate to ease passing and to hold a used utensil so it doesn't rest in the vessel or on the table.

At even semiformal and informal gatherings it's best to do this. No product labels at the table. Condiments should be brought to the table just before serving the course or with the first plate, so that the first diner served may serve themself and then pass the condiments along. (For more on individual utensils, see Reference Guide: Utensils, page 142, and Utensils, page 142.) Here is a sample menu for an informal dinner party:

FIRST COURSE

Chilled pea velouté with crème fraîche

SECOND COURSE

Gems salad with breakfast radish; shaved asparagus
with mint-lemon vinaigrette

MAIN COURSE

Grilled pork tenderloin with pickled apple and parsnip
puree; grilled fennel with lemon and olive oil

DESSERT

Apple tartine with whipped cream

Note that the salad in our sample menu is served before the main course, thus the salad fork and knife are set on the outside of the main course utensils. If the salad was served after the main course, the salad fork and knife would be placed to the inside of the main course utensils.

We will offer our guests a choice of red and/or white wine. Some hosts set the table with both red and white wineglasses and either leave both so that guests may switch wines with courses, or remove the unused glasses once a guest chooses a wine. Hosts with fewer glass options may rinse a glass if a guest decides to switch, or might choose to offer only one type of wine. Courtesy and practicality can go hand in hand. Our place setting would look like this:

Things to note: You do not flip a setting for left-handed guests; the forks remain on the left and the knives and spoons on the right. If you are using many glasses and your table is tight, it's okay to group the glasses instead of set them in a line cascading out from above the knives. Try to group them so that the glasses that go with earlier courses are in front of the glasses for courses later in the meal.

TABLE LINENS

Stellar table settings don't require that all table linen options be used. Many hosts are known to set a gorgeous formal table without a tablecloth. There are two rules to follow with table linens:

1. Napkins always. Never set a dinner-party table without napkins. No other linen is actually required.

2. Do not use anything you would cringe to see stained. If Grandmother's hand-embroidered century-old heirloom is too precious to be soiled, then let it be too precious to be dined upon. Keep it safe. While no guest should make a true mess of any host's linens, accidents do happen.

TABLECLOTH. The tablecloth can have any design, but should hang down nicely from the table. You can fold a large tablecloth to help it fit a small table (diners don't want to feel like there is a blanket in their laps), and this is fine for casual or semiformal meals at home. However you arrange it, do your best to make sure the tablecloth hangs evenly on all sides. The tablecloth should be ironed (or pressed by a dry cleaner). Avoid the mistake of ironing right on your table, which could adversely affect its surface. You don't need to put a placemat or runner on top of a tablecloth; however, it can be done for added color and decoration. A charger plate may be used with a tablecloth or a placemat or even the bare table.

NAPKINS. Obviously, you want one for each guest. It's a good idea to keep a few extras available if a guest needs a replacement. While many a banquet staff member has spent an afternoon preparing intricate napkin folds (some more appealing than others), they are all virtually unnecessary. A simple fold or two (or three) resulting in a rectangle or triangle is all that is needed. (Emily herself had some thoughts on the absurdity that napkin folding can take on.) For formal and semiformal meals at home, the napkin is usually to the left of the forks; alternatively, it can be in the center of the setting or on the charger. For informal or casual meals, a napkin ring may be used, and in informal settings or at a tight table you might choose to put your napkin under the forks. In doing so, diners will be required to move the forks to access their napkin. Some people are taught that this is not as proper as putting the napkin to the left of the forks. In formal situations napkin rings are not used.

RUNNER. A runner is a narrow swath of cloth that is placed in the center and runs down the length of the table. Runners can be simple (white linen with embroidered edges) or intricate and colorful. Candles and flower arrangements are placed on them, and they can prevent wax and pollen from damaging the table. They can be placed on top of a tablecloth or a bare table.

SILENCER. This is a cloth, often felt, that goes under the tablecloth and helps silence the noise of items being picked up and set back down again. If you are serving family-style, a silencer can protect the table from hot dishes that are not on trivets or from heavy dishes being set down multiple times. They shouldn't be so thick that glasses will stand uneasily on them; a clean, thin fleece blanket also works well.

PLACEMATS. Placemats can be a fabulous way to set a casual or informal table. Some placemats are simple; others are elaborate and paired with napkins as sets. They create a bit of protection for the table and help to define a diner's space nicely. Placemats and a runner can create a nice look together, without going full tablecloth.

For dishware, glassware, and flatware, please see Glasses, page 145; and Utensils, page 142. For centerpieces, see Plan Your Décor, page 288.

SERVINGWARE

Here are some of the most common servingware pieces. They not only are practical but also can help elevate the presentation of your meal. (For more on tableware, see Utensils, page 335, and Glassware, page 335, as well as the sections Utensils, Plates and Bowls, Glasses, and Extras, starting on page 142.)

- Serving spoons and forks
- Carving knives and forks
- Salt and pepper shakers or cellars
- Tongs and ladles
- Flat spatulas or pie servers
- Large and small platters
- Bread baskets
- Fruit bowls
- Chafing dishes, hot plates
- Carving platters
- Gravy boats and small pitchers
- Water pitcher or carafe
- Large and small bowls
- Small pots, dishes, underplates for condiments and spoons, forks or spreading knives

Tablescapes, centerpieces, lighting! Decorating for a dinner party is fun, and there are so many places to find inspiration these days. (Though with so much to draw from, sometimes we can go overboard or lose our sense of theme or purpose, so it's best to avoid going too far down the rabbit hole.)

When it comes to décor for your party, less is often more—but more can be so much fun! One need only search "dinner party tablescapes" or "dinner party decorations" to find innumerable inspiring ideas. The key is to choose something that fits both the style of your party and your skill level (let the Pinterest searching begin). It's also important to note that beyond a centerpiece (which doesn't have to be floral), you don't need extra items for a dinner party. Ask yourself if the decorations are nice touches or if they take undue attention away from the guests, either during your preparations or the event. It can be fun to dress up a table or room in different ways; we know one host (*ahem,* Tricia Post) who is an artist with silver and gold confetti stars as well as frosted fruits on her New Year's Eve table. But don't feel you need to overdo it to make your party "more." You, the food, a clean space, and good conversation are all you need for a dinner party with friends.

FLORAL ARRANGEMENTS are the most classic dinner-party centerpiece and décor. Fresh flowers in the entryway and main gathering space (living room or outdoors), on the dinner table, and in a small vase in the bathroom are classic uses for arrangements to spruce up each of these rooms.

CENTERPIECES are terribly fun to come up with, and there are so many ways to utilize them. Typically, a centerpiece is an arrangement of flowers or fruits, or it is an ornament like a large silver or china piece. It is essential that your centerpiece be an enhancement to the table, not a hindrance to the diners. Floral centerpieces should not block the views of diners. Keep them well out of eye height; we suggest below, but some people love to prop up an enormous vase and raise the arrangement above eye level. It can be done, but be aware that the vase is like a column and still creates a visual barrier. When selecting flowers for your centerpiece, it cannot be overstated that you should select blooms that don't have much aroma. At the dinner table, their scent will compete with that of the food and possibly even confuse the diners' senses and experience of the meal.

Depending on the size of your table, you might choose to have small arrangements running down the center at intervals, or possibly a set of three arrangements in the center. A romantic approach is to weave very small arrangements or even the flowers themselves throughout the table from one end to another. While this starts to be less of a centerpiece and more of a free-form decoration, it can be very effective.

CANDLES may be used in a variety of ways. From the classic set of two tapers in candlesticks to candelabras, small votives, hurricanes, or even a collection of different candles grouped together can make a cozy or romantic centerpiece. Candles can be of any color, and even electric versions are okay if they look good with the rest of your setting. Don't use scented candles for the table, as they will compete with the food and confuse diners' senses. It should also be noted when using candles that they are open flames at the table. Keep them in toward the center and not close to diners, where a cuff, sleeve, or someone's hair might easily catch fire.

Don't be intimidated by the options. Have fun with your décor: colors, themes—go for it! Balance common sense and whimsy, as odd as that may sound. You do want to get creative and build upon or show your personal hosting style, but stay practical; people still need to be able to dine easily.

HOSTING THE CLASSIC DINNER PARTY

The dinner party is very special. It's a "time out" from food as fuel, food as function, food on the go. It's a celebration and honoring of food and hospitality. "I'm just so busy" is the lament of the modern-day person. We are indeed busy. Our lives are filled with many options for things to do and things we have to do and things we should be doing that we are indeed so busy—every one of us, in some way or another. And in all that busyness, we are still inspired to put in the effort: to clean up our space, to prepare a meal, and to host our guests in hopes that they are filled with enjoyment. We want to grace their lives with the soul-nourishing effect of people gathering together for food and conversation. Hosting a dinner party can truly be an act of love.

GREETING GUESTS

Refreshed and ready after your 15 minutes of relaxing, you hear the first knock at the door, the buzz of the buzzer, the ding of the bell. It's time for the dinner party to begin! (Also, yay! At least one or two guests are definitely going to be there!) Greet your guests at the door. "Welcome! Come on in! May I take your coat? Feel free to take a seat if you need to switch out of boots and into indoor shoes." "Thank you, Mrs. Kindhart. I'm so glad to be here!"

If a guest brings a hosting gift, you may open it right then or save it for later. If you do open it, take the time to thank the giver. It's okay to save the gift, even one of food or wine, to enjoy at a later time.

For your first guest, greet them at the door and welcome them in, then follow up once they're inside (after any coats and whatnot have been removed) by offering them a drink and hors d'oeuvres: "Hi! Welcome! I'm so glad you could make it [*guest removes coat or issues a greeting in return*]. Please come in [*move toward living room*]. You're the first one here. May I start you with something to drink?" "That'd be great! What are you serving?" Stay with them until the next guests arrive. To leave a single guest without anyone to interact with while you busy yourself with additional preparations is not polite. It's fine, of course, to leave them to greet the next guest, or to take their coat and indicate they may head into the living room while you go hang it up or store it in a designated bedroom if you're low on closet space. After this, as other guests arrive, greet them as they arrive and then welcome them into the party, offering to make introductions if need be, fix them a drink, or say, "Help yourself to the bar and hors d'oeuvres." If time allows, spend a moment talking or helping them join another conversation before heading off to greet the next guest.

If you are cohosting, it's perfectly all right to have one host manning the door and the other helping guests to get into the swing of the party. Play to your strengths in deciding who should do which task, or let it happen organically. Try to share the workload. Avoid having one host default to pack-mule status, having their role consist solely of carrying coats and bags to the bedroom or closet (unless this is what they prefer).

THE COCKTAIL HOUR

Once all your guests have arrived and you've handled any meal prep issues you might need to tackle quickly, your cocktail hour will likely be 15 to 30 minutes into its hour, and it's probably time to refresh platters of hors d'oeuvres and guests' drinks. Take a moment to also clean up any messes that might have started to form: chips outside a bowl, dip drips, drink rings and spills. With that taken care of, now it's time to really join your party!

Fix yourself a drink, mingle with your guests, have a bite of shrimp cocktail or some onion dip (or something from the harvest board, you chic host, you). It's smart to keep an eye on the time, either by making sure you know which song in your playlist means "go check on dinner" or by setting a timer for yourself. Obviously, the former is a little more discreet, but requires you to pay attention; two Manhattans in and some of us might not remember which song was meant to be our warning signal. (Note to self: you're the host, you're in charge, so it's best to not find yourself in this circumstance. Water down your own drinks or time them so you can remain comfortably in control.)

While it is a host's role to generate conversation among guests, if your guests are already enjoying themselves, don't feel you have to force it. Take the freebie and enjoy not having to do the heavy lifting. If, however, you're noticing some awkward or uncomfortably quiet moments for guests, then it is on you as the host to try and engage your guests. (Easy does it: you don't have to put on your old cheerleading costume, Rachel Green.) Consider what you know about your guests—the reliable, tier-I conversation topics, not the gossipy, salacious ones—and start asking questions. (See the Three Tiers of Conversation, page 61.) "Boris, you're a big football fan; what's your take on Brady's glory? I know Dan has some thoughts!" Remember, though, that this sort of line only works when you know you're serving up topics the person is bound to talk about. Shared hobbies and interests in the arts or pop culture can make great starting points. Asking Boris about his thoughts on privacy issues with drones wouldn't do if you've never heard Boris speak about this.

After about an hour, you'll want to start the transition between the cocktail hour and the dinner hour. Since guests do not bring their cocktails to the table, it's nice to give a 15- to

20-minute heads-up on when dinner will be served. This gives them a chance to refresh drinks one last time or enjoy what they have left before moving on to dinner. The same is true of the hors d'oeuvres; a guest might not go scarf down those stuffed mushrooms if dinner is coming shortly. Or maybe it'll encourage someone to tuck into the baked brie one more time before it's whisked away.

COMING TO THE TABLE

When it's time to call your guests into dinner, it is on you, the host, to make the announcement. In Emily's day, upon hearing the announcement, each gentleman would escort his dining companion (the female guest whose name was on the dinner card he had been given) into the dining room and hold her chair as she took her seat. This woman was typically not his spouse.

Today, we have no such standards for at-home dinner parties (although it could be a real hoot if you wanted to play up your dinner party old-school-style). Instead, the host announces, "Dinner is served. Please come take your seats," or "Please come find your place at the table," or "Dinner is served!" If a buffet is to be served, the host may say, "Dinner is served. Please take a plate and begin serving yourself." Or, if the plates are on the table: "Dinner is served. Please find your plate and begin the buffet." Regardless of whether the host is serving a buffet, family-style, or a plated meal, they should always take their food last. This allows a host to assist if there are any issues with the buffet and ensure that their guests have enough to eat before serving themself.

At very formal dinners, once everyone is served, it's the host's job to "lift their fork" to officially start the meal. At casual and informal dinner parties, if there's no grace being said and service will take more than a few minutes, it's more common for a host to invite guests to start once they are served (or have served themselves from the buffet). This is often the case at the Post family table. (See When to Begin, page 147, for more on when to begin under which circumstances.)

SERVING AND CLEARING COURSES

There are some longstanding traditions when it comes to serving and clearing courses (and condiments), and they are often rooted in practicality and presentation. It's not wrong if they aren't followed, but most of them make the serving and clearing of courses orderly and more manageable, and that can help a host.

ALREADY SET. Since your menu and serving choices will vary, you'll have to make decisions that make sense for your table. However, for most dinner parties, the bread and butter will already be on the table (at each place if it's formal). Sauces and condiments are placed only if needed for the specific course they accompany. When possible (beyond seasoning with salt and pepper), the dishes should be "ready" for diners.

SERVING THE FIRST COURSE. If you are serving your guests plated courses, you should wait until everyone is seated to serve the first course. Certainly don't try to have the first course on the table before the guests get there. Food sitting out is never attractive and begs for dust, hairs, and other debris (or worse, something with wings) to find their way onto the dish amid the shuffling of guests. Not to mention it means that a hot dish will cool as it sits waiting for its diner. No, no—instead, serve the first course once all your guests are seated. Always start with the guest of honor, or if there isn't one, with the person seated to your (the host's) right. Then work your way around the table, serving a cohost and yourself last.

SIGNALING FOR SERVICE. Review the flow of the meal with your servers (if you've hired any) ahead of time. Many experienced servers will easily follow your direction; for example, to serve a first course after people have taken their seat or after a toast, or to clear when everyone has finished eating and won't need any signals from you during the meal. Should you need to signal, eye contact and a nod to your server should do it. Whatever you do, do not signal that dishes be brought or cleared by snapping your fingers. In Emily's home in Edgartown, Massachusetts, she had a discreet button that she could tap with her foot to signal to the staff. These early "smart home" buzzers were quite common in houses of hosts who did a lot of entertaining, even in the 1950s and '60s.

WHEN TO CLEAR. When it comes to clearing courses, always wait until *all* the diners are finished. To remove plates from some and not all would make those not yet finished feel rushed which is not a host's goal. The "all finished" utensil placement is a big help for hosts and servers to know for certain that their guests are finished with a course. (See Where to Place Utensils, page 172). While some may have food still on their plate, take notice of when all your guests have generally stopped eating before having anything cleared.

LEAVE LEFT, RETRIEVE RIGHT. When serving individually plated courses, you leave (serve) from the left, and retrieve (clear) from the right. Always start with the guest of honor, or the guest to the host's right, continue to the right, and serve the host(s) last. Plates (or bowls if it's a soup course) should always be placed delicately. You don't have to be so cautious that you linger in slow motion, but never allow the plate to drop or clatter as it's placed (as it's often messy, loud, and unpleasant). Do not line plates up your arm; the likelihood of spillage is high, even for those who have had professional experience. Instead, as a host (or server), carry one in each hand. If there is a sauce or addition to the dish, it should be brought out with the course and placed near the guest of honor or in front of the host to offer to the guest of honor, and then be passed to the right around the table. If you're hosting on your own, for a more informal dinner at home you might take a guest up on their offer to help serve. If you don't have someone who can play cohost for you, don't rush—it's okay to take your time, and will likely mean fewer spills or elbows bumped. If a host or servers are going to be presenting and offering dishes to guests at the table, they stand to the guest's left, close enough so that the guest does not have to turn too much to serve themselves.

When removing completed courses from the table, you remove the plate from the right side of the diner. Hopefully guests will know to put their utensils with the handles at the four if the plate were a clock face. This makes it easy when retrieving from the right to place your thumb over the utensils so they don't slide and clatter or, worse, drop onto your guest or the table or floor. Each implement is removed once its purpose has been served for its course (used or unused), and you'll want to remove any sauces or course accompaniments as well.

PASSING. Any item needing to be passed at the table should be passed to the right. Having one direction keeps things simple, and for the majority of people (who are right-handed—sorry, lefties!) it makes it easier to serve yourself. In passing to the right, the diner passing the item may offer to hold it for the guest on their right. If you're holding a dish and serving yourself, receiving it in your left hand leaves your dominant right hand free to serve. Passing plates to the left forces your right arm to tuck in, like a T. Rex forearm or chicken wing, as you try to serve yourself. Of course, at a table with a majority of left-handed diners, you could certainly pass to the left.

SERVING DISHES AT THE TABLE. Sometimes in a formal situation a host might choose to serve guests by having their staff offer each platter or serving bowl to a guest by standing at the guest's left and holding the dish while the guest serves themself. This type of service is not well suited to a tightly seated table. The server should try to hold the dish very steady and close enough to the guest and table that food isn't likely to spill or drip as it is transferred from the dish to the plate, but not so close that a guest can't move their arm well when taking their portion. A host might also choose to serve this way for an informal or casual meal. However, do think about how long it will take and if it's really necessary. A family-style, buffet, or plated service is often a better choice for hosts who haven't enlisted help for the evening.

CONVERSATION AT THE TABLE

Dinner-table conversation that vacillates between guests being deeply enthralled and enthusiastically animated, quiet with fascination, or boisterous with laughter is indeed a dream. The key to making it happen is a well-curated guest list and the confidence to facilitate the conversation without micromanaging it.

As the host, seed conversation with small-talk topics like popular culture and current-day entertainment, sports, technology, and hobbies (See The Three Tiers of Conversation, page 61). Among those you know well, you can also request specific tales from your guests. "Sharif, you just got back from a visit home to Charleston, didn't you? Care to tell us about the trip?" or "I'm curious if any of you have tried one of those sleep-monitoring beds or apps? I've been thinking about getting one." Of course, you want to say something like this only if you know your guests are hot to trot on tech. If not, such a prompt will likely fall flat, with guests looking around to see who might pick up the conversation, because they certainly won't be.

In Emily's day, ladies were meant to speak with the person on their right until the hostess literally "turned" the table by turning to speak to the gentleman on her left, and all the ladies would then turn to speak with the gentleman on their left. Even our formal gatherings no longer stick to this rule (and are rarely so gendered). However, as a host (and a guest too, for that matter), you should spend time talking to each of the guests next to you, though not to the exclusion of the rest of the table. How awful is it to sit at a table with a host lost in hushed giggles, smiling only at the diners directly around them? Don't be that host. Instead, feel confident speaking to those sitting a little farther away, though remember that the more distance there is between you, the more people will be involved in the conversation.

For smaller gatherings of up to eight (or maybe even ten) guests, you're likely to have the entire table engaged in one conversation. Once you start to break into the ten-plus range, smaller conversations at the table will likely go on among multiple groups seated near each other. As the host, it's not bad to stir up a table-wide conversation once or twice during the meal, but it's also not necessary.

If you see that someone is looking left out, direct a question to them or ask for them to chime in with their opinion: "Tara, what do you think about that?" or "Tara, you read Dune, didn't you? What do you think of the new movie?" (Of course, if you know this guest to be painfully shy, don't put them on the spot: let them be "the listener.")

If the conversation turns ugly, while anyone can help to rein in an unpleasant conversation, it's the host's responsibility to redirect it. Feel confident taking the reins should this happen. "Mark, I'm going to ask that we not discuss this at the table. I'd love to hear about what you've baking lately instead." (See Disengaging from an Unpleasant Conversation, page 73, and Difficult Guests, page 184.)

DESSERT

Dessert is usually served at the table, and certainly served at the table during formal dinners at home. All dishes, including the bread plates, butter knives, and salt and pepper shakers, should be removed from the table before dessert. If the table is messy with crumbs, you can always use a crumber (a small brush or scraper-like utensil used to quickly clean up crumbs). A little bit about the crumber: it used to come with a rectangular box that had a handle and hinged lid that opened by pressing down with your thumb. The box was held in the left hand, the crumber in the right; the box was opened, the crumbs swept in, then the box was closed. No mess on your guest. Today crumbers come in a few shapes and sizes, from simple scrapers or brushes to ones that have a compartment for the crumbs. You would not offer your guest a crumber to use themselves (you've already cleared their plates, so what would they do with the crumbs?!). While they are a great option for cleaning the table, they are most often used in restaurants.

Set any sauces, creams, or sugar on the table first before bringing the desserts. Then place the guest of honor's dessert plate down and say, "Please help yourself to the raspberry sauce and whipped cream." Then, moving to the right, serve the next guest, and so on until you've served the person sitting to your left or at the other head of the table, and finally yourself. Emily told a delightful story of Mrs. Three-in-One, her famed character who played host, cook, and maid, who put the ice-cream maker under her chair so she could take it out and serve ice cream while remaining with her guests at the table.

Only the dessert fork and spoon, place card, and the water and wineglasses should remain. Guests will pull their dessert fork and spoon down into place if they've been set at the top of the setting, with the fork on the left and the spoon on the right (or just take them from their place at the top of the setting once dessert begins). If you haven't set the table with the dessert utensils, you will bring them out with each dessert plate. If dishes aren't plated and dessert is served family-style or at the table, bring out and set the dessert utensils for each guest before you serve the dessert. Coffee or teacups aren't usually set during meals at home and are instead brought out with dessert or after dessert.

COFFEE

Coffee (or tea if a guest wishes that instead) after dinner is a custom we refuse to let fade away. Even though it is less commonly offered nowadays at more casual dinners, it can cap off an evening nicely at an informal or semiformal dinner and is an expected component for a formal dinner party. Coffee and/or tea is often served with dessert, or if a dessert wine is served with dessert, these might be served after dinner in a sitting room, living room, or den. A thoughtful host offers decaffeinated options as well, since caffeine can interfere with digestion and sleep.

Cups with saucers should be used rather than mugs. If possible, brew a pot of coffee and place it in a decorative pot to serve at the table or wherever you've gathered guests after dinner. Or, if you don't have a decorative pot, pour the coffee in the kitchen and then bring each saucer and cup to the table. Cream (milk or alternatives) and sugar (or sugar substitutes) should also be placed in a small decorative pitcher and bowl and brought to the table even if you've asked your guests how they take their coffee or tea. Spoons should always be served with coffee (and tea). You'll want to take the cups and saucers into the kitchen together if you are giving guests a refill.

If a guest asks for tea and you have only tea bags on hand, steep their tea in the kitchen and remove the bag before serving it, especially if this is for a semiformal or formal dinner. For a casual meal, you might bring out a teacup of hot water and offer a small array of teas to choose from. The guest can use their saucer for the tea bag or you may provide a small plate (like a bread plate) for them. It's also nice to offer a lemon wedge along with sugar and cream or milk when asking how your guest takes their tea. (See Tea and Coffee, page 319.)

After-dinner liquors like brandy, sherry, or port are either offered once dessert has been cleared, or along with the coffee and tea when served in another room. It really is best to have the proper glasses for these after-dinner drinks so they can breathe. Brandy out of a rocks glass or sherry or limoncello out of a pint glass just isn't quite right. It's not that you can't do it, but the presentation and feel of the correct glass adds to the atmosphere at the end of the meal in a delightful way.

Saying good night well is important for a host. It's like tying the bow on a gift. It simply pulls everything together. As your after-dinner hour winds down, typically the group will collectively sense that it's time to leave, and one guest will admit that they must indeed be making their way back home. It's fine for guests to take the lead in leaving. Sometimes the guest speaking up will cause a mass exodus and everyone will get up, gather their coats, make offers to help (at casual or informal dinner parties), and exchange thank-yous and compliments on how nice the evening was. "Thank you so much for coming." "Thank you so much for having us! The pork was superb, and I want that chocolate torte recipe!" "You were so kind to bring the flowers, and thank you so much for helping me with the coffee this evening. You brew the perfect pot!" This is a great time to practice your "helping someone put on their coat" skills. They might ask you, appreciatively, to hold something while they put it on themselves. If they take you up on your offer, hold the coat open by the collar facing them, up at about shoulder height, presenting the arm holes. Continue to hold the coat up and open as they slide one arm in, turn, and find the other sleeve. If they decline, just smile and hand them their coat.

It's wonderful when the exit just happens naturally. If a guest gulps down their coffee, stands, and says, "Well, all, this has been lovely, but I'm going to head out," rather than call him out on leaving early, instead say, "Oh, what a shame you can't stay any longer, but if you must leave, let me help you with your coat."

On the other hand, if your guests won't leave, or haven't picked up on your subtle cues (closing down the bar, putting away the coffee, turning up the lights, and turning down the music), then it's time to get more direct. "Well, it has been absolutely wonderful to have you all here tonight, but I must get myself to bed for an early day tomorrow!" If your guests still aren't getting it, you can be more direct: "My friends, I am so glad that you want to stay so long into the night, but I must insist that we bring this party to an end."

Once the last guest has left, take a moment to be proud of yourself. You just hosted a real—and likely fabulous!—dinner party. (For more on departing guests, please see Say Good Night, Gracie, page 200.)

FORMAL HOSTING

When it comes to entertaining at home, few of us need to memorize or become well acquainted with truly formal hosting. However, for those whose ambitions or circumstances encourage them to rise to the task, it is undoubtedly an amazing experience to provide a formal dinner at home for your guests. Elegant and sometimes intimate, it evokes sophistication, indulgence, and awe.

To achieve a truly formal effect requires a greater degree of precision and coordination. This attention to detail, combined with an elevation from the everyday in our attire, the space and décor, the food, and even our own behavior, is what makes a formal event stand out from our more everyday semiformal and casual gatherings at home. It takes work. But it's worth the effort to create an experience that is truly formal.

When we entertain formally, it's not that we are putting on airs, but that we are choosing to create an experience that is fancier, more refined, or elevated from even our special dinner parties.

For the formal at-home dinner party, you're going to focus on the same preparations and good hosting skills you would for any dinner party at home, but the following are specifics for taking your dinner party up to the formal notch.

FORMAL PREPARATIONS

Formal preparations often take longer and require more time to ensure they are correct, so the big, overarching rule for any formal party at home is to start far—*far!*—in advance. Two to four weeks before you even attempt to send out invitations, you should have most of the party planned and any staff you'll be needing booked.

Your guest list is going to be tighter than usual. For a formal occasion, you want to spend extra time getting the guest list right (that is, if you have a choice in the guest list). A formal dinner party where the guests will be business associates or a group from an organization you belong to will likely have a pretty specific guest list. When you do have a choice, look to invite people who will truly enjoy the experience.

FORMAL INVITATIONS

For a formal dinner at home, the proper invitation is a printed or handwritten one. It may be sent by mail or hand delivered. Formal invitations are not sent digitally unless the host, guests, or organization is making an effort to have a more sustainable event and digital invitations are required in order to reduce the carbon footprint. Even then, they should be of the highest quality available, and the service should never show ads to the invitees or share guest list information. Remember, too, that there are options for reducing the carbon footprint of a mailed paper invitation; today's stationers are happy to present you with options to help you meet your goals. (See Invitations, page 93, for more on formal invitations.)

FORMAL MENU

For the formal at-home host who is also an amateur chef, the menu is usually both elegant and sensible. This is not the time to try something startlingly new, but a time to impress with consistency and, especially, quality. For those who are balancing a budget, this means wisely choosing dishes that you can afford and can execute extremely well—your tried-and-true dishes. It is also very common for a formal at-home dinner party host to hire a caterer. A formal meal can have as few as three or four courses (though typically four is the minimum) and as many as six or more. Below are some examples of what a formal menu for an at-home party might look like. Please note that you would not serve all of these items for each course; they are examples of what could be good individual choices.

FIRST COURSE
Soup, fruit cup or melon, shellfish, or salad.

SECOND COURSE
Traditionally fish or sweetbreads, or omitted altogether if fish is served in the first course. Today, we might see a small-plate option here, like a pâté, or a duck-confit or risotto cake, or a small portion of vegetables, often served with a sauce. You might also see a soup, salad, or a small pasta dish served as a second course.

ENTRÉE, OR MAIN COURSE
Usually meat or poultry with vegetables, but today fish is also common. Sometimes you'll see a vegetarian dish as the main course. We think this will be increasingly likely in formal situations, as more people are adopting vegetarian and plant-based diets.

FOURTH COURSE
Salad (usually something light; think vinaigrette rather than a creamy dressing) or assortment of cheese

FIFTH COURSE
Dessert such as cakes, tartes, a trifle or mousse, pastries—though not of the breakfast variety—berries or fruit with cream or sauce, and ice creams or sorbets are all typical options. Try to avoid anything eaten with the fingers like biscuits or cookies. An assortment of cheese with fruit can be an alternative to dessert.

SIXTH COURSE
Coffee, tea, and cordials (port, sherry, liquors, or dessert wines), and possibly cheese with fresh fruit

WORKING WITH HIRED STAFF

You may choose to entertain your close friends or family at a formal level as a solo host—a true Mrs. Three-in-One—but while it can be done, this is only for an experienced host with excellent forethought and a low-stakes guest list who know and love you. The more formal (and large) the occasion, the more likely you are to hire staff to help execute the evening so that you may entertain and lead your guests through the party. This could mean one assistant to help you plate and serve, or a full run of valets for parking cars; chefs and servers for the cocktail hour, dinner, and after-dinner drinks; and even a butler to help with welcoming guests and assisting them at the end of the night. When it's a work-related formal at-home dinner party, or the guest of honor is a prominent figure or someone you personally are very honored to host, hiring help can allow you to focus on your very important guests. Few of us have the necessary staff on hand, so that means hiring out for the evening.

The more formal the dinner party and further removed the guests are from you, the more professional you'll want your staff to be (rather than your college-age kid and their roommates). Sometimes a caterer will have servers who work with them. Other times you might enlist the help of someone you've known and trusted for such occasions over the years. (If you don't know of someone, ask around for recommendations from friends or colleagues who you know have entertained with staff.) You'll want to review with them how you would like staff to receive guests and serve throughout the cocktail hour, and discuss your choices for dinner service, such as the serving style of the meal and when to bring and clear courses. Also don't forget to go over how to handle departing guests when saying good night. With professional staff, be sure to respect their experience and trust that they will get the job done and done well. Everyone should be on the same page for the evening. (For more information on service, see Serving Style, page 282.)

WELCOMING YOUR GUESTS

You might choose to do valet parking for the evening, in which case make sure you, the host, are covering tips for the evening and attendants know to refuse tips offered by guests. Once guests have exited their cars, the front door should be open if possible and guests will be greeted either by a door attendant or you, the host (or both). Guests' hats and coats should be taken; for American entertaining, you would never ask guests to remove their shoes at a formal dinner unless there is a cultural reason to do so.

Welcome your guests by saying, "Welcome, please come in! I'm delighted to have you here!" You could carry on with "Alfred will take your coats. There are drinks and hors d'oeuvres in the living room, right this way . . ." and escort your guests into the cocktail hour area, have your bartender fix them something to drink, and either you or a server offer them hors d'oeuvres. If it's obvious where the party is, you don't need to fully escort guests in during the "arrival rush" (that moment when multiple guests show up at once); simply gesture to the cocktail area. You might add, "Please head in; Joseph will fix you anything from the bar, and I'll be in in a moment."

If your party is large, after the first twenty minutes or so of guests arriving, and if you have a door attendant, you may now focus more on the guests who are at the party than those arriving. This isn't because those arriving are now late and not deserving of a welcoming greeting, but instead because you now have an obligation to those gathered in the cocktail area to mingle and guide them through the evening. If you see that guests have arrived and you don't have help greeting them (either hired staff or a cohost), by all means excuse yourself to the door to welcome them and bring them into the party. If you do have help, they will take care of it by saying something like "Welcome; Mrs. Kindhart is in the living room with the rest of the guests. Please come in and I'll take you there." If the distance is short, a door attendant need not accompany a guest, but can simply gesture toward the room.

THE COCKTAIL HOUR

If you're hosting a smaller formal function and are managing without any hired help, be sure to have your cocktail hour well set up. A pitcher or two of premixed drinks (alcoholic or non-alcoholic) makes it easier to pour and serve for multiple guests. Hors d'oeuvres that are simple and can sit out on their own (not needing to come fresh from an oven, pan, or fryer) will also make serving without help much easier. Otherwise, the cocktail hour is often staffed by a bartender and server, and, as mentioned in Welcoming Your Guests (page 299), possibly someone to greet guests and take coats. Hors d'oeuvres at a formal function are typically passed by servers, though you might have something like a raw bar set up with a mix of seafood items from which guests can help themselves. At a formal at-home party, try to avoid other kinds of stations (leave the slider bar for a more casual night). A crudité platter or small bowls of nuts may be left out for guests to serve themselves—just don't forget to include a discard bowl nearby if your platter includes something like olives with pits. Never in a formal situation should a guest have to wonder where to put a toothpick, shrimp tail, or the like. Food passed during the cocktail hour should be easy to eat in one or two simple bites that don't get messy. A cocktail napkin should always be offered.

ANNOUNCING DINNER

At a formal dinner, you will bid your guests to "Please come in to dinner." This is not done by clinking a glass and announcing to everyone at once, "I bid you, come in to dinner," but instead by the host going to their guests in their little groups and saying, "Dinner is served. If you would please make your way to the dining room."

While a formal dinner often means everyone dons their best attire and manners for the occasion, these elements don't necessarily dictate the tone of the party. As the host you set the tone of the dinner party. You can be dressed up and using your best table manners while also encouraging your guests to relax, engage in conversation, and have fun during the evening. Set the example yourself by being relaxed, chatting with both the guests seated to your right and left, and stimulating some whole table conversation. Never forget the power of a smile and laughter to help put others at ease—even when we are being fancy. (See Hosting the Classic Dinner Party, page 289, for more on how a host can skillfully lead their guests through the evening.)

AFTER-DINNER DRINKS, COFFEE, OR TEA

At a formal dinner, you'll want to leave time for after-dinner drinks. In the days of old, this was the "gendered" portion of the evening, with the women retiring to the drawing room to play cards or talk and the gentlemen remaining at the table or retiring to the study for cigars, brandy, and possibly cards. Today, we are all welcome to enjoy each other's company after dinner.

Once the dessert has been finished, the host should announce that it's time to have after-dinner drinks in the den, study, drawing room, or living room (or in the summer, possibly out on the patio if it's mosquito-free and a comfortable temperature): "I have coffee for us in the den. Shall we?"

Offer guests after-dinner drinks such as brandy, port, liqueurs, and coffee/tea. Cheese and fruits can be served at the table at this time; but when served elsewhere, it's less likely you'll offer anything that needs a plate.

Guests will have their after-drink, chat for a bit, and take their leave, or stay well into the night talking (and hopefully laughing) until you must ask them to leave. Yes, even for a formal evening, it's a win for a host if their guests do not want to go home.

BIDDING YOUR GUESTS GOOD NIGHT

When your guests indicate that they must take their leave, escort them to the door and either retrieve their coats and anything else that was put away after they arrived or ask the door attendant to do so. (See Saying Good Night, page 295, for more on how to help someone with their coat.) Chat with your guests about how grateful you are they could join you while they put on their coats. Give them a hug, handshake, or kiss on the cheek, and warmly say good night: "Thank you so much for coming! It's been wonderful to see you, and have a good evening!"

You may need to say goodbye to a group of guests who didn't come together. Even though it's a group, be sure to thank each person individually. It's delightful to make a personal comment such as, "That story you told was just the best!" or "I will be sure to find a way to get you that recipe," or "I'll have to brush up on my internet history for the next time we get together so I can hold my own with you!"

For very close friends and family, a follow-up thank-you text or call to your guests the next day is wonderful. And hopefully, your guests will be reaching out to you as well.

OTHER PARTIES AT HOME

Following are some of the most common parties you might host at home. The formality and style of each will vary, and the basic considerations are a little different from those of a dinner party.

BRUNCH

In her 1922 edition of *Etiquette,* Emily opined about a few things, and one of them was brunch. She bemoaned the idea of brunch, explaining that she would rather have had a late breakfast extend into the lunch hour, or see it served amid a luncheon spread. She also stated that as a portmanteau of *breakfast* and *lunch*, it was an appallingly lazy way to name the meal. Clearly this opinion did not stick with her readers, because today brunch is beloved by many, and brunches at home with close-knit groups of friends and family are commonplace. (Visit our website for more on wedding brunches.)

Brunch is usually served on a weekend day, and Sunday brunch is now traditional. This meal can range from comfortably casual and relaxed to formal and elegant. At home, it's generally served between 10:00 a.m. and 2:00 p.m.; a brunch beginning at 11:00 a.m. could easily last into mid-afternoon, with guests relaxing and returning to the buffet or spread throughout the gathering.

Invitations might be as casual as after a church service offering for friends to come over for brunch at your house, or deciding when you're out at a club that you all want to meet up at your place the next morning. Or you might choose to plan your brunch ahead of time—an obvious tack for formal brunches—and send out invitations 2 to 4 weeks in advance.

A host has the usual options for how to serve the meal: plated and served individually, family-style, or from a buffet. As for what to serve, standards include eggs, toast, bagels or baked goods, breakfast meats, fruit salad, green or mixed vegetable salad, polenta or grits with various fixings, waffles, pancakes, and hollandaise in a gravy boat. Quiche is a regular on brunch menus—a great cross between a breakfast and lunch dish, it is easy to make ahead of time, easy to heat, and easy to serve. Go quiche!

Fresh juices, mixed juices, spritzers, iced or hot teas, and coffee (decaf and caffeinated) are all superb offerings for brunch. Alcohol is often on the menu, with mimosas and Bloody Marys (or Bloody Shames, without alcohol) being the most popular options. Light wines or sparkling wines can be served. Beer, soda, and red wine are not traditionally served at brunch.

LUNCHEON

While we certainly have had friends over for a casual lunch, hosting and inviting guests to a formal luncheon is really more like hosting a midday dinner party. Rare though it may be, a luncheon is a lovely tradition, and it's a pleasure to host one and set a more formal tone for lunchtime. You might host a committee gathering, a close group of friends, or a bridesmaids' luncheon. Or you might host your soon-to-be in-laws and your parents for a first-time meeting. In some areas, you might invite over a new employee and their partner or family for a welcome luncheon. And in many places, though you won't likely send out invitations, a Sunday luncheon is a multigenerational family tradition not to be missed, whether it's formal, casual, or somewhere in between.

Most luncheons are between 11:30 a.m. and 2:00 or 2:30 p.m., with the meal served between 12:00 and 1:00 p.m. If you start too early, your guests won't feel ready for a large or multicourse meal. Yet if you start too late, your guests will be rumbly-grumbly and wondering how long this luncheon will end up lasting.

Since a luncheon is more formal than a brunch or a casual lunch (this isn't sandwiches and potato chips), you're more likely to send out printed or handwritten invitations. While you might go digital, it's less common; if you do, be sure to use a service that mimics a real invitation and doesn't send guests ads. Regardless, don't forget to follow up on any outstanding RSVPs.

A true luncheon usually consists of three courses and often delicate and plate-friendly items are served. You want a luncheon to be filling but light, so your guests aren't in a food coma for the rest of the day. Aim to serve in the style of a dinner party. Below is a sample menu.

FIRST COURSE
Seasonal soup

MAIN COURSE
Chicken, lobster, or seafood salad over fresh greens, or grilled fish or meat and a fresh salad

DESSERT
Lemon meringue or fruit tarts (while you may choose a chocolate-based dish, consider it might be a heavy way to end the meal)

DRINKS
Tea; iced tea or coffee; light white, rosé, or sparkling wine

TEA PARTIES AND AFTERNOON TEA

In 1922, Emily described an afternoon tea as being delightful, whether served by a butler with all the trimmings or by a host themself in a simple and neat presentation. And as many a parent knows, tea parties are fabulous for almost any child. A tea party can be a very nice way to do a bridal or new child shower and is something a bit different from the usual luncheon, brunch, or cocktail party with hearty hors d'oeuvres. Teas are excellent for holiday gatherings as well as for making introductions. They can be casual or formal, and since they don't require much heavy lifting in the kitchen for the host, they can be planned long in advance or happen last-minute.

Tea is usually served in the afternoon around 3:00 or 4:00 p.m. and lasts two hours at the most.

In Emily's day, teas were formalized ways for people to hang out, be introduced to one another, and honor someone. "Tea" may not have the same draw as "pizza at my place" for some, but a warm cup of tea and a sweet cookie or slice of cake in the afternoon has an undeniable appeal. (For how to set up your tea and serve it, please see Tea and Coffee, page 319.)

Traditionally, casual invitations to tea, whether to see a friend or be introduced to someone, were put on a host's visiting card (much like a personal business card in size, but with less information on it). In the 1922 edition of *Etiquette,* Emily wrote, "The invitation is a visiting card of the hostess with "to meet Mrs. So-and-so" across the top of it and "Jan. 10th Tea at 4 o'clock" in the lower corner, opposite the address. Since tea can be as casual or as formal as you wish, the invitation will reflect the style of tea you want to host.

EMILY'S CASUAL INVITATION ON A VISITING CARD	EMILY'S FORMAL TEA OR RECEPTION AT HOME
to meet Mrs. So-and-so Ms. Gilding 1841 Rosco Road *Jan. 10th Tea at 4 o'clock*	Mrs. Grantham Jones Miss Muriel Jones will be at home on Tuesday the third of December from four until six o'clock One Thousand Fifth Avenue.

REFRESHMENTS

While it's called afternoon tea, you can also serve coffee, iced tea or iced coffee, as well as hot chocolate or other nonalcoholic drinks. For a formal tea, brew a strong pot of loose-leaf tea and keep an extra pot of hot water so a guest can dilute their tea if needed. For an informal tea, you might offer an assortment of tea bags and keep hot water at the ready. Milk, sugar, sweeteners, and lemon are traditional tea accompaniments. As for food, choose anything that can be easily eaten with the fingers in a few bites: biscuits, cookies, tiny savory sandwiches, grapes or berries. Slices of cake are also traditional, but require a small plate and dessert fork.

THE COCKTAIL PARTY

The cocktail party is a fabulous way to entertain when you don't want to throw or host a full dinner, but you do want to gather guests for a good time. It's also a great party to throw when you need or want to reciprocate a number of invitations at once. A dinner party or afternoon get-together can be reciprocated with a cocktail party invitation. Cocktail parties can be short and kept roughly to the cocktail hour and with an open house–styled invitation ("Please join us for cocktails, Friday, June 16th, from 6 to 8 p.m., 2245 Appleton Street, Clarkton"). Or a cocktail party can have a set start time, with no indication of when the party would conclude ("Please join us for cocktails, Friday, June 16th, at 6:00 p.m.").

Since a cocktail party isn't a full dinner party, it's okay to stick to offering small bites and hors d'oeuvres, whether passed or set out on tables or a buffet. If it's a large party, consider hiring a bartender and servers to pass and refresh drinks and the hors d'oeuvres. While a full bar is wonderful to be able to offer, a smaller offering of signature cocktails or a few types of liquor and a variety of things to mix them with is another option for your cocktail party. Wine and beer may also be served, but don't have to be.

As the host, stay focused on mingling with your guests and keeping drinks and hors d'oeuvres refreshed. Typically, music and mingling are all the entertainment you need, but if dancing breaks out, consider yourself a host who has won the hosting game!

If your cocktail party has an end time because you and your guests will either be going to dinner or a show together, or going your separate ways to other social gatherings, it's okay to give your guests a 30-minute heads up so they can think about preparing to leave. "Just a heads-up that it's 7:30 now, if that helps with prepping for the next adventure in your evening," or "A heads-up that it's 7:30, and we should all plan to leave here for the theater right at 8."

(For more on cocktails or the cocktail hour, please see The Cocktail Hour, page 290.)

CHILDREN'S BIRTHDAY PARTY

Birthday parties are still popular in North America. Whether for children or adults, it's a heartwarming tradition that you are celebrated on the day you were born into this world. Children's birthday parties are often a mix of magic and meltdowns. When aiming to create the magic, a few tried-and-true guidelines will help you create a party you and your child can both manage and enjoy. Today, the classics—punch and party foods, goodie bags, games, and gift opening—still go over well. When it comes to kids' birthdays, keeping it simple and making sure the focus stays on the kids (especially the honoree) is often what makes for a great party. On the following page are some tips for successful and manageable children's birthday parties.

- Invite one more guest than your child is old. (Five years old? Invite six guests. This isn't a rule, but a suggestion.)

- Avoid giving out invitations at school or at group activities if you aren't inviting every kid in that group.

- Have a few suggestions ready for parents who ask about gift ideas. Registries should not be used for a birthday party.

- Opening gifts at the party allows all the kids to practice good gift-exchange etiquette. If gifts are part of the party, don't skip this valuable teaching moment!

- For refreshments, serve snacks and kid-friendly drinks, maybe an easy meal, and cake (or some kind of festive dessert).

- Dialing it down usually leads to fewer tears and meltdowns than going all out. Often this means toning down the entertainment and cutting back on how much sugar you're offering, or reducing the number of guests. A party doesn't have to be a private carnival to be a big success. In fact, if you go too big, you might lose some of the focus on the honoree.

Aim for a party that lasts about two hours; three might be needed for some older kids, but four is often too much party time (for kids and parents). Usually, an afternoon party on the weekend is best, but an after-school party might also be an option.

GUESTS AND INVITATIONS

A smaller guest list is the easiest and fastest way to both cut costs and drama at your child's party. That said, sometimes inviting the whole class or team really is the best option. Think hard about your child's attention span and ability to deal with excitement and chaos before making a big guest list. Also, consider how much space you have to work with.

The younger the kids, the more likely parents are to be included in the invitation. Siblings are not typically invited unless the birthday child is close with them. Once kids are old enough to be dropped off at a friend's house for a playdate without a parent, then they are old enough to be at birthday parties without parents, too. At this age, think about how many kids you can reasonably manage without their parents around to help.

The only gift information you would put on a child's birthday party invitation is *No gifts, please*. If you are okay with gifts, spread good gift ideas via word of mouth instead of on the invitation (see Gifts, facing page; Creative Gift Requests, page 208; and Sample Invitations, page 110, for more). If there are any directions to convey, do this on the back or bottom of the invitation: "Our mailbox is across from our driveway," or "We're apartment 4A, but on the elevator press the button for floor 3."

GIFTS

Gifts are often a part of kids' birthday parties. Sometimes it can feel awkward trying to word gift requests, even when gifts are an expected part of the party. Etiquette suggests the polite thing to do is to wait to be asked by guests and word gift requests as a hope rather than an instruction. "So glad Ora can make it! You asked about gifts in your message. We know a lot of people like the 'fiver' idea, and you're welcome to do that if it works for you, but we've also been suggesting books" or "Jackie loves anything from the LEGO space world." Keep your price range suggestions low, and be sure to offer a variety of ideas.

Gifts should be opened at the party in front of those who brought them. It really is a great experience for kids to practice (as a guest) watching another child open their gifts and being happy for them, and (as the honoree) receiving gifts well and showing gratitude by saying thank you to the person who gave it (even if it's not the gift they were hoping for). These are all experiences and lessons worth making time for. When it goes well, gift opening is wonderful! However, gift openings can be long and sometimes result in tears. But just as sitting at the table doesn't always result in a smooth meal, it's still a good idea and it's practice to help build a good habit. As your child opens their presents, make a list of the gifts and givers so that the thank-you notes are easy to write. (See page 217 for a sample list and page 106 and page 107 for sample thank-you notes.)

FOLLOW UP

Even though kids will open their gifts at their birthday party and thank the giver in person (the most personal thank-you), we still suggest they write thank-you notes for their birthday gifts, with as much parental help as needed. Sitting down with a stack of cards and even the gift itself if possible and taking the time to remember each gift and giver is an excellent practice in gratitude and not terribly difficult to accomplish. Each guest should be thanked for the specific gift they gave, and the note should be written and signed by your child and mailed. (For more on thank-you notes, see Teaching Kids to Write Thank-You Notes, page 214.)

BIRTHDAY PARTY FOR ADULTS

It's an easy image to conjure: a group of friends putting candles into a cake, the family singing to dad, the boyfriend setting the table for a special birthday dinner. The birthday party is a tradition we all know. However, American adults are divided on celebrating birthdays. For some, a birthday is the one guaranteed day of celebration in their life, a day to truly feel special and be celebrated by family and friends, while for others, the idea of birthday parties beyond adolescence is embarrassing or completely unnecessary. Put us firmly in the camp of those who love to celebrate (30! 42! 58! 75! 100!!) birthdays. Honoring each other and taking the time to remember where those around us are on life's journey is not just worthwhile, it's fun! Even with the basics of the happy birthday song and a cake with candles, you can help make someone's birthday special. Traditionally, and certainly in Emily's day, adults did not throw parties for themselves because it was considered self-serving. *You* asking for others to celebrate and (possibly) get a gift for *you* just because you were born. *Gauche.* But this way of thinking leaves those who want to celebrate, but don't have anyone offering to host, feeling rather stuck and possibly a little bummed too.

Today, it is acceptable to throw yourself a party (if not you, then who?), with a few caveats. Most importantly, if you are going to throw your own party, be prepared to pay for it and do not ask for gifts or assume they will be given. You absolutely cannot say, "I want us all to go to dinner to celebrate me, and you all will cover the tab." No. (See Hosting vs. Organizing, page 186.) On the other hand, it's fine to say, "Come over to my place to help me celebrate my 30th! 7 p.m., 213 Barclay Ave. Apt 7D," or "I'll be at Smith's tonight from 9 p.m. on celebrating my 30th. Pop by for a drink and some cheer!"

No matter who hosts, let the formality level direct the invitations, refreshments, and entertainment. The sky's the limit.

SHOWER

Showers are special. Friends and family gather to make sure that you enter a new stage of life (marriage or the arrival of a child) ready and prepared. What a beautiful and generous tradition to show love and support. These are parties where gifts are the purpose of the event, though showers should not be seen as an opportunity to get as many gifts as possible, and the gifts you do register for should be related to the occasion you're celebrating. Whether for one honoree or two or three, a shower is typically a two- to three-hour event, usually held on a weekend afternoon and sometimes in the evening.

HOSTS AND HONOREES

Showers were traditionally hosted by friends or extended family, never a sibling or parent. When a friend or distant relative hosted, it felt more like the party was a gift from the community to the person being celebrated, instead of like an immediate family member asking for gifts for their child or sibling. However, times have changed, and sometimes a parent or sibling is the only sensible person to host and they can feel confident doing so. Today, the keys to hosting a great shower are simple: celebrate the honoree and open the gifts.

Good communication is important. Ask the honoree what they are hoping for, but do not place tasks on their shoulders beyond talking with you about details and helping you with the guest list and registry information. There are many showers where the host gets carried away and the honoree feels they can't speak up since so much is being done on their behalf. If you prepare a gorgeous, amazing party, but it's a far cry from the personality and preferences of the honoree, you're not being a thoughtful host. If this is a surprise shower, get some of the honoree's other friends or family to help you, maybe even by doing a little digging to determine their favorite foods and personal party preferences. If the honoree detests games, don't play them. In the event that an honoree may act spoiled or demanding, handle it with a candid and respectful conversation. The same goes the other way: as an honoree, if a host is not respecting your basic wishes, have a polite conversation with them about your concerns. Start with gratitude and work toward redirection, or at least being heard.

GUESTS AND INVITATIONS

If you are throwing a wedding shower, all guests invited to the shower must also be invited to the wedding. The exception here is when a couple is not inviting their office mates to the wedding, but their coworkers decide to host them a shower to celebrate. (The same could be true for any interest groups or teams the couple may be involved in.)

The idea is for the honoree to select a small group of close friends and/or family—the people in life close enough to want to help set the honoree up well for this big change. The very last thing you want for a shower—where gift opening is part of the party—is to have too large a guest list. Even a guest list of twenty to thirty will take time when it comes to both mingling and gift opening. For this reason, guest lists should be smaller. It's fine for the honoree to have more than one shower, and this usually means a different host for each one. Large guest lists often break naturally into smaller groups, such as work friends, friends from growing up, or family (sometimes splitting into sides if your family is large). Opening gifts at this party is the main event, and opening fifteen gifts is far easier (and quicker) than opening forty-five. If you're the honoree, you might say, "Oh, but having to go to all those parties and coordinate with all the hosts . . ." Boo-hoo. Parties are being thrown in your honor to celebrate you and "shower" you with gifts. Now is not the time to complain. Instead, think about how much easier it will be to spend time with your guests and express your gratitude for their support and encouragement when the guest lists are smaller or stick with one shower at a reasonable size.

Putting registry information on an insert with the invitation is perfectly appropriate. Some fill-in cards have a space for registry information, and if you're going the casual route, this is fine to use, as is a link on a digital invitation. This is the only type of invitation that allows for this, as the party is specifically about giving gifts. (See Registries, page 207.)

Since accepting a shower invitation requires the guest to bring a gift, it's kind to send invitations out 4 to 6 weeks before the shower, and having the extra time as a host to coordinate and organize is helpful. This is one party that benefits from a long lead.

While it's not mandatory for any guest (even bridal attendants) to attend showers, many people do their best to get to a shower. If a live stream of the event is offered, those who are not able to attend in person can still participate.

REFRESHMENTS

A shower spread can be as simple as an afternoon tea with sandwiches and light sweets, or it can have more of a luncheon or brunch buffet feel to it. Because this is supposed to be a special occasion, it's a good idea to spruce up whatever you do serve. So, if your honoree loves fried chicken or pizza, serve fried chicken or pizza, but do serve it from a platter (not the box) on real plates, with utensils (even if guests use their fingers) and cloth napkins. Classic shower food includes chicken or seafood salads, small sandwiches, quiches, all kinds of hors d'oeuvres, cake, cupcakes, pies, tarts, and macarons or other cookies. Often Champagne or a Champagne-based drink or punch is served along with nonalcoholic options.

GIFTS

While the honoree selects the gifts to add to the registry, the host manages guests' questions about gifts. They also manage gifts sent to the party directly (for an in-person party, they should be sent to the host, or if it's an all-virtual party, to the honoree), and keep everything organized when the present opening begins! Gifts are expected for this party, and while guests are not obliged to send a gift if they RSVP "no," many choose to do so. Be prepared to open these gifts as well if time allows.

It is expected that all shower gifts are opened during the party, and this means that the host should help guide the process (note the word *guide*, not *micromanage*—this is supposed to be fun!). Here are some tips to help make it all go smoothly:

- Try to spend about 1 to 2 minutes per gift, max—it's more time than you might think. This gives the honoree time to unwrap it and connect with the giver, commenting on how useful or wonderful it is. And for the giver to respond if they need or want to.

- Have the gifts organized so you know who the gift is from as you hand it to the honoree.

- If you can, suggest to the honoree that they read any long or sentimental cards later—definitely not out loud. "Taryn, thank you! I'll read your sweet note in full when I have a little more time." Funny cards are often passed around.

- Record what each gift is and who gave it. (Use the Gift Ledger on page 217 to make it easy.)

- Keep track of the overall timing of the party and adjust your pacing if you have to.

Hopefully you've invited only enough guests for present-opening to take 30 minutes to an hour at most. If by chance your timing is off or the guest list is huge and you find yourself in a pickle, see if there are guests you know who would be okay with having their gift opened later. Set those gifts aside and once you're through the rest of the gifts, if you have time, the honoree can start opening these, or you can thank everyone and begin your goodbyes, and the honoree will make time to open the held gifts later.

Remember to give the honoree the gift list/ledger before the end of the party so they can send their thank-you notes promptly. On the issue of shower thank-you notes: do not ask guests to self-address their own thank-you notes; it's a disturbing trend born of good intentions that goes too far by implying the thank-you note is too much of a chore for the honoree. If an honoree is so burdened that they cannot do the task themselves (which might be the case, especially for an expectant parent), you as the host might choose to help by pre-addressing thank-you notes yourself. But you never ask a guest to pre-address their own thank-you note. It is neither polite nor in the spirit of gift giving and receiving.

GAMES

Games are often a part of showers, but they don't have to be. Always defer to the honoree about any games that might be played, and never force guests to participate. Wedding showers may include creating toilet paper wedding dresses or outfits, a Q&A game about the honoree(s), matching games (match a classic "Annie tale" with the age she was when it happened), writing notes of encouragement or advice, or taking a moment to offer a silent intention for the marriage, or child. New-child showers often involve decorating onesies or quilting squares, predicting a baby's birth date or size, and writing wishes and/or words of wisdom for the child or family.

GRADUATION PARTY

Graduation parties are a wonderful tradition celebrating a great academic achievement (it's not about the grade; it's about the completion of the program). Typically, they are held for completing high school, undergraduate, and graduate degrees. We do see some kindergarten, fifth-, and eighth-grade graduation parties, but they are typically held within a family or household.

Graduation parties are often backyard or park cookouts and potlucks. Casual parties with buffets are also common, as is a group meal at a restaurant. If you want a formal event, you can certainly throw one, but it's not the usual nor what is expected, so make the formality clear to your guests with your invitation.

The party itself is usually a lunch, afternoon, or early evening event. For an open-house-styled graduation party, you might list the hours as "2:00 p.m. till 6:00 p.m." or "2:00 p.m. until we drop," but then don't be surprised if some guests drop by at 10:00 p.m. to see if the party's still going. Typically, the party is held on graduation day, but if people's schedules don't permit that, you might have a graduation party in the weeks after. You don't hold this party before the actual graduation, as it's a bit presumptive—call us superstitious.

It's worth considering throwing a group party for multiple graduates, but if you do this, be sure to honor each graduate. While you might offer a toast to the group, spend time as a host congratulating and speaking with each honoree, and do make sure that if you display any names or achievements (on cakes, banners, and so on), that you do so for all the honorees.

If you want to throw yourself a graduation party either because no one is offering or you're not looking for someone else to, go for it! As the host, however, you should supply and coordinate everything. Like with a self-thrown birthday party, you wouldn't expect gifts, but if someone asks, you may tell them your thoughts.

GUESTS AND INVITATIONS

The honoree(s) should help you with the guest list. One of the hard things about graduation parties in small towns and school communities is that since so many friends in a group are celebrating the same thing at the same time, either everyone converges or people gather with their individual families. Any of these would be a fine option, and all are appropriate. But do be careful; it would be awkward to leave one member of a friend group out.

Invitations should be sent out 2 to 6 weeks before the party. They can be sent via phone, social media, email, or mail as fill-ins or handwritten or printed cards. It really depends on the formality of the event and the way you know most of your guests communicate. We always advocate for paper invitations because we think people take them a bit more seriously, and they set a special tone. But there's no reason not to use the best method for getting responses, which could very well be a group text or social media invitation. (See Sample Invitations, page 111, for samples.) Hosts, remember not to confuse an invitation with an announcement. The invitation is about getting people to the party. The announcement comes after the graduation and serves only to spread the news.

REFRESHMENTS

Anything your graduate loves is probably the best way to go for the menu. While you could certainly have a celebration that was lower key (a punch-and-cookies party, if you will), we're more used to classic party staples that are easy to serve and refill throughout the party: pizza or pasta dishes, burgers and hotdogs (meat and veggie options), chips and dips, and fruit salads and, of course, cake.

GIFTS

Gifts are optional for guests who are invited to a graduation party. Many guests will bring just a card or flowers, but others will be excited to get a gift for the honoree, and as the host it's good to have a few ideas in mind if guests ask when they RSVP (this is often a time when an Emily Post Etiquette book makes a great gift!). (See the Gift Guide, page 215.) You do not create a registry for a graduation party.

Gifts are opened when the guest list is small and intimate enough to handle the opening of gifts. Otherwise, as gifts are not the central focus of the party, it's better to open them after the party, particularly when the party is for a group of graduates. By not opening gifts you avoid two things: a potentially very long gift opening, and any awkwardness for guests who did not bring a gift. Don't forget to send thank-you notes for those who did get you a gift.

HOUSEWARMING

Housewarmings are great fun! The whole idea is to make a new home feel warmed by the presence of your family, friends, and neighbors. Housewarmings can be held for any new space you move into (business or home). You should expect to give tours of the space, which usually means more than just the living room, kitchen, and bath. However, you don't need to leave your entire home open for people to walk through, and it's fine if you choose to close a few doors.

Housewarmings can happen for each new place you move into. For some, that could be a yearly occurrence. Others may make only one big move in their life. They can also be for any type of home: apartment, condo, townhouse, tiny house, and single-family home.

Housewarmings are usually held as open houses, meaning that guests can show up when they want and leave when they want within the stated time frame. List the hours that you'll be receiving people. Often this is from lunchtime or early afternoon into the early evening (1:00 to 6:00 p.m. for example), and usually on a weekend.

GUESTS AND INVITATIONS

This is a come-one, come-all type of party. Unless you like to keep a tight circle, you may invite neighbors, or new colleagues if you feel comfortable. Typically, though, you invite friends and family in the area so that your new space starts to feel warm and friendly to you.

Plan on sending out invitations about 2 to 4 weeks in advance. This invitation can also serve to highlight your new address. Because of the casual nature of this party, any form of invitation will do: social media, text, phone call, fill-in, handwritten, or printed. Open houses don't use an RSVP because it's a drop-in party. Certain fill-in or online invitations come with automatic RSVPs, so if it's there and unavoidable, cross it out, or leave it blank.

REFRESHMENTS

This is a party that can survive on punch and cookies or some light hors d'oeuvres. Because it's an open house, it could also feature a simple buffet. Any guest arriving within the hours listed should feel confident grabbing a plate and digging in. There is no "you missed the meal" here. Remember to set yourself up for success by choosing foods that don't need constant attention or replenishment. You're likely going to be busy giving tours and talking to guests.

Be prepared for guests to bring food, but don't count on them to fill out a buffet table. You should still prepare your menu. It's common for guests to bring some homemade cookies or treats to a housewarming, so being ready for that is smart. You can choose to either serve or save any offering, or a mix of both, depending on what gets brought. It's always thoughtful to ask the guest who brought the item if they mind if you serve it, just in case they were hoping you'd save it to enjoy yourself.

GIFTS

Housewarmings do not require guests to bring a gift. While it may seem convenient to have a registry, avoid the urge; since gifts are not expected, it would be presumptuous. If you suspect your guests will get you a gift and will be asking you for ideas, it's fine to prepare a wish list, but only share it with those who ask. And never put this information anywhere for a guest to find without having asked you first. No links, no inserts. While some might really want to help guide what items enter their home, it's best to remember that (a) it's the thought that counts; and (b) gifts for this type of party are traditionally in the range of a small houseplant or a platter of cookies (with the platter, unless otherwise specified or clear by its make, most likely needing to be returned). Close family and friends might get you an appliance you need or some décor they know you'd love, but that is really more about your relationship than it is about a gift for this party. Since the party is a mix of people, you don't want some guests feeling like their plate of brownies—a lovely gesture—was somehow lacking compared to the standing mixer your aunt brought you. Keep the focus on people warming the space. It's best to remember it is not a shower; it's a housewarming. Do remember to send thank-you notes for any gifts that may come your way, and also for any treats that were brought to the party.

RETIREMENT PARTY

Retirement parties are wonderful, even if a bit bittersweet. To reach a point in life where you are walking away from the daily world of your career is a huge accomplishment that deserves to be honored with recognition. Retirement parties can be hosted by an employer or by a spouse, loved one, close colleague, or friend of the retiree. They can be held at home or at a restaurant or event venue. It all depends on the host's and the honoree's preferences.

This party is held once the honoree has retired, and is often an evening event lasting 2 to 4 hours. Now all this is not to say that if the honoree prefers something more casual, you couldn't do an afternoon backyard barbecue; that would be a wonderful celebration.

Guests are associates from work, immediate family, and close friends. If it's a very large company, you might stick to one department. If it's a small team, invite everyone, including a boss. You might have to be a sleuth, or you can ask your honoree for suggestions, especially when it comes to family and friends whom they'd like to have attend or colleagues from work that a family member who is hosting may not know.

Invitations typically go out 4 to 6 weeks in advance. These are classic party invitations, see page 115 for a sample. Remember to have the formality of the invitation match the formality of the event. A backyard barbecue might have a fill-in party invitation, while a formal dinner at someone's house or a restaurant might have one that is printed and mailed.

REFRESHMENTS

Most retirement parties consist of either hors d'oeuvres and a cake, or a meal and a cake. (Cake is just so celebratory!) The party can be big or small, casual or formal. There are also many "office" retirement parties that are held at work—please visit our website for specific information on those.

Dinner is almost always served: for larger parties, a buffet; for smaller parties, either a plated meal or heavy hors d'oeuvres. If it's casual, you're more likely to have a buffet with casual fare. Serve something the honoree loves; it is their night. Toasts, speeches, and even the presentation of a gift to the honoree might be part of the evening.

GIFTS

You don't see many guests bringing gifts to retirement parties. A loved one, or the company, a boss, or the team might get the honoree something, but other guests don't. They do, however, bring cards of congratulations and sometimes flowers. Be prepared as a host to help collect these and send them home with the honoree. You might open and read cards at a casual or intimate retirement party, but choose not to if it's a larger group.

FOOD AND DRINK

Emily never had to consider much variety when advising hosts about what food to serve to their guests. Even Delmonico's, Emily's standard for fine dining, had a very limited (if rich) menu on any given night. Today, our options are nearly limitless! As a host, keeping food and drinks on hand that you enjoy and feel confident preparing and serving is probably one of the best pieces of entertaining advice. While we are all going to have different items that tickle our fancy, we can look at our personal pantries as an extension of our entertaining style. In Alka's home you'll always be greeted by the smell and taste of warm spiced nuts, fresh fruits, and crisp vegetables. Over at Wallace's house, his love of Italian culture will permeate every aspect of his menus— cured meats, cheeses, bread, and seasoned oils will greet you. It's wonderful to expand your comfort zone, but as a host you want to be sure you can confidently execute your plan well for the gathering you're hosting.

Today we respect that everyone has different eating habits, dietary requirements, and tastes. A host who asks their guests about any food restrictions or allergies is truly being kind and considerate. Emily didn't write about allergies and food restrictions. It's not that they didn't exist back in 1922, but they weren't dealt with in books on etiquette. If you were outside the "standard," *you* had to figure it out. Nowadays we want to make sure our guests can attend our event without food being a barrier. Thinking *tough patooties* if someone is allergic to strawberries is not in keeping with kindness and consideration (not to mention potentially dangerous!).

As a host, you aren't expected to have mastered dishes for every type of diet, or to understand how to work around every kind of restriction. But if you are someone who can eat without restrictions, do challenge yourself in the kitchen by learning to prepare dishes for other people's diets or consider them when curating a menu, and do get one or two winning recipes (or catered/ pre-made selections) under your belt that match a number of dietary needs. This allows you to reassure a guest with confidence that you've got them covered (while also thanking them for their offer to bring a dish). When it comes to choosing a menu, do not do as Emily's famed character Mrs. Newlywed did and attempt dishes that, while sounding nice, are beyond your skill level or familiarity. Stick to what you know and trust. (This is true even if you are ordering out; order from places where you know the menu well.)

THE WELL-STOCKED HOST

By being well-stocked at home (and this doesn't have to break the bank) a good host will be ready to host anytime. We can entertain impromptu parties and drop-by visitors confidently and say "yes" in the moment when we know our house is stocked and ready. A well-stocked pantry can also save the day when catastrophe strikes. Rather than just having a box of mac & cheese, a smartly stocked house can provide drinks, snacks, and/or a full but simple meal in a pinch.

THE IMPROMPTU PANTRY

Following is a list of items we think can help you host even under unexpected circumstances, and from which you might easily pull together an offering for a tea, an impromptu cocktail hour, a simple but satisfying dinner and easy classic dessert, or even a spontaneous moment of celebration. Substitute your own favorites and go-tos for your pantry.

- Biscuit cookies
- Bottle of Prosecco or Champagne
- Bottle of red wine
- A boxed cake either frozen or prepackaged
- Butter
- Canned or preserved diced tomatoes
- Chocolate or caramel sauce
- Crackers or crostini
- Dried fruits
- Dry pasta
- Frozen cooked shrimp
- Frozen lasagna
- Frozen peas
- Fruit preserves

- Garlic
- A jarred pasta sauce you like
- Kosher or sea salt
- Nuts
- Olive oil
- Olives
- Parmesan cheese
- Peppercorns for a pepper grinder
- Seltzer, juice, and ginger ale
- Tea and coffee
- Tinned fish
- Tomato paste
- Vanilla ice cream

BEER, WINE, SPIRITS,
AND NONALCOHOLIC DRINKS

As a host, offering alcohol is completely optional. There are plenty of homes where it's not permitted at all, or where guests are welcome to bring their own but also to take it when they leave. And in some homes the host will provide alcohol for guests even if they don't partake themselves. Whether you are serving alcohol or not, keeping your favorite beverages on hand is usually a host's best bet.

FOR NONALCOHOLIC OPTIONS: There is always water, of course, but you should really have at least two other non-alcoholic choices for guests. Fruit juices, iced teas, lemonade, seltzer, herbs for infusions, and soft drinks like ginger ales and colas offer variety and make for a well-stocked bar. If you can't make a freshly squeezed juice, keep some quality fruit juices on hand. A good host never pressures a guest to drink alcohol. "Oh, come on—you've just got to try this bottle of Tignanello I brought back from Tuscany. I insist!" No. Instead, make sure a guest is enjoying their beverage, and ask if they need anything else.

FOR BEER: Try to have at least two options when you throw a party, one that's generally liked and one that's more of a specialty or local beer. Always serve beer in a glass for more formal occasions. For casual ones, you can offer a bottle or glass. For super casual gatherings, a can, a recyclable cup, or straight from the bottle is fine.

FOR SPIRITS (LIQUOR): A fully stocked bar can be a bit of a wow factor (also see A Well-Stocked Bar, page 341). It allows a host to offer almost anything to their guests. For consumables, consider stocking vodka, gin, tequila, bourbon, whiskey, scotch, rum, Campari, vermouth, sherry, port, brandy, tonic, seltzer, fruit juices, ginger ale, cola, lemons, limes, oranges, olives, cocktail onions, maraschino cherries, citrus twists, aromatics, and bitters. For equipment, it's nice to have on hand a shaker, ice bucket, tongs, long spoon, knife, cutting board, strainer, jigger, and mortar and pestle. This is a big list and is not always doable or affordable. The good news is that it's not all necessary in order to be a great host. If you can't do a full bar, start by stocking your favorites, and if you can, the favorites of some of your regular guests. "Angela, I've got your favorite gin; would you like a G&T?" will certainly make a guest feel taken care of.

FOR WINE: Try to pair wines with the meal you're serving, or choose your favorites. Keeping a favorite red and white on hand should have you pretty well covered. When pouring wine, angle the bottle so that a smooth stream flows out, and turn or twist the bottle gently as you finish the pour to help stop drips. Do not hold the bottle too high or the wine will splash.

When serving special wine, make sure each person can receive two servings per type of wine. For regular wine that you aren't worried about savoring, still try not to overpour. People can always help themselves, or ask for more. As the host, you never want to overserve your guests.

If you truly want your wine to breathe, decant it. It can also breathe in the bottle, but it might take longer. (A clean glass vase can make a wonderful decanter in a pinch!) Of course, pouring it into the glass will get it breathing quickly. (For information on which type of wine to serve in which type of glass, and tips for serving and pairing, see Pouring, Serving, and Pairing Wine, page 340).

TEA AND COFFEE

Offering someone a hot beverage creates tangible warmth in your hospitality. Whether it's a service or repair person, a friend or family member who stopped by briefly or a friend coming over to hang offering coffee or tea is a classic consideration. While we may not serve full tea trays or offer coffee after dinner as much as we used to, we are big fans of embracing coffee and tea as a staple in your hospitality skill set.

SERVING TEA

There is so much ritual and tradition in serving tea or coffee that one could spend a lifetime researching it. Learning to serve a proper pot of tea is a skill worth knowing. However, 60 percent of Americans say they have never served tea from a teapot. So let's turn to Emily's 1922 description of afternoon tea for guidance on how to present and serve a proper pot of tea: "The everyday afternoon tea table is familiar to everyone; there is not the slightest difference in its service whether in the tiny bandbox house of the newest bride, or in the drawing-room of Mrs. Worldly of Great Estates . . ."

It matters not whether you can serve for twelve from the finest china, or whether your teapot shows its usage. A clean and tidy presentation with the elements to allow your guest to enjoy their cup while sharing good company is the true goal.

Rather than serving tea at the dining table, it is served while seated on a couch or chair, whether you're serving it outside or in. Here is what Emily imagined as she set the afternoon tea table: "There are really no 'correct' dimensions; any small table is suitable. It ought not to be so high that the hostess seems submerged behind it, nor so small as to be overhung by the tea tray and easily knocked over."

Today, what we call a coffee table, or other small, low side table, would serve nicely. Emily suggested covering the table with a tea cloth, typically white and edged with either embroidery or lace, though a colored or patterned cloth would work, too. It should either just reach the edges of your table or hang 6 to 12 inches over the edge. On top of the cloth, you set your tea tray. As mentioned above, this shouldn't hang over the side of the table, but be large enough to hold all the elements comfortably. Here is Emily's tea tray: ". . . on it should be: a kettle which ought to be already boiling, with a spirit lamp [burner] under it, an empty tea-pot, a caddy of tea, a tea strainer and slop bowl, cream pitcher and sugar bowl, and, on a glass dish, lemon in slices. A pile of cups and saucers and a stack of little tea plates, all to match, with a napkin (about 12 inches square, hem-stitched or edged to match the tea cloth) folded on each of the plates, like the filling of a layer cake, complete the paraphernalia." We might not break out a burner for our tea trays today, but a tea cozy on a kettle or a teapot that is well insulated are other great options. The goal is to have all that you need so you may sit and enjoy tea with your guest and not be fussing in the kitchen. This may not be an issue for a casual drop-by cup, but if you've invited a guest "over for tea," it's nice to prepare it in a way that lets you spend as much time as possible with your company, especially if it's one-on-one. Emily went on in great detail about what food to serve with tea. And while her detail may make even an ambitious host have to steel their nerves, the gist of it is to serve the classics: warm breads; small, light "party" sandwiches (not to be confused with deli sandwiches); and tea cakes. Keep the offerings light and with little need for extra utensils or fuss. You'll want everything you serve to fit on the tea tray. Keeping it simple serves every host well. (See Tea Parties and Afternoon Tea, page 304, for more on what food to offer with tea.)

A host should ask their guest whether they like their tea weak or strong, and then steep it accordingly. If you err on the strong side (meaning it steeps longer), you can always offer your guest more water if they need to dilute the tea. You may also choose to offer both regular teas and decaffeinated options to your guests. It's thoughtful to remind guests of this option, as they might otherwise wonder why they are so wired at midnight and unable to fall asleep. A host should next ask whether the guest would like milk, lemon, or a sweetener (sugar, honey, or a substitute—today there are so many options beyond "One lump or two?"). For a drop-by visit, you might suggest your guest dress their cup as they see fit, offering them lemon slices, sugar, and milk. Many people nowadays use substitutes for sugar or dairy. If you don't already have a nondairy option or a sugar substitute, it's worth keeping a small amount of each on hand, especially if you plan on or find yourself offering tea regularly.

Tea bags are a great quick option if someone drops by and you aren't properly set up for a full pot. If you serve tea during or after dessert at a dinner party and use tea bags, steep the cup(s) of tea in the kitchen. This helps eliminate both the guest sitting with a cup they have to wait to enjoy while it steeps in front of them, and the issue of where to put the used tea bag.

When serving coffee, you could keep it simple or go down the rabbit hole of beans, roasts, grinds, percolation methods, pours, temperature, and strengths. While it's nice to offer something sweet with your coffee service, it's less expected than with tea, though it helps to absorb the acidity of the coffee. (*Mmmm,* biscotti!) We do recommend brewing (pouring, pressing, or steaming) a fresh pot for guests you're inviting over for coffee; it has more of a host-guest feel than a coffee pod shot loudly through a machine.

As with tea, coffee can be served elegantly in cups with saucers either after dinner or when inviting a friend over. You can pour and serve from the kitchen, or brew a pot and serve from a tray either at the table during dessert or after dinner in the living room, den, on the patio, or other seating area. Offer your guests the option of decaf or regular, and sugar (or sugar substitute) or cream (or nondairy milk). While any milk is fine for everyday casual coffee offerings, when you're serving coffee in a more formalized way (say after dessert at a dinner party) it's best to have at least one high-fat option like cream or half-and-half for those that enjoy it.

For a drop-by visit, a mug will be fine, but if you're setting the scene for a nice cup of coffee with your friend, do just that: set the scene. A cup and saucer also allow guests to have a place to put their spoon should they take their coffee with cream or sugar.

Share what you love and would make for yourself as a treat: fresh drip, pour-overs, espresso. You can certainly get fancy if your equipment and skills allow, but resist the urge to go full barista with foam artwork for your guests. Don't let the service takes so long or so much for your attention that your guest(s) might feel awkward, or worse, ignored.

HOSTING HOUSEGUESTS

Hosting guests overnight in our home gives us a chance to really flex our hosting skills. Due to the extended nature of the visit, it both gives us an opportunity to relax around our guests and challenges the endurance of our hosting skills. It is very rare that someone would host houseguests formally today. Typically, we host people we know well or friends of friends.

Most houseguest hosting is done either for an overnight, a long weekend, or a full week. Two weeks isn't an impossibility, but anything beyond that should really be looked at as a long-term stay. The classic adage—"Fish and houseguests stink after three days"—can certainly be true. It also reminds us that even a week-long visit could test the patience of any host. It's wonderful if you have the resources (and personal stamina) to fully host someone for a week or longer, but it should never be expected. At some point, your guest stops being a guest and starts being a resident. We are fans of one host's saying to her children's friends when they came for sleepovers:

"Night one, you're a guest. Night two, you're family." Meaning that on night one, don't even think about lifting a finger, whereas on night two, feel free to help with the dishes, dear. Without being quite so bold, let's explore the right things to do when hosting a houseguest.

When thinking of perfect hosting for houseguests, we can't help but remember and love the humor in Emily's depiction of a houseguest in a less-than-desirable situation. In 1922 she wrote:

"If you go to stay in a small house in the country, and they give you a bed full of lumps, in a room of mosquitoes and flies, in a chamber over that of a crying baby, under the eaves with a temperature of over a hundred, you *can* the next morning walk to the village, and send yourself a telegram and leave! But though you feel starved, exhausted, wilted, and are mosquito bitten until you resemble a well-developed case of chickenpox or measles, by not so much as a facial muscle must you let the family know that your comfort lacked anything that your happiest imagination could picture—nor must you confide in any one afterwards (having broken bread in the house) how desperately wretched you were."

This is very much so *not* the experience you want to create. As the host, you want to explain or mention anything that might cause issue for your guests, "Yes, we'd love to host you; I should let you know our extra bed is a fold-out couch, is that okay?" or "We'd love to have you; the baby isn't sleeping through the night yet, so we also understand if you'd rather stay nearby." Nor is it what you should do if as a guest you find yourself in a less than desirable houseguest experience. Instead of deceiving your host, say that you are sorry but you must cut the trip short, if it's truly so bad you're going to leave.

FROM THE GET-GO

It can be exciting to think about entertaining houseguests. Just like sleepovers when you were kid, there's something special about having a guest stay overnight or even for an extended period of time. The best seasons for visitors to come as well as special occasions or annual gatherings can all be great reasons to extend an invitation (usually by phone, but text, email, or even a handwritten note could all be welcome) and then you can get excited about planning the visit.

As a host, there are two things you must know before inviting or committing to hosting anyone overnight: (1) What space do you have to offer? A futon in the basement? A guest bedroom? A pull-out couch in the living room? A guest house? and (2) When and for how long can you reasonably offer to host? Once you know this, you will be in good stead for inviting guests to come stay or to saying yes when a friend or family member comes to town and might need a place.

Timing a houseguest visit can be challenging. Now, sometimes the idea of a visit is sprung upon you and it all happens very fast: "Lara! I'm so glad you picked up! Zeb and I are going to be in your neck of the woods, and we are looking for friends we might be able to stay with for a few days. Any chance you'd be game?!" (Yes, she did just invite herself to stay. No, it wasn't an egregious error, because she explained why the "ask" was happening and made no assumption that Lara was able to host.)

Typically, you'd want a friend to let you know they'll be in town, and have the chance to offer whatever works for you: a meetup, a meal, a place to stay. Then your friend can accept or suggest what might work with their travel plans, and so on. It's that beautiful little host-guest dance. But when that doesn't happen, rather than feeling put-upon and flustered or flummoxed, simply say, "Oh, Sabrina, that's wonderful news! Let me check with Janet about our schedule, and I'll get back to you this weekend with what works for us." Now you have time to make a plan and offer what feels right to you.

If your friend counters with dates that work better for them, you can certainly accommodate them, or respond with what would work for you, or you might choose to try to schedule the visit for another time. Be willing to work through a few back-and-forths, but if it starts becoming too much of a game of Twister, try for another time. Sometimes a guest's dates might shift due to things beyond their control, or you might find yourself dealing with someone who is changing their plans capriciously leading up to the visit. Only accommodate what you truly can. If someone is starting to impose on you, don't be afraid to speak up. "Sabrina, I understand that you've got about 2 weeks' worth of vacation you're planning. Janet and I will only be able to host you through Monday. But I can recommend a couple of friends' Airbnbs for the rest of your visit if you'd like to stay in the area longer." As a final component of the planning process, and one of the most important, make sure that you discuss a departure date. Some circumstances might warrant a decision being made later on, but absent of that, confirm a departure date. Just in case that didn't register: *set a departure date.* One way to get this discussion going is to ask questions about your guests plans for departure early on. "I can give you a ride to the airport on Sunday, what time is your flight home?" Keep the focus on helping them make the flight or to get on the road in a timely manner and you will likely strike the right tone and not sound like you are pushing to get someone out.

PREPARING FOR A HOUSEGUEST

Whether you can offer your guest an official bedroom or a designated area to stay, like an office, living room, or den, it's important to make sure you provide them with the following:

BEDDING. Whether it's a bed, couch, or blow-up mattress on the floor, making up a bed for guests is a sign of welcome, especially for someone who has been traveling. Clean sheets, pillowcases, and a warm blanket are the basics. Quilts or comforters are great additions. Try to have two pillow options: one firm, one soft. And keep an extra blanket or quilt handy in case a guest needs it.

BATHROOM. Aside from a clean bathroom, you should provide towels for each guest—at least one large bath towel and one face towel—as well as liquid soap or a fresh bar of soap. While in Emily's day traveling guests expected to have certain items provided for them, today's guests often bring all the toiletries they need. That being said, a good guest-bath kit includes shampoos, conditioners, body and face washes, and lotions along with a spare disposable toothbrush, toothpaste, floss, mouthwash, tampons and pads, cotton swabs, tissues, and a disposable razor and shaving cream. Not to mention, nail clippers, tweezers, and needle and thread for bonus points.

STORAGE AND WORK SPACE. Think about where your guest will put their things: on a luggage rack, or in a dresser or closet? If they are visiting while on business, find a good place you can designate for them to work or spread out their work items.

WI-FI AND OTHER CONSIDERATIONS. We've come to a time when providing access to your Wi-Fi is not only easy, but often essential. Most of us can operate on cellular networks, but more and more folks are requiring and relying on Wi-Fi services. As hosts, we must move with the times. Keeping a card handy with your Wi-Fi network and password on it, or using your phone to directly set up a guest is definitely good hosting. Some hosts even set up a separate guest network. (See A Good Host, page 177, for more on how to handle tech, like smart speakers and security with your houseguests.)

Other things to consider for your guests' comfort, whether they are in a private room or a makeshift guest space, include tissues, a TV/remote (along with any passwords or instructions), a small dish for change or jewelry, and a water carafe and glass.

Don't forget: a good host always asks, "Is there anything else I could get you?" and they also feel confident saying, "No, I'm sorry I can't provide that but I can do this . . ."

YOUR GUEST ROOM

The very best way to set up a guest room, hands-down, is to put it together as you see fit and then stay in it for a night or two. Pay attention to noises, textures, and comforts. You'll quickly figure out exactly what your guest will experience: scratchy or smooth sheets, an annoying ticking fan or the perfect gentle breeze. Make any adjustments necessary. Emily suggested that if you don't spend a full twenty-four hours in the room, at least imagine what it would be like, and definitely check that the faucet in the guest bath runs smoothly, the shades pull and the curtains draw easily, the bed doesn't squeak, and the drawers don't stick.

In her 1922 edition of *Etiquette,* Emily declared that each guest should have their own room, with three exceptions:

"1. A man and wife, if the hostess is sure beyond a doubt that they occupy similar quarters when at home.

2. Two young girls who are friends and have volunteered, because the house is crowded, to room together in a room with two beds.

3. On an occasion such as a wedding, a ball, or an intercollegiate athletic event, young people don't mind for one night (that is spent for the greater part "up") how many are doubled; and house room is limited merely to cot space, sofas, and even the billiard table."

A bed, nightstand, and dresser or closet are the main components of a basic guest room. Beyond that, a vanity, a chair, or a small writing desk are all welcome and classic elements. Try to avoid cluttering a guest room with knickknacks.

Do be sure to have quality lighting in your guest room, and air the space out before your guest arrives. These rooms can sit empty or closed up for long stretches of time. While it can be tempting to use sprays, candles, or oils to freshen a room, fresh air alone does wonders. If there isn't a window, use a fan and an open door to assist air flow. Many scents can be overwhelming for people, and since we all react differently to aromas, it's best to err on the side of caution and use limited scent or none at all. You can always leave a candle or oils out as an option for a guest to use during their stay.

EXPECTATIONS

While we've talked about setting start and end dates for your visitors, it's also important to speak up in an inviting way about any expectations you may have, or parameters that need to be put in place for the visit.

CHILDREN

Kids can have so much fun being house guests, but they can also run amok—such is life. Be sure to be very clear in your invitation as to whether or not children are being included: "I just booked my summer rental, and I'd love to invite you and Cooper for an adults-only weekend while I'm up at the lake, if you can make it!" When you do invite kids, help make them feel more comfortable by setting up clear spaces for them, talking to parents about best sleeping arrangements, and by letting the parents do the parenting. While you should certainly explain any house rules to both parents and their kids together, it's important to let the parents do the disciplining if anything goes wrong. It's also very important to be patient. When kids are in a new space, they can get shy or excited; so be flexible (not a doormat, mind you, but flexible).

PETS

Pets can be a joy or a deal breaker when it comes to house guests, whether the animal is yours or your guests'. Some people never travel anywhere with their pets; others never go anywhere without them. Some hosts love pet visitors and some would rather they not come. Some folks with allergies can't stay with or host people with pets. And then there are therapy and guide animals (who truly aren't pets), which are necessary and should be accommodated by hosts whenever possible. There's no right or wrong position. Just be clear with your guests on the expectation at your house. Here are some options for wording your decision:

- "Nadia, thank you for asking. Unfortunately, we are a pet-free household, so if you can come without Shushu, that would work for us."

- "Nadia, I'm so glad we're planning this visit. I just wanted to be clear that Shushu is absolutely welcome."

- "Nadia, I'm so glad we're planning this visit. My cats are dog-friendly. Is Shushu a cat-friendly dog?"

- "Nadia, I'm so glad we're planning this visit. I know Shushu usually comes everywhere with you, but with Suzie's allergy I have to ask that she sit this one out."

- "Nadia, I'm so glad we're planning this visit. Our new puppy is not good with other dogs yet, so we are asking friends not to bring their pups over until he can socialize better."

If you're going to accommodate someone's animal companion, be sure to be just as welcoming to the pet as you are to the guest. Offer them bowls for food and water, help keep doors shut to rooms you don't want them going into, and engage with the animal if appropriate.

If a pet shows up unannounced, it's up to you to decide if you can make the accommodation, or if you have to ask your friend to find another spot to stay that is animal friendly. If the latter, offer to help them find a good place to stay. While it's not your fault that you didn't know your friend (a) had a pet; and (b) was going to bring it along, a good host is as helpful as possible. It's kind of a record scratch moment, but by handling it graciously it can help get you back on track for a great visit.

TIME TOGETHER AND TIME APART

It's really nice when a host balances both time together and time apart during the visit. Creating some space is good, whether it's just to take a walk or have a cup of tea on the porch. That said, you don't want to leave your guests so alone that you are only serving them meals.

If you can, chat about a general itinerary with a couple of contingency plans ahead of the visit, this will make your life as host (and often, tour guide) much easier. Plan out a few things each day. Obviously, this depends on the nature of the visit. Think about the weather and the busy times of day at any attractions or venues you're looking to visit. Try to pick one or two things to commit to, along with at least one meal. If you won't be able to share all your meals with your guest, let them know as soon as possible so they can make arrangements for themselves. "Friday night I'll be getting home after you arrive. I'll leave a meal in the fridge as well as take-out menus. Then on Saturday and Sunday, I'm all yours. We can plan outings or lounge, whatever you'd like!"

PREPARING FOR YOUR HOUSEGUEST

When a guest room is kept prepped and ready, there's little a host has to do aside from a thorough cleaning of not only the guest room, but the rest of the house as well. Vacuum, dust, mop—now's the time to make it all shine. Everyday house mess is completely normal and understandable, but when a guest arrives, your house should be as clean and tidy as possible. Surfaces should have been wiped down, mirrors cleaned, and floors and seating free of dirt, dust, and pet hair. Make sure the guest's space doesn't feel like storage during their visit.

Prepare your housemates, whether they are family members or roommates. It's very important to let everyone know what to expect when it comes to a guest visit. And remember, especially if you have roommates, the conversation with them should happen before you issue the invitation or say yes to the request to come stay.

Be sure to have enough food on hand so that your guest could at least have something like tea and toast at home. Beyond a bare minimum, having something available for each of the standard meals as well as some snacks is a good idea.

HOSTING YOUR HOUSEGUEST

Once your guest arrives, help them with any luggage or bags and show them to their room. From there, you can proceed with a tour of the house if necessary. Even if your guest has already seen your home, you can offer a refresher tour.

Offer your guest some refreshment: tea, coffee, a snack, a cold drink, or water. A little something after travel can be restorative. Then let your guest unpack and settle in: "I'll bring you up that tea as soon as it's ready; feel free to take your time. If you want a shower or bath to freshen up, there are towels in the guest bath for you. I'll be down here preparing dinner. Come down once you're settled."

Cultivating an inviting but informative tone as a houseguest host is worthwhile. There will be so many little moments of communication, and sounding invested but not too eager, informative but not bossy, will help facilitate the visit: "If you would like . . . ," "I wanted to mention that . . . ," "Which would you prefer . . . ?" "If you're interested . . . ," or "A few options are _____, let me know what works for you!"

Feel confident excusing yourself when you need to recharge, or letting your guest know you have other obligations. "I'm hoping to go have a lie-down until about 4:30, and then I'll get started on dinner. Is there anything I can get for you before I head up?" Or "I have a video conference at 7 tonight, but I can meet you all after your dinner for the movie at 8." Make sure your guest is taken care of during your absence.

You should also feel confident letting your guests know what they are welcome to in your home and what should be left alone. Whether it's a bathroom that's not guest-friendly, an office that's not to be played in, a cake that's being saved for an event, or not letting the cat out, communicating these things to your guest is important—otherwise, how would they know? Certain things you may have to continually remind guests of, and it's important to do so with grace and a gentle tone each time. Don't let your impatience get the better of you; remember, this person doesn't live here. They don't think about or know the things that you do.

While it's not your responsibility to provide hotel-quality service for any guest, being a great host means paying attention and doing what you can, within reason, to accommodate your guest and make them feel comfortable. Should you be met with requests or behavior that doesn't jive with your house rules or desired hosting experience, use a calm tone to convey what is possible instead: "While I can't change the menu for the evening, we can certainly go to the store tomorrow and get fixings to do Grandma's gumbo on Sunday," or "I should have mentioned that I ask guests to please smoke and vape outside. Let me set you up with a dry spot, since it's raining," instead of, "James, really? What made you think I wouldn't smell that? Take it outside, man." Scolding rarely, if ever, builds relationships.

Here are other common corrections that while reasonable for a host to make are best said with a patient and kind tone rather than a blunt one.

OVERLY BLUNT	PATIENT AND KIND
"Hey, no swearing around my kids!"	"We're working on our language around the girls. Any help to curb your swearing when you visit would be so appreciated."
"Take your shoes off, I don't want dirt coming in."	"Please excuse my vigilance, but don't forget to take your shoes off once we're inside."
"Don't use your phone around our kids, it sets a bad example."	"We're limiting our screen time, so any help you can give by not watching or scrolling something in front of the kids would be so great."

As your visit comes to an end, focus on and remind yourself of the good times, and try to let go of any issues that may have occurred. While hosting houseguests can be stressful, most of the time we are happy to have had the chance to spend so much time with our guests. Help your guest gather anything they may need to pack, and to sort out travel logistics for leaving town, whether driving directions or help with catching other transportation. While you are not obligated to do an airport, train, or bus pickup or drop-off, it is awfully kind whenever possible.

As a nice final touch, thank your guest a day or two later with a call or text (you can even send a note if you really want to shine) that reflects on what a great time you had.

REFERENCE GUIDE

ENTERTAINING CHART

	TYPE OF GATHERING	INVITATION TIMING	INVITATION TYPE	TIME OF DAY
SUPER CASUAL	Easy hangout, drop-in visit, open-ended visit ("We're home, stop by"), a casual coffee or tea	Impromptu/last minute to 1 week or more in advance, depending on the gathering	In-person, phone call, text, email, direct messaging or invitation features via social media	Any time, though usually afternoon or evening
CASUAL	Potluck, barbecue, cookout, a last-minute or extended hangout, a casual coffee or tea, picnic, boil, roast, bonfire, brunch, celebration parties: birthdays, housewarmings, graduation parties, holiday gatherings	Anywhere from a couple of days to a few weeks in advance, though last-minute (within a week) might be appropriate given the casual circumstances	Email, Evite or social media invite, text or group text, phone call, fill-in invitation, a personal blank that you fill in from your personal stationery	Any time, though often you're usually operating around mealtimes
INFORMAL	Shower, luncheon, brunch, afternoon tea, dinner party, potluck, outdoor parties that notch it up from casual, and celebrations: birthdays, graduations, housewarmings, holiday gatherings	Eight weeks (at the outset, for a shower) to two weeks in advance for something like a brunch or luncheon	Email, Evite, phone call, fill-in invitation, printed invitation, personal blank, handwritten invitation. Consider your guest list and the occasion	More often than not, late afternoon to evening, but some of these gatherings might take place late morning or over lunch
SEMI-FORMAL	Dinner party; luncheon; weddings; celebration parties for graduations, retirements, religious milestones, achievements, milestone birthdays, showers, holiday gatherings	Anywhere from 8 weeks (at the most, for a shower) to 2 weeks in advance (brunch or luncheon). A semi-formal afternoon tea can be sent 2 weeks in advance	Printed or handwritten invitations. Digital invitations only if the gathering focuses on environmental efforts, and then they should be of high quality, not through social media or containing any ads	Typically evening for a semiformal event at home; however, luncheons may also be semiformal
FORMAL	Formal dinners, formal luncheons, balls, celebration events: engagements, weddings, milestone anniversaries and retirements, or a very high achievement/promotion	Twelve weeks to two weeks in advance; typically we see eight to four weeks for formal events	Printed or handwritten formal invitations. Consider using a calligrapher. Hand-delivered or mailed	Evening gatherings, usually starting after 6:30 p.m. except for formal weddings, which might start as early as 4:30 p.m.

FOOD	DRINKS	ENTERTAINMENT	SERVICE STYLE	ATTIRE EXPECTATIONS
Offering snacks is thoughtful, and a bare minimum. A full meal isn't expected but might emerge as a good option	Offer water. But you may offer anything beyond that that you feel like and that is appropriate to the time of day	A range: it might be the conversation, music, TV/movie/ sports, video games, crafts, board or card games	Serving from or offering guests the bag/jar/box/ can/bottle is fine but offering a glass/plate is a thoughtful touch	However your guests come; however you are
A must for a casual get-together. Offer anything from snacks to a more substantial dish, if not a full meal	Definitely have a couple of options of beverages to offer, both alcoholic and nonalcoholic	You might splurge on entertainment or have none; anything from games, to friends playing music or hiring professionals is possible	Potlucks, buffet, family-style meals, and heavy hors d'oeuvres are options. Host organizes the refreshment service, typically it's self-serve, not plated or served by hired staff	Casual attire. Pretty much anything goes, suitable to the weather
A must, even for an informal tea. Use bowls, platters, and boards. Take items out of their packaging and arrange nicely. No labels at the table	Definitely have a couple of options of beverages to offer, both alcoholic and nonalcoholic	Music (musicians or DJ), dancing, performers, and even artwork; possibly lawn games	Either self-serve (buffet/ family-style/heavy hors d'oeuvres) or plated food for a dinner. Presentation is worth considering, any takeout should be on platters	The dressier side of casual. Can range from dress shirts and jeans to suits and dresses
Provide and serve a full meal/menu. Cocktail party: heavy hors d'oeuvres. Dinner/celebra-tion: sit-down meal, typically two to four courses. No labels on the table	Whether open bar or limited offering, have options for your guests to choose from, both alcoholic and nonalcoholic	Music (musicians or DJ), dancing, performers, and even artwork; possibly lawn games	Host or hired staff may serve. If serving buffet, use more formal touches. Nothing served out of its container	From jeans with jackets to suits, and from skirts or dress pants to cocktail dresses or dressier maxi dresses
A full spread. Food must be presented well. Dinners and celebrations: hors d'oeuvres and at least a three-course meal. No labels at the table. Highest quality your budget allows	A full open bar is traditional. If not pos-sible, then ensure a variety for your guests to choose from, both alcoholic and nonalcoholic	Music (musicians or DJ), dancing, performers, and even artwork; possibly lawn games	Cocktail hour: Passed hors d'oeuvres. Dinner: plated in kitchen and served, plated in the din-ing room and served or served tableside by staff from platters. No labels or product containers. For highly formal func-tions: no buffet	Formal attire expected. Suits, cocktail or long dresses, pos-sibly tuxedos and gowns, or white tie

TABLE-SETTING DIAGRAMS

FORMAL SIX-COURSE MEAL Here we display all six courses worth of utensils for a meal that consists of an oyster dish, soup, fish course, entree course, salad, and dessert. You could also, as Emily suggests, place only three (not counting dessert) courses worth of utensils out at a time and possibly bring out the soup spoon and oyster fork with their respective dishes. You might have more than one wine glass (and of course sherry and Champagne glasses are only set if they are to be used).

1. Bread plate & butter knife
2. Dessert fork
3. Dessert spoon
4. Water glass / goblet
5. Sherry glass
6. Wineglass
7. Champagne glass
8. Napkin
9. Fish fork
10. Entrée fork
11. Salad fork
12. Charger/place plate
13. Salad knife
14. Entrée knife
15. Fish Knife
16. Soup spoon
17. Oyster fork

FORMAL FOUR-COURSE MEAL For a four-course meal, we are likely to see all utensils on the table, though it isn't a must. Remember to set only the glasses you will be using. As always, the dessert spoon and fork could be set out or brought out with the dessert.

1. Bread plate & butter knife
2. Dessert fork
3. Dessert spoon
4. Water glass
5. Wineglass
6. Wineglass
7. Napkin
8. Salad & appetizer fork
9. Entrée fork
10. Charger/place plate
11. Entrée knife
12. Salad & appetizer knife
13. Soup spoon

INFORMAL THREE COURSE MEAL As a three-course meal could be casual, semi/informal, or formal, you may or may not see a bread plate and butter knife, the dessert fork and spoon, or the charger. You might have more than one type of wine but you will typically just be served one, either red or white.

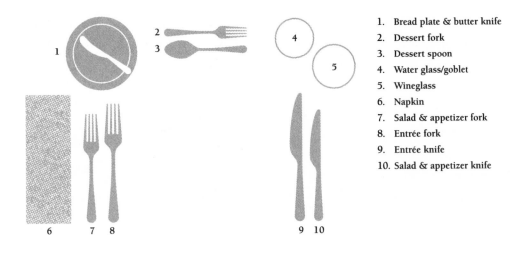

1. Bread plate & butter knife
2. Dessert fork
3. Dessert spoon
4. Water glass/goblet
5. Wineglass
6. Napkin
7. Salad & appetizer fork
8. Entrée fork
9. Entrée knife
10. Salad & appetizer knife

CASUAL/FAMILY ONE-COURSE MEAL A casual setting might utilize a placemat (though they can be used for semi/informal meals as well) and only our napkin, entree fork and knife, and a water glass will be set. It's unlikely that for a casual meal we will use a charger or underplate. In casual settings, sometimes the fork is placed on the napkin.

1. Water glass/goblet
2. Napkin
3. Entrée fork
4. Entrée knife
5. Placemat

SEATING CHARTS

When seating your guests, any guests of honor are seated to the right and left of the hosts, with the first guest of honor on the host's right and the second guest of honor on the host's left. From there a host should place guests around the table based on who they think are likely to enjoy each other's company.

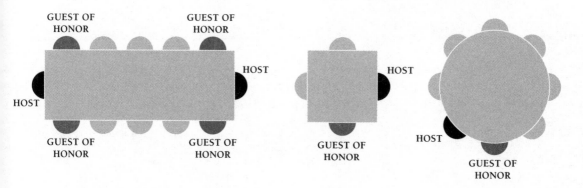

SAMPLE MENUS FOR MULTICOURSE MEALS

The following are examples, use your skill, comfort level, and interest to build your own menus.

PASSED HORS D'OEUVRES, MAIN COURSE, DESSERT

Hors d'oeuvres
Cheese, crackers, crudités and dips

Main
Maple-glazed Brussels sprouts, pickled pear and walnuts with beef Wellington and potato puree

Dessert
Berries with cream and mint

HORS D'OEUVRES, THREE-COURSE MEAL

Hors d'oeuvres
Dolmas, dips (muhammara, hummus, baba ghanoush) with pita and fresh veggie crudités, mini lamb kofta skewers

First
Curried cauliflower salad, pickled raisins, cilantro, yogurt

Second
Lettuce wraps, ground lamb, crispy chickpeas, whipped/ crumbled feta, marinated cucumbers and sumac

Third
Honey baklava

SIX-COURSE FORMAL MENU

First
Crab vichyssoise seasoned with Tabasco sauce

Second
White asparagus, pancetta crisps, beurre blanc

Third
Braised halibut and leeks, whipped potatoes, sunchokes, paprika, white wine and lemon sauce

Fourth
Frisée, fennel, Castelvetrano olives, and toasted almond salad with orange vinaigrette

Fifth
Assortment of cheeses, water biscuits and a stone fruit spread

Sixth
Lemon meringue tart

GLASSWARE

WATER GOBLET
RED WINEGLASS
WHITE WINEGLASS
CHAMPAGNE GLASS
COUPE
ROCKS GLASS
HIGHBALL GLASS

MARTINI GLASS
TEA OR COFFEE CUP (USE WITH SAUCER)
PINT GLASS
SHOT GLASS
SHERRY GLASS
BRANDY SNIFTER
DESSERT WINEGLASS

UTENSILS

ENTRÉE FORK
SALAD & APPETIZER FORK
DESSERT FORK
OYSTER FORK
ENTRÉE KNIFE
SALAD & APPETIZER KNIFE
FISH KNIFE
BUTTER KNIFE
STEAK KNIFE

DEMITASSE SPOON
DESSERT SPOON
SOUP SPOON
ICED TEA SPOON
GRAPEFRUIT SPOON
SHELLFISH CRACKER
SHELLFISH PICK
ESCARGOT TONGS

FOOD RESTRICTIONS

Food restrictions are important to pay attention to as a host. Some people strictly observe dietary restrictions, while others are more flexible (especially if it's not life-threatening). They are not something to judge, but something to respect. Here are some common ones:

ALLERGY: Allergic reaction to whatever the culprit is. Be sure to ask your guest if it's just a specific preparation or the item as a whole, and whether cross-contamination is an issue. Common allergies include shellfish, dairy, peanuts/tree nuts, chocolate, strawberries, sesame, and gluten.

GLUTEN-FREE: No products of any kind containing gluten from wheat.

GRAIN-FREE: No grains of any kind.

FLEXITARIAN: Generally sticks to one type of diet, but makes exceptions, either for ease or to enjoy in moderation. Like a vegetarian who chooses not to worry about the chicken stock in the stuffing at Thanksgiving dinner, or who eats the steak her friend serves at a dinner party rather than bringing a dish or having her host offer to make a dish that meets her needs.

HALAL: A term describing Islamic dietary laws, the most common of which ensure that meat is processed and prepared in accordance with the laws. Pork is not eaten, and alcohol is typically abstained from.

KOSHER: Indicates food that has been butchered or prepared in accordance with Jewish dietary laws. Milk and meat are not cooked or served together, and generally pork and shellfish are not eaten.

PESCATARIAN: Will eat fish and vegetables, but no meat. Some might eat shellfish only, or no shellfish, but will eat swimming fish.

VEGAN: Eats vegetables but no animal products or byproducts (no cheese, eggs, butter, animal milks, or honey). Certain food dyes and gelatins are also avoided.

VEGETARIAN: Does not eat meat; eats vegetables, grains, legumes, mushrooms, and typically eggs, cheese, and animal milks.

BRUNCH

TIMING: Begins around 10:00 a.m., ends around 2:00 p.m.

GUESTS: Anyone

INVITATIONS: Printed, handwritten, digital, in-person, or via phone, text, or social media platform. Can be sent any time from the night before or morning of to 4 weeks in advance.

FOOD: Egg dishes; breakfast meats and smoked fish; roasted, grilled, or fresh vegetables; toast, breads, pastries; polenta or grits, salads of all kinds (fruit, pasta, mixed vegetable, green); heartier dishes can sometimes be fish- or meat-based.

BEVERAGES: Juices, mixed juices, spritzers, coffees, teas, mixed drinks like mimosas and Bloody Marys/Bloody Shames, and sparkling or light wines

LUNCHEON

TIMING: Begins between 11:30 a.m. and 1:00 p.m. and ends between 1:30 p.m. and 2:30 p.m.

GUESTS: Anyone

INVITATIONS: Printed, handwritten, digital, in-person, via phone. Can be sent between 2 and 4 weeks in advance. (See the sample invitations for luncheon, below.)

FOOD: Typically, a three-course meal at least. Roasted, grilled, or fresh vegetables; soup; salads; fish, meat, and poultry dishes. Desserts: fruit tarts, assorted cookies, fresh fruit (usually lighter items).

BEVERAGES: Juices, mixed juices, spritzers, coffees, teas, mixed drinks like mimosas and Bloody Marys/Bloody Shames, sparkling or light wines.

FORMAL INVITATION
(on personal stationary)

1292 Lovely Lane, Charleston
*Ms. Mary Guerry
requests the pleasure of
Ms. Monique Weathers's
company at luncheon
on Sunday, the sixth of June
at noon.*

CASUAL INVITATION
(printed or handwritten)

*Please come for a luncheon
on Sunday, June 6th at noon.*
1292 Lovely Lane
Charleston
RSVP Mary
342-576-9097

CASUAL TEXT: *Lunch at my place (1292 Lovely Lane, Charleston) Sunday, June 6th, 12pm. Don't worry about bringing anything. I've got it all taken care of!*

WEDDING SHOWER OR NEW CHILD SHOWER

HOST: Usually a friend, cousin, aunt or uncle, can be anyone, though.

TIMING: Typically, an afternoon party, though could be any time from the luncheon hour to early evening. Usually runs 2 to 3 hours.

GUESTS: For a wedding shower, guests must be invited to the wedding unless it's an office shower that the office has elected to throw knowing they aren't invited. Avoid showers larger than fifteen to twenty-five people; hold multiple showers for more specific social groups instead of one large one if you need to.

INVITATIONS: Printed, handwritten, or digital, sent 4 to 6 weeks in advance. For a virtual shower, add the link to the video call with a digital invitation (with instruction on whether or not it may be shared); for printed or handwritten invitations, make a note of it on an insert or at the bottom of the invitation. Registry information may be included with the invitation because it is a shower. (See the sample invitation, below.)

FOOD: Mixed light and heavy hors d'oeuvres to a fuller spread. Often a buffet instead of a sit-down meal.

BEVERAGES: Juices, mixed juices, spritzers, coffees, teas, mixed drinks like mimosas and Bloody Marys/Bloody Shames, sparkling or light wines.

GIFTS: Should be opened at the party; givers thanked in person and later with a handwritten note, even for virtual showers.

GAMES: Only if the honoree wants them.

FOLLOW-UP: Honoree thanks host with note and often a gift. Honoree sends a specific handwritten (not printed/generic) thank-you note to each guest. Envelopes are never pre-addressed by the guests during the party.

SAMPLE INVITATION

Please join us in celebrating
Abha and Brendan
with a baby shower
Saturday, June 20th at 4 o'clock in the afternoon
243 Pollander Road
Claremont

RSVP: Jaya or Kojo
214-890-3345

Abha and Brendan are registered at purenaturebaby.com

GRADUATION PARTY

HOST: Usually a parent, guardian, or other relative of the graduate

TIMING: Afternoon to early evening, lasting through the night; often can be open-house style

GUESTS: Anyone close to the graduate(s)

INVITATIONS: Printed, handwritten, or digital, sent 2 to 6 weeks in advance. (For sample invitations, please see Sample Invitations, page 111.)

FOOD: Often a buffet of heavy hors d'oeuvres and crowd-pleasers like burgers and hot dogs, pasta salads, chicken wings, and chips and dips, but could also be a selection of the graduate's favorites or a favorite meal.

BEVERAGES: A mix of nonalcoholic offerings and perhaps beer and wine for those over 21. More formal parties might have cocktails, but they are less common at mixed-aged parties, especially for a high-school graduate.

GIFTS: Can be opened or saved for later.

FOLLOW-UP: Honoree thanks host with note. Honoree thanks guests with handwritten specific notes.

Retirement and anniversary parties would follow in a very similar suit to graduation parties or showers (minus the gifts), though often as more formal occasions. (See Sample Invitations, page 115, for invitation ideas to both of these parties.)

SAMPLE INVITATION

Please join the family of
Van Angelo
in celebrating their graduation from
San Diego State University with a Master of Fine Arts
Saturday, June 11th,
at 4 p.m.

223 Van Buren Boulevard
Riverside

RSVP: Arrianna, 951-229-8791

POURING, SERVING, AND PAIRING WINE

TYPE OF WINE	GLASS USED	TIPS FOR SERVING	PAIR WITH
Light-bodied reds	Large bowl, stem (more formal) or no stem (casual)	Pour to the widest part of the bowl of the glass. Allow to breathe	Barbecue, grilled summer veggies and meats, cheese boards, and grilled red meats
Full-bodied reds	Large bowl, stem (more formal) or no stem (casual)	Pour to the widest part of the bowl of the glass. Allow to breathe	Hearty winter dishes, meat pies, heavy Italian dishes, anything with tomatoes or tomato base, well-seared steaks, mushroom-based dishes
Light-bodied whites	Standard wine-glass with stem	Pour to the widest part of the bowl of the glass. Allow to breathe	Salads, lighter summer meals, delicate seafood and shellfish dishes, salty fried snacks (tempura, fries, fried cheeses)
Full-bodied whites	Standard wine-glass with stem	Pour to the widest part of the bowl of the glass. Allow to breathe	All pork and poultry, roasted dishes, lighter meat pies, heavy cream-based dishes, funky cheeses, charred vegetables
Rosé	Standard wine-glass with stem	Pour to the widest part of the bowl of the glass. Allow to breathe	Everything under the sun. Rosé is a catchall that plays well in all food realms. Pair a lighter-bodied, higher-acid rosé with lighter food, and a heavier, more tannic rosé with heavier foods
Sparkling (red, white, and rosé options)	Standard wine-glass with stem, coupe, or flute (the flute will help preserve the bubbles)	The coupe is pretty and vintage; a flute keeps the bubbles but won't let you swirl or the wine breathe (which it should!). Pour a small amount and let the bubbles settle, then pour to just below the rim (coupe) or about an inch below the rim (flute)	Similar to rosé, it can go with almost anything. Definitely a favorite for all things brunch
Dessert wines	Any fun, vintage glassware, short flutes (like sherry glasses) are often used	Two- to three-ounce pours; this is not a full glass	Desserts, anything sweet, and cheeses, especially blue cheese or mascarpone. The sweeter the dessert, the sweeter the wine should be

A WELL-STOCKED BAR

	SIMPLE BAR	FULLY STOCKED BAR
Beverages	Three liquors, usually at least one either dark or clear	Vodka, gin, tequila, bourbon, whiskey, scotch, rum, Campari, vermouth
Mixers	Seltzer	Tonic, seltzer, fruit juices, ginger ale, cola
Garnishes	Lemons (for twists and wedges)	Lemons, limes, oranges, olives, onions, maraschino cherries, citrus twists, aromatics, bitters, herbs
Equipment	Shaker, ice bucket	Shaker, ice bucket, tongs, long spoon, knife, cutting board, strainer, jigger, mortar and pestle

HOSTING HOUSEGUESTS CHECKLIST

☐ Set start and end dates for visit.

☐ Know who is coming (humans and pets).

☐ Organize arrival to and departure from your home.

☐ Prepare guest bedroom and bathroom.

☐ Clean or tidy up your home.

☐ Stock extra food to share.

☐ Prepare a list of suggestions for things to do.

☐ Plan downtime.

CHAPTER 11

About Town

"Consideration for the rights and feelings of others is not merely a rule for behavior in public but the very foundation upon which social life is built. Rule of etiquette the first—which hundreds of others merely paraphrase or explain or elaborate—is: Never do anything that is unpleasant to others. Never take more than your share—whether of the road in driving a car, of chairs on a boat or seats on a train, or food at the table."

When we are out and about in the world interacting with those beyond our personal orbits, it's good to be polite. It's a wonderful and interesting fact that as a species we have developed this notion. In fact it might even be necessary to our existence. Even though we have a strong sense of "to each their own" today, we also know that there are common and basic courtesies that help us interact with others—usually strangers, and often briefly—when out and about in the world, doing things like running errands, dining out, attending sporting events or live performances, working out, going to the movies, and enjoying the scenery. Even virtual encounters, like pre-date dates, online classes, gaming, and virtual parties require us to use our about-town manners. In Emily's era the goal was not to disturb others in public, and the same can be said today. When we are out and about, in real life or virtually, politeness is one of the very best tools we can use to make our journey and our impact on the world around us a positive one.

When we are courteous to those around us, especially those whom we see regularly in our communities (the grocery store clerk, a barber, a shop owner, the garbage collector), we start to develop not only positive relationships, but a sense of community as well. A "friendly neighborhood" isn't friendly because it's perfectly clean, or the people in it are all the same—far from it. It's friendly because people repeatedly choose to be welcoming and aware of each other. And that trend becomes a characteristic of the area. Even when we are visiting other places, we want to act as good guests and strive to interact with others kindly and respectfully. Whether as longstanding members or visitors we can make a positive impact on the community around us.

BASIC COURTESIES
WHEN OUT AND ABOUT

Greetings and goodbyes are the most basic of basic courtesies when you're out in the world. When you encounter someone, eye contact, a nod, or even a friendly "Hi" are the bare minimum—and might be just perfect for these brief friendly but not close interactions. (For more about greetings, see Chapter 2: Greetings & Introductions.)

Goodbyes are just as important as greetings. As you leave the register, head for the door, or disengage from a chat in line or a waiting room, saying "goodbye" to those you've chatted with is courteous. "Nice chatting with you," "Thank you, take care," "Thanks and have a good day!" are all heard as people exit gas stations, dog parks, community centers, restaurants, and shops of all kinds. And all of them close the interaction and leave it on a positive and respectful note.

COURTESY IN STORES

Beyond greetings and goodbyes, there are some common courtesies to observe when you're in any store.

ASKING FOR HELP. A simple "Excuse me, could I get your help with something?" or "Excuse me, could you please direct me to . . ." is easy enough and should get you the help you need. After someone has helped you, be sure to say thank you. If they are wearing a name tag, saying their name is always respectful. Even if you have not been introduced to them, their name tag acts as a visual form of introduction.

RESPECTING THE MERCHANDISE. It's polite to treat the merchandise you haven't yet purchased with respect. Clothing should be refolded or rehung properly on its hanger. Return items you have decided not to buy to where you found them, rather than on the nearest shelf. Yes, store clerks are there to do these tasks, but treating the items well is a sign of respect for them (especially since you don't own them yet), the store, and the next customer.

AT THE REGISTER. If you are at a register, stay off your phone. Whether you put the call on hold or end it, do not have someone talking in your ear while a clerk rings you up. When they start working on your items, focus on them and your purchase. Even at the self-checkout, don't be texting, scrolling, posting, or doing anything that slows down your self-checkout. Always check with a clerk first before running to grab a forgotten item.

The flip side of this is, if you're running a register, avoid wearing earbuds or looking at your phone. It's still important to interact with your customer, even if they're buying only a pack of gum. Saying, "One dollar and twenty-five cents, please," instead of nothing or just pointing at the register read-out and saying "thank you" and "goodbye," all make for a courteous transaction from the clerk's end as well.

STANDING IN LINE

Line manners help keep us orderly and polite under sometimes stressful circumstances. Ms. Outta Line has terrible line manners. She cuts in front of people, acting as if she didn't see them there, uses an express lane when she has more than the item limit, and—possibly most unpleasantly—huffs and puffs about how slow the line is moving. She also has the habit of chatting up people in line who clearly don't want to talk. She is the epitome of poor line manners.

There are times when you aren't sure who's in line or for what—like when people are grouped around a counter or entry area of a restaurant. Some might be waiting to put their name in to be seated, others might be looking to pick up takeout. It's okay to ask, "Are you in line for takeout?" to figure out where you fit into the group. When you're standing in line, give the people around you space (though not enough to allow room for someone to cut in). Of course, when social distancing practices are in place, we may allow greater spacing between people, and if this is the case, it's important to recognize that the line may not look traditional. A simple "Is this the end of the line?" will help you come across as observant and respectful to others waiting.

It's nicer for those around you if you're not on the phone while in line; however, realistically we know many people will take or make calls while waiting in line. If you do, keep the conversation public space–friendly, and avoid discussing potentially controversial topics or personal information. It's also important to keep your voice down and remember that you do have a captive (and rarely captivated) audience. End or pause the call when it's time to engage at the register.

Avoid saving spots. Sure, a date might hold a space for you while you park the car, but for one person to hold a space for three or more others is impolite. It's one thing if everyone in the line already has a ticket with an assigned seat and being the first in doesn't make a difference. But when it's first come, first served, or not assigned seating, saving spaces in line for a group is not considerate to the people behind you. If you want your group to stay together, you can all go to the end of the line.

When you're out shopping, don't continue to shop from the line. In a long line, it's okay to go back once for a forgotten item—if the person behind you doesn't mind holding your spot—or to send your kid as a go-for. But if on your own, don't do this more than once.

GETTING AROUND

"Getting around" means all kinds of things, from maneuvering on a sidewalk, path, or through tight aisles in a store to taking public transportation and driving. How we move through life—literally—can be full of good etiquette moments when we are aware of ourselves and the space and people around us. In Emily's day, there were very specific manners for getting around, however today we don't see or need to be as concerned with which side of one another we walk on, who is carrying whose parcel or bundle, or assisting someone over a muddy puddle by laying down a perfectly good coat. Today, we keep it simple but still polite. In the United States, most people walk on the right when faced with oncoming pedestrian traffic. Calling out "on your left" when passing on a recreation path (less commonly on sidewalks) is not only considerate, but also safe! It's also important to *give people as much space as you can while passing them.* Whizzing by someone or coming even within a foot of them is considered close enough to startle them or disrupt their personal space. Remember that 18-inch (½-meter) comfort zone most Americans like to operate within? Well, unless the space is crowded (which plenty of public sidewalks, transportation stations, and malls can be), people expect the same 18 inches *at least* when passing. When out with a group on a sidewalk, trail, or path, it's important to shift yourselves so that you aren't more than two people abreast, or even drop down to single file if it's a tight squeeze between parties. When social distancing is in order, the polite distance is increased so it never feels like a close call.

Many of us use mobility devices to get around, such as crutches, walkers, wheelchairs, motorized units, and canes. These devices make mobility possible and serve as extensions of people's bodies. It's important to respect them as such. To stare, point, or make comments about people using mobility devices is rude behavior. Never question the necessity of these devices, and never touch or move any device unless the person who uses it has asked or invited you to. "Here, let me just move your crutches so I can get by," is not appropriate. Instead try, "Excuse me, would you mind moving your crutches so I can get by?" If it's easier for the person to have you move them, they will offer this suggestion or ask for your help. As with other courtesies, offer your help rather than impose it: "Would you like me to get the door for you?" instead of, "Here, let me get that for you."

No matter how we end up getting around our town, the magic words, our patience, and our awareness of those around us will serve us well and help us contribute to making our public spaces more polite.

DOORS, ELEVATORS, AND ESCALATORS

There are many comical scenes of madcap mishaps with characters navigating doors, elevators, and escalators. When we want life to go smoothly, our magic words and a little awareness can do wonders to help us politely communicate our intent and avoid minor awkward moments.

DOORS. For standard doors, you typically allow people to exit before you enter. It makes the most sense to let people out before you try to go in. Anyone may hold a door for someone else (traditionally this was based on gender and age, whereas today it depends more on who can more easily hold the door in each situation). Sometimes this means moving through the door first to then hold it open for those following. Other times it means opening the door and stepping back to allow others to proceed. Remember if someone holds a door for you to say "thank you" as you pass through.

For a set of doors, you might find a couple of different maneuvers helpful. If you're going to hold the door for someone who is encumbered say, "Here, I can get that for you." Then step up to the door, open it, and as they pass through you can now say, "One second and I'll get the next door for you as well." If they are not encumbered, you might find that you each hold a door for the other. You might hold the first one open for the other person to pass through, and as they reach the second door, they then hold it for you. Or more casually (and very commonly), you hold the first door for the other person, they then open the second door for themselves and as they pass through, they keep their hand on the door and give it a push so it stays open long enough for you to grab it (and prevents it from shutting on you just as you reach it.)

REVOLVING DOORS. If you're going to try to assist someone with a revolving door, you enter the door first and push to get it moving so the other person doesn't have to make the effort. Go slowly so that it's easy for them join you (if there's room) or to enter the next open spot. Do not try to enter a section of a revolving door that is crowded. Slow down if you see that the person on the other side is managing a lot, like a stroller or a dog, or carrying a number of bags or packages.

ELEVATORS. Always allow people to exit an elevator before stepping on. Tradition saw ladies and the elderly exiting first, while men led the way when entering to secure the space and assist. Today, anyone may offer to let someone go first. The politeness is displayed by not rushing or pushing your way on or off. When there is room, avoid standing with your back to another passenger. If an elevator is crowded, don't get on; wait for the next available lift. You want to be careful not to crowd anyone with a dog or stroller, and especially careful not to crowd anyone who uses a wheelchair—it can be extra uncomfortable to be in a tight space with people standing when you are seated. If someone calls out "Hold the elevator!", accommodate them if possible. It's polite if you're near the button panel to offer to push a button for another passenger. "What floor would you like?" is easy enough. If no one has offered and you're too far from the panel to reach it yourself, you may ask someone to push a button for you. "Would you mind pressing 4 for me please?" is polite with a stranger. A quick, "Four please" will also do, if this is your building and circumstances are such that you know the person near the panel or they are at least a familiar-enough face. Don't forget to say thanks for a button pushed, a door held, or space made.

ESCALATORS AND MOVING WALKWAYS. Escalators are for riding, and while some might choose to walk up or down them to move faster, pass someone only if there is room to do so. For moving walkways, stand on the right and walk or pass on the left. If you're standing with many items (luggage, shopping bags, etc.), do your best to create space for others to pass.

PUBLIC RESTROOMS

Public restrooms are set up in many ways, from porta-potties to having multiple individual stalls to being a single restroom complete with your own sink and baby-changing station. No matter where the restroom is, whether you're at a fair or festival, mall or airport, restaurant or salon, bus or train terminal, or in the finest of hotel lobbies, you should always employ proper line manners, be discreet (this refers more to talking loudly across stalls or about private topics than to any bodily function), and don't leave a mess. Don't take your phone out in a public restroom—it's a private space and people shouldn't be wondering if someone is recording or can hear them.

When it comes to accessible stalls, there is a mixed range of suggestions for using them properly. In general, they should be left available for people who need them. Many people have different accessibility needs, not all of which are apparent, so you want to avoid judging someone because they are using the stall. If you are next in line, and the accessible stall is one you don't personally need but it's the only open stall in a busy bathroom, you can always ask if anyone else in line needs the accessible stall before you use it. "Does anyone need or want to use the accessible stall?"

OUT TO EAT

Our dining-out options range widely, from sandwich shops and cafés to Michelin-starred restaurants whose service is as impeccable as their food. We dine out alone, in groups, for business meetings, as celebrations, and when we're on the go. Sometimes we play a host or guest role, and other times we are simply dining together. However we do it, Americans like to eat out.

Feeling confident navigating any type of dining-out experience will allow you to relax and enjoy your time with others. When you're confident in your social skills in a given situation, the focus can be on the good time you're all having. Knowing the ropes is half the battle. Dining out without making a mess or disrupting others is the rest of the challenge.

Note: If dining out is possible when social distancing measures are in place, your politeness and willingness to follow an establishment's rules or protocol are key to a smooth and likely safer experience. Always respect the rules of the restaurant.

ARRIVING

If using a valet service, pull your car up, get out, and give the valet the keys (or the spare key) and say, "Thank you." If there is anything to note about a sticky clutch or odd door handle, it's best to say so. You offer a tip (usually $2 to $5 or more) when you collect your car, not when you leave it with the valet. (Remember, you are not bribing them for good service, you are thanking them for the service they provide.) If you're hosting a group, you'll want to arrive a little bit early (say, 10 minutes) so you can be there to greet your guests. If there is a coat check, you can leave your coat and take your ticket; like the valet, you'll tip the attendant upon picking up your coat. If your table isn't ready, you may be asked to wait in the bar or in the lobby or greeting area of the restaurant. Be patient. The restaurant usually has a reason for not seating someone right away. Service can get hectic, and it's best to give them the benefit of the doubt rather than assuming the worst. Often a restaurant won't seat you until all or most of your group has arrived. If you're hosting, it's polite to wait for your guests. If the restaurant host offers to seat your group before everyone has arrived, you may seat those who are present and then return to the lobby to wait for the rest of the group. If late guests have yet to arrive after 5 or so minutes, take your seat at the table with the guests who are present and ask the host to please show anyone else for your group to the table. Welcome any late guests with warmth, not glares or remarks about how far into the meal you are. If you are the late party, apologize for being late and take your seat. If you're super late, do your best not to disrupt the dinner in progress; instead join in whatever course is being served. The most important part is to apologize.

THE BAR

At the bar, you always want to be kind and respectful to your bartender, especially if they are busy. You can ask for any specific drink you like, but be polite and flexible if they don't have the ingredients or quality you're seeking. No one from Best Society would be a snob about it. If your tab from the bar is transferred to your table, be sure to tip your bartender in cash (usually 10 to 15 percent, or $1 or $2 per drink) when you leave to be seated. Not doing so doesn't guarantee a tip for the bartender unless the restaurant pools tips, and how are you to know that? If you don't have cash on hand to tip, it's best to settle up rather than transfer your tab so that you can be sure to leave a tip.

WHERE TO SIT

When you're dining out, whether as a host or guest, you want to pay attention to where to sit. As the host, be prepared with a seating plan or make one up on the spot. Usually, you give the guest of honor the best seat available at the table, the one either facing the view, or facing the room if there is no view. Often seats near doorways or high traffic areas are less desirable, and the host is likely to choose this seat for themselves. Guests should look to hosts, and even ask if no one has mentioned it yet: "Alan, where would you like us to sit?" If there is no host-guest dynamic at play, feel free to sit wherever you'd like, and be accommodating if others have preferences or accessibility needs, especially if you don't.

YOUR SERVER

Regardless of whether this is a local diner or the highest-rated fine-dining restaurant, your server is going to take care of you, and it's best to start by giving them the utmost respect and consideration as they do their job. Try to be efficient with your server and ask for things all at once rather than repeatedly calling them over, which slows down overall service in a restaurant. Ways to treat your server well include the following:

- Saying hello and listening for any specials or other information your server may have rather than jumping straight into placing your order.

- When you ask for substitutions, or questions about preparation, be patient or understanding if something cannot be accommodated. "Would you be able to . . . ?" or "Would it be possible to . . . ?" instead of "I want" makes a difference, as do the magic words *please* and *thank you.*

- Make eye contact and, if necessary, half-raise your hand to signal a server over. Do not snap, point, or call out to them.

- Don't make dismissive gestures instead of actually speaking to a server. For example, don't wave someone off with your hand; instead, turn to them and say, "No, thank you," or "I'm all set, thanks."

- When a server is pouring wine or water, avoid covering your glass with your hand to indicate you don't want any, and there is no need to turn an empty wineglass upside down to signal you don't want wine. Simply speak to your server when they make the offer: "No, thank you."

- Always tip. If you have a problem with the service, it should be dealt with by telling management, not by stiffing someone on a tip. The minimum for a standard tip is 15 percent, and it should be applied even if you're upset with the service. Speaking to the manager is the way to handle a problem—let your words speak for you, not your money.

- Always say thank you after each interaction.

ORDERING

Ordering for ourselves is usually easy enough—we just have to remember to say *please* and *thank you*. And we want to especially remember our *p*'s and *q*'s if we are asking for any special accommodations for our meal. When it comes to ordering for someone else or the table, there are a couple of courtesies to keep in mind. If you'd like to order for someone and you are a host, ask first if they would like you to order for them, especially if it's a first date. Traditionally the person who's done the asking out (officially the host) would also do the ordering. This doesn't mean that they choose menu items for the other person, but it does mean they will ask what the person would like and then communicate that to the server: "The lady will have the lobster risotto and I will have the lamb chops." We try not to refer to people as singular pronouns when we are right there with them. Saying "my guest," "the gentleman," "my friend," "the lady," "my colleague," or "my/the kids" is preferable to "she/he/they will have . . ."

When ordering for a larger table, family, or family-style meal, try to be ready with as much information as possible, so you can communicate it clearly and efficiently. If you do not have a specific order for each person, be sure to get some basic suggestions or restrictions from the group first and then choose a mix of dishes. Be especially careful to not order just one vegetarian, gluten-free, or other special diet dish. You don't want the person with the restriction at the table to be limited to one option (which others are sharing in as well). Keep an eye on how quickly food is getting eaten and order more if you need to. For a list of possible courses you might encounter, see Chapter 5: Table Manners.

If someone is treating you to a meal, they may let you know what's okay to order by saying something like: "Please feel free to order anything on the menu." And this usually means *anything* on the menu. Your host might also say, "I'm going to order an appetizer as my entrée, but please feel free to order both courses if you see any items you'd like." If your host hasn't said anything, you may either pay attention to what the host orders in terms of courses, or you can ask, "What are you planning on ordering?" If your host has made no indications of what to order, most people will order a mid-price item off the menu. However, as the host, be prepared for a guest to order anything, including the most expensive item. While most guests might need encouragement to order it, it's best to be prepared that they might, rather than count on them not.

If you have a dietary restriction or allergy, it's best to state this up front. Some people carry cards that explain their allergy, and many chefs welcome receiving them, as it makes communication easy and clear rather than a mini game of telephone.

BEHAVIOR AT A RESTAURANT

When dining out, the goal is to have a wonderful time, but not at the expense of others. Stay seated as much as possible; getting up frequently or letting your kids run around the restaurant is distracting to others. Keep your conversation to your own table. While a good joke or sentimental toast might elicit laughter or an "aww" for a moment, you want to keep it contained so you don't disrupt others. Use your indoor voices. (For more about good table conversation, see Things Not to Do at the Table, page 164, and The Three Tiers of Conversation, page 61.) For keeping kids well behaved at the table, a mobile device can seem like the perfect pacifier, but make sure they use headphones or the sound is off, whichever makes more sense. No one should hear "Baby Shark" while dining out. Restaurants work hard to create a certain atmosphere, and part of why people go out is to enjoy that atmosphere. Respecting that is the height of good taste when dining out.

THE BILL

The question of the bill was just as awkward in 1922 as it can be today. As Emily wrote:

"Everyone has at some time or other been subjected to the awkward moment when the waiter presents the check to the host. For a host to count up the items is suggestive of parsimony, while not to look at them is disconcertingly reckless, and to pay before their faces for what his guests have eaten is embarrassing. Having the check presented to a hostess when gentlemen are among her guests, is more unpleasant. Therefore, to avoid this whole transaction, people who have not charge accounts, should order the meal ahead, and at the same time pay for it in advance, including the waiter's tip. Charge customers should make arrangements to have the check presented to them elsewhere than at table."

These days the bill is not quite so ugly a thing as Emily described. People are aware of and not ashamed at all by the fact that someone will have to foot the bill for the meal. However, Emily's points of not making a show by tallying everything up in front of guests, and leaving a tip, are still appropriate today. If something is wrong with the bill, take the issue to the host's stand, or at least address it away from the table, rather than bringing the whole table's attention to the mistake.

When splitting the bill, you could leave the restaurant out of it altogether, with one person paying and others reimbursing them. This is simple and easy as long as everyone does reimburse the person paying. More common, though, is to simply get separate checks, allowing for each person or group to pay their own way (on tax and tip as well). If you are going to do this, it's best to ask about separate checks before you place your order. If you've forgotten and are asking for separate checks at the end of the meal, be patient, clear, and helpful when reminding a server who had what to eat. If the restaurant cannot split the bill, then it's up to you all at the table to come up with a solution—divide it evenly or by each person's order. Don't forget that, however you handle the expense, and especially when dining out in large groups, you cannot shortchange the server. Always make sure the tip is correct and the tax is covered. Standard for restaurant tipping is 15 to 20 percent. You can always leave more if you' like. (For more, see Tipping, see page 365.)

Note that when you are figuring out how to split a bill, if someone has eaten much less or not consumed alcohol, it's kind to speak up for them and adjust the breakdown of the bill. "Marykate, you had an appetizer as your dinner and didn't have any of the wine; let's make sure you don't have to pay the same full split." If no one has spoken up, it's okay for you to speak up for yourself.

Some people feel like they have to make an offer to pay even when they are being treated. This can get awkward for the host (or even others present). If someone has said they will pay, and has done the inviting for the meal, it's best to let them pay. The best time for a guest to offer to share the cost is when they reply to the invitation. If you'd like to make an offer to contribute when at the table, do so graciously, not forcefully. "Misha, this has been such a great meal, may I offer to split the bill?" More likely than not the host will say, "That's kind of you; however, this is my treat." If that's the response, do not push to pay the bill. Remember, you can always use this moment as inspiration to treat this person some other time. When you ask, you should always be prepared to make good on your offer in the rare case that someone says, "That would be lovely, thank you for offering."

The only time as a host you really can't insist on paying a full bill is when you are on a date and your date asks that you split the check. It's very important to listen to your date when they ask to split the bill. Many people want dates, especially early on, to feel like they are on equal footing and not like one person owes the other person anything. (To be clear: No one owes anybody anything on any date—except consideration, respect, and honesty—but many express feeling this way when someone has bought them a meal.) While it's best to say you'd like to split the cost when you first set the date up, it's common for this exchange to happen when the bill arrives. If your date says to you, "This has been great; I would really appreciate splitting the bill," you can offer to treat them one more time: "Are you sure? I really am happy to treat tonight." But if they decline again, split the bill with them. Take note: you should not offer to split the bill unless you truly want to.

When you are sure you are hosting and there's not going to be any bill splitting, if you want to be really smooth, do as Emily suggests and make arrangements for the bill not to be brought to the table. Take care of everything ahead of the meal, or excuse yourself for a moment near the end of the meal and handle it.

When treating someone to a meal it is okay to use a gift card if you have one. Remember, a tip is still expected and should be given separately from the gift card (meaning you shouldn't use the gift card to tip).

WHEN SOMETHING IS WRONG

If there is something wrong with your meal, signal for your server and quietly let them know what the issue is. Often, the rest of the table will ask what's going on, and you can either tell them, or not. Remember to be discreet, depending on what the issue is. Meat is too rare? Not a big deal. Ask for it to be cooked a little longer. A worm or Band-Aid in your meal? Best to keep it quiet so as not to spoil others' appetites; you can either excuse yourself and tell the server away from the table, or tell them quietly at the table. Should anyone ask, you can say, "There was something in my salad, but they are handling it," to help avoid grossing others out by saying exactly what was wrong. Typically, the restaurant will take care of the issue right away. It should also be noted that you should never ask for a meal to be comped. The restaurant will offer if it's warranted. If something is just not to your taste, well, that's a risk we all take when we order something. If it's truly not a dish you can enjoy, but there is nothing wrong with it, it's okay to quietly order something else instead.

WHEN A MESS IS MADE

If you've spilled something too large to easily fix with your napkin, hopefully the nearest server will come over quickly. Much like a mess at home, you want to deal with it promptly and with as little fuss as possible. If no one from the restaurant has noticed the spill, mess, or other disaster, calmly go find someone to help if you need it. If you are the one who spilled or made the mess, apologize to the table and thank the servers who are helping to clean it up.

For items that fall to the floor, leave them there. When you are dining, especially dining out with others, never touch the floor and then bring your hands back to the table. It can be hard not to dive in and try to help clean up a mess—it feels like it might be good etiquette, but this is one case where the task is best left to those prepared to deal with it. If you're dining at a casual place that has no servers (counter service) and you drop something, pick it up and throw it out or bring it to a bus bin if there are any, and then go wash your hands before returning to your table or seat at the counter.

FORMAL DINING OUT

Formal dining out is a treat indeed, as everything is top notch, and it's important to honor the sentiment that we are stepping everything up when we dine out formally. Usually our attire, the atmosphere, and the cuisine are all meant to be elevated from our everyday experience. As patrons we want our manners to reflect this too.

For a true formal dining experience, the reservation process might be a bit more involved. Plan on making reservations at least a few weeks ahead and maybe more for a hot spot. The restaurant may call you back to confirm, which is a great opportunity to ask any questions you may have about the menu (which may be available online), cost, and protocol (including attire) at the restaurant.

Upon arrival you will be greeted by a host, and they will either guide you straight to your table or invite you to wait at the bar or lounge while they ready the table. Once you're seated, servers might switch out your napkin for one more closely matching your outfit (usually just a difference between black and white), and may refold or replace your napkin if you excuse yourself from the table. You will *never* be asked to hold on to dirty silverware between courses, and crumbers are often used between courses to keep the table looking neat and tidy.

Your place setting may be set with a full complement of flatware and glassware, in which case the server will remove any unneeded items once you have ordered your meal. In other restaurants, the appropriate utensils for your order will be placed before serving each course (if you've ordered a steak, a steak knife will be set just before your entrée arrives).

The menu may be extensive, including à la carte options, or it may be prix fixe or a "chef's menu." When dining à la carte, you do not have to order every course available to you. Choose what would be pleasing to your palate and your appetite. Sometimes a tasting menu is offered, which is basically a sampler of the restaurant or chef's specialties. It may have many courses, but the portions will be on the small side. When it comes to restrictions or allergies, it's okay to speak up. While some menus might be fixed, and you certainly wouldn't micromanage or over-direct at an upscale establishment, it's okay to indicate any allergies you have or inquire if there's a substitute for a particular item that you can't eat or truly don't care for. "I am quite allergic to almonds, please let me know if there are dishes on the menu I should avoid."

If a sommelier is on staff, they are not there simply to pour. Feel free to ask them questions, or for their opinion on pairings before ordering. Wine and Champagne will always be presented to you if you have ordered them by the bottle. Check the label of the wine to be sure it is what you ordered. Once you've approved the selection, the server will pour a small amount for you to taste to make sure it hasn't gone bad (a condition sometimes referred to as "corked"). There's no need to assess or grade the wine in this moment. If it has gone bad, the vinegar-like taste will be obvious, in which case you would say, "It appears this bottle is off. May we try another?" If the selection tastes good to you, you simply nod your head or comment, "Very nice." And the server or sommelier will pour the rest of your glass and then for the rest of the table.

The type of service you might encounter in a formal dining venue can vary from a single server (or table manager) dedicated to your table or group to two servers assigned to each diner. Feel free to ask questions if you are curious about anything—the décor, the menu, the service—or if you are unsure of what is expected of you. Food might be cooked out of sight or in an open kitchen right in front of you. It could be presented on a cart (French service), brought out plated and served to each diner (American service), or served from platers presented at the table (Russian service). If food is presented to you and you are asked to make a selection, pick the item, piece, or cut that looks best to you. With as many as two servers per diner, food can be presented to everyone simultaneously at the start of a course. New items may be presented as previous ones are cleared, always leaving the diner with something at their place. Service can become a performance and go in many directions. (You may even find yourself transported to nineteenth-century Paris, with silver domes pulled off plates at the table, revealing fine delicacies, releasing savory aromas, and indicating that the course has begun.) Whatever the style of service, be ready to engage in and enjoy a truly spectacular formal dining experience.

CASUAL DINING AT THE COUNTER

Oftentimes we will dine out in a super casual setting. Lunch counters, bars, cafés, sandwich or to-go shops, and fast-food restaurants all provide casual dining experiences. Good table manners are still required regardless of the formality level. You may or may not make conversation with those around you, and even though it may not be a full-service venue, you still want to make sure to be courteous with the staff by saying "please," "thank you," and "Have a good day" when you depart.

At a lunch counter or bar, your server will clear your place, whereas at fast-food joints, cafes, and many sandwich, burrito, and pizza shops, you'll be expected to bus your own table—bringing your plates and cups to bus bins and throwing out any garbage or recycling your drink bottles, etc. If you're unsure of the policy at the eatery, simply ask at the counter: "Should I bus my own table? I wasn't sure, and didn't want to just leave a mess." While you should clear away as much of your mess as you can, you don't have to go so far as to grab a rag and spray bottle; leave that to the staff. Do return your dishes and tray, and appropriately dispose of any garbage, recycling, or compost.

For counter service where you sit down and are served, always tip the standard 15 to 20 percent. For service where you pick up your food and bring it to your table, the tip is discretionary, and these days is often added to a tab via a tablet. You can also put loose change or a dollar or two into the tip jar. (See Tipping, page 365.)

TO GO AND DELIVERY

When you aren't dining at a restaurant but getting your food to go, pay attention to any pickup or take-out protocols so the restaurant can keep running smoothly. This might mean waiting until you are called to pick up and/or pay for your order, paying when you place the order instead of when you pick it up, standing in a particular line, or sometimes waiting outside until your order is ready. For takeout, tipping is still discretionary, but is usually either a few dollars or 10 percent of the order. You can always tip more.

When you're ordering for delivery, always relay any oddities about where you live or how to get to your door, such as, "Number 35 is actually behind number 37 but they use the same driveway, and we are the upstairs door on the unit." A customary tip for delivery is 10 percent of the order, or $5 to $10. Remember, your tip is not the same as the delivery fee; often that fee is not given to the delivery people. The same is true of room service in a hotel. The service fee listed on the bill may not include a tip that goes directly to the person bringing the food. You can always double-check if your service fee is going to the server; if not, you should leave a tip.

COFFEE SHOPS

You may be popping in to pick up your favorite steamy beverage to go, or you might be setting up camp to get some work done, have a nice catch-up with a friend, or just enjoy a break. For whatever reason you find yourself headed to the coffee shop, here are some things to consider when you get there.

If you're a regular, avoid considering a particular table or chair yours. Switch it up. Also, be aware of how much space you're taking up if you're bringing an office's worth of stuff with you. It's fine to set up your laptop or tablet, or lay out a textbook, notebook, and pens, but keep it limited to just what you need to get your work done.

As always, tidy up your space before you leave. If you don't see someone busing tables, look for marked bus bins to put your empty dishes in, and recycle, compost, or throw out any waste. If you're unsure where to bring them, rather than taking your dirty dishes to the counter where people's orders are placed, ask first.

Coffee shops will often jokingly be referred to as someone's "other office" or their "other living room." Most businesses like having regulars, but if you do frequent a particular establishment, it is more respectful to be a paying customer. Many coffee shops now have policies preventing people from hanging out for hours and purchasing only a cup of coffee or something even smaller while using the free Wi-Fi and monopolizing a table. Instead of trying to game the system, why not show your gratitude by supporting your favorite venue instead; for example, by buying a coffee *and* a scone?

GROUP CLASSES AND MEETUPS

There are as many groups to engage with as there are interests in our culture: team leagues; pickup games; language and yoga classes; crafting, chess, and cosplay groups, etc. No matter the subject or activity, group classes and meetups are times when adults rely on their school-day manners to be courteous and ensure the class or activity is enjoyable and serves its purpose.

KEEP YOUR COMMITMENT. Whether or not it's a paid activity, if you've reserved a space for yourself, you must play the role of good guest and either keep your commitment and attend, or change your status so someone else can take your spot. Last-minute cancellations should be for true emergencies only. If you treat the activities you sign up for as important commitments, you'll be courteous both to those organizing and those participating.

SHOW UP ON TIME AND READY TO GO. Showing up early is sometimes better than being right on time. Be sure to pay attention to any agenda, required materials, attire, or equipment, as well as to any parking or entry information the organizer has given you. Not doing so might negatively impact the group, either because you can't participate well or properly, or are late because you were waiting at the wrong door or went to the wrong place.

LISTEN AND PARTICIPATE. Listening to your instructor, leader, or other participants when appropriate is really important. This is not a private lesson or session; it's about all of those involved. Paying attention and participating well will help make the group experience more efficient, and hopefully enjoyable and productive.

THE GYM

Whether it's a public outdoor workout space or an indoor gym that you pay to use, there are some common courtesies to observe.

WAIT YOUR TURN. Each gym or workout space usually has its own rules for how to get your workout time on each apparatus. Whether it's by signing up; first come, first served; or time limits, be sure to pay attention to the order of operations. If someone is going over their allotted time, you can catch their attention and, with a friendly tone, say, "Hi, I signed up for the 6:30 time slot," or something similar to indicate their time is up. If this doesn't get someone to budge and there are no other machines available, get a staff member to assist.

WIPE DOWN THE MACHINES. It's considerate to wipe down your equipment and machines when you are finished with them using the supplies provided. Not only is it hygienic, but it also helps keep odors from building up. Always wipe down what you've touched or sweated or breathed heavily upon.

DO NOT WEAR SCENTS. On the days when you are going to work out, do not wear perfume or cologne. The aroma of perfumes and colognes is amplified when you start to heat up and sweat. Not only can it be overpowering, but it can give people instant headaches or make them feel nauseated. If you wear scent regularly, try using a cleansing wipe on your neck or wrists (or wherever you apply the scent) to help remove it before a workout. Be understanding if people have to move away from you. Scented deodorants are not usually a problem.

IN THE LOCKER ROOM. Locker room etiquette isn't so much about your towel being on or off as it is about keeping the facility clean and not taking up too much space with your stuff. While the locker room is there for you to take the time to get ready for your workout or class or the rest of your day, it's best to be respectful of others waiting to use the showers, sinks, or mirror space. While chit-chat is perfectly okay, this is one of those spaces where conversations are easily overheard, so be mindful of the topics you choose to discuss. As a privacy courtesy, don't use your phone in the locker room.

PUBLIC TRANSPORTATION

On buses, trains, subways, trams, and other forms of public transportation, we want to use our best public manners. We experience these spaces with others when we are all on the go: a combination that makes them ripe for rudeness, but that can just as easily give us opportunities to exhibit polite behavior. When getting on or off a bus, train, or subway car, always let those who are exiting go first. This is only logical. The smaller space needs to be emptied before there can be room for the new passengers. Make room for passengers who need extra time or who are carrying large or cumbersome things. You might even offer to help them, but whatever you do, avoid pushing by them.

When it comes to taking a seat, it's still considered polite for those who are young and spry to leave seats for those who could really use them (a pregnant person, an elder person using a cane . . .). If you're already seated, you should stand up and offer your seat rather than offer it from a seated position, as you're much more likely to be taken up on the offer. If you need a seat and no one is offering you one, you can certainly ask: "Pardon me, would you be willing to let me sit?" While offering your seat is considerate, we must never judge people who aren't offering their seat. Remember that not all disabilities and health conditions are visible. Glaring or scowling at someone who hasn't offered their seat isn't polite.

When you're standing on a bus, subway, or train car, it's best to be aware of both safety and how you impact others' personal space. In tight quarters the magic words are your friend. An "Excuse me," "pardon me," or "sorry" goes a long way when reaching for a strap, bar, or handle or when moving past others. Whenever possible, make room for passengers who are entering or exiting.

If there is a driver or attendant that you pass, say hello when you see them and say thank you to them as you leave. Public transportation is an amazing part of our world, and while it may or may not always function like a well-oiled machine, we can always express our gratitude to the people who make it happen.

RIDE SHARES AND TAXIS

Rideshares (like Uber and Lyft) and taxis are more private than subway, bus, or train transportation, and come with their own expected manners.

When hailing a cab, try to make eye contact with your driver if you can, and never ever push someone out of the way to get a cab. If there is a dispute, unless it's an emergency it's best to let it go and find the next taxi. For rideshares or taxis that you have called or preordered, double-check that this is your ride (both as a safety measure and out of consideration for others who might be waiting nearby for their rideshare as well). Always say hello to your driver and ask how they are doing. It's a small courtesy that makes a difference. If you are not able to chat, it's fine to be on your phone, or even just look out the window. Say something like "I'm going to listen to some music now." Avoid eating in a cab or rideshare. If you are so hungry that you cannot wait, ask the driver first if it is okay.

You tip a rideshare and a taxi the same: roughly 10 to 20 percent (see Tipping, page 365). Never stiff a driver on a tip. For rideshares you can also leave a rating, and always remember that good etiquette counts, and don't forget your driver can rate you as well!

AT THE PARK OR BEACH

Our public parks and beaches can be some of the most wonderful places in our communities. Whether huge national forests or postage-stamp oases in the concrete jungle, parks and beaches are for all to enjoy. For the most part, people do a good job keeping to themselves, and taking care with these spaces, but there are a few things to consider in order to help ensure a good visit.

PICKING A SPOT. A good spot is a satisfying thing to find. Think about what you'll be doing and how it might impact those around you. Don't forget to check ahead of time about reserving things like grill spaces and fire pits. While not all parks take reservations for these, it's best to know before you assume and end up disappointed. Think about what you want to do while you're at the park: Are you going to be tossing a frisbee or playing football or catch? How much room do you need to sprawl out and enjoy the activities you plan to do? It doesn't make much sense to plop down 3 feet from a couple who is relaxing and start tossing your frisbee over them when there are other spaces where you won't bother anyone. Be particularly mindful at the beach about not getting sand on others.

SMOKING, GRILLING, AND MUSIC. Smoke from cigarettes, cigars, pipes, cannabis, grills, or camp-fires can negatively impact others. When it comes to smoke whose source you can control (for example, a cigarette), find a way to be downwind from others, especially children. When you're set up near a grill or firepit area, you should expect the possibility of smoke. If you're playing music loudly, be considerate about its content. Pick songs that would get regular radio airplay rather than the explicit lyric versions. Loud music is bad only if people nearby are bothered by it. One thing you can do is ask some of the people around you if the music is too loud. This can feel risky, but it shows you're considerate and can prevent dirty looks and negative assumptions. If someone is being too loud or playing music too loudly, it's best to try and find another spot first. If there's nowhere else to go, you can certainly try to ask someone to turn their music down. Kind folks will politely oblige.

LEAVE IT BETTER THAN YOU FOUND IT. Some people call this the "campsite rule." Picking up after yourself, leaving no trace, and maybe even doing a little something extra to clean or improve the area for the next person can feel so good and helps care for our shared spaces. All trash, recycling, and compost should go into the proper bins or be carried out if no bins are present. Leaving your garbage for others and nature to deal with is the height of rudeness. Even in 1922, Emily lambasted litterbugs: "People who picnic along the public highway leaving a clutter of greasy paper and swill (not a pretty name, but neither is it a pretty object!) for other people to walk or drive past, and to make a breeding place for flies, and furnish nourishment for rats, choose a disgusting way to repay the land-owner for the liberty they took in temporarily occupying his property."

ATTENDING PERFORMANCES

Performances run the gamut, from occasions where we have to be dressed to the nines and on our super best behavior, to raucous events where anything goes. The spectrum is broad, to say the least. To help narrow it down, we'll cover both seated venues and standing or festival-style events.

SEATED VENUES

Seated performances can be anything from children's recitals and school plays to sold-out stadiums for major stars to a night on Broadway. Symphony orchestras, plays, musicals, operas, and dance performances from contemporary to ballet all fall within the seated performance category.

Different performances come with different levels of expected attire. Kids' recitals, school plays, and daytime musicals are often considered more casual affairs, while opening nights, symphony and opera performances, and evening plays and musicals deserve dressed-up attendees. For some, this might be a jacket with your jeans; for others, it means a full tuxedo. If you're unsure of what might be appropriate to wear, we suggest calling your host or the ticket office to ask what is expected for the date and time of the performance you are viewing.

As an audience member at a seated performance, your biggest goal is not to disrupt anything—neither the performers nor the people seated near you. This definitely means turning cell phones off and double-checking to make sure they are. Don't be that person whose phone rings in the middle of a performance. Don't bring in anything to eat or drink that isn't allowed, and even if it is allowed, avoid anything with a noisy wrapper or that will rattle in a box. Silent foods, if any, are the best choice, but usually you can't eat during the show.

Ushers may be present at a theater or larger venue to help you find your seat or guide you in and out of the theater when the lights are low or the show is going on. They can also help if you have a question or need assistance. If you are late and missed the dimming of the lobby lights that indicate the show is about to start, an usher may have you wait until a natural break in the performance and then help you to your seat. If an usher asks you to be quiet during a show, it's important to politely take their cue.

Once the show starts, you should avoid getting up at any time other than intermission. Of course, if you are having a coughing fit, excuse yourself. Otherwise always wait until the intermission to use the restroom (emergencies aside) or to step out to "check something." If you do have to get up for an emergency, apologize quietly (mouthing "Excuse me" and "I'm sorry") as you move by others to exit your row. Be sure to do so while facing the stage. To turn your back on the performers is rude, even if they cannot see you. If you need to balance yourself, you can *lightly* touch the back of the chair row in front of you, but do not disturb the people sitting there.

Usually applause is saved for the end of a show, set, or scene but really there are few rules about when someone might feel compelled to break into applause. Mostly, you want to be sure your applause is showing the genuine appreciation and excitement it is meant to convey and is not a distraction to others in the audience, or worse, the performers. An "Encore!" or "Bravo!" is warranted for an excellent performance, and (should you feel compelled) you can shout it out along with your applause. If someone receives a standing ovation, join in if you are able.

Some of us are tall. Please never sulk or complain about a tall person seated in front of you; it's absolutely rude. Lean to one side (you may have to switch later to the other side) to see around them. You should never make someone feel bad for their height. While it's equally kind for tall people to try and help someone see around them, it shouldn't be their constant lot in life to always be treated like they are "in the way."

STANDING/FESTIVAL VENUES

While outdoor concerts and festivals are fabulously free-spirited, they are not without etiquette, which is primarily to respect the rules of the event when it comes to chairs, blankets, and tents. Set up what you can, but don't try to push the limits.

All-ages festivals are great for kids but remember to help your little ones mind their festival manners by keeping them in control. If you're at a show with a child and want to put them up on your shoulders, be sure to move around a bit so the view isn't completely blocked for the person behind you. If you've just been blocked by someone's shoulder ride, do your best to move around them to see.

Moving through a crowd to find a new spot can be done with grace. Don't shove or go fast to get it over with or gain momentum. You'll get farther faster and with fewer glares if you break out your magic words, use a sweet tone of voice, and give people a big ol' smile: "'Scuse me, pardon me, mind if I sneak by?"

If allowed by the venue, smoking and vaping are common at outdoor concerts and festivals, and while nice to be able to enjoy them at a show, step away from the crowd to do so if you can, especially at a mixed-ages event. Venues would be wise to create smoking and vaping sections that still have good views of the show, when possible.

Always clean up after yourself. Cups, food wrappers, and leftovers should be brought to the trash, recycling, and compost cans rather than just left on the ground.

Say thank you to any ticket attendants, vendors, or security staff you encounter. They so appreciate kind concertgoers.

OUT AND ABOUT ONLINE

Even while sitting in the privacy of our own home we might find ourself in very public online spaces. Most of us engage with the world through digital devices and virtual spaces, and it is wise to think of our behavior at these times as part of our public life. Our profiles, accounts, sites, comments, and posts are filled with different versions of ourselves; moments in our lives both lasting and fleeting. It's easy to think of our online interactions as private or forget the impact and reach they can have, but any time we post or message someone online, our behavior matters. Consider too, that what we say and do online can be not only public, but also permanent. It's not always possible to delete the impression something creates—even if you take a post down. We are at the mercy of screen captures and stored data that could allow a post to resurface. In some ways, we've come to live with this and accept it. In other ways, we can be so foolish. A few key pointers below will help us navigate our online life well.

LET CONSIDERATION, RESPECT, AND HONESTY GUIDE YOUR INTERACTIONS. Any time your words start to become less than considerate or respectful, consider signing off or not hitting Send. Avoid getting drawn into arguments or making negative comments, especially online when your tone can easily be incorrectly delivered or misinterpreted. (See Cultivating Kindness in Language, page 67.)

TREAT OTHERS WITH DIGNITY. You may not like someone's point of view or comment, and may even choose to challenge their perspective, but take the etiquette high road and always respect their dignity. We must always learn and follow the rules that make our forums and threads safe and keep the conversation focused. It can be easy to forget that there's a real person behind what's being posted and that insults, judgmental opinions, and personal attacks can cause real harm. This also means respecting someone's wishes if they ask you not to post something about them, or to take down something that includes them.

FILTER WHAT YOU SHARE. Share only things online you would be comfortable with your employer, child, coach, neighbor, or parents seeing. This is not to say that you can't express yourself, but to be polite, we have to consider our entire audience. Because these are public spaces, any of these folks might see what you post. Just thinking about them offers us good, natural checks on our attitude and the expression of our thoughts and feelings.

CHECK YOUR SOURCES. If you choose to share articles or statistics, make sure they are legitimate. Truth should be the goal, not winning an argument or impressing others. Can you find two other credible sources to verify your information before you share? Is the information from a reputable organization that transparently indicates how they produce their content? It might be faster to just copy and paste a link to prove your point, but we all know how quickly misinformation spreads. Do your part if you're debating and sharing online by checking your sources properly before you post.

KEEP YOUR INFORMATION CURRENT. This is important for businesses, especially brick-and-mortar locations. Maintaining your social and business networks online is part of contemporary life. Having outdated information or an old profile on LinkedIn, for instance, is like handing out an old business card. An old address on a Google profile could lead navigation apps to send customers to the wrong location. Not good.

COMMENT ETIQUETTE. Part of being considerate is being aware of context in posts and comment threads. Not all online comments and discussions are going to be positive. That's okay. But we can still be polite. Stick to the focus of the post, and never hijack someone's post or thread by changing the topic, especially in reference to yourself or something connected to you. Start your own conversation if you have a different perspective you want to explore.

YOUR FEED, YOUR SANITY. You are in control of your own attention. If there are videos or posts you don't agree with, it's usually better to just move on than to get in an online argument about them. If you're reading something, engaged in an exchange, or following someone whose posts are making you uncomfortable, it may be time to refresh, step away, or unfriend, mute, or unfollow for your own sanity. This is perfectly okay to do.

THE TROUBLE WITH TONE. Tone is very hard to read when we've got only words on a screen. Emojis, emoticons, text formatting, and font can all help, but they're still limited. Be sure you're saying what you mean. Double-check your own tone. Read what you've written aloud before hitting Send to see if you need to adjust anything. Be prepared for people to interpret a post or comment differently from how you meant it.

DON'T RELY ON DIRECT MESSAGE. While most people will respond to a DM they receive, it's not always possible, and you shouldn't expect it. People use social media in so many different ways, there is no single standard you can count on. No one is obligated to "heart" every story or mention they receive on social media, especially if it's something that expires after a period of time. For important messages, look for more direct communication methods. It should be noted that while many businesses use social media, for most, reaching out to them via private or direct message (DM) is *not* always the most effective or professional way to go. Use the email or website links provided to get in touch with them first. If you can't reach someone, then DM them.

ON TROLLS. Finally, trolls are rude. Don't feed the trolls. It's just not worth it. If you are going to clap back, be prepared to stop after you've said your piece. Getting into a back and forth with someone who is only looking to get you going plays right into their game.

TIPPING

In 1922, Emily wrote:

> "A quarter is the smallest possible tip in a first class hotel. If your meal costs a quarter—you should give the waiter a quarter. If it costs two dollars or more than two dollars, you give thirty or thirty-five cents, and ten per cent on a bigger amount. In smaller hotels tips are less in proportion. Tipping is undoubtedly a bad system, but it happens to be in force, and that being the case, travelers have to pay their share of it—if they like the way made smooth and comfortable."

Tipping is a time-honored tradition in American culture. It started out as a small something extra to show our appreciation, and ballooned over time into a Byzantine system. No matter the situation or the amount being tipped, good tipping etiquette still stems from giving a little extra to show our appreciation and recognize good work. We tip people from a variety of service sectors—from hair stylists, taxi drivers, valets, and baristas to, of course, servers at restaurants and the many service people we encounter when traveling. We also have an annual custom of tipping some people who work with us throughout the year at the end-of-the-year holidays. Such people include snowplow drivers, mail carriers, apartment building staff, personal trainers, nannies, garbage collectors, and newspaper delivery people to name a few. There are even situations where you might feel inspired to tip but a cash tip would be inappropriate, like with a teacher or doctor. It can feel like there is a lot to keep track of, but by keeping the gratitude in our gratuity, we give the gesture meaning and prevent it from being just another fee to calculate. Instead it remains true to its origin of being a little bit extra given to show our appreciation. (For a detailed list of who to tip when and how much, please see our Reference Guide, page 381.)

EVERYDAY TIPPING

For many of us, tipping is part of our everyday lives when we are out and about, and some-times even at home. There are many places where tipping is completely discretionary, and other situations when we either have a minimum we should meet, or a range that is most common. Remember to always budget for a tip, and don't feel you have to tip beyond the standard to impress anyone. A sincere "thank you" given along with your tip can go a long way toward communicating your appreciation. (For more information on tipping specifics, see Tipping on page 381.) Here are some common places we encounter tipping and how to handle them:

- **THE TIP JAR.** This is a place where tipping is entirely discretionary. You can leave your change from the total, or maybe what loose change you have in your pocket. Or you can leave a dollar or more, depending on your order. You do not have to tip when you see a tip jar.

- **FOR A PERSONAL SERVICE.** For hair, nails, waxing, personal training, massages, or treat-ments at a spa, you usually add a tip of 15 to 20 percent when you pay for the service.

- **FOR DELIVERY SERVICES.** For deliveries of groceries or other daily items, or takeout from a restaurant, tip around 10 percent or $5 or more per order. For curbside pickup of groceries or food, a couple of dollars is kind ($5 if it's a large load or order).

- **AS PART OF WEEKLY, MONTHLY, OR EVEN DAILY SERVICE.** A regularly occurring service usually has a set rate that works for both parties, and tipping is often left to the end of the year. However, this shouldn't stop you from tipping your babysitter, dog walker, cleaning person, or gardener if you really appreciate their service or they go above and beyond 1 week.

- **WHEN DINING OUT.** For a sit-down meal, it's important to understand that tipping isn't an option; it's an expectation. Even if the service isn't good, you still leave a minimum 15 percent tip. Many people regularly tip between 15 and 20 percent for standard service, and you're always welcome to tip more if you feel inspired. If you have a problem with the service, don't listen to that little voice that says, *I'm not going to tip*. Instead, leave 15 percent and speak to the manager.

- **TAKE AWAY** can be a full meal, a quick snack, or even just a beverage and tipping for it is discretionary. Sometimes you'll add your change to a tip jar, other times you'll add a buck or two to either a sales slip, tip jar, or payment screen. It's up to you. For big or complicated orders consider leaving up to 10 percent. You can always leave more if you wish.

THE SMOOTH TIPPER

Mr. Smooth Tipper always keeps small bills on hand so if a cash tip occasion arises, he is at the ready. By knowing in which situations he usually tips and what amounts are standard, he can have his tip already in hand as he approaches or even before the situation unfolds. He isn't left rummaging through his pockets, wadded-up dollar bills, or his wallet in order to tip.

He *never* flashes a large bill (or any bill for that matter) to get better service. While doing so is portrayed on TV, in real life it is often an insult to a maître d', host, or other service industry worker. Mr. Smooth Tipper knows a tip is always a thank-you, not a bribe. He knows his tip doesn't have to be super secret, covertly hidden in his hand, but he makes no show whatsoever of giving a tip. He always looks the person he is tipping in the eye and says, "Thank you very much" when he gives them the tip.

HOLIDAY TIPPING
IS HOLIDAY THANKING

It's customary to give a tip at the end of the year (usually around the holidays) as a thank-you for a year's worth of great service (not a bribe for the year ahead). Some providers, like nannies, babysitters, dog walkers, and house cleaners, often receive cash tips in the amount of one visit's or 1 week's worth (or month's worth) of service. For others, like teachers, staff at a nursing home, or an in-home caregiver, it's traditional to give a gift instead. There may be instances when your holiday thank-you is being given to a group, such as all the workers in an apartment building. Other times you might be part of a group gift, like when a gift to a teacher is from all the parents and students in the class. (For more Group Gifts, see page 210.)

Cash, a check, or a gift—however you decide to thank your year-round service providers, be sure to stay within your budget. The amounts and people listed in the Holiday Tipping Guide in the Reference Guide (page 384) are suggested guidelines, and your choices may vary based on where you live, your budget, and your relationship with the particular service provider. Reviewing a list like this long before the holiday season can help with budgeting when tipping season arrives. Year-end tips should be provided in a card with a note thanking your service provider for their work throughout the year and wishing them a happy new year to come. If you see them when they perform the service, you may also give an in-person thank you along with your holiday tip.

If there is a year when you can't tip as much but are still able to engage the service, it's okay to reference this in your note or card:

12-14-22

Dear Gauthier Guys,

Thank you for a wonderful year of service! We apologize that this isn't our usual end-of-the-year tip. It is not a reflection of your excellent service, and we hope to be able to do more to say thank you in the future.

Happy holidays to you and yours,
Saul and Alexa

COMMON TIPPING QUESTIONS

Do I have to tip on the tax for a meal or service? No, but many people do, and it's an easy way to tip a little more if you aren't keeping a tight watch on your budget.

What about tipping on alcohol? Yes, you tip on both food and beverages, including alcohol.

What if the person hosting me doesn't leave a tip, or leaves an insufficient tip? This is so awkward. You can only say something or offer to add more if it was an absent-minded mistake, and you can't know if it was a mistake without broaching the subject. If you're being hosted, you cannot say anything; it creates too awkward of a situation for there to be a polite way to mention it. If it's really upsetting to you, take note of the server's name; you could choose to go back another time to help make it right.

Why do some people tip rideshares like Uber and Lyft and others don't? Services like Uber and Lyft started with the premise that the drivers set their rates and therefore tips weren't necessary. As the services changed and gained drivers, however, it became harder for drivers to truly set their own rates, and tipping became more essential. While you might not have tipped when you first started using the services (even if you left awesome reviews), you should *always* tip these services now.

Do I have to pick one of the suggested tip percentages on a screen? No, you do not. It can be a confusing moment when standing at the counter and the very nice person who just got you food turns the screen to face you so you can sign and there are suggested tip amounts from 20 to 40 percent. At a cafe or for take-out food service, it's up to you how much you tip. The percentages on the screen are only suggestions. No one should feel embarrassed about choosing either the lowest amount or choosing a custom amount instead. Nor should you feel you have to explain if you choose "no tip." Similar tip suggestions are also seen on taxicab payment screens; while you shouldn't feel pressure, unlike at a coffee shop, taxi tipping isn't purely discretionary. There is a custom of tipping cabs 10 to 20 percent.

What is the biggest mistake people make when tipping? Forgetting the gratitude. About the only way a proper tip can truly fall flat is if it doesn't feel like a genuine gratuity. If you toss your tip at someone callously, or don't look them in the eye as you hand them a cash tip, or if your signing of the slip isn't accompanied by a thank-you (or at least a thankful attitude) it takes the appreciation out of the tip and the gratitude out of the gratuity.

Why is tipping at a restaurant different from other tipping situations? It is widely understood that the majority of restaurant waitstaff do not make the same minimum wage that applies to most other service jobs—even those that involve food and/or drink. Their pay is based on a smaller hourly wage than any other profession (below the usual minimum wage) and the assumption that they receive a tip on each customer's bill to balance their total take-home pay. These tips are an important part of how we collectively pay for service in restaurants. To tip less than 15 percent for sit-down restaurant service is not appropriate. A few restaurants are experimenting with service that is not based on tips by paying their servers more in line with other restaurant employees. If you are eating at a restaurant where this is the case, it will be a clear part of their presentation (on their advertising, menu, an information card or insert, and in service scripts) and the bill. In these instances, you can take the establishment at its word and don't need to add an extra gratuity (unless you want to). You can always ask the restaurant for more information if you are curious or unsure about their practice.

WHEN TRAVELING

Emily wrote in 1922: "One might say the perfect traveler is one whose digestion is perfect, whose disposition is cheerful, who can be enthusiastic under the most discouraging circumstances, to whom discomfort is of no moment, and who possesses at least a sense of the ridiculous, if not a real sense of humor!" These words are as true today as they were then. Emily was well-traveled, both at home and abroad. She was one of the first women to cross the United States by car, chronicling the event in *Collier's* magazine and later publishing her 1916 book, *By Motor to the Golden Gate*. Even though she had not yet begun to write about etiquette formally, it was on this trip that Emily learned that New York manners were not for everyone, and that each part of the country had its own particular social customs to express respect and consideration. As an even younger woman, she traveled to Europe and wrote fabulous letters home to her family, which later would become the inspiration for her writing career and inspire her novels such as *The Title Market*.

When we travel, either at home or abroad, we must think of ourselves as guests and act accordingly, not only for our hosts ("the locals," as they say), but also for the other guests (fellow travelers). Let's look at how we can be our best selves and use our best etiquette when traveling.

YOUR MINDSET

Don't forget to pack your patience and your smile! Any trip, whether solo or with family or friends, for pleasure or for business, at home or abroad, will go a lot more smoothly if you start off with a positive, can-do mindset. Meditation, prayer, a mantra or checklists: whatever it is that helps you feel reassured, confident, and positive about your trip will definitely be helpful in making sure you are a courteous traveler and a more enjoyable travel companion. It's not bad to think about and prepare for potential pitfalls; however, locking on to negativity can lead to more stress, which leads to more rudeness. Traveling near and far can be a time when we want to remember that two rudes don't make anything polite. You can always choose the etiquette high road—even when someone is being rude to you. By finding ways that work for you to start your trip off on a positive or confident note, you're setting yourself (and the trip) up for success.

WHEN TRAVELING WITH OTHERS

When traveling with others, even those with whom you've traveled before or regularly, it's imperative to discuss details, travel preferences, and styles well ahead of departure. It's best when we can choose our travel companions, and picking based on travel style can be important to the success of the trip. Someone who is a planner fits well with someone who loves to be a tag-along, but not so well with a free bird who wants no structure and to make decisions for themselves. There are times when you don't have a say in whom you are traveling with, then it's best to find ways to both compromise where you can and carve out space and time for yourself when you need it. Here are some other points to consider when traveling with others:

DECIDE UPON SHARED BUDGETS AND EXPENSES AND WHO IS COVERING WHAT. This should be clear from the get-go, with all parties in agreement. The last thing you want to have ruin a great trip is confusion over who pays, or worse, a discrepancy in the total tally for each party.

AGREE ON A CLEAR ITINERARY TO KEEP EVERYONE ON THE SAME PAGE. Travel details and information as well as meet-up times for departures should all be known and confirmed between travel companions. Have backup plans in place if people get separated.

SPEND TIME TOGETHER AND TIME APART. Allow for some downtime apart, and take notice of your travel buddy(ies) and what they are looking for. This isn't just about getting a reprieve; freedom and independence can be a delightful part of an itinerary when traveling with others.

DROP THE JUDGMENT. As we've mentioned, not everyone is a good traveler or has perfect packing skills. If a travel companion is tiring easily or has forgotten an essential item, rather than berate them for it or hold a silent grudge, try to drop the judgment, put yourself in their shoes, and see if there is anything you can do to help. Can you share some of your toothpaste, or is it easy to make a trip to the pharmacy? What about offering to get lunch for you both while your panicked travel buddy deals with canceling their credit cards after having left their wallet at the last stop? Guilt-tripping or shaming someone who's already frazzled won't help the situation, and it certainly wouldn't be polite.

AS A HOUSEGUEST

Being a good houseguest is not that different from being a good guest, you just do it for a bit longer. However, stepping up your manners and staying aware of a few considerations can make for an easy stay and often an invitation to "please come stay with us again soon" (the goal of any houseguest).

Our visits can take many forms, from the incredibly casual "couch crash" to being treated to a luxurious stay by a host while joining them on vacation. Sometimes we will stay with family or friends with whom we can be our most casual selves, and other times we will be the houseguest of a boss or client or someone we need to put on our most formal manners with. Sometimes our visits will be at a specific time, such as when an event or occasion is bringing us to the area, and other times it will be at the discretion of the host's and guest's calendars. There's a wide range of possibilities, to say the least. The good thing is that you will have a sense of where you are in that range for the visit or trip you're making, and if you're in any doubt, you may always ask your host what you should expect. "Parker, I can't wait for this trip—thank you so much for inviting me! I've never been to Fisher's Island before; what do I need in terms of attire, or for any outings you may have planned?"

Take note: while staying at an Airbnb (especially with a host who is onsite) or traditional bed and breakfast, we use many of our good houseguest behaviors. Even though the setup and payment don't always mimic the usual social host-guest relationship, the manners we exhibit as guests should: respecting the host's schedule and house rules, leaving the space we've occupied clean and tidy before we go, and communicating well with our host. Here are some good house-guest behaviors to pay attention to:

RESPECT YOUR HOST'S AVAILABILITY. For some visits we will be invited clearly for a specific amount of time, and the answer will be either yes or no. But there are plenty of other times where there is a bit of a dance as the host and guest try to find a good time for the visit. We can call to let someone know we are going to be in their area, and then it's up to them to say, "You're welcome to come stay here for the weekend!" We will have relationships with some folks that allow us to ask if we can come stay, but for most others we do not, and therefore need to be delicate with how we present the idea of our visit. If your host lets you know dates that will not work for them, be understanding and don't try to say things like, "Well I could just stay an extra night even if you won't be there, right?" Your host will offer this if it's even an option. If you're able to choose your dates together for the visit and schedules aren't lining up well, don't try to force it. You may simply need to find another time for the visit. By respecting your host's schedule from the start, you are being a good houseguest even before you arrive.

COMMUNICATE WELL. It is imperative that you determine the nature of your visit and communicate well with your host about it. We visit for different reasons; sometimes we're invited so that we can visit and spend time with our host and other times we are conveniently crashing because we have a business meeting or a wedding to attend in the area. No matter the nature of your visit, you shouldn't be expected to bring things like your own sheets or towels. Still, it's not a bad idea to ask ahead of time if there's anything you should bring or know about staying with your host.

RESPECT THE HOUSE RULES AND SCHEDULE. While you are a guest and your host wants to make you feel comfortable, by respecting the house rules and schedule a guest can also help keep their host comfortable in their own home. If you're an early riser and the household is still asleep, being quiet, taking a walk, or getting breakfast nearby could be ways not to feel like you have to wait to get up until the rest of house does, and also not to disturb others' slumber. (Being as quiet as possible is very important when anyone is sleeping.) If some house rules are hard for you to remember (taking your shoes off, limiting water use due to a drought, not letting the cat out), apologize for your forgetfulness and invite your host to remind you any time.

KEEP YOUR BELONGINGS NEAT AND TIDY. When you are shown where you'll be sleeping and the bathroom you'll be using, be sure to stow your items neatly. You may have a full private guest room and bath, or you might be stationed in the living room on a pull-out and have to use the same bath everyone else uses. In either case, keeping your items neatly tucked away in a drawer, closet, or your suitcase will respect the space. Make your bed each morning. It's also important to make sure you don't leave a trail of your things throughout the house. Whether you're fixing yourself a sandwich, spreading out some work for business, or having coffee in the yard, take care of any dishes you're using, and clean up your personal items or any messes you might make.

BALANCE DOWNTIME AND HOSTED TIME. As a guest you can help to create a balance between time together with and time apart from your host. A good host will leave a guest ample time to relax on their own, but even the best host can get excited about a visit and plan too much. If this should happen, simply ask them for some downtime: "Michelle, I'd love to make time for my run today. Would it be all right to head out around 3 so I've got time to run, shower, and get ready before we leave for dinner?" Any good host will say "Of course," but they may make a suggestion about your timing, like "You may want to head out about a half hour earlier since it takes us a half hour to get to the restaurant."

TIME TO GO. When it's time to leave, ask your host if there's anything you can do to help leave the space in good condition as you prepare to go. Always ask your host how they'd like sheets and towels handled. Stripped and remade? Left as is? Different hosts have different preferences.

HOSTING GIFTS AND SAYING THANK-YOU TWICE. As a houseguest, it is customary to give your host a gift for hosting you. You can bring a gift with you—often a favorite treat from your hometown is delightful. (See Houseguest Gifts, page 216, for more ideas.) Alternatively, you can treat your host to something on the trip, or you can send something after the trip. If you decide to treat your host to a dinner out or other experience, make it clear that this is a thank-you for the visit: "Isabelle, I'd love to take you and Morgan out to dinner as a thank-you for hosting me; is there a good night this week?" It's also important to say thank you twice: once when you are leaving and saying your goodbyes of course, but also by sending a thank-you note (sometimes called a bread and butter note; see page 96).

AT HOTELS

For as long as there have been travelers, there have been places for them to stay while on the road. Hotels can be some of the most elegant, elaborate, and formal places on Earth—we call it "puttin' on the Ritz" for a reason. They can also be some of the most modest, efficient, and practical places to rest one's head. But no matter the style, they all serve a similar function: they provide us with a place to stay away from home. In any hotel the ultimate etiquette goal is to be a good guest.

Our friend Ms. Travelswell is a delightful hotel guest. No *Fawlty Towers* hijinks with her. She arrives luggage in hand and is happy to have the bellhop assist her, knowing to give them a tip once they reach the room. She is pleased as punch with her room accommodations, and if anything is amiss (like that time she was shown to an unmade room, or when she—a light sleeper—was placed in a room next to the elevator), she asks sweetly if there are other options that might suit her needs. If the establishment is able, they are more than happy to accommodate her. If she can't be accommodated right away, she often has to wait only a bit (with her bags in the lobby storage) for the right room to become available. Naturally, she seizes the free moment to acquaint herself with the concierge, introducing herself and explaining a bit about her visit while inquiring about the best coffee shop she might venture out to in the morning. (Of course, when the concierge follows up with a tip on a show and some hard-to-get tickets, Ms. Travelswell is delighted and remembers to tip for the extra favor when she picks up the tickets the concierge has procured.)

She never makes a mess of her room once she's settled into it. Her trash makes it into the bin, her take-out food is neatly wrapped back into its take-out bag and disposed of. She piles the towels she won't be using again into a corner in the bathroom (as requested) and hangs the ones she will continue to use on the rack. Her clothing is kept neatly near her suitcase, or she uses the drawers and closet. She tips the bellhop when they arrive with the toiletry kit and ironing board she's requested. And she *always* leaves a tip every day for the housekeeper, knowing that it's often not the same person who readies her room each day. She never blares her music or the TV, and is especially careful not to talk loudly in the hallway, no matter how many glasses of Champagne she's had or how giggly she is with her travel companions. She does her best not to disturb other guests, knowing that each room might contain someone desperately trying to sleep in a foreign space. She smiles and says hello to the staff she sees and interacts with, and she is sure to say thank you to each of them for any assistance they have provided. Ms. Travelswell does indeed travel well, and she is every hotel staff's dream guest. Do as she does and you too will be the perfect hotel guest.

ON AIRPLANES

Emily saw the arrival of commercial air travel in her time, and while the following quote from 1922 was pre-airline industry, we think it has wonderful applications to air travel in particular today:

> "The perfect traveler . . . is one who possesses the virtue of punctuality; one who has not forgotten something at the last minute, and whose bags are all packed and down at the hour for the start. Those who fuss and flurry about being ready, or those whose disposition is easily upset or who are inclined to be gloomy, should not travel—unless they go alone."

Minding our manners throughout the entire air travel experience is incredibly helpful to the crew of people both in the air and on the ground who help make it possible. When we are courteous, orderly, and follow directions well, we contribute to everyone's safety and comfort.

First of all, get to the airport early. Delays can be caused by more reasons than just heavy traffic. If you're unfamiliar with an airport, definitely look online to find out the suggested arrival time for your departure flight. As soon as you enter the airport, prepare yourself for good line etiquette and bring a healthy dose of patience. Mind your p's and q's at the ticket counter where you check your bags and get questions answered. Follow the directions of the TSA staff (shoes in the bin or on the belt? Electronics separate or in one bin?) and be courteous to your fellow travelers, especially while waiting in line. Hold on to that patience through one more line starting at your boarding gate, and you will find your seat waiting. There could be wins or delays at any point. Hope for the best and ignore the rest, and you'll keep your stress levels down. (For tipping practices at the airport, see Travel Tipping, page 386.)

When you're waiting at your gate for your flight to depart, there are some ways to be a polite and courteous fellow traveler:

- Keep your luggage close to you at all times—not only for security, but because it's cumbersome and can easily block spaces where people are trying to walk or sit.

- Try to occupy only one seat for yourself. Put people before luggage and pets, and offer to move your bags for someone who is standing or to make room for groups or families traveling together.

- Try to use only one outlet at a time if there are others who are looking to plug in.

- *Always* use headphones. It is not appropriate at the gate or in any line to play music or entertainment through your device's speakers, or take a call on speakerphone.

- Stay seated until your zone or row number is called, and avoid rushing if the line is already long or not even moving. You can always ask a flight attendant to help you find a spot for your carry-on once you get onboard.

Once you're on board, here are a number of considerations to take into account for a polite flight:

STOWING YOUR LUGGAGE AND PERSONAL ITEMS. When stowing luggage, try to put it in an overhead bin near your seat, and only stow the items that are too big to fit under the seat in front of you. Wait to stow any purses, smaller or less-packed backpacks, or coats until others have had a chance to get their carry-on into the overhead compartment. Be very careful when hoisting your luggage up into the overhead space. Many a head has been banged by someone clumsily or carelessly trying to put their luggage away. If you're able, this is a great opportunity to offer to help someone. Never take someone's luggage out and put yours in instead. It's first come, first served always. A flight attendant can help you if there is no space near your seat. Try not to stow large items under the seat in front of you. The added bulk can be a safety hazard, and it adds to the already cramped quarters.

GETTING IN AND OUT OF YOUR SEAT. When getting into your seat you want to take care with the people around you. A quick, "I'm 17A" often gets passengers already seated in your row to rise and let you get situated. If someone doesn't exit the row to let you in, you'll have to shuffle over them. When doing so, do your best to not lean too hard on the seatbacks of the row in front of you. If you need to lean on them for balance, let the person sitting in that seat know first. Then hold the seatback as gently as you can to balance yourself. If no one is in your row and you need to balance yourself, it's better to do so by holding on to your own row's seats, rather than the seatbacks of the passengers in front of you. Take note that once everyone is seated and before takeoff, someone might offer or request to switch seats with you. There is no obligation to agree to this request. It's up to you whether to say yes.

If you need to get out of your row, it's polite to get the attention of your rowmates and say or signal that you'd like to get up. "I'm going to use the restroom; do you mind popping up for a moment?" Most people oblige quickly and politely. If they don't and you have to get past others or need to balance yourself, just as when taking your seat, do so as gently as possible. It's also polite to let your seatmates know that if you're asleep and they need to get by, it's okay to wake you, or to do so in a particular way. Some people will mention if they are prone to getting up frequently so their seatmates know to expect it.

TALKING WITH YOUR SEATMATES. Once seated, it's polite to say hello to your rowmates. You'll quickly get a vibe for whether or not they'd like to chat. If you see someone break out their headphones, book, or device, that's a signal they'd like to keep to themselves for the time being. If they want to chat and you do not, and taking out a book or your headphones hasn't clued them in, you can say when you have a chance, "It's been nice to meet you; I'm going to listen to my music (or tuck into my book/movie/show)." You don't really close out this conversation, because it's likely you'll communicate with this person at some point again during the flight; however, it's not rude to politely disengage. (See The Basics of Conversation, page 55, for how to decline a conversation with strangers.)

RECLINING YOUR SEAT. Oh boy, here we go. Just because you can recline doesn't mean you should. The only time a recline is 100 percent polite is when there's no one behind you. Airplane space is tight, and unless it is a long flight or you have back or leg issues, try to avoid reclining at all. In this case, especially in tighter seating arrangements, your comfort is someone else's discomfort. If you do recline, be sure it's not during a mealtime, and check first to see if the person behind you is working on a laptop or leaning forward. Some people will check in: "I'm just going to lean my seat back for a bit." Others slowly and gently start to recline so as not to startle the other person. If you are reclining, remember you don't have to recline all the way. See if just an inch or two can give you the comfort you're seeking.

THE MIDDLE SEAT. In the middle seat? There's not much to say except do your best to share the armrests and stay within the limited space afforded this seat. While it's tempting to carve out both armrests as middle seat territory, the polite move is to try to share them. Remember, you can always put your elbows further back or forward to create room to share the armrest.

FOOD. When it comes to bringing food on board, avoid anything that has a strong odor that people can be bothered by, like fish, bananas, or cruciferous vegetables (such as Brussels sprouts). Also avoid anything that might make a mess. You don't have to offer to share your food unless you'd like to.

PERFUME, COLOGNE, AND OTHER SCENTS. Another aromatic consideration is to avoid putting on any perfume or cologne the day of a flight. Strong scents (including unintentional ones like smoke) can give people headaches or create nausea for those who are sensitive to fragrance and have to share a close space. *Eau de foot* is also not a pleasant experience on a plane. If you'd like to remove your shoes, bring slippers with you to put on just in case odor might be an issue.

ON TRAINS AND BUSES

Train and bus etiquette is quite similar to plane etiquette, especially in terms of eating, talking, storing luggage, and moving around other passengers. The biggest difference is that on trains and buses, even if it's a long-distance trip, people get on and off. As a courteous traveler, you want to make sure to keep your bags and things out of the way for those who are trying to get on or off. Also keep your bags off the seats and place them in proper storage areas so others can take a seat if they need to.

If you don't have a reserved seat, always ask before just sitting down directly next to someone. "Is this seat taken?" or "Mind if I sit here?" are both polite. On subways, city buses, trams, and shuttles where standing is common it's polite to give up your seat to those more encumbered. This common and traditional courtesy still stands (pun intended). For trips where everyone has an assigned seat, this isn't an issue.

ON CRUISE SHIPS

Your behavior on a cruise should be similar to that at a hotel, theme park, concert venue, restaurant, or spa; cruise ships are basically floating cities.

EXCURSIONS. Probably the most important piece of advice when on a cruise is to show up on time for your departures throughout the trip. When you have made plans to venture off the ship, if you have to cancel, do so early so others on the waitlist can take your place. Know where the excursion is going and what attire you will need to wear. The same is true for onboard lectures, presentations, shows, and entertainment.

TIPPING. The cruise line will give you a breakdown of expected tips, and may even offer envelopes to put your tips in. Tips are given at the end of the trip, but be ready by asking ahead of time and budgeting for them.

DINING. When dining, you may be seated at a table with other passengers. This is an opportunity to meet people and strike up new friendships or at the least a conversation. (See Chapter 5: Table Manners, The Self-Introduction, page 29, and The Basics of Conversation, page 55.) If you are invited to dine with the captain, get ready to enjoy a few maritime traditions, with the opportunity to take your attire up a notch. Bring clothes that would be appropriate for such an occasion: semiformal attire should do, unless more formal attire has been specified for the dinner. It's perfectly fine to accept or decline. Just be sure to respond.

TRAVELING ABROAD

When we travel abroad we should be on our very best behavior, as more than any other time, we truly are guests as well as representatives of our home country. It's an avoidable tragedy that Americans have received such poor marks as travelers abroad. We must try to correct this. Before you travel out of the country, read up on where you are going. Beyond vaccinations, safety tips, and the currency exchange rate, geek out on the culture's etiquette! Countries, states, regions, cities, and towns often have tourism websites set up by their governing bodies. Starting here is great because you are hearing from the locals what they consider important to know when visiting. Wikipedia and the U.S. State Department website also have loads of information on many countries. Travel sites and resources can help narrow it all down to a visitor's most expected questions. Most commonly you'll want to know the following:

- Words and gestures for greetings, goodbyes, and for demonstrating gratitude, as well as the magic words. Learning the proper pronunciation of common phrases and practicing them is smart and shows respect for the culture you're visiting

- What's considered appropriate attire; for example, for the weather or customs such as if shoes should be on or off indoors, and which parts of the body are supposed to be kept covered (head, shoulders, entire body)

- Gifting customs and traditions, especially if visiting for business or visiting a specific person

- Standards of conduct. Each country has its own laws and standards. Knowing that alcohol is forbidden, or that spitting or public displays of affection could get you arrested, or that certain hand gestures are considered offensive is important

- The dining customs of the country you are visiting, since they vary widely across the globe

- Tipping customs for the country you are visiting

Pay attention to dates and times for holidays, festivals, and religious occasions, all times when the usual services might not be running or available. These can be opportunities to participate in the local culture or make your drive to the airport impossible depending on your preparation.

While you won't be able to learn everything, proper preparation will help give you confidence as you travel. A good guidebook will include information on customs, holidays, legalities, and some basic vocabulary and will never run out of batteries. If you are an experienced traveler on a return visit, recommit to these basics of good manners abroad.

REFERENCE GUIDE

HOLDING DOORS

Getting in and out of spaces when we are about town can be tricky. When in doubt, ask if someone would like a door held or a revolving door started for them.

Elevator
Allow those exiting to get out first. Traditionally, men went first and held the door for women and the elderly. Today, anyone may hold the elevator for others. Don't crowd or push. Avoid getting on a crowded elevator. Offer to push the button for someone who can't reach it.

Personal car
Open and hold the door for anyone more senior or a person you'd like to honor (often a spouse or partner).

Regular door
The person who is better able to easily operate the door should make the effort. There's no need to run ahead, but you can call out, "I can get that for you if you'd like." All things being equal, the first person there may choose to hold it for the next.

Revolving door
Traditionally men entered first to get it going. Today anyone can take the lead, but you should communicate an offer to help. Go slowly, and watch others using the door so you don't go too fast. Avoid jumping in with others.

Subway, train, or bus
Allow those exiting to get out first. Hold the door for those who may need extra time. You may offer a hand to someone descending the bus stairs who may need help. It's okay if they decline.

Taxi/Uber/Lyft
The person making the gesture holds the door for the other, and that person enters and slides across the back seat. Sometimes those in skirts or dresses prefer not to slide and may suggest they go second, taking on the responsibility of closing the door. Never steal someone's taxi, Uber, or Lyft.

TIPPING

The following are suggested amounts for tipping in various situations. For any tipping scenario you are always welcome to tip more. If you're unsure whether someone accepts tips, ask: "Do you accept tips?"

EVERYDAY TIPPING

WHO/ WHERE	TIP	NOTES
Barista	Discretionary; change for the tip jar or $1 or $2 is fine.	This is an up-to-you tip, not a mandatory tip. But remember, all tipping helps those who are working.
Bartender	$1 to $2 per drink or 10 to 20% of your tab	The bare minimum is $1 per drink. Anything more is up to you, and is always appreciated, especially for someone who is making complex drinks. If you didn't like the service, leave a $1 tip and speak to the manager.
Caterer	15 to 20%	Be sure to check your contract, as the gratuity may already be included. If the caterer has a waitstaff, tip the caterer the entire amount. If you hire separate waitstaff, tip them on top of the agreed-upon service (usually 15 to 20% is tipped to the whole group).
Coat check	$1 to $5 per item	Tip is given when you retrieve your items.
Counter service	Discretionary (usually change from the transaction or $1 or $2).	While you may sit and dine in the establishment, if they aren't serving you at the table, the tip is discretionary. You can always tip more for larger or complicated orders.
Rideshares/ Uber/Lyft	10 to 20%	Tipping is no longer optional; it's standard. Not tipping could impact your rideshare rating.
Server	15 to 20% or more	The minimum is 15%. If you didn't like the service, tip 15% and speak to the manager. A tip of 20% is common, as it's easy to calculate, and more than 20% says you were very impressed or extra grateful for the service.
Taxi	10 to 20%	The point-of-sale screens in taxis often pre-suggest higher amounts like 25 or 30%. It's okay to tip the standard 10 to 20% even if you see this.
Valet	$5 to $20	Tip is given when you pick up your car.

SALONS, BARBER SHOPS, AND SPAS

WHERE	TIP	NOTES
Barbershop	20%	Give the tip when you pay for the service, or after it has been performed.
Hair removal services	15 to 20%	Give the tip when you pay for the service, or after it has been performed.
Hair stylist	20%	If multiple people work on you, ask at the desk if you need to divide and tip individually or if the salon takes care of it.
Nail technician	15 to 20%	For elaborate or longer services, tip closer to 20 percent. Give the tip before your nails are painted.
Spa massage therapist	20%	Not all massage therapists accept tips; ask when you pay, or after your appointment. If tipping, give the tip when you pay for the service, or after it has been performed.
Spa treatments	20%	Check to see if gratuity is built into the cost already. If it is but you still want to offer a gratuity, ask if it's allowed and then leave what you wish. At this point it's discretionary.

DELIVERY OR SERVICE

SERVICE	TIP	NOTES
Appliance or furniture delivery	Not usually tipped; situational	If they deliver to a fourth-floor walk-up, unpack and set up the new furniture, and take away the old, then you might tip $10 to $20 per person.
Bike messenger service	Not usually tipped	Since the service charges what it needs to, this group more often sees holiday tips from a regular client than a per-run tip.
Cannabis delivery service	Up to 15% of your order	Depending on the service and the order, a tip may or may not be needed. If someone just drops off your order, no tip is necessary unless you'd like to. If they help with any instruction, then offer a tip.
Food delivery	10% or $5 or more	*Always tip the person who hands you the food.* Food delivery fees are not the same as tips, and often don't go to the delivery person.
Grocery delivery	$5 or more, or 10% of the bill	You can always tip more for large orders or if someone has to carry a large order up many flights of stairs.
Movers	$10 to $20 per mover for small jobs; $30 to $60 for the head mover on a larger job; $25 to $50 for each crew member on a larger job	Give it to the head mover to disperse among the crew. A small job is around ten lighter boxes and few if any furniture items. A large job would be furniture and heavy boxes in and/or maneuvering through tight spaces, several flights of stairs, or a small elevator.
Pool cleaner	$10 to $20 for a single service	For more regular service, tip the amount of one full service at the end of the year.

Holiday tipping is about saying thank you at the end of the year to the service providers we work with regularly throughout the year. A card is usually given with each tip or gift.

WHO	TIP OR GIFT	NOTES
Building doorperson	$20 to $100 per door person	Amounts will vary based on the city, building, and your budget.
Building elevator operator	$20 to $50 per operator	Amounts will vary based on the city, building, and your budget.
Building superintendent	$20 to $100	Amounts will vary based on the city, building, and your budget.
Cannabis delivery service	$10 to $30 or a gift to share	Consider giving your regular delivery person a tip or gift.
Country club staff	$20 per staff member	Not always given, but kind to do so. You might not tip every single member of the staff, or you might tip per group (bartenders, locker attendants, backroom/bag/equipment staff). *Check the tipping policy at the club. Some clubs have a no-tipping policy.* Attempting to give a tip at one of these clubs can be a serious breach of the rules, with consequences for members and staff. Many clubs have a holiday fund that is split among the employees.
Dog walker	A week's worth of pay	A gift or card from the dog is kind, too.
Gardener	Up to a week's worth of service	Good to tip each individual $20 to $50 or the group a week's worth of service.
Hair stylist	The cost of one visit or a gift	If you tip well throughout the year, a gift is more common.
Home nurse or caregiver	A week's worth of pay and a card from the person they care for	Ask the organization they work for first if they can accept tips. If more than one person visits, a gift to the organization might be best.
Mail carrier	Gifts under $20 value	The USPS is quite clear that carriers may not accept gifts of cash or gifts worth more than $20. Sending a gift (usually a consumable, such as cookies) to your local branch is also an option.

WHO	TIP OR GIFT	NOTES
Massage therapist	The cost of one visit or, if you go multiple times per week, a week's worth of pay, or a gift	A card with your tip is thoughtful.
Nanny or au pair	A tip from you and a gift from your child	Usually a full week's (or even month's) worth of pay
Package delivery person	Not usually tipped	If you decide to, check the company policy first and give $10 to $30 or a gift.
Personal shopper	A week's or instance's worth of service	Given with a thank-you note.
Personal trainer	The cost of one visit, or a gift	
Regular babysitter	A tip or gift from you, or a gift or card from your child	Usually a night's or weeks' worth of service or more
Residence staff or caregivers	Often a consumable gift for the staff as a group is best. For a cash tip, give a week's worth of service or whatever you can do	Ask the organization they work for first if they can accept cash tips or gifts. If more than one person visits, a gift to the organization might be best. Or something that can be shared by staff.
Teacher	Gift only (for ethical reasons, no cash, and no elaborate or extravagant gifts)	Keep it moderate. Classroom items are often helpful, since many teachers pay for them out of pocket. Avoid mugs!

TRAVEL TIPPING

WHERE	TIP	NOTES
Airport/hotel shuttle	$1 to $2 per bag	Tip if they help you; if they don't, it's discretionary.
Bellhop	$1 to $2 per bag, or $2 to $5 for bag storage	
Bus driver	Not usually tipped	If a bus driver helps you with luggage, $1 to $2 per bag
Cruise ships	Many types of crew members are tipped on cruises. On average, it ranges from $10 to $15 per day for room and restaurant staff combined	Often the ship's informational packet lists whom to tip and standard amounts. This should be taken into account when budgeting the trip.
Hotel concierge	$5 to $20 for services or assistance	You don't have to tip for every conversation or question easily answered. But if a concierge gets tickets or reservations for you, or assists in similar ways, tip them for the help per instance.
Hotel doorperson	$1 to $2 per bag or per taxi hailed	Door people can help in many ways. If they answer a question, don't worry about a tip, but if they help you with bags or hail you a taxi, offer a small tip.
Hotel housekeeping	Roughly $2 to $3 per person staying in the room and per day of stay	Leave the tip each day and make sure it's clear that it is for the staff. A note on the pad of paper in the room might say, *Housekeeping—Thank you!* A couple of crumpled bills on the dresser might get left untouched.
Mobility assistance	$5 to $20 per assistant	
Room service	15 to 20% of the bill before room-service fees and taxes	Be aware: Room service often has a room-service fee and taxes. You add a gratuity separate from that.
Skycap	$1 to $2 per bag	
Tour guide	$5 to $50 or possibly $50 to $500 for multi-city or country tour guides	For a short tour you just picked up, $5 to $50 is great—more if you're a group or they did a great job. For a tour guide who accompanies you through multiple cities or countries, $50 to $500. Given at the end of the tour or trip with a thank-you.
Train attendant	$1 to $2 per bag	

HIGH-LIFE TIPPING

Highly luxurious experiences are a treat indeed. Whether it's your everyday lifestyle or a once-in-a-lifetime opportunity, here are some considerations when tipping in luxury scenarios.

EXPERIENCE	TIP	NOTES
Driver/guide	20% of the cost of the trip, or $50 to $500 per day with the option of a small gift	Given at the end of the trip. No tip is needed if the driver or guide was provided by your host, or a company.
Private jet crew	$50 or more per pilot (if you choose to tip your pilot); $50 or more per crew member (who should always be tipped), per person traveling with you.	Given at the end of the flight, possibly in an envelope on your way out with a proper in-person thank you.
Town car/limousine	20% of the cost of the car for the trip	This is always taken care of by a host. If someone has said, "My driver will take you to the airport," they are paying. If you hire the car yourself, you are paying.
Yacht or boat with private crew	$100 to $1,000 for the captain, $50 to $500 per crew member. For charters, tip 10 to 15% of your weekly fee to the captain and the crew.	Given at the end of the stay, often in an envelope, and always with an in-person thank you. If you're being hosted, you may not have to offer a tip, but it's kind to do so. If you have chartered the boat or a host has offered the use of their yacht but cannot be on board with you, you should offer a tip at the end of your trip.

TO RECLINE OR NOT?

Since space on planes and buses is usually tight, here are some things to consider before reclining your seat:

- Is anyone behind you, either an adult or child?

- If someone is behind you, are they eating a meal, leaning forward, or working on a laptop?

- Are you in serious pain, and reclining rather than walking about the cabin will bring relief?

- Are you on a red-eye, international, cross-country, or long trip where it is likely that most people are reclining or will want to recline?

- Has the person in front of you reclined and that means you need to?

While the function is there, do your best to recline only when it truly won't impact others. Note that reclining partially is still reclining, and while an inch or two might not have as much impact on the person behind you, you should still be cautious and considerate when partially reclining.

USING SOMEONE'S SECOND HOME

Some Americans have second (or sometimes third and fourth) residences that they make available to friends, family, or colleagues (sometimes with a fee associated, sometimes not). The scenario of being offered their use will vary for each situation. Here are some things to consider as the guest that will help toward not only treating this very generous offer with respect but might even get you invited to use the beach house, cabin, or ski condo again.

- Get clear start and end dates for the visit. Be sure to know where hidden keys are or what the access code is, before you depart your own home for the trip.

- Get the lowdown on what is available for you to use and what isn't. Ex: "Happy to have you use the lake house, but please do not take the sailboat out." Or "Happy to have you and Joselyn come, but we ask that you not invite other guests."

- Ask about cleaning and expectations for how the house should be cared for during your stay and left before you go. (As a general rule, always avoid leaving food that will spoil or anything wet behind.)

- Be understanding about fees that your host may ask you to pay—such as a cleaning fee, or nightly rate. Remember you can always politely decline the stay if you cannot meet this requirement. "It sounds like it would be out of my budget but I so appreciate the offer and hope I can take you up on a future offer."

- Always say thank you to the homeowner both when you accept their offer and once your stay is over—a handwritten note is best.

- Find out who to contact in case of a problem and always communicate any issues you may be having or have had to the homeowner (or caretaker).

THINKING FORWARD

Far from static, Emily Post etiquette evolves as American society changes. For all of the traditions that inform our advice, there are also current trends. The way we speak, the general attitudes around formality and familiarity, the specific actions we deem courteous, and of course our methods of communication are all subject to change. As we celebrate 100 years of Emily Post's *Etiquette,* we can't help but wonder what the next 100 years will bring. What will remain important? What will be new? What from today's modern etiquette advice will become traditional and what will be antiquated by the time the next generation (if they are willing) is ready to take on the mantle? Etiquette is always evolving.

Consideration, respect, and honesty will forever be good principles to guide us when we don't know what to do, but we use them along with feedback we hear from you to identify what's working and what isn't. Below are a number of topics that we can imagine seeing changes to in the future. We'd love to hear your thoughts on the etiquette surrounding them. We welcome your feedback on the following topics, any thoughts they might inspire, and the future of etiquette at *ThinkingForward@emilypost.com.*

- **TIPPING IN RESTAURANTS** Restaurant service is the only service where workers' take-home pay is dependent upon the gratuities they receive. There's a social expectation around restaurant tipping that is not outwardly stated, it's simply understood and trusted. Would changes in hourly wages that reduce the expectations around tipping in restaurants be welcome? Would a more European style of tipping in restaurants, where gratuities are truly just a "little bit extra" and discretionary, work for us in America?

- **THE OBLIGATORY WEDDING GIFT** Wedding gifts are traditionally given if you are invited to a wedding, whether you attend the wedding or not. Is obliging guests to give a wedding present if they decline the invitation too much to ask of guests? Could a suggestion to send a congratulatory card if you don't attend a wedding be a more practical piece of advice?

- **WEDDING ATTENDANTS AND GIFTS** Much is asked of those who agree to be part of a wedding party. Should wedding attendants (who often pay for multiple trips, parties, and their wedding attire) be required to also give a gift to the couple? Or could their participation be seen as the gift?

- **MARRIED TITLES** Currently only one title identifies an individual as being both an adult person *and* married, the title of *Mrs.* Do more people wish they could use a title that functions this way? Would men and nonbinary people appreciate titles that allow them to identify as married when they are not presented with their partners? What might this look like?

- **RESPONDING TO A CHANGING CLIMATE** Droughts, storms, flooding, fires, shortages, and even disease are stretching our social systems in new ways. What are the areas of etiquette that could see change in response to a changing climate? Will it impact our host and guest roles when we visit those who live in climates very different from our own? Could disaster preparedness and response become a more regular consideration in our social expectations of each other?

Whatever changes we see in the future, it is all of us, our friends, our families, and our communities who will determine "the right thing to do." We hope that by looking at etiquette as something that exists in service to a society and that is meant to change, we can all participate in building a kinder, more considerate, and more respectful world, together.

EMILY POST

JAMES MONTGOMERY FLAGG

EMILY POST AND
HER LEGACY

Emily Post became America's primary source for etiquette advice in the twentieth century through both her bestselling book *Etiquette* and radio shows on the topic. She was a prominent woman in New York society from the early 1900s until her death in 1960. Born in Baltimore, the daughter of famed architect Bruce Price, she would marry, have two children, get divorced, become a novelist, and chronicle a cross-country road trip before she ever became famous for writing *Etiquette*.

Though much of Emily's early work was fiction, she seized the opportunity to write about manners and etiquette presented by her publisher. The more she dove into the topic, the more she found she had to say. Upon its publication in 1922, when she was 50, Emily's book *Etiquette in Business, in Society, in Politics, and at Home* topped the nonfiction bestseller list, and the phrase "according to Emily Post" soon entered the American lexicon as the last word on the subject of social conduct. *Etiquette's* first edition was not only a practical guide, but also a look into the world of high-society American culture. With the book's success in the 1920s and Emily's national radio program, *The Right Thing to Do*, in the 1930s, Emily Post was cemented as an American icon. She was *the* source for American etiquette and manners advice.

Emily included wartime supplements to the book in the 1940s, and continued to write and update the advice she gave until her death. In 1946 she established the Emily Post Institute, Inc. with her son Edwin, allowing for her family to carry on her legacy and work. Emily lived to see the horse and buggy become the car, the first coast-to-coast highway built, the rise of iconic brands such as Coca-Cola, and the invention of the airplane, telephone, and the television. Through it all, she kept her finger on the pulse of American life. Her work was adapted and changed with each decade, and although she passed away in 1960, a Sterling Brands survey revealed that most people think Emily Post is alive and well and about ten years older than they are. Legends never die.

A hundred years and five generations after Emily wrote the first edition of *Etiquette,* her great-great-grandchildren Daniel Post Senning and Lizzie Post now run the Emily Post Institute from Vermont, managing the company's publishing efforts, website, and social media, as well as training services and the *Awesome Etiquette* podcast. The legacy of Emily Post, still America's go-to source for etiquette, continues, and now rests (quite literally) in your hands as well.

ACKNOWLEDGMENTS

It took many thoughtful minds and willing hearts to create this book, and we could not have done it without the help of the following people.

First and foremost, we would like to acknowledge our great-great-grandmother, Emily Post. We would not be doing this without her, and are honored to continue to represent her material. We would also like to thank our grandparents, Mud and Poppy, who stewarded Emily's legacy through the most turbulent times, and who always gave us their support. And to the fourth generation of the Post family, who kept her legacy alive to pass down to us, we would especially like to thank Tricia Post and Peter Post, whose editing contributions were not small and were essential to this work. And thank you to Cindy Post Senning and Peggy Post, for their thoughts and encouragement throughout this process.

We would like to thank Kaitlin Ketchum, Julie Mazur Tribe, Leigh Saffold, Carolyn Keating, and Mikayla Butchart, not only for their excellent editing of this book, but also for their love of etiquette and sense of care for the Emily Post tradition. We are incredibly grateful to have worked with you. We'd also like to thank Lizzie Allen for her skillful design work, and the rest of the team at Ten Speed Press: Ashley Pierce, Want Chyi, Dan Myers, David Hawk, and Andrea Portanova for their support and fine work bringing this book together and getting it out into the world.

Thank you to Katherine Cowles, our literary agent, for your unwavering support, encouragement, and guidance. And to the team at Emily Post—Susan Iverson, Chris Albertine, Bridget Dowd, and Renee DeBell—thank you for your support, patience, and good humor throughout all the stages of writing and editing this book.

This work was informed by a number of sources that we recommend to those interested in diving deeper into the world of etiquette, protocol, and its history, including Laura Claridge's *Emily Post: Daughter of the Gilded Age, Mistress of American Manners;* Margaret Visser's *The Rituals of Dinner: The Origins, Evolution, Eccentricities, and Meaning of Table Manners;* Robert Hickey's book *Honor & Respect, The Official Guide to Names, Titles, & Forms of Address* and its corresponding website; and Suzanne von Drachenfels's *The Art of the Table: A Complete Guide to Table Settings, Table Manners, and Tableware.*

We'd like to express our grateful appreciation for the efforts of those we interviewed and asked to review our material: Amy Silverman, author of *My Heart Can't Even Believe It;* Michelle Acciavatti, end-of-life specialist and funeral director; Trenton Endres, professional chef; and Kayla Silver, certified sommelier and owner of Salt & Bubbles in Vermont. Thanks are also due to custom clothier Colin Ward; to Hazel Kreider for help with our military titles section; and to Gillian Weeks, Kelly Williams Brown, Ann Blunk, Arriana Arroyos, Van Angelo, Jesse Cauchon, Silvia

Doyle, and Jon Nix for their support and willingness to answer very random but nonetheless important etiquette questions.

We'd also like to thank the Emily Post audience, especially our podcast listeners; stationers from around the country; and the wedding and event professionals who regularly reach out to tell us what they are seeing and experiencing in regard to etiquette. Your questions, thoughts, and suggestions can be found on many of these pages.

Finally, we'd like to thank our families, especially Dan's wife, Puja, and his children Anisha, Arya, and William, Lizzie's parents, Peter and Tricia Post, and her sister Anna for their love and support throughout this process.

ABOUT THE AUTHORS

LIZZIE POST

Lizzie Post, great-great-granddaughter of Emily Post, is a co-president at the Emily Post Institute. She manages the company's publishing efforts and delights in being a cohost of the Institute's weekly podcast, *Awesome Etiquette*. Lizzie has authored and co-authored several books on etiquette, covering a range of topics from weddings to legalized cannabis use. A regular source on the topic of etiquette in the media, she has been featured by *The Today Show*, NPR's *1A*, the *New York Times, Here & Now*, *NFL Films*, the *Wall Street Journal*, the *Associated Press,* and others, and has written for *The Atlantic, Good Housekeeping, Women's Running,* and *Houzz.com*. She lives in her home state of Vermont.

DANIEL POST-SENNING

Daniel Post Senning, great-great-grandson of Emily Post, is a co-president at the Emily Post Institute. He manages the company's training programs and enjoys answering questions as a co-host on the Institute's weekly podcast, *Awesome Etiquette*. Daniel has authored and co-authored several books on etiquette, covering topics from business to digital manners, and delivers seminars and speeches on these topics around the world. An active spokesperson for the Institute, he regularly speaks with media outlets about business, technology, and dining etiquette. Daniel has appeared on *The Today Show, The History Channel,* and *ESPN,* and has been interviewed by publications including the *New York Times, GQ, Time Magazine,* and the *Wall Street Journal*. Daniel lives in Duxbury, Vermont, with his wife, Puja, and their children, Anisha, Arya, and William.

INDEX

communication with, 260
difficult, 264
helping each other, 260–61
loaning and borrowing
items, 261
meeting new neighbors,
258–59
sample scripts for, 267
visiting, 263
nonbinary individuals
"mx" title, 17, 30
pronouns, 25–26, 29,
35–36
respecting, 36
notes and cards
sample notes, 106–08
structure, 95
types, 96, 118–19

O

obituaries, 228, 239
offensive behavior, 185, 199
"othering," 70
overindulgence, 185–86

P

parks and beaches, 360–61
performances, attending,
361–63
personal space, 59, 345
pets, 252, 265, 326
phone calls
conference calls, 81–82
ending, 78–79
the mute button, 82
technology issues, 77–78
timing of, 76–77
voicemail, 79
volume and tone, 77
work calls, 80–81
place cards, 147
place settings. *See also* dining;
table manners
for the classic dinner party,
284–87
favors, 147
glasses, 145–46
memory aids for remember-
ing, 173
napkins, 141–42
place cards, 147

plates and bowls, 144
salt and pepper, 147
table setting diagrams, 171,
332–33
using someone else's
items, 169
utensils, 142–43, 149–51,
160–61, 171–73, 335
plates, 144
"please," 57
"plus-ones," 193
police officers and firefighters,
32–33
Post, Elizabeth (Emily's granddaughter-in-law), 10
postcards, 95
postponements, 184
potlucks, 272
pregnancy, grieving a lost,
226–27
privacy
direct messages (DMs),
102–03, 364–65
respecting, 190, 246
Tier III conversations, 62
privilege, 70–71
profanity, 65–66
professional titles, 31–33, 48
pronouns, 25–26, 29, 35–36
public parks and beaches,
360–61
public transportation, 358–59

R

reciprocity
of gifts, 204–05
of invitations, 192
reference guides
attire, 136–37
dealing with the
unexpected, 199
ending the event, 200
entertaining chart, 330–31
food restrictions,
335–36, 350
funerals, obituaries, and
condolences, 238–41
gift guide, 215–17
glassware, 335
goodbyes, 43
government titles, 50–52

greetings, 42
grooming and hygiene
checklist, 137
holding doors, 380
hosting houseguests checklist, 341
how to ask or respond
appropriately, 106
making introductions,
43–44
military officers, 52–53
neighbors, 266–67
party guides, 337–39
pets, 265
pouring, serving, and pairing wine, 340
professional titles, 48
religious titles, 49
roommates, 265
sample invitations, 110–15
sample menus for multi-
course meals, 336
sample notes, 106–08
sample scripts for hosts and
guests, 197
seating charts, 334
social titles, 45–47
table manners, 171–75
table setting diagrams,
332–33
tipping, 381–86
traditional gifts, 216–17
utensils, 335
video calls, 109
weddings, 200–01
a well-stocked bar, 341
what not to say, 104–05
work emails, 109
registries, gift, 94, 194,
207, 309
religion
attire for religious ceremonies, 133
readings at a funeral,
230, 231
reference guide to titles, 49
respect
of nonbinary and transgender individuals, 36
of others' personal property,
246–47

of other's privacy, 190, 246
on social media, 363–64
restrooms, public, 347
retirement parties, 115,
314–15
rideshares and taxis,
359–60, 368
roommates
considerations before choosing, 251–52
establishing house rules,
243–44
and hosting guests, 186
parting ways, 253–54
reference guide, 265
setting boundaries, 253
shared property, 246–47
types of, 250–51
RSVPs, 89, 178, 194,
279–80, 313

S
salad course, 153, 156–57
sandwiches, 158
scents
avoiding personal fragrance
at the gym, 358
avoiding personal fragrance
on planes, 377
from flowers or candles,
288–89
seating charts, 283–84, 334
semiformal attire, 129–30
servingware, 287
shellfish, 159
shoes, removing, 180, 189
showers, 94, 114, 207,
308–11, 338
smart devices and virtual
assistants, 248–49
smiling, 24
smoking and vaping, room-
mate agreements about,
252, 253
sneezing, 168
social distancing
appropriate gestures and
greetings, 18
following an establishment's
rules, 348

social media
after death, 236
commenting on, 102, 103
direct messages (DMs),
102–03, 364–65
online behavior, 363–65
public posts, 101–02
social titles (honorifics),
29–31, 45–47
soup course, 153, 157
speech
shouting, 164
speaking to a voice-activated
device, 248–49
vocal tones, 59–60, 126
volume, 60
speeches
eulogies, 230, 231
toasts, 148–49, 174
spills, 168–69, 181–82
splitting the bill, 352–53
spoons, 143
stores, courtesy in, 344
suffixes, 31
sunglasses, 134–35
sympathy notes, 235, 241

T
table linens, 286–87
table manners. *See also* dining
bone-in foods, 158–59
bread and butter, 156
at buffets, 175
charcuterie boards, 160
chewing, 163
cleaning your plate, 165–66
common mistakes, 164–65
coughing, sneezing, and
burping, 168
courses of the meal, 152–54
devices at the table, 165
drinking properly, 154–55,
161–62
ending a meal, 169–70
excusing yourself, 166
finger foods, 160–61
food stuck in your teeth,
166–67
food that is too hot, 167
holding a chair, 140
making toasts, 148–49, 174

pacing your eating, 155
passing food, 162–63,
164, 293
place settings, 141–47, 169,
284–87, 332–33
reference guide, 171–75
removing something from
your mouth, 168
salad, 156–57
sandwiches, 158
saying grace, 148
serving and clearing,
292–93
serving yourself, 163
sharing negative news during a meal, 165
shellfish, 159
soup, 157
spills and dropped items,
168–69
taking a seat, 139–40
unpleasant surprises in
food, 167–68
utensils, holding and using,
149–51, 160–61, 172–73
when to begin, 147–48
tea, 154–55, 161–62, 295,
301, 319–20
tea parties, 304
technology
device usage, 165, 247
digital invitations, 188
home management systems,
248–49
online condolences, 235
phone problems, 77–78
video calls, 85, 86, 225
virtual funeral services, 233
Wi-Fi network and pass-
word, 324
texting
conversations, 87–88
emojis and abbreviations, 87
group texts, 89
informality of, 88
introductions, 38–39, 89
replying to a text, 87–88
"thank you," 57, 191–192,
196, 204
thank-you notes, 196, 212–14,
217, 307

EMILY POST'S ETIQUETTE

Published in the United States by Ten Speed Press, an imprint of Random House, a division of Penguin Random House LLC, New York.
TenSpeedPress.com
RandomHouseBooks.com

Ten Speed Press and the Ten Speed Press colophon are registered trademarks of Penguin Random House LLC.

Illustration on page 394 by Jamee Montgomery Flagg, courtesy of the Post Family.

Typefaces: Monotype's ITC Berkeley Oldstyle Pro and Jean-Baptiste Levée's Columbia Sans

Library of Congress Cataloging-in-Publication Data
Names: Post, Lizzie, author. | Senning, Daniel Post, author. | Post, Emily,
        1872-1960. Etiquette.
Title: Emily Post's etiquette / Lizzie Post and Daniel Post Senning.
Description: 20th edition, First Ten Speed press edition. | Emeryville,
        California : Ten Speed Press, 2022. | Includes index.
Identifiers: LCCN 2021042568 (print) | LCCN 2021042569 (ebook) | ISBN
        9781984859396 (hardcover) | ISBN 9781984859402 (ebook)
Subjects: LCSH: Etiquette--Handbooks, manuals, etc.
Classification: LCC BJ1853 .P6 2022 (print) | LCC BJ1853 (ebook) | DDC
        395--dc23/eng/20220613
LC record available at https://lccn.loc.gov/2021042568
LC ebook record available at https://lccn.loc.gov/2021042569

Hardcover ISBN: 978-1-9848-5939-6
eBook ISBN: 978-1-9848-5940-2

Printed in USA

Editor: Kaitlin Ketchum | Production editor: Ashley Pierce | Editorial assistant: Zoey Brandt
Designer: Lizzie Allen | Production designer: Faith Hague
Production manager: Dan Myers
Copyeditor: Carolyn Keating | Proofreader: Mikayla Butchart | Indexer: Amy Hall
Publicist: David Hawk | Marketer: Andrea Portanova

1st Printing

First Edition